LONGMAN LINGUISTICS LIBRARY

A SHORT HISTORY OF LINGUISTICS
Third Edition

A Short History of Linguistics

Third Edition

R. H. Robins

LONGMAN
London and New York

Longman Group UK Limited,
Longman House, Burnt Mill, Harlow,
Essex CM20 2JE, England
and Associated Companies throughout the world.

Published in the United States of America
by Longman Inc., New York

First published 1967
Second edition 1979
Third edition 1990

British Library Cataloguing in Publication Data
Robins, R. H. (Robert Henry), *1921–*
A short history of linguistics. – 3rd ed. – (Longman
linguistics library).
1. Linguistics, history
I. Title
410.9

ISBN 0-582-29145-3

Library of Congress Cataloging-in-Publication Data
Robins, R. H. (Robert Henry)
A short history of linguistics/R. H. Robins. – 3rd ed.
p.   cm. – (Longman linguistic library)
Includes bibliographical references.
ISBN 0-582-29145-3
1. Linguistics – History.   I. Title.   II. Series.
P61. R6   1990
410'.9 – dc20   89-13771
CIP

Set in Linotron 202 10/11pt Times
Produced by Longman Group (FE) Limited
Printed in Hong Kong

Contents

From the preface to the first edition

In this book I have attempted to give a brief account of the history of linguistic studies up to the present day. For the reasons stated in the first chapter, the narrative is organized around the history of linguistics in Europe, but it is my hope that due notice has been taken of the contributions that the subject has drawn from work originating outside the European continent.

The current interest shown by linguists in past developments and the earlier history of their subject is in itself a sign of the maturity of linguistics as an academic discipline, quite apart from any practical applications of linguistic science. It is my hope that this book will go some way towards fulfilling teachers' and students' needs in the field, both in deepening their appreciation of what has been done in the study of language and in suggesting profitable areas of further research.

In venturing on a book of this scope, one is at once made conscious of a number of difficulties. In the first place, no one person can achieve anything like equal familiarity with the entire range of linguistic work that such an undertaking requires of him. Secondly, the extent, the nature, and the present state of the source material varies widely from one period to another. There are lamentable gaps in our knowledge of some of the early pioneers of linguistics, while in the contemporary history of current trends the problem is an opposite one, that of trying to select from the great mass of published material that which is likely to be of permanent historical significance. Between these outer limits there are considerable differences in the availability, accessibility, and editorial condition of the primary texts.

If one looks outside Europe to the linguistic scholarship on which Europeans drew so heavily and so beneficially, the need for editions and commentaries is no less urgent. Much of Chinese, Arabic, and Indian linguistic work has been extensively studied already, but largely from the standpoint of its place in the cultural and literary history of the peoples themselves. Scholarly treatments that relate individual writings in these fields to current linguistic theory and practice will fill a considerable gap in our understanding of the world's cultural history.

For all these reasons, in addition to the inadequacy of the author's knowledge and abilities in relation to this self-imposed task, readers are likely to find substantial grounds for disagreement and disappointment with what is here written. But if this book should stimulate further detailed research into our sources for the history of linguistics, it will have achieved a part of its purposes.

In trying to cover so wide an area, one is made more than usually aware of one's debt to contemporary and to earlier scholars who have laboured in this field. This debt is partially acknowledged in the bibliographical references that follow each chapter. More personally, I am happy to express my thanks to colleagues in London and elsewhere whom I have consulted, and in particular to Professor David Abercrombie, for his painstaking help in reading and checking the text of this book and for his important comments and corrections, and to those who have been kind enough to read drafts of chapters dealing with topics in which they are far better qualified than I am: Dr Theodora Bynon, Mrs Vivian Salmon, and Mr K. L. Speyer. The book is the better for their help and advice; I remain responsible for any remaining errors and blemishes. Finally, I have been greatly assisted by the kindness and patience of my wife, who read through the entire book in typescript, making numerous valuable suggestions on diverse points of detail.

London, 1967   R. H. ROBINS

Preface to the second edition

In preparing a second edition of this book I have tried to take into account the friendly and helpful comments of reviewers and colleagues, and to take proper notice of current work in the history of linguistics both as a whole and with reference to specific times and places. The amount of such work is a gratifying demonstration of the growing interest in this field of linguistic studies, as is the appearance of a specialist journal, *Historiographia linguistica*. But much still remains to be done before we can look for a satisfactory full-scale historical treatment of linguistic science.

London, 1979   R. H. ROBINS

Preface to third edition

In the ten years since the publication of the second edition of this book much work has been done in studies related to the history of linguistics. Recognized as an important part of general linguistics and as a valuable component in courses in linguistics at university level, it figures in first degree and postgraduate degree syllabuses at several universities in Europe, America, and elsewhere. In Britain an established lectureship has been designated explicitly for the history of linguistics.

The enlargement of interest in this branch of linguistics can be regarded from a somewhat different viewpoint as a broadening of the comprehension of the history of science, or, more generally, of the history of ideas. Not surprisingly, a number of societies and organizations have come into being to serve the history of linguistics. Since 1978 a triennial International Conference on the History of the Language Sciences has met and published its papers; the Société d'Histoire et d'Epistémologie des Sciences du Langage, also established in 1978, holds regular colloquia and symposia, also followed by publication; more recently in Great Britain the Henry Sweet Society (1984–) and in America the North American Association for the History of the Language Sciences (1987–) provide forums for the exchange of research findings, lines of enquiry, and diverse interests in a field of intellectual investigation making contacts at different points with cultural and general history. The periodical *Historiographia linguistica* (1974–) continues to provide its invaluable service as an outlet for specialized articles and reviews in the whole field of studies.

Needless to say, all this activity has necessarily involved a reconsideration of several traditional views on linguistic work at different times and in different places, and the challenging of a number of *idées reçues* on the development of linguistic thought through the ages. Such reconsiderations are only to be welcomed;

without them any body of studies risks becoming little more than a static and unquestioned set of names of persons, schools, and modes of thinking, linked together in an unexamined sequence or progression.

In the present edition I have done my best to draw attention to the major breaks with traditional views that have appeared in the past decade or so, not necessarily accepting the conclusions of their proponents, but, I hope, giving readers the inclination and the means to follow up the relevant literature and to come to their own conclusions. Otherwise, rightly or wrongly, I have left the organization of the subject as set out in the 1967 edition.

In the preface to the first edition (1967) it was my pleasant duty to acknowledge the patient help in various aspects of the preparation of that book freely given by my wife, Sheila. Before work on the present edition could be brought under way her life on this earth ended, and I have had to do my best without her ready and informed guidance and assistance. Had she lived, the reader like the author would have benefited from her help. As this cannot now be, this book in its present form is dedicated, for what it may be worth, to her memory in undying gratitude and affection.

London, 1989   R. H. ROBINS

'Pereant qui ante nos nostra dixerunt',
Aelius Donatus apud St. Jerome (*To the devil with those who took the words out of our mouths*)

'Alles Gescheidte ist schon gedacht worden, man muss nur versuchen es noch einmal zu denken', Goethe
(*Everything worthwhile has been thought of already, one must just try and think of it once more*)

In memoriam uxoris dilectissimae

Chapter 1

Introduction

During the greater part of our lives, we accept our use and understanding of our native language without awareness, comment, or questioning. Memories of early childhood and experience in bringing up young children may cause us temporarily to ponder the complexity of every normal person's linguistic ability, and the learning of one or more foreign languages after mastering one's first or native tongue reveals just how much is involved in mankind's faculty of communication through language.

However, despite this general acceptance of the gift of articulate speech, most cultures in the world have engendered among certain of their members some realization of the scope and power of language. This linguistic self-consciousness may be first stimulated by contacts with foreign speakers, by the existence and recognition of dialect cleavage within a speech community, or by a particular orientation of man's inherent and disinterested curiosity about himself and the world around him. From this source springs 'folk linguistics', speculation or dogmatic pronouncement about the origin of language, or of one's own language, and its place in the life of the community. It may take the form of pejorative comments on other dialects and other languages; but many cultures contain aetiological myths purporting to describe the origin of language as a whole or, at least, of the favoured language of the people. The conception of language as a special gift of a god has been found in several diverse and unrelated cultures, and is itself significant of the reverence rightly accorded by reflective persons to this priceless human capability.[1]

In certain cultures, namely those that are for this and for other reasons credited with the title of civilizations, curiosity and awareness of one's environment have been able to grow into science, the systematic study of a given subject or range of phenomena, deliberately fostered and transmitted from one generation to another by persons recognized for their skill and knowledge in a particular activity of this sort; and all mankind owes a great debt to those cultures that have in one way or another fostered the growth of the sciences.

Among the sciences that arise in this fashion, folk linguistics has developed in different parts of the civilized world into linguistic science. The term *science* in the collocation *linguistic science* is used here deliberately, but not restrictively. Science in this context is not to be distinguished from the humanities, and the virtues of exactness and of intellectual self-discipline on the one hand, and of sensitivity and imagination on the other are all called into operation in any satisfactory study of language.

The sciences of man, which include linguistics, arise from the development of human self-awareness. But equally these sciences, or more strictly their practitioners, may become aware of themselves for what they are doing and for what they have done. When this scientific self-awareness includes an interest in the origin and past development of a science, we may recognize the birth of that specific discipline known as the history of science. In recent years the rapid and at times bewildering growth in linguistics as an academic subject, both in the numbers of scholars involved and in the range of their activities, has led to a corresponding growth in the interest of linguists in the past history of the subject. In part this may be due to the feeling that some understanding and appreciation of the problems and achievements of earlier generations may be a source of stability during a period of unprecedentedly swift changes in theory, procedures, and applications.

Linguistic science today, like other parts of human knowledge and learning, and like all aspects of human cultures, is the product of its past and the matrix of its future. Individuals are born, grow up, and live in an environment physically and culturally determined by its past; they participate in that environment, and some are instrumental in effecting changes in it. This is the basis of human history. Like a people and like an intellectual or moral conception, a science (in the widest sense) has its history. Scientists do not start from scratch in each generation, but they work within and on the basis of the situation which their science, and science in general, has inherited in their culture and in their age. Historical thinking about science or about anything else in human affairs consists in the study of the temporal sequences of persons and events, and the causal connections, influences, and trends, that may be discovered in them and may throw light on them.

It is tempting, and flattering to one's contemporaries, to see the history of a science as the progressive discovery of the truth and the attainment of the right methods, something of a counterpart to what has been called 'Whig history' in political historiography.[2] But this is a fallacy. The aims of a science vary in the course of its history, and the search for objective standards by which to judge the purposes of different periods is apt to be an elusive one. 'The facts' and 'the truth' are not laid down in advance, like the solution to a crossword puzzle, awaiting the completion of discovery. Scientists themselves do much to determine the range of facts, phenomena, and operations that fall within their purview, and they themselves set up and modify the conceptual framework within which they make what they regard as significant statements about them.

Brief historical sketches of a subject, such as are often included in introductory textbooks, inevitably look at the past through the eyes of the present, concentrating on those aspects of earlier work that seem either peculiarly relevant or, on the other side, shockingly irrelevant, to present-day approaches. This is quite proper, indeed it is almost inevitable, in such a short notice; but it carries with it the danger of evaluating all past work in a subject from the point of view in favour at the present, and of envisaging the history of a science as an advance, now steady, now temporarily interrupted or diverted, towards the predetermined goal of the present state of the science.

This does not mean that one should exclude the evaluation of past work against later achievements and against the present position in the same field, where there is reason to see therein a definite advance. Indeed, such comparisons may be rewarding, in that they show which aspects of a science were most favoured by particular circumstances and in particular periods and areas of civilization. What is needed is an attempt to discern the evolution of the past into the present and the changing states of the science in its changing cultural environments. One should strive to avoid the deliberate selection of only those parts of earlier work that can be brought into a special relationship with present-day interests.

If history is to be more than just an annalistic record of the past, some subjective judgment is inevitable in the ordering and in the interpretation of events; hence the classic statement that there can be no unbiased history. In the history of a science, and in the present case in the history of linguistics, there is the additional subjective element involved in determining what activities and aims on the part of earlier workers shall be deemed to fall within its sphere and so to belong to its history. In order not to impose the standards of linguistics today on the decision on what to admit as linguistic work from the past, we may agree to understand as part of the history of linguistics any systematic study directed towards some aspect or aspects of language envisaged as an interesting and worthy object of such study in its own right.

Changes and developments in a science are determined by a number of causes. Every science grows from its past, and the state reached in a previous generation provides the starting point for the next. But no science is carried on in a vacuum, without reference to or contact with other sciences and the general atmosphere in which learning of any sort is encouraged or tolerated in a culture. Scientists and men of learning are also men of their age and country, and they are participants in the culture within which they live and work. Besides its own past, the course of a science is also affected by the social context of its contemporary world and the intellectual premises dominant in it. Applications of the science, its uses for practical purposes and the expectations that others have of it, may be a very important determinant of the directions of its growth and changes. In linguistics, as elsewhere, attempted and projected applications, practical ends to be achieved, have often preceded the statement of the theoretical positions on which they implicitly depend.

Scientists are not all alike in ability, motivation, and inspiration. Every practitioner must learn his craft and master the state of his science as it is presented to him when he enters upon it; and if it is to continue, some must teach it in turn to others. Probably most scientists must be content to do no more than that, but every lively branch of knowledge attracts a few men of outstanding enterprise who are able to take some control of its direction and to respond positively to the challenges that the present inherits from the past. Such persons think more deeply and question accepted theory and practice more searchingly. If a culture is not to be entirely static they are a necessity, and in our own European history it is fortunate that ancient Greece of the classical age produced men of this character in hitherto unprecedented numbers and of unprecedented qualities, in so many spheres of human thought and activity.

When some lead, others follow; and leaders and innovators in a science, given favourable circumstances or making for themselves favourable circumstances, become the founders of schools, with disciples and followers continuing the exploitation of the lines of thought or practice developed by the founder or leader. Changes in scientific thinking and in scientific attitudes may arise from outside or from inside the science whose history is being traced. The existing state of a science, the starting point for any change, is the product both of external and internal factors. The general contemporary intellectual and social context, whether favouring stability or encouraging change, is largely external to the particular science itself, although each science and branch of learning is a part of the whole context along with all the others and along with the general cultural attitude towards learning.

When the dominant innovators in a science respond to the challenge of a situation that demands some change in its practice, this may take a number of forms, and rival schools may grow up around different leaders responding differently to a particular situation. These rivalries may be reinforced and perpetuated by the use of standard textbooks in the teaching of newcomers to the field. Any science whose subject matter involves the empirical study of observed data (and on any interpretation linguistics is included in this class) must be able to cope with its own phenomena, and once any observation is accepted as relevant its theory and modes of description and analysis must be able to handle it, and to handle it with scientific adequacy, of which exhaustiveness, consistency, and economy are canons. Fresh data, or the extension of a science to new but relevant fields, may require the further elaboration and articulation of existing theory along lines similar to those followed in the past and logically implied to them; it may, on the other hand, demand a radical recasting of existing theory and existing models of description. The Copernican heliocentric universe is a classic example of the recasting of existing theory when it was becoming incapable of handling economically some of the newly-observed astronomical data. Equally well, the data considered relevant to a science and the methods of that science in dealing with the data may be fundamentally altered by the response that one or more of its leaders makes to what he accepts as the dominant situation in which he is working or to the practical and intellectual needs that he is persuaded it is to the task of his science to fulfil. Throughout the history of linguistics all these factors can be seen at work in different ages and among different groups, as the science experienced changes in its objectives, its methods, and its theoretical positions.

Interest in language and in practical linguistic problems led independently to linguistic science in more than one centre of civilization. Each had its own merits and its own achievements, and in the course of history each has come into contact with the European linguistic tradition and has contributed to it. In some important respects it is difficult to believe that European linguistics would be in the position it is today without the insights brought to it by linguistic work from outside Europe, in particular the work of the ancient Indian linguists on Sanskrit grammar and phonology. But since in the present age European science has become international science, and linguistics is no exception here, we can trace several streams of linguistic studies flowing into the European tradition and becoming part of it at different times, thus to constitute linguistic science as the world knows it today.

This statement may provide and justify the framework on which to organize a history of linguistics. To build it around the history of linguistics in Europe in no way implies a claim to European superiority in the linguistic field. Indeed, in much phonetic and phonological theory, and in certain aspects of grammatical analysis, European scholarship was manifestly inferior to that of the ancient Indians. But in the European tradition we are in a position to follow a continuous line of development from the origins of the subject in ancient Greece, whereas we know little of the origin and early stages that lie behind the mature Sanskrit work of the Indians. The practical and theoretical results of Greek linguistics were taken over by Rome (with so much else of Greek intellectual life), and passed on by Rome at the hands of the Latin grammarians to the Middle Ages, to be received from them in turn by the modern world during and after the Renaissance, together with the vital contributions from outside Europe. At no stage is there a break that amounts to discontinuity in the European tradition of linguistics. Changes of theory, aims, methods, and concepts are repeatedly found, and they are the material of the history of linguistics; but each generation of European linguists has had at its disposal a knowledge of the existence and some of the work of its forerunners.

It is, therefore, reasonable to make the history of European linguistics the foundation for a history of linguistics as a whole. This procedure is not based on any evaluation of the relative merits of European and extra-European work, but it does determine the place at which linguists outside Europe receive attention. They and their achievements will be described at that period wherein they made their first significant impact on European linguistics, and thus entered the stream leading to world linguistics of the present day.

In the history of a science, as in more general historical studies, there is the constant temptation to discern and extract pervasive themes or patterns running through and manifested in the succession of events and activities. Where such themes may legitimately be revealed they can prove enlightening interpretations of the historian's narrative, and certain very broad correlations suggest themselves. For example, the failure of western antiquity to evolve an adequate theory of historical linguistics, despite the fascination shown for etymology, may be linked with the failure of ancient historians to envisage the fact of change as more than the revelation of what was innately present all the time in a political system or in a person's character[3]; and the all-embracing synthesis of language, thought, and objective reality involved in late mediaeval 'speculative grammar' appears as a facet of the synthesis of knowledge and learning within Catholic theology that characterized the scholastic age.

But at the present stage, at least, of our knowledge and research in much of the history of linguistics, our aims must be more modest. The importance of the history of a science is that it helps to place the present in perspective. Linguists today are not alone in their achievements, their disputes, and their problems. They are the heirs to more than two millennia of the wonder that the 'strangeness, beauty, and import of human speech' has never failed to arouse among sensitive and enquiring minds.[4]

For further consultation

The bibliography for this chapter will necessarily include items relevant to the book as a whole. They may be divided into three sections:

1. Other histories of linguistics and general studies in this field.
2. Studies in the theory and practice in historiography and the history of science that touch on points raised in this book.
3. Collections of articles or chapters dealing in greater detail with specific topics in more than one of the chapters in this book.

I.

T. A. AMIROVA, B. A. OL'CHOVIKOV, and JU. V. ROŽDESTVENSKIJ, *Abriss der Geschichte der Linguistik*, Leipzig, 1980. This book, translated from the original Russian, provides a comprehensive and fairly detailed history of linguistics in 484 pages up to Vossler and the aesthetic school, but subsequent twentieth-century linguistics receives only summary treatment.

H. ARENS, *Sprachwissenschaft: der Gang ihrer Entwicklung von der Antike bis zur Gegenwart*, Freiburg/Munich (second edition) 1969, covers the history of linguistics as a whole, principally through extracts from representative writers of each period linked by commentaries. Arens devotes most space to nineteenth-century comparative work and to historical linguistics; but twentieth-century descriptive work is surveyed up to the 1960s.

W. AYRES-BENNETT, 'Linguistic historiography', *Linguistic abstracts* 3 (Oxford, 1987), 113–25.

A. BORST'S exhaustive *Der Turmbau von Babel*, Stuttgart, 1957–63, treats in great detail the history of men's ideas and beliefs in different parts of the world on the origin and diversity of languages and peoples in relation to current religious and philosophical opinions.

K. GROTSCH, *Sprachwissenschaftsgeschichtsschreibung: ein Beitrag zur Kritik und zur historischen und methodologischen Selbstvergewisserung der Disziplin*, Göppingen, 1982.

E. HOVDHAUGEN, *Foundations of western linguistics*, Oslo, 1982, provides and introductory account of the development of linguistics in Europe from Greece to the year 1000, with lengthy translations from original texts, and a good coverage of linguistic work in the first half of the Middle Ages.

G. MOUNIN, *Histoire de la linguistique*, Paris, 1970.

P. SCHMITTER, *Untersuchungen zur Historiographie der Linguistik*, Tübingen, 1982.

P. A. VERBURG, *Taal en functionaliteit*, Wageningen, 1952, deals with the period from the Middle Ages to the beginning of the nineteenth century, examining the changing attitudes towards the functioning of language in human life.

2.

H. BUTTERFIELD, *The Whig interpretation of history*, London 1950.

R. G. COLLINGWOOD, *The idea of history*, Oxford, 1946.

W. C. DAMPIER, *A history of science and its relations with philosophy and religion*, Cambridge, 1948.

T. S. KUHN, *The structure of scientific revolutions*, Chicago, 1962.

S. F. MASON, *A history of the sciences*, London, 1953.

G. SARTON, *A guide to the history of science*, Waltham, Mass., 1962.

C. SINGER, *A short history of science*, Oxford, 1941.

3.

H. AARSLEFF *et al.* (eds.), *Papers in the history of linguistics*, Amsterdam, 1987.

S. AUROUX *et al.* (eds.), *Matériaux pour une histoire des théories linguistiques*, Lille, 1984.

H. E. BREKLE, *Einführung in die Geschichte der Sprachwissenschaft*, Darmstadt, 1985. This is not an 'introduction' to the subject in the usual sense of the term, but a collection of highly interesting essays on themes relating to successive periods in the history of linguistics.

T. BYNON and F. R. PALMER (eds.), *Studies in the history of western linguistics*, Cambridge, 1986.

D. HYMES (ed.), *Studies in the history of linguistics: traditions and paradigms*, Bloomington, 1974.

E. F. K. KOERNER (ed.), *Progress in linguistic historiography*, Amsterdam, 1980.

——, *Practising linguistic historiography: selected essays*, Amsterdam, 1989.

H. PARRET (ed.), *History of linguistic thought and contemporary linguistics*, Berlin, 1976.

T. E. SEBEOK (ed.), 'The historiography of linguistics', *Current trends in linguistics* 13 (1975), is a comprehensive two-volume compilation of chapters, with full bibliographies, giving accounts of the work done and the material published up to 1975 in linguistics in different parts of the world through the centuries. In subsequent chapters this will be cited as 'Sebeok, *Historiography of linguistics*'.

P. SCHMITTER (ed.), *Geschichte der Sprachtheorie 1: Zur Theorie und Methode der Geschichtsschreibung der Linguistik*, Tübingen, 1987.

During the past twenty-five years the history of linguistics has established for itself a recognized and distinctive place in the teaching and research comprised by general linguistics. It has been allocated places in the degree structures of linguistics in European and American universities, it appears regularly among the courses offered in Linguistic Institutes and in other similar schools, and it has its own section in the CIPL *Bibliographie linguistique*.

Since 1978 an International Conference on the History of the Language Sciences (ICHoLS) has met every three years with its *Proceedings* published. The following societies are specifically devoted to the study of the history of linguistics: La Société d'Histoire et d'Epistémologie des Sciences du Langage (SHESL, 1978), The Henry Sweet Society for the History of Linguistic Ideas (HSS, 1984), and The North American Association for the History of the Language Sciences (NAAHoLS, 1987).

A considerable number of books have been published, some of which are listed in the bibliographies of the chapters of this book. Articles on the history of linguistics and reviews of books appear in most linguistics periodicals, but the following may be regarded as the specialist serials in this field, and they should be consulted by those with particular interests in this branch of linguistics:

Studies in the history of linguistics (volume 32 and after, *Studies in the history of the language sciences*) (*Amsterdam studies in the theory and history of linguistic science* III, 1973).

Historiographia linguistica (1974)

Histoire épistémologie, langage (1979)

Notes

Bibliographical references to publications listed in the titles 'for further consultation' at the end of a chapter are given in the form of the author's name followed by the date of the work in question; other references are given in full in the first instance, but are repeated more briefly on repetition within a chapter.

1. cp. BORST, 1957–63, volume I.
2. cp. BUTTERFIELD, 1950.
3. cp. COLLINGWOOD, 1946, 42–5.
4. L. BLOOMFIELD, *Language*, London, 1935 vii.

Chapter 2

Greece

For the reasons given in the preceding chapter, it is sensible to begin the history of linguistic studies with the achievements of the ancient Greeks. This has to do, primarily, not with the merits of their work, which are very considerable, nor with the deficiencies in it that latter day scholars, looking back from the privileged standpoint of those at the far end of a long tradition, may justifiably point out. It is simply that the Greek thinkers on language, and on the problems raised by linguistic investigations, initiated in Europe the studies that we can call linguistic science in its widest sense, and that this science was a continuing focus of interest from ancient Greece until the present day in an unbroken succession of scholarship, wherein each worker was conscious of and in some way reacting to the work of his predecessors.

This is not to deny or to ignore significant work in applied linguistics (to use a later terminology) carried out in the Near East during the centuries preceding the Greek achievements. Writing, originally in a pictographic or character script, was devised in Egypt and in other parts of the world as well, independently, as in China and in Central America. The syllabic scripts which later became the source for the Greek alphabet[1] were probably created from the Egyptian script, progressively modified.

Any development of a system of writing that makes it possible to record visually a language as spoken and understood is a massive accomplishment, usually over several generations, in linguistic analysis specifically applied or directed to very practical needs. But, apart from the prior invention of writing and following from it, we have examples of ancient grammatical texts from

Babylonia, dating from about 1600 B.C. and later, written on tablets in cuneiform script, which set out in paradigm form the inflections of Sumerian pronouns, verbs, and other classes of words, with their correspondences in the Akkadian (Babylonian) language. The purpose of this work was the preservation of knowledge of Sumerian, a language becoming obsolescent but one in which much of the earlier Babylonian literature had been written.[2]

It was, however, in ancient Greece that theoretical linguistics had its European origin, in part from the service of practical requirements; but it was there that we have our first records of linguistic speculation arising from, but going far beyond, folk linguistics and practical applications.

The European tradition of linguistics has passed through several different stages, and has changed its main impetus and direction several times, being sensitive both to internal developments and to external situations. In the course of its history it has made contact with the major contributions of groups of linguistic scholars who started their labours outside the European tradition and developed their own insights independently of it. European linguistics has learned much from them. Indeed, without them present-day European linguistics (and this now inevitably means present-day linguistics in the world as a whole) would be poorer in content and less advanced in technique than we have the right to think it is. In starting from Greece and following the course of linguistic studies in Europe we can take in the work of scholars outside Europe at the point where it became known to Europeans and thereby entered and enriched the subject as the world knows it today.

By the time at which we have any record of linguistic science in Greece, the beginning of the classical age in the sixth and fifth centuries B.C., the Greeks had been settled for many generations in the habitable parts of the Greek mainland, the western coastal areas of Asia Minor, the islands of the Aegean, the east coasts of Sicily, and a few places in south Italy and elsewhere. The settlement of Greece by the Greeks was the result of successive movements of invaders from the north coming down into Greece and spreading outwards from it. The last such invasion was the arrival of the Dorians, probably around the end of the second millennium, disrupting the earlier Greek civilization of the 'Mycenaean age' achieved by other groups of Greek-speakers who had settled the mainland and some of the islands in the preceding centuries.

It is, of course, not just in linguistics that the Greeks were the

European pioneers. The intellectual life of Europe as a whole, its philosophical, moral, political, and aesthetic thought finds its origin in the work of Greek thinkers, and still today one can return again and again to what we have of Greek activity in the intellectual field for stimulus and encouragement. With the Greeks as with no other earlier or contemporary civilization modern man feels an undeniable intellectual kinship. Just what circumstances, environmental, cultural, and biological, gave rise to this brilliant flowering of the human intellectual and artistic genius in the Greece of the classical age we shall never know with certainty. We can only be thankful that it all happened.

The Greeks were not the first group of civilized men in the area that they entered. They learned much from established civilizations with which they came into contact in and around the eastern end of the Mediterranean and the 'fertile crescent' of Asia Minor, the cradle of civilized man in the west. But with the Greeks and in Greek civilization there developed for the first time in human history an insatiable demand for questioning the world around and the ways of men in the world. Among the Greeks there were those who insisted on enquiring into things that others failed to notice or in which they were uninterested. The Babylonians, whom we have already noticed in connection with applied linguistics, had also made use of geometry for land surveying and of arithmetic and astronomy for the calendrical measurement of time, but in Greece we find astronomy, arithmetic, and geometry studied as abstract independent sciences for the first time, and built up on the basis of systematic observation and the establishment of postulates and principles. In taking notice of the Greek achievement in linguistics, Bloomfield remarks of their peculiar brilliance of intellect: 'The ancient Greeks had the gift of wondering at things that other people take for granted'.[3]

Among the factors that were observed in the preceding chapter as giving rise to an interest in language as part of human life, the Greeks of the classical age were already aware both of the existence of peoples speaking languages other than Greek and of dialectal divisions within the Greek-speaking population. There must have been considerable linguistic contacts between Greeks and non-Greeks in trade, diplomacy, and in much of everyday life in the Greek 'colonies', settlements of Greeks on the coastal fringes of non-Greek-speaking areas in Asia Minor and Italy. We know surprisingly little about this. Herodotus and others quote and discuss foreign words, Plato admits in the *Cratylus* dialogue the possibility of the foreign origin of part of the Greek vocabulary, and we know of the existence of bilingual speakers and of professional interpreters. But of serious interest in the languages themselves among the Greeks there is no evidence; and the Greek designation of alien speakers as *bárbaroi* (βάρβαροι whence our word *barbarian*), i.e. people who speak unintelligibly, is probably indicative of their attitude.

Quite different was the Greek awareness of their own dialectal divisions. The Greek language in antiquity was more markedly divided into fairly sharply differentiated dialects than many other languages. This was due both to the settlement of the Greek-speaking areas by successive waves of invaders, and to the separation into relatively small and independent communities that the mountainous configuration of much of the Greek mainland and the scattered islands of the adjoining seas forced on them. But that these dialects were dialects of a single language and that the possession of this language united the Greeks as a whole people, despite the almost incessant wars waged between the different 'city states' of the Greek world, is attested by at least one historian; Herodotus, is his account of the major achievement of a temporarily united Greece against the invading Persians at the beginning of the fifth century B.C., puts into the mouths of the Greek delegates a statement that among the bonds of unity among the Greeks in resisting the barbarians was 'the whole Greek community, being of one blood and one tongue'.[4]

Not all the dialects were reduced to writing, but by the classical age the major dialects were, and we have inscriptional evidence of them, giving us a more detailed knowledge of the ancient Greek dialect situation than is available elsewhere in antiquity. Apart from the spoken dialects, educated Greeks were aware that the language of the Homeric poems, the Iliad and the Odyssey, was not precisely identifiable with any living dialect of the time. These poems held a special place in Greek education; they were publicly recited, and regarded and quoted in sources of moral precepts. 'Homeric scholarship', the establishment of acceptable texts of the poems and their critique, had begun in Athens during the sixth century.

The first achievement of linguistic scholarship in Greece, essentially part of 'applied linguistics', necessarily occurred before records appeared. Early in the first millennium B.C. an alphabetic system for writing the Greek language was worked out, and this served as the basis for the Greek alphabet of classical Attic (Athenian) and the other literary dialects, and, together with the Roman alphabet, derived from a western Greek variety of the Greek alphabet, became the parent of the most widely diffused means of writing in the world today.[5] We now know that writing was developed in Greece at two separate periods. During the second millennium the Mycenaeans made use of a syllabic writing system that included some logograms (symbols for individual words). This is also known as Linear B, and for long remained undeciphered. Like early Sumerian writing, it appears to have been largely confined to uses in administration and accountancy. The interpretation of this script and the almost certain identification of the language it recorded as an early variety of Greek constituted one of the outstanding events of recent classical scholarship, with a profound effect on our linguistic and historical knowledge of early Greece.

However, during the dark ages accompanying the Dorian invasions the knowledge of writing was lost, and the Greek alphabet as we know it today was independently developed from an adaptation of the Phoenician script. It is not certain whether this is historically connected with the original Egyptian form of writing, which, like that of ancient (and modern) China and of the Aztecs, was in the nature of a set of characters, signs or logograms, partly pictorially representative, standing for individual words or morphemes.

When the Greeks made use of the Phoenician system, it was largely a set of consonant signs, the vowels being in general supplied by the reader from his sense of what was written. The Greeks cannot claim to have invented writing; but by devising an alphabet, in the modern sense of the term, separately representing every distinctive segment, vowels as well as consonants, they can claim marked progress in their application of linguistic science. Essentially what the Greeks did was to apply certain consonant signs of the Hebrew system standing for consonant sounds not used distinctively in Greek to represent the Greek vowel sounds. Thus ℵ (*aleph*) standing for /ʔ(a)/ in Phoenician became the Greek letter A *(alpha)* standing for the vowel phoneme /a/. This very significant historical event is recorded mythically: Cadmus is said to have introduced writing from overseas, an acknowledgment of the alien origins of the historical Greek alphabet.

Broadly the Greek alphabet was phonemic. It was not completely so, and no alphabet is; hence the need for phonemic transcriptions. In particular, the suprasegmental features of distinctive pitch (the accents) and of juncture, which were observed and described later, with the accents graphically represented, had no symbolization in the classical period. But the devising of an alphabet for the segmental phonemes of Greek depended on an unconscious phonemic analysis of the language (or of its individual dialects). We have little knowledge of the steps by which this was achieved, but the appearance in certain inscriptions of the letter ♀ for /k/ before back vowels (from Phoenician ♀ standing for /q/ a distinct phoneme in that language) indicates a stage of incomplete phonemic analysis, since the varieties of velar position in Greek, being dependent on the nature of the adjacent vowels, are all allophones of one phoneme /k/, written κ in the classical alphabet.[6]

That the development and use of writing was the first piece of linguistic scholarship in Greece is attested by the history of the word *grammatikós* (γράμματικός); up to and including the time of Plato and Aristotle the word meant simply one who understood the use of letters, *grámmata* (γράμματα), and could read and write, and *téchnē grammatiké* (τέχνη γραμματική) was the skill of reading and writing.[7] The later extension of the meaning of this and of its formally associated terms follows the further development of linguistic science, specifically in the field of grammar, by later generations.

In the classical age of Greek literature and afterwards we can follow the progress of conscious linguistic speculation, as men reflected on the nature and the use of their language. Looking backward in history we may think ourselves to be tracing the growth of part of linguistic science towards a preconceived end; but from the point of view of each generation of thinkers we are seeing what those who came after did with what they found left by their predecessors, without any ultimate systematically organized subject in mind. The term *grammatiké* meant no more at first than the understanding of letters, and much of what one thinks of today as early linguistic enquiries fell under the general heading of *philosophía* (φιλοσοφία), itself covering a much wider field in ancient Greece than 'philosophy' does today, and initially embracing virtually the whole realm of human knowledge.

Observations on language, always with reference to the Greek language, are found in the records we have of the pre-Socratic philosophers, the fifth-century rhetoricians and Socrates, and in the writings of Plato, and Aristotle; but one must wait until the time of the Stoics for the separate recognition of linguistic studies within the much wider field of *philosophía*.

Our knowledge of the pre-Socratics and of the early rhetoricians is fragmentary and derived from secondary sources. From the end of the sixth century B.C., philosophers in Ionia and elsewhere ranged widely over astronomy, physics, mathematics, ethics, and metaphysics, and they included language within their purview. In the fifth century, the rhetoricians became well known in the Greek world, among them Gorgias from Sicily. These persons made a professional study of oratory, and some of them travelled about giving instruction for fees and writing books on their subject; they formed part of that body of itinerant purveyors of instruction of all kinds known as the Sophists.

Our knowledge of Socrates is also indirect. He left no writing himself, but his arguments and viewpoints are reported in some of the writings of Xenophon and in the more famous *Dialogues* of Plato, though in these latter it is always an open question how much of what we have is directly taken from Socrates and how much is the thought of Plato expressed as the speech of Socrates. Certainly Socrates stood for fearless criticism and for total freedom of speech; he went to his death for his ideals. In the somewhat totalitarian polity sketched out in Plato's *Republic* and put into Socrates's mouth he might soon himself have endured suppression or expulsion.

One dialogue, the *Cratylus*, is devoted to linguistic questions, though in some ways it is disappointing in its content; and references to language and its analysis are found in several other Platonic dialogues in which Socrates is the main speaker. Though Plato does not gather together his separate observations, he is credited with some part in initiating grammatical studies in Greece by the later writer Diogenes Laertius, who says that Plato first investigated the potentialities of grammar'.[8]

Aristotle (384–322 B.C.) knew the works of Plato, on which he developed his own thinking. His was probably the most remarkable intellect in antiquity; almost all fields of human knowledge then recognized fell within his scope. His writings range from ethics, politics, and logic, to physics, biology, and natural history, and in a survey of the forms of life he in some ways anticipated the nineteenth-century evolutionary tree model of the living universe.[9]

As with the works of Plato, we must assemble Aristotle's linguistic doctrine from statements scattered among several works on rhetoric and logic, where they appear incidentally and in other contexts. This makes it difficult to state Aristotle's position on any detail with exactitude and certain questions are likely to remain controversial. Nevertheless the outlines of Aristotle's linguistics are fairly clear, and it may be seen that his work marks a development from the positions reached by Plato.

The Aristotelian age marked the end of an era in Greek history. Aristotle had been appointed tutor to the young Alexander of Macedon, and, if his political teaching is reflected in his political writing, he preached to his pupil the merits of the small independent Greek 'city state' such as had been the typical polity for several centuries. But Alexander's conquests, that in fact brought all Asia Minor and Egypt as well as the Greek homeland under Macedonian control, altered the Greek world irreversibly. Though his empire was divided among his successors, who were often at war with each other, Greek administration and Greek ideas spread over the eastern Mediterranean area, and Asia Minor, and a variety of the Attic dialect known as *koinē* (*diálektos*) (κοινή (διάλεκτος)), or common dialect, became a standard language for government, trade, and education over the whole area, gradually displacing the local dialects of earlier periods.

Alexander himself and most of the Macedonian rulers of his successor states justified their rule and their imperial position by asserting the benefits of Greek culture and Greek civilization that they were now imposing on the moribund remains of what had been the Persian Empire. Greek education was fostered at all levels. As Greek was now the language of senior administration, the professions, and of social advancement, the teaching of Greek to non-Greeks (i.e. 'Greek as a foreign language') became for the first time a widespread activity with its own techniques and requirements. This was all part of the process known as Hellenizing, and the period following the Macedonian conquests is designated the Hellenistic Age. In cities such as Pergamum in Asia Minor and Alexandria in Egypt, Greek-speaking universities were established and fostered by the Macedonian rulers, with endowed libraries and salaried scholars, in which higher instruction and research were undertaken in Greek literature and in the classical Greek language of Homer and of the Athenian poets and prose writers of the fifth and fourth centuries B.C. At the same time Athens itself remained the academic centre of the Greek world.

Among the philosophical schools that grew up in Athens after Aristotle, the most important in the history of linguistics is the Stoic school. The Stoics, founded by Zeno (*c.* 300 B.C.), worked in a number of fields in which Aristotle had worked, but in certain aspects of philosophy and rhetoric they developed their own methods and doctrines.

Under the Stoics linguistics achieved a defined place within the overall context of philosophy, and linguistic questions were expressly treated in separate works devoted to aspects of language, and treated in an orderly manner. The position of language in the Stoic system can be summarized in three quotations: 'First comes the impression, then the mind, making use of speech, expresses in words the experience produced by the impression'; 'All things are discerned through dialectic studies'; 'Most people are agreed that it is proper to begin the study of dialectic from that part of it dealing with speech'.[10]

The Stoics formalized the dichotomy between form and meaning, distinguishing in language 'the signifier' and the 'signified', in terms strikingly reminiscent of de Saussure's *signifiant* and *signifié*. The relevant texts are hard to interpret, but it seems that 'the signified' was not just a mental impression, but something in the speaker's and the hearer's mind corresponding to an utterance in language, somewhat akin to the Saussurean union of sound and thought by the operation of *la langue*.[11]

They gave separate treatment to phonetics, grammar, and etymology, to which they devoted considerable attention; but their most notable contribution, as is the case with the whole of western linguistics during antiquity, was in the field of grammar, in which a progressive development through more than one stage of theory and terminology can be traced.

Though it was among the Stoics that linguistics, *grammatikḗ* (γραμματική), was first accorded independent recognition within philosophical studies, it is now difficult to reconstruct with any certainty many of the details of their linguistic theory. We do not have their contemporary writings extant, except for some fragmentary texts, but we do known of the authors and their titles through later writers and notably through Diogenes Laertius (*c.* third century A.D.), who compiled an encyclopeadic set of short accounts of the life and work of notable Greek philosophers (*Vitae Philosophorum*), including several prominent figures in the early Stoic schools. It is to be noted that they promulgated a theory of syntax or sentence structure based on the analysis of the different types of predicates available in the Greek verbal system, e.g. transitive, intransitive, and impersonal (as in *metamélei Sōcrátei* (μεταμελει Σωκράτει), (it) repents (to) Socrates, i.e. Socrates regrets. But several problems of interpretation remain.[12]

Stoic philosophical schools and Stoic teaching in philosophy in general and in linguistics continued throughout antiquity, and their ideas contributed to the thinking of other schools; but as far as concerned linguistics, the Stoics were not accepted as part of the mainline tradition, and for this reason as well as through the loss of their early writings we are less well informed of the details of their work than we are of the Alexandrian scholars, who effectively set their seal on the teaching of linguistics, especially of grammar, through the Greek, Roman, and mediaeval worlds.

The Stoic school was founded in the Hellenistic age, the post-Alexandrian age, whose characteristics were mentioned above. Linguistically this period, more than the earlier centuries, was marked by increasingly close contacts between Greek-speakers and speakers of other languages (the first translation of the Old Testament into Greek, the Septuagint, was carried out in this age); it was also characterized by the divergence of current spoken Greek, the *koinē*, from the language of the Athenian classical authors, the literary standard, apart from Homer, of all educated Greeks. Some have held that the attention paid to linguistic questions by the Stoics and the insight that they showed in analysing the semantics of the Greek verbal tense system (pp. 33-4 below) may be attributed in part to the fact that Zeno, their founder, was himself a bilingual whose first language was a Semitic one and who had learned Greek in later life.

Up to this period the context in which linguistics had developed had been philosophical, and in particular logical, enquiries; the linguistic science of the Stoics formed a part, though a distinct and articulated part, of their general philosophical system. But from this time on another motivation made itself felt in ancient linguistics, the study of literary style; firstly, there was a concern for 'correct' Greek pronunciation and grammar, that is classical Greek as against much of the current *koiné* and the changes caused by the large-scale acquisition of Greek by previous speakers of other languages; and secondly, in the widespread study of classical literature and of the works of Homer, commentaries on the language and the content were required by many readers within the newly Hellenized world. To the Hellenistic period belong a number of glossaries of different non-Attic dialects, evidence of the systematic study of the differences between varieties of Greek that had a representative writing system.

The written accent marks of Greek writing date from the Hellenistic age, as guides to the correct pronunciation of words, and the description of accentual and junctural features graphically represented by word boundaries and punctuation marks, under the general heading of prosodies, *prosōdíai* (προσωδίαι) was part of the movement in favour of correctness, or Hellenism, *Hellēnismós* ('Ελληνισμός), as it was called. Homeric scholarship reached an advanced stage during the Hellenistic age, and a number of important grammarians engaged in linguistic research were best known for their work in the establishment of correct Homeric texts and their exegesis.

Having taken notice of the principal scholars concerned in the first stages of Greek linguistics, we may return to consider the main lines on which their work was organized and developed. Once again, we should try to see this not as a series of tentative anticipations of what we know became the culmination of Greek linguistic thought, but as successive movements from the positions reached as lines of thinking and modes of statement were tested, extended to new material, and adapted in the light of experience.

From the outset it is found that questions about language, concentrated entirely on the Greek language, were considered within the terms of two somewhat interrelated controversies. These were the rival claims made on behalf of nature, *phýsis* (φύσις), as against convention, *nómos* (νόμος) or *thésis* (θέσις), in the first place, and of regularity or analogy, *analogía* (ἀναλογία), as against irregularity or anomaly, *anōmalía* (ἀνωμαλία), in the second, in the control of man's speech and our proper understanding of its working. These two dichotomies represent opposing viewpoints, one being favoured by some and the other by others, rather than continuous formalized debates with rigidly distinguished adherents locked in permanent argument.

The *phýsis-nómos* question seems to have been the earlier controversy; the one between the analogists and the anomalists persisted throughout antiquity, though its relevance became less as time wore on. Both put linguistic questions within the context of wider-ranging arguments, and each side could draw on obvious support from the facts of the case.

A principal topic of discussion among the pre-Socratic philosophers and among the later Sophists, and one that appears in several dialogues of Plato, was to what extent accepted standards, institutions, and judgments of what is right and wrong, just and unjust, and so on, were grounded in the nature of things and to what extent they were essentially the products of a tacit convention or even of explicit legislation. The theme of the *Cratylus* is a debate on the origin of language and on the relations between words and their meanings: are they based on a natural affinity between word form and word meaning or are they the result of convention and agreement?[13] Both views are given due consideration in the mouths of the participants, without a definite conclusion being reached. The naturalist argument leaned as it must on the weight of onomatopoeia in a vocabulary and on a more general sound symbolism in the phonological structure of some words, and a good deal of play was made with the sort of etymologies proposed for some Greek words by which it was hoped to trace them back to an allegedly 'natural' source, since it was admitted on the naturalist side that time had wrought changes in the 'first' forms of words.[14] The conventionalists pointed out that vocabulary can be changed at will and that the language is equally efficient once the change has been accepted.[15]

In itself the nature-convention discussion does not seem properly framed or very fruitful as far as language is concerned. Language is a universal capability of every normal human being, and in terms of total complexity, orderliness, and cultural adequacy there are no valid means of grading languages in a scale or of picking out alleged survivals of primitivity. In this sense the capability of communicating by speech (de Saussure's *langage*) is natural. But a wider acquaintance with different languages than was envisaged by the early Greeks shows how limited a role onomatopoeia and sound symbolism play and that in the greater part of the vocabulary of any given language (*langue*) the arbitrary and conventional status of the relation between form and meaning prevails (*l'arbitraire du signe*), though the convention is tacit, not explicit, like the social contract adduced as the basis of social organization. Speculation on whether in its origin language was far more onomatopoeic than in any known period remains and will remain largely unverifiable speculation, and was rightly subject to the sarcastic criticism of Max Müller in the last century.[16]

Historically the importance of the controversy is due to its place in the early development of linguistic theory and to the stimulus it provided to more detailed examination of the Greek language. In maintaining and in criticizing each side of the argument people were led to examine more closely the structures and the meanings of words and the formal patterns that words exhibited. In such examinations lies the beginning of precise linguistic analysis.

Later scholars took up more definite positions than we find in Plato. Aristotle firmly adopted a conventionalist point of view: 'Language is by convention, since no names arise naturally.'[17] Onomatopoeia need not invalidate this, since onomatopoeic forms vary from language to language and are always cast within the phonology of the particular language. Aristotle's view of language is summed up at the beginning of the *De interpretatione*: 'Speech is the representation of the experiences of the mind, and writing is the representation of speech.'[18]

Epicurus (341–270) took up a middle position, holding that word forms arose naturally but were modified by convention. More importantly in the history of linguistics, the Stoics favoured the natural status of language, again relying heavily on onomatopoeia and sound symbolism: 'In the opinion of the Stoics names are naturally formed, the first sounds imitating the things which they name.'[19] This attitude fitted well with their more general emphasis on nature as the guide to man's proper life; and in their etymology much weight was placed on the 'original forms' of words, *prôtai phōnaí* (πρῶται φωναί), which were said to have been onomatopoeic but later to have suffered changes of various kinds.[20]

These opposing views of Aristotle and the Stoics are important since they lead to the second linguistic controversy of antiquity, analogy versus anomaly. This was not set out formally, with the opposing arguments marshalled against each other, before the extended treatment accorded to the question by the first-century B.C. Latin writer Varro; and one must not envisage the two views as the exclusive tenets of sharply and continuously opposed partisans, but rather as two attitudes to language, each in itself reasonably justified by part of the evidence and each favoured by some individuals and groups.

It seems clear that Aristotle favoured analogy and the Stoics favoured anomaly as the dominant theme in language. Later analogists tended to concentrate on linguistic questions for the purposes of literary criticism and the maintenance of standards of correctness (*Hellēnismós*); Stoic interests were more broadly based. The division may have been sharpened by the rivalry of Alexandria and Pergamum under Macedonian rule as two main centres of learning, Alexandria dominated by analogists and Pergamum by Stoics. Chrysippus, the Stoic, wrote a treatise on linguistic anomaly.[21]

Once more it may be felt that the controversy was expressed in terms that one would not resort to today; but, like the nature-convention argument, it was part of the context within which the detailed investigation of Greek and Latin grammar took place, and a lack of historical sympathy is perhaps shown by those who would dismiss it, as Classen did, as not worth so much as a yawn.[22]

In considering both these controversies it is important to remember that they largely took place before the publication of any grammar books or dictionaries of the Greek and Latin languages. They were indeed part of the way in which those who thought about language were developing their ideas in debates and disputes with their fellow thinkers as the subject of descriptive and theoretical linguistics gradually took shape. These controversies were historically part of the context of early linguistic enquiry. Classen's brusque dismissal was made against a very different background in the early years of the nineteenth century, when grammatical theories had long been worked out and expounded and when grammars and dictionaries of Greek, Latin, and other languages were readily available.

Broadly, the analogy – anomaly controversy turned on the extent to which orderliness and especially proportional regularity held sway in the Greek language, and by implication in language as a whole, and to what extent irregularities, 'anomalies', characterized it. The regularities looked for by the analogists were those of formal paradigms wherein words of the same grammatical status had the same morphological terminations and accentual structure, and those involving the relations between form and meaning, whereby words that were comparable morphologically could be expected to bear comparable, 'analogical', meanings and *vice versa*. These sorts of analogies lie at the heart of morphology, and without them paradigms of different word classes, and their subclasses (declensions and conjugations in Latin and Greek), in which repetitive patterns are summarized, would not be discoverable. They are moreover the basis of any attempted semantic labelling of grammatical categories such as singular and plural and the nominal cases. To this extent, as the later grammarian Dionysius Thrax pointed out, the morphological component of grammar largely consists of 'the working out of analogy'.[23]

Analogical arguments were sometimes used to prefer one word form over another as correct Greek and to establish the proper text of a Homeric line.[24] Some analogists went further than this and tried to reform Greek irregular paradigms in the interests of analogical regularity (a process that in some respects took place of its own accord in the passage from classical Attic through the *koiné* and Byzantine Greek to the modern language); the forms *Zeós* (Ζεός), *Zeí* (Ζεί), *Zéa* (Ζέα), etc. were suggested in place of the actual but 'anomalous' forms *Zēnós,* etc. as the oblique cases of the word *Zeús (Ζεύς)*. Such attitudes were attacked by Sextus Empiricus, writing in the second century A.D. when grammarians were identified with the analogists, who challenged their whole work, accusing them of fabricating more unknown 'analogical' forms such as *kýōnos* (κύωνος), instead of *kynós* (κυνός), from *kýōn* (κύων), dog; and a later Latin writer was led to protest that to speak Latin and to speak grammatically were now two different things.[25]

While it may now be seen that the entire basis of an economical description of Greek morphology rested on the recognition and systematization of formal analogies, the anomalists had no lack of counter-examples with which to maintain their thesis. Most nominal and verbal paradigmatic classes admit exceptions, irregular members, which cannot be expurgated from the languages at the behest of grammarians. Proportional semantic relations between formal categories and their generic meanings are upset by such anomalies as single cities being designated by formally plural nouns (*Athênai* ('Αθῆναι), Athens; *Thêbai* (Θῆβαι) Thebes), and positive states or attributes like immortality being referred to by negatively prefixed words (*athánatos* ('αθανατος); Latin *immortālis*). Sextus, in a genial attack on grammarians as a class, makes much of the semantic anomalies of gender, pointing not only to the masculine and feminine genders of nouns denoting inanimates and abstractions and the use of a single masculine or feminine (and sometimes a neuter) noun to refer to both sexes of an animate, but also to dialectal variation between the genders of some nouns.[26]

The anomalist case appeared at first more cogent when no adequate distinction was made between inflection and derivation within grammatical word form variations. It is a characteristic of Greek and indeed of most languages that the inflexional paradigms are much more regular and apply to entire classes of stems, whereas the incidence of derivational formations is more irregular. Almost all Greek nouns had forms for five cases, singular and plural, but derivational suffixes were restricted to specific noun stems; thus we find *patér* (πατήρ), father, and *pátrios* (πάτριος), paternal, but no corresponding form **métrios* (μήτριος) with *métēr* (μήτηρ), mother. Likewise English derives nouns from adjectives by such varied formations as *true, truth, happy, happiness, hot, heat, high, height,* and *possible, possibility,* and some speakers would hesitate between (*un*) *grammaticalness* and (*un*) *grammaticality*.

Carrying their semantic analyses further, the Stoics would point out also the fallacy of any clear-cut one-form, one-meaning correspondence in the Greek, and by implication in any other, language. Sometimes as the result of divergent historical processes a single word form could come to bear several very different referential functions. Augustine, setting out Stoic views, points to the different meanings of Latin *aciés mīlitum* (soldiers), line of battle, *ferrī* (sword), sharp edge of the blade, and *oculōrum* (eyes), keenness of vision.[27]

The consonance of the analogical attitude to language with Aristotle's general philosophical position is not hard to illustrate. Proportionality (*análogon, analogia*) appears in several places in his works as a guiding principle in conduct and in reasoning.[28] It was moreover logically associated with the conventionalist view of language, which he espoused, since the more regularity there is to be found in any arbitrary, conventional system of communication, the more efficient it will be.

The Stoics, however, regarded language as a natural human capability to be accepted as it was, with all its characteristic irregularity. They took a broader view of what was good Greek (*Hellēnismós*) than the analogists, and were interested in linguistic questions not principally as grammatical and textual critics; they were philosophers for whom language served as the expression of thought and feeling and for whom literature held deeper meanings and insights veiled in myth and allegory (the Greek word *allēgorikôs* (ἀλληγορικῶς), allegorically, is first known to have been used by the Stoic Cleanthes[29]).

Linguistics, like other sciences in antiquity, lay under the general influence of Aristotelian scientific method, but in the contrasting tendencies of the Stoic philosophers and the Alexandrian literary critics one sees the opposition between philosophical and literary considerations as the determining factors in the development of linguistics. With the later full development of Greek grammar, literary interests predominated, but throughout antiquity and the Middle Ages this conflict of principle, now tacit, now explicitly argued, can be observed as a recurrent feature of the history of linguistic thought and practice.

The three main aspects of linguistic study that received specific attention among early Greek scholars were etymology, phonetics (pronunciation), and grammar. The first, etymology, aroused much enthusiasm, research, and speculation, and was stimulated by the nature-convention controversy about the origin and development of language. But the term *etymology* was understood and etymological enquiries were carried on under different ideas on the subject from those prevailing today. The time scale for any historical study of languages was much briefer than is ours; within a few centuries human beings and therefore human language went back to their ancestors among the heroes and gods and goddesses of accepted mythology, and efforts were principally directed at answering the question how the limited stock of phonetically appropriate primary words, first given or taught by the gods, were multiplied to produce the vast numbers of words in the vocabulary, first of Greek and then of Latin, to cope with the requirements of a literate and literary civilization. A Greek definition of *etymologia* (ἐτυμολογία) clarifies this conception: 'The unfolding of words, through which their true meanings are made plain.'[30]

From the start etymological investigation was directed towards attempts at tracing the forms of words back to the forms of other words by which the meaning of the former could, it was thought, be explained. This produced the fanciful etymologies proposed in all seriousness, some of which appear in Plato's *Cratylus*, for example *ánthrōpos* (ἄνθρωπος), man, from *anathrôn hà ópōpen* ('αναθρῶν ἃ ὄπωπεν), looking up at what he has seen, and *Poseidôn* (ποσειδῶν) from *posì desmós* (ποσὶ δεσμός), restraint to the feet (presumably in walking through water, Poseidon being the god of the sea). But it is fair to add that Plato does treat some of these etymological suggestions quite playfully.

Similar efforts continued to characterize etymological scholarship throughout antiquity and the Middle Ages. Mainly because of this different understanding of etymology before the Renaissance, this aspect of linguistic research in antiquity and in the Middle Ages has been dismissed with ridicule – a dismissal sometimes extended, quite unjustly, to Graeco-Roman linguistics as a whole. We should not forget that ancient and mediaeval linguists themselves saw the ease with which this sort of etymologizing could pass into mere comic conceits: the grimly humorous derivation of *cadāver*, corpse, as *ca(rō) da(ta) ver(mibus)* is all too well known.[31]

Greek phonetics and phonology, in so far as these two can properly be separated with reference to this period, were built upon the composite unit of writing and speaking, the basic element of articulate speech, the *grámma* (γράμμα), best considered as a letter of the alphabet together with its phonetic values.

Some articulatory classifications were attempted, the syllable was introduced as a structural unit of phonological description, and by the time of the Stoics a rudimentary picture was grasped of speech as the effect of articulatory interference with egressive air from the lungs. Only Greek was studied. Foreign words were written as best they could be with the Greek letters, but no scholarly concern was evinced over alien sounds or alien sound systems. The descriptive framework for Greek phonetics was the Greek alphabet, and statements took the form of accounts of the pronunciation of the letters in it.

One objection to such a letter-based approach to phonetics is that the recognition of allophonic differences within the Greek phonemes was obstructed; commentators refer to different conjoint realizations of vowels with different accents and with and without aspiration and length, but they make no mention of different qualities of vowel sounds themselves though such differences must have accompanied different segmental and suprasegmental environments.[32] Nor were the phonetic differences between the dialects described other than those differences that were represented by different spellings. More seriously, an improper analogy was accepted between the relation of discrete letters to a text and that of allegedly discrete sounds to a spoken utterance. This fallacy was not challenged, and it appears explicitly in Priscian at the end of the classical period, writing on Latin: 'Just as atoms come together and produce every corporeal thing, so likewise do speech sounds compose articulate speech as it were some bodily entity.'[33] The relations are otherwise: letters actually do compose written sentences; speech may be analysed into speech sounds.

Plato made a number of distinctions among classes of segmental phonemes in Greek, grouping together vowels in contrast to consonants and distinguishing within them between continuants and stops, the latter not being pronounceable without an adjacent vowel sound. He was also aware of accentual differences between words having similar sequences of segments, or letters; he compared *Diì phílos* (Διὶ φίλος), a friend to God, with the name *Diphilos* (Δίφιλος) in respect of their different pitch sequences.[34]

Further advances were made in phonetics by the Stoics, who recognized the study of speech sounds as a distinct part of the study of language. They distinguished three aspects of the *grámma*, thereby confirming its phonetic-orthographic unity: its phonetic value, e.g. [a], its written shape, e.g. α, and the name by which it was designated, e.g. *alpha*.[35] These three properties of letters continued to be distinguished throughout antiquity, their Latin names being *potestās* (power), *figūra* (shape), and *nōmen* (name).

The Stoics studied the syllabic structures of the Greek language, and made the threefold distinction between sound sequences actually occurring as meaningful parts of discourse, sound sequences which could occur according to the rules of syllable formation but in fact do not (e.g. *blítyri* (βλίτυρι)), and sequences excluded as being phonologically impossible in the language.[36]

A number of precise and correct observations on the phonetics of Greek were made by ancient scholars, and they are of great value in reconstructing the pronunciation of Greek (and so are the phonetic statements of the later Latin grammarians); but several serious omissions of factual observation as well as a lack of adequate descriptive theory remain, and in the history of phonetics Greco-Roman work is not of prime significance. In particular, their classifications and descriptions were couched mainly in impressionistic acoustic terms, for which they had no adequate technical terminology, rather than in terms of articulations such as were used more successfully by the ancient Indians and the Arabs (pp. 156–8, 111–12 below). Nineteenth-century phonetics, which saw such rapid progress in this aspect of linguistics, owed its main inspiration to the descriptive techniques of the Indians and to the observational methodology of the empirical tradition of the preceding three centuries.

It was in the field of grammar that the Greek (and the Roman) world did its best work, with the most effective and lasting influence on the future. In this we not only see the purposeful and fruitful building of later generations on their predecessors' results, but we know of authoritative books written on Greek and on Latin grammar, several of which are extant, and the grammatical descriptions provided in them were maintained by a continuous tradition through the Middle Ages and the modern world to become the basis of the standard grammars of these languages today. Moreover the theories, categories, and terminology evolved by ancient scholars in relation to the grammar of their own languages have become part of the general grammatical equipment of descriptive linguists of our own day.

The framework of grammatical description in western antiquity was the word and paradigm model.[37] Despite the richness of classical morphology, a theory of the morpheme was not achieved, and classical grammatical statements exhibit the strengths and the weaknesses of a word based morphology. As Greek phonology was based on the pronunciation of the letters of the Greek alphabet, so Greek grammar concentrated on the written language, mostly the Attic Greek of the classical authors, though always with a proper attention to its implication of utterance in reading aloud.

A word based grammar involves three main procedures: the identification of the word as an isolable linguistic entity, the establishment of a set of word classes to distinguish and classify the words in the language, and the working out of adequate grammatical categories to describe and analyse the morphology of words entering into paradigms of associated forms and the syntactic relations obtaining between words in the construction of sentences.

Though there are general grammatical arguments in favour of treating syntactic relations as the central component of grammar (they are, for example, dealt with in earlier rules than those covering word morphology in a generative grammar), in the history of western grammatical theory morphology appears to have been formalized first; our first extant description of Greek mor-

phology antedates our first extant description of Greek syntax by
two centuries, and the latter is based on the former in its statements.

Logically one might argue that in working out a word based
grammar one should proceed first with the formal identification
of the word unit, then with the classes of words, and finally with
the categories relevant to them. This, in fact, is the order of
treatment in Greek grammar attributed to Dionysius Thrax. Historically, however, we find what were later to be part of the
system of grammatical categories discussed first, sporadically by
the fifth-century Sophists. Protagoras considered the nominal
category of gender in Greek, and is reported to have wished
mênis (μῆνις), anger, and pélēx (πήληξ), helmet, to be masculine instead of feminine, presumably on the grounds of a
semantic association with male characteristics and activities rather
than with female.[38] Socrates may himself have discussed this
category, as Aristophanes makes fun of him in his comedy The
Clouds for suggesting new formally feminine words like
alektrýaina (ἀλεκτρύαινα), hen, instead of the use of alektryōn
(ἀλεκτρυών) in both the masculine and feminine genders for
'cock' and 'hen', and for worrying about words like kárdopos
(κάρδοπος), trough, one of the few second declension nouns
ending in -os that were feminine.[39]

Protagoras also set out the different types of sentence in which
a general semantic function was associated with a certain grammatical structure, e.g. wish, question, statement, and command.[40]
This lay within the field of rhetoric, but it provided the material
for more formal syntactic analysis of sentence structures by later
generations.

Plato and Aristotle make scattered references to grammar, but
do not deal with it consecutively or as a specific topic. Plato, however, is said to have been the first to take the subject seriously,
as in his dialogues we encounter a fundamental division of the
Greek sentence into a nominal and a verbal component, ónoma
and rhêma (ὄνομα, ῥῆμα), which remained the primary grammatical distinction underlying syntactic analysis and word
classification in all future linguistic description.[41]

Aristotle maintained this distinction, but added a third class of
syntactic component, the sýndesmoi (σύνδεσμοι), a class covering
what were later to be distinguished as conjunctions (and probably
prepositions, though this is not apparent from the examples
cited), the article, and pronouns.[42] This tripartite analysis of the
sentence was probably intended to distinguish the components of
the declarative statement, apophantikòs lógos (ἀποφαντικὸς

λόγος), in which as a logician Aristotle was most interested and
which he took as basic. Aristotle additionally gave a formal
definition of the word as a linguistic unit: a component of the
sentence, *méros lógou* (μέρος λόγου), having a meaning of its
own but not further divisible into meaningful units.[43] Plato had
not explicitly stated whether his *ónoma* and *rhêma* referred to
words or to phrases or to both. Aristotle's definition is remarkably like Meillet's 'association of a given meaning with a given group
of sounds capable of grammatical employment'[44]; in fact neither
is wholly adequate, since both exclude the morpheme from consideration, which itself is always 'capable of grammatical
employment' and often enough carries an isolable meaning. The
sentence (*lógos*) involved more for Aristotle at the semantic level,
since unlike the isolated word it affirmed or denied a predicate,
or made an existential statement.[45] He further defined the *rhêma*
as additionally (i.e. unlike the *ónoma*) indicating a time reference
and as representing the predicate.[46] This second part of the definition allowed him, like Plato, to include adjectives such as *leukós*
(λευκός), white, and *díkaios* (δίκαιος), just, among the *rhēmata*,[47]
since they frequently serve in Greek as predicates (*leukòs ho hip-
pos* (λευκὸς ὁ ἵππος), the horse is white), and, with the
copula *estí* (ἐστί), is, 'understood', and always available for inser-
tion, it could be said that they carry (present) time reference as
well. For this reason the translation of *ónoma* and *rhêma* by *noun*
and *verb* at this stage in the development of Greek grammatical
theory may be misleading.

Aristotle, like Protagoras, recognized the category of gender in
nouns and listed typical gender marking terminations,[48] but other
formal differences in word shapes are treated under the category
of *ptôsis* (πτῶσις). In Aristotelian usage this term covers a number of grammatically relevant alterations of a descriptively basic
form of a word; oblique cases of nouns, comparative and superlative forms of adjectives, the deadjectival adverbs in *-ōs*, like
dikaîōs (δικαίως), justly, verbal tenses other than the present,
and other verbal inflections are all *ptóseis*, shaped from the basic
form of the inflecting word concerned.[49]

It is easy to see the inadequacy of Plato's and Aristotle's grammatical frames of reference; but what is more significant is to
notice the first stage, taken by them, in forging a technical
metalanguage for the description and analysis of Greek, from the
lexical resources of the language, which had not hitherto been
required to serve in this way. This is part of the fascination
of following the progressive development of the Greek
grammarians' descriptive apparatus. *Ónoma*, on its way to be-

coming the translation of English *noun*, had originally meant 'name', and *rhêma*, 'predicate', later 'verb', had been used to mean 'saying' or 'proverb'[50]; *ptôsis*, literally 'fall', of which the technical etymology is obscure, was used by Aristotle as a logical term as well as a very general grammatical term.[51] This term was to have a very long history; its restriction in meaning to that of English *case*, Latin *cāsus*, was one of the distinctive advances in theory made by the Stoic grammarians.[52]

Successive generations of Stoic philosophers achieved a great deal in grammar; some scholars indeed would say that grammar in the modern sense only began with them, but the work that has just been surveyed provided them with their starting point. The Stoics, whose philosophical attitude led them to pay great attention to language, contributed significantly to the development of the descriptive analysis of Greek and to the refinement of grammatical concepts for this purpose, as their work, appearing in the various specialist writings already mentioned (p. 19, above), was taken up and further developed by later grammarians of the dominant Alexandrian school.[53]

Although it later took second place to the mainstream Alexandrian tradition, it is important to take note of the main outlines of the Stoic achievement.

The Aristotelian system of word classification and grammatical categories was further articulated by the Stoics in two directions: the number of word classes was increased, and more precise definitions and additional grammatical categories were introduced to cover the morphology and part of the syntax of these classes. Later writers saw the developing word class system as the progressive subdivision of the previous one[54]; it seems that the Stoics proceeded in three stages. Firstly, among Aristotle's *sýndesmoi* the inflected members (later pronoun and article) were separated jointly as *árthra* (ἄρθρα) from the invariant uninflected members, to which alone the term *sýndesmos* was applied (the later preposition and conjunction); secondly, Aristotle's *ónoma* was divided into proper noun, to which the term *ónoma* was applied, and common noun, *prosēgoría* (προσηγορία); and, thirdly, from within this the class of adverbs was split off and named *mesótēs* (μεσότης), literally 'those in the middle', perhaps because they belonged syntactically with verbs but were mostly associated morphologically with noun stems.

Of these Stoic classes all were taken over by later writers except for the *prosēgoríā*, which was reunited with the *ónoma* as a single class under a single definition, *prosēgoría* being recognized within it as a subclass only. The Stoics defined the distinction between their two classes of noun semantically by reference to individual quality ('being Socrates') as against general quality ('being a horse'). This is logically and semantically important, but it is not a morphological distinction, and attempts to assign separate paradigms to common and proper nouns are not borne out by the facts of Greek, though a more delicate syntactic analysis may provide a formal basis for a subclass of proper nouns.[55]

Case in its modern usage as an inflectional category of nouns and other words inflected like them was the creation of the Stoics; thereafter *klísis* (κλίσις) was used generically of grammatical word form variation. By restricting *ptôsis* to nouns and words likewise inflected, the Stoics were able to make case inflection the *fundamentum divisionis* between *ónoma* and *rhêma*, which it remained (with the result that Greek (and Latin) adjectives were treated as a subclass of nouns, *onómata*, henceforth) and between their *árthra* (case inflected) and their *sýndesmoi* (uninflected). Within the category they extended the use of the term to cover all the forms of case inflected words, and divided them into *ptôsis eutheîa* (εὐθεῖα) or *orthế* (ὀρθή), nominative (Latin *cāsus rectus*), and the *ptôseis plágiai* (πλάγιαι), oblique cases (in Greek the accusative, genitive and dative). The position of the vocative in the Stoic system is uncertain. It was seen that the nominative, as the subject case, in concord of number with the finite verb, contrasted with the three oblique cases, all of which construct with verbs in different syntactic relations and with prepositions, and the genitive with other nouns as well.

The restriction of *ptôsis* to nominal words both required separate terminology for the verbal categories and provided criteria for its use. Active transitive verbs (*rhếmata orthá*), passives (*hyptía* (ὑπτία)), and 'neutral' (intransitive) verbs (*oudétera* (οὐδέτερα)) were each defined by their constructing, respectively, with an oblique case (usually the accusative), with *hypó* (ὑπό) and the genitive, and with neither.[56] The partially common terminology, *ptôsis orthế* and *rhêma orthón*, was not accidental; the syntax of active and passive verbs in the classical languages were closely linked with differences of case.[57] Other verbal categories and distinctions appeared in the Stoic system, but their most important contribution to the analysis of the Greek verb was the abstraction of the temporal and aspectual meanings inherent in the tense forms.

The indication of time, recognized by Aristotle, is only part of the semantic function of the Greek verbal tenses. As in many languages, two dimensions are involved, time reference, and com-

pletion as against incompletion or continuity. Four tenses can be
arranged in relation to these two categorial distinctions like this:

Aspect Time	present	past
incomplete	Present tense gráphei (γράφει) is writing	Imperfect tense égraphe) (ἔγραφε) was writing
complete	Perfect tense gégrapha (γέγραφα) has written	Pluperfect tense egegráphei (ἐγεγράφει) had written

The future (méllōn (μέλλων) grápsei, γράψει, will write) and the
aorist (aóristos (ἀόριστος) égrapse, ἔγραψε, wrote) fall outside
this symmetrical system, and for this reason they were regarded
as indeterminate, méllōn with reference to the future and aóristos
with reference to the past; the morphological similarity of stem in
many future and aorist forms may have reinforced this semantic
interpretation.[58] The Greek future perfect was regarded as a feature largely peculiar to the Attic dialect and not much used in
that.[59]

Stoic linguistic work went on among the members of the Stoic
philosophical schools; but in the history of linguistics, the changes
made by Alexandrian scholars in the Stoic positions brought the
subject, more particularly in its grammatical aspects, to the state
in which the later Latin grammarians, and through them the
European tradition, took it over.

Unlike the Stoics, whose concern for language was primarily
from a philosophical viewpoint, linguists working in or connected
with Alexandria were predominantly interested in language as a
part of literary studies, and were adherents of the analogist position. They applied analogist principles to textual emendation and
to the determination of standards of acceptability (Hellēnismós).
Homeric studies received special attention in Alexandria, and
one of the most famous Alexandrians, Aristarchus (second century B.C.), has been considered a founder of scientific Homeric
scholarship; he is also credited with a number of developments in
grammar, and was the teacher of Dionysius Thrax (c. 100 B.C.),
who is credited with the authorship of the first surviving explicit
description of the Greek language.

The extant Téchnē grammatiké (τέχνη γραμματική), as it is
called, runs to fifteen printed pages and twenty-five sections, and
comprises a summary account of the structure of Greek. Its major
omission is any statement of Greek syntax, although the word

class system and the morphological analysis that are set out in it
formed the basis of later syntactic statements. Basically it was an
Alexandrian work, but its author was obviously aware of Stoic
linguistic studies and some marks of Stoic influence have been
detected in it.

Some doubts on the authenticity of the text as we have it were
raised in later antiquity and have been revived in modern times,
and these cannot be lightly dismissed, though they are by no
means universally accepted. Certainly there was a grammarian
called Dionysius Thrax, a pupil of Aristarchus, working and
teaching in Alexandria and in other places around 100 B.C., who
was the author of a short grammar of classical Greek. The first
section of the *Téchnē* as we now have it, historically of the
greatest interest, is clearly genuine, since Dionysius is quoted by
name by Sextus Empiricus (second century A.D.) from it, and the
first part of his definition is translated with one small addition
into Latin by his later contemporary, Varro (116–27 B.C.).
Evidence from Greek grammatical papyri in Egypt, dating from
early in the Christian era, indicates that by that time the grammar
of Greek was being regularly presented and taught in the manner
set out in our text of the *Téchnē*; and the system of word classes
and grammatical categories given in the *Téchnē* was used without
alteration by Apollonius Dyscolus in his syntactic works (second
century A.D.). It would appear, therefore, that something like the
grammar of Greek as it is set out in the text that we have of the
Téchnē was, in fact, taught by members of the Alexandrian school
in the first century B.C. on the lines laid down in a brief textbook
compiled by Dionysius. If, indeed, it was as popular as ancient
and modern evidence implies, it is very likely that successive versions embodying various alterations and adaptations (as with new
editions of modern textbooks) should have been produced, and
it may well be that much of the actual text that we have dates
from later, perhaps as late as the third or fourth century A.D. The
question of the authorship and authenticity of the *Téchnē* text in
its present form is a matter of classical philology and cannot be
pursued further in an elementary textbook. Reference may be
made to the relevant publications cited in the notes.[60]

In fact the description given in the *Téchné* was regarded as
definitive. It was translated into Armenian and Syriac early in the
Christian era, and was the subject of a considerable amount of
comment and exegesis from Byzantine critics, or scholiasts. It
remained a standard work for thirteen centuries, and a modern
writer has declared that almost every textbook of English grammar bears evidence of a debt to Thrax.[61] Its orderliness, brevity,

and explicitness make it well worth the serious study of anyone with a knowledge of ancient Greek, whether from the point of view of general linguistics or from that of classical scholarship, and a brief notice of its main features is appropriate in any history of linguistics.

The *Téchnē* begins with an exposition by Dionysius of the context of grammatical studies as this was seen by the Alexandrians. He writes: 'Grammar is the practical knowledge of the general usages of poets and prose writers. It has six parts: first, accurate reading (aloud) with due regard to the prosodies; second, explanation of the literary expressions in the works; third, the provision of notes on phraseology and subject matter; fourth, the discovery of etymologies; fifth, the working out of analogical regularities; sixth, the appreciation of literary compositions, which is the noblest part of grammar'. This extensive definition was intended to make quite clear what grammar, and indeed linguistic studies as a whole, were about and why such studies should be undertaken. It was left unchallenged, either assumed or repeated in part in later grammars of Greek and Latin in the mainline tradition. It set its mark on the practical and literary orientation of linguistic studies in Europe, as opposed to a philosophical one, up to the emergence of speculative grammar in the scholastic period. We may notice that at the beginning of his treatise on syntax, Apollonius introduces it as being 'most essential for the interpretation of poetical works'.[62]

We see that his attitude was observational; the material was drawn from the written texts of accepted authors, and their usage justifies his descriptive statements. Such an empirical attitude finds many supporters today, but some later commentators had their feelings hurt by his use of *empeiríā* (ἐμπειρία), practical knowledge; and drawing on an accepted scale of accomplishments from *peîra* (πεῖρα), skill, the lowest, through *empeiríā* and *téchnē*, science, to *epistémē*, (ἐπιστήμη), understanding, the highest, they complained that he had cheapened the subject he professed.[63] This controversy, reported by the scholiasts, may be perceived as one of the first shots in a continuing dispute, very active still today, between (a) those who see linguistics as essentially the accurate recording and the meticulous analysis of languages as they are revealed in the speech and writing of native speakers and (b) those who look more deeply for a theory of language able to explain and to justify the very existence of grammars, and to account for the capacity of human beings for the acquisition and use of their native language, and to reveal in part the nature and the working of the human mind or brain (*psyché* (ψυχή) in Stoic terminology).[64]

We see further how grammar in the strict sense was part of a wider scheme of propaedeutic studies leading to a proper appreciation of classical Greek literature. Only the fifth division, the working out of regularities in the language, or of analogy, covers what both then and later was regarded as the central province of grammar, and this is the only division that actually receives detailed development in the text. The first extant formulation of Greek grammar, and the pattern for centuries of later work can thus be seen as a product of the analogist-anomalist argument.

The description begins with an account of the phonetic values of the letters of the Greek alphabet. Letters, *grámmata* (γράμματα), are defined as elements, *stoicheîa* (στοιχεῖα), a term already in use for the ultimate constituents of the physical world,[65] and specified linguistically by a writer of about 20 B.C. as the primary and indivisible elements of articulated speech,[66] a definition consistent with the definition of *grámma* given above (p. 27–8) and bearing comparison with early definitions of the phoneme in our own century. Such had been the framework for Greek phonetic and phonological studies hitherto, and the *Téchnē* draws heavily on the work of its predecessors. It confines itself to the description of the segmental phonemes and the distinction of length in vowels and in syllables, despite the mention of prosodic features, a subject taken up by later commentators. These sections provide valuable evidence for the reconstruction of ancient Greek pronunciation. Allophonic differences are not mentioned, but a later commentator, referring to the three-fold distinction of sound, shape, and name (p. 28 above), already made by the Stoics, pointed out that there was more than one pronunciation to a single letter shape.[67] In both classical Attic and in Hellenistic Greek the written vowel letter sequences *ei* (ει) and *ou* (ου) almost certainly represented long monophthongs, [eː] (later [iː]) and [oː] (later [uː]),[68] but no mention of this is made in the *Téchnē*. A scholiast, however, later explained that *ei* (ει) and the 'subscript diphthongs', in which the letter *i* was written below the other vowel letter, ᾳ, ῃ, and ῳ, had a pronunciation of the same quality as that indicated by the simple letters ε, α, η, and ω.[69]

The author identified the consonantal triads of Greek, *p, ph, b, t, th, d,* and *k, kh, g,* as sharing the same sets of articulatory distinctions. He differentiated the aspirated and unaspirated

members as 'rough' (*daséa* (δασέα)) and 'smooth' or 'bare' (*psilá*
(ψιλά), thus linking the differentiating feature with the difference
between aspirated and unaspirated vocalic onset, as in *heîs* (εἷς),
one, and *eis* (εἰς), into. Mysteriously he referred to the voiced
members of the triads as 'middle' (*mésa* (μέσα)). The exact
meaning of this term is uncertain, but it seems clear that like the
rest of antiquity in the west he and his later commentators had
not understood the articulatory basis of the voice – voiceless contrast. The term *mediae* (*litterae*), the Latin translation of the
Technē's mésa (*grámmata*), lingered on in some nineteenth-century writings in reference to voiced consonants; and the
present-day, apparently phonaesthetic, designation 'liquid' for [l]
and [r] types of sound can be traced back to the *Téchnē* use of
hygrá (ὑγρά), liquid, to refer to Greek *l* (λ), *r*(ρ), *m* (μ), and
n (ν).

Alexandrian scholars had devised the graphic marks, in
general use today in the writing of classical Greek, for the three
distinctive Greek accents or pitches: acute (high)´, grave (low)`,
and circumflex (high falling to low)^. These were listed without
comment or explanation, but further elaboration is to be found
in the observations of the scholiasts.[70]

Passing to the strictly grammatical sections the *Téchnē* makes
the two basic units of description the sentence (*lógos* (λόγος)),
the upper limit of grammatical description, and the word (*léxis*
(λέξις)), in western antiquity the minimal unit of grammatical
description.[71] The sentence is defined notionally as 'expressing a
complete thought'.[72] The term *méros lógou* (μέρος λόγου), whence
the modern 'part of speech', recurs in the listing of the different
grammatical classes of words. It had been first used by Plato, so
far as is known, where it stands for constituents of the sentence;
only with the growth in the numbers of classes of words distinguished by Greek linguists did the expression take on its later
meaning of 'word class'.

Eight word classes are distinguished, whose number, with one
change necessitated by the absence of an article word in Latin,
remained constant to the end of the Middle Ages in the grammatical description of Greek and Latin, and with very marked
influence on the grammatical analysis of several modern
European languages. This word class system was regarded as one
of Dionysius's chief claims on the memory of posterity.[73] The
Stoic common and proper nouns were reunited into the single
ónoma class, the participle (*metochḗ* (μετοχή)) was separated from
the verb to become a word class in its own right, and the Stoic
sýndesmos and *árthron* were each split into *sýndesmos*, conjunction, and *próthesis* (πρόθεσις), preposition, and into
árthron, article, and *antōnymía* (ἀντωνυμία), pronoun, respectively. The adverb was renamed *epirrhḗma* (ἐπίρρημα), in place

of the Stoic *mesótēs*. The eight class names are worth quoting
with their definitions as an example of the conciseness of terminology that had been achieved by this time and the application to
linguistics of Aristotelian methods of classification:

> *ónoma* (noun): a part of speech inflected for case, signifying
> a concrete or abstract entity,
> *rhêma* (verb): a part of speech without case inflection, but
> inflected for tense, person, and number, signifying an activity
> or process performed or undergone,
> *metochḗ* (participle): a part of speech sharing the features of
> the verb and the noun,
> *árthron* (article): a part of speech inflected for case and
> preposed or postposed to nouns,[74]
> *antōnymía* (pronoun): a part of speech substitutable for a
> noun and marked for person,
> *próthesis* (preposition): a part of speech placed before other
> words in composition and in syntax,
> *epírrhēma* (adverb): a part of speech without inflection, in
> modification of or in addition to a verb,
> *sýndesmos* (conjunction): a part of speech binding together
> the discourse and filling gaps in its interpretation.[75]

It will be seen that refinements in diagnostic criteria were used
by the Alexandrians to give a greater number of discriminations;
some of the features involved had been noted by the Stoics but
not formàlized by them as the basis of separate word classes. Two
principal discrepancies are apparent between the Alexandrian system and that of current presentations of Greek grammar. Firstly,
the separate recognition of the participle, which aroused comment in antiquity since all participial roots were verbal roots, and
vice versa, was due to the high place accorded since the time of
the Stoics to case inflexion as a *fundamentum divisionis*. The two
primary parts of speech, noun and verb, are differentiated by this
feature and its absence, but the participle is both case inflected
and tense inflected, and shares (*metéchei* (μετέχει), 'partakes'
(Latin *participat*)), in the syntactic relations contracted by both
nouns and verbs. Secondly, the adjective, whose morphology and
syntax were more similar to those of nouns in both Greek and
Latin than they are in English, was included in the *ónoma* (noun)
class. This allocation is reflected in the terms *noun substantive*
and *noun adjective* still occasionally encountered in current use.

Each defined word class is followed by a statement of the
categories applicable to it. The *Téchnē's* term for these is *parepómena*
(παρεπόμενα), consequential attributes, and the use of this
word can be compared to Aristotle's use of *symbebēkóta*

(συμβεβηκότα), accidents, in logic.[76] The *parepómena* refer collectively to grammatically relevant differences in the forms of words, and include both inflectional and derivational categories. The five *parepómena* which apply to the noun class will serve as illustrations:

1. *Génos* (γένος), gender: masculine, feminine, or neuter.
2. *Eîdos* (εἶδος), type: primary or derived. The adjective *gaiéios* (γαιήιος), of the earth, is given as an example of a derived noun, and referred to the primary noun *gê* (also *gaîa*), earth. Among other subclasses of derived nouns are listed adjectival comparative and superlative forms. (e.g. *andreióteros* (ἀνδρειότερος), braver, and *andreiótatos* (ἀνδρειότατος), bravest). Thus the forms that could have served as one criterion for distinguishing adjectives as a separate class were themselves assigned their own specific place within the noun class.
3. *Schêma* (σχῆμα), form: simple or compound, according to whether the roots of more than one noun could be identified within a single noun stem. Examples are given from proper nouns; *Mémnōn* (Μέμνων) is simple, *Philódēmos* (Φιλόδημος) is compound (*philo* + *dēmos*).
4. *Arithmós* (ἀριθμός), number: singular, dual, or plural. The distinct dual forms of both nouns and verbs, inherited from Indoeuropean, had a limited use in classical times and ultimately disappeared.
5. *Ptôsis* (πτῶσις), case: nominative, vocative, accusative, genitive, or dative. The five cases of the Greek noun (and adjective) are listed, and named by reference to part of their semantic function (e.g. *dotiké* (δοτική), dative ('giving to')). It is interesting to notice that the Latin *cāsus accūsātivus*, our *accusative case* arises from a mistranslation of the Greek *aitiātikè ptôsis* (αἰτιατικὴ πτῶσις), the object case, referring to the recipient of some action caused to happen (*aitiā*(αἰτία), cause). Varro, who was responsible for the Latin term, appears to have been misled by the other meaning of *aitíā*, accusation or charge.[77]

The *parepómena* of the verb are mood, voice, type, form, number, person, tense, and conjugation. The systematization of the Greek tenses in the *Teéhné* differs somewhat from that of the Stoics. Three basic time references are distinguished: present, past, and future. Of these, past time alone is assigned more than one tense form, four in fact: imperfect, perfect, pluperfect, and aorist. The six tenses are further linked into three pairs:

present   imperfect

> perfect pluperfect
> aorist future.

The first two links (*syngeneîai* (συγγενεῖαι)) are the same as linked pairs of tenses within the aspects of completion and incompletion set up by the Stoics, though the terminology of the two schools differs in part, and the aorist and future were also associated by the Stoics as being both indeterminate tenses. Morphologically the forms of regular Greek verbs show proportional correspondences (*analogíai*), the first pair being built on the present stem, the second on the perfect (reduplicated) stem, and the third each having a 'sigmatic' (−*s*−) stem, though the two were probably not etymologically connected.[78] Despite the similarities between the two systems, this failure to give proper recognition to the aspectual dimension in the semantic structure of the Greek tenses must be considered a definite loss of insight. The compression of the Greek tense meanings into the single dimension of time led to attempts by later commentators to distinguish the meanings of the perfect and pluperfect tenses, for example, in terms of the distance in time of the action from the present just does not fit, whereas the distinction between completion at the present time and completion with reference to an anterior time does: *gégrapha* (γέγραφα), I have written, could be five years ago or more, provided its reference is to the present state of affairs: 'During my lifetime I have written ten novels.' *egegráphein* (ἐγεγράφειν), I had written, could be five minutes ago: 'I had written a note to you when your letter was brought to me.' Equally, the essential meaning of the imperfect tense, *égraphon* (ἔγραφον), I was writing, is that though it refers to the past it also refers to some unfinished activity: 'I was writing to you, when you telephoned me.'[79]

The five inflected word classes are defined and described first; the last three, uninflected or invariable word classes, are distinguished on syntactic grounds, though their syntactic functions are not further dealt with. The adverb is designated *epírrhēma* (whence the Latin *adverbium*, and English *adverb*) from its principal syntactic association with verbs (Greek grammarians seem to have ignored the possibility of its immediate constituency with members of any other word class, though this is quite common in Greek). The Stoic term *mesótēs*, no longer in use for the whole class, appears in the *Téchnē* as the name for a subclass of adverbs, namely those formed deadjectivally with the suffix −*ōs*.

Later work in Greek grammar took the form of developments from the linguistic description summarized in the *Téchnē* and of

comments on specific passages in it. Its main omission from the
standpoint of modern linguistics was the absence of any sections
on syntax, although the term *syntaxis* (σύνταξις) was employed
and syntactic analysis was partly presupposed in some definitions
given in the *Téchnē*. Syntax was dealt with extensively by Appol-
lonius Dyscolus writing in Alexandria in the second century A.D.
He wrote a large number of books, only some of which survive,
and it would appear that despite earlier writings on Greek syntax
his was the first attempt at a comprehensive syntactic description
and analysis of the Greek language. His importance, together
with that of the *Téchnē* was realized by his successors, and the
great Latin grammarian, Priscian, some three centuries later
referred to him as 'the greatest authority on grammar', and explicitly imposed Apollonian methods on his own full-scale
description of the Latin language.[80]

Apollonius worked with the material supplied by the *Téchnē*
and the syntactical observations of earlier writers, many deriving
from rhetorical studies. He made use of the same set of eight
word classes as those given in the *Téchnē*, but he redefined some
of them, more particularly to make greater use of notional terminology and to establish a common class meaning for each word
class.[81] He defined the pronoun not merely as a noun substitute
as the *Téchnē* had done, but additionally as standing for substance (*ousiā* (οὐσία)) without qualities, a statement repeated by
Priscian and of considerable importance later in mediaeval linguistic thought (p. 66, 89, below).[82]

Though he worked on the basis of the morphological description of Greek set down by the Alexandrian school, his general
outlook on linguistic matters was more mentalist than theirs and
owed something to Stoic influences. He sharply distinguished
form and meaning (*schêma* (σχῆμα) and *énnoia* (ἔννοια) in his terminology), and justified grammatical classifications by reference
to content rather than to morphological form.[83]

Just as the nominal and verbal constituents of the Greek sentence were the first to be recognized as distinct and were always
regarded as the most fundamental division in the grammar of the
language, Apollonius expressly built his syntactic description on
the relations of the noun and the verb to each other and of the
remaining classes of words to these two.[84] In describing these relations he relied on the cases of nominally inflected words in their
different interconnections with each other and with verbs, and on
the three classes of verbs, active (transitive), passive, and neutral
(intransitive), with their separate relationships to the nominal
case forms. One finds under the active verbs the statement that

they designate an action 'passing over to something or someone else', whence the Latin *verbum transitīvum* and English *transitive verb* may be said to originate.[85]

These developments foreshadow the distinction of subject and object and of later concepts such as government (rection) and dependency. Such however do not appear to have been part of Apollonius's descriptive apparatus. He devotes considerable attention to concordial relations (*katallēlótēs* (καταλληλότης), *akolouthiā* (ἀκολουθία)), which hold, for example, between a finite verb form and a nominative case noun or pronoun in respect of number and person, but not between a finite verb and an oblique case form.[86] Of more abstract syntactic relations, such as can be established for all languages and not merely those morphologically similar to Latin and Greek, he mentions the relationship of constituent structuring (*paralambánesthai* (παμα-λαμβάνεσθαι) to be taken together) to refer to the construction of participle and main verb in a sentence, or of noun or pronoun and verb.[87] Substitution (anthypágesthai (ἀνθυπάγεσθαι)) occurs when a word of one class, e.g. a pronoun, can be used in place of one of another class, e.g. a noun.[88] In his use of *symparalambánesthai* (συμπαραλαμβάνεσθαι), 'to be taken along in addition', something like the modern concepts of immediate constituency and hierarchical ranking seems to be envisaged, as in one of his analyses of the sentence *tachỳ elthòn paidíon ōnēsen hēmâs* (ταχὺ ἐλθὸν παίδιον ὤνησεν ἡμᾶς), quickly coming up, a boy helped us, in which the adverb *tachý*, quickly, is immediately associated with the participle *elthón*, having come, which in turn is associated with the main verb *ónēsen*, (he) helped.[89]

However a good deal of Apollonius's discussion of grammatical questions was directed not so much towards the elaboration of a theory of syntactic description as to attempts at explaining particular features of Greek constructions. Thus the fact that two verbs, meaning 'to love', *phileîn* (φιλεῖν) and *erân* (ερᾳν), take respectively the accusative and genitive case is referred for explanation to the more passionate and therefore less controlled nature of the love involved in *erân*[90] and the true explanation of the peculiar Greek concord of singular verb with a neuter plural subject noun (*gráphei tà paidia* (γράφει τὰ παιδία), the boys are writing) quite escaped him, arising, in fact, as is now known, historically in the origin of the nominative neuter plural case ending from a singular collective.[91]

Overall one gets the impression from reading Apollonius of a detailed and painstaking account of the syntax of the Greek language, rather than of a general theory of syntax exemplified in

Greek. For such a general theory (exemplified from Latin) one must wait until the later Middle Ages (pp 90–6).

Apollonius's son, Herodian, is best known for his work on Greek accentuation and punctuation, covering the field of the *prosōdíai* referred to by Dionysius Thrax. The *prosōdíai* were described in more detail by later scholiasts and came to include the distinctive pitch levels symbolized by the accent marks on written words, length and shortness in vowels and quantity in syllables, aspiration and non-aspiration of vocalic onset at the beginning of words ('rough' and 'smooth breathings'), and such junctural phenomena as vowel elision, pitch changes in word compounding, and word boundary markers of the type that could distinguish *estì Náxios* (ἐστὶ Νάξιος), he is a Naxian, from *estìn áxios* (ἐστὶν ἄξιος), he is worthy (perhaps comparable with the features available to keep apart English *a notion* from *an ocean*). It is interesting to see the Greek word *prosōdìa* covering very much the range of phonetic phenomena to which the term *prosody* has been applied in recent Firthian phonological analysis.[92]

The *analogíai* of the morphology set out in the *Téchnē* found their ultimate consummation in the lists of nominal and verbal inflections, known as canons (*kánones* (κάνονες)), on which later paradigms were modelled. The best known is the complete set of all the theoretically available forms of the verb *týptein* (τύπτειν), to hit, of which, however, in classical Greek only a limited number were actually in use.

The *Téchnē* and the syntactic works of Apollonius formed the foundation of linguistic scholarship in the Byzantine world, that is to say in the Greek-speaking eastern half of the once unified Roman Empire, whose capital was Byzantium, renamed Constantinople (now Istanbul) after the refounding and rededication of the city in 330 A.D. The Byzantine Empire, as it is called, persisted through a thousand years of tribulation from within and without, losing territory to the Arabs, the Turks, and invaders from the west, until the final fall of Constantinople to the Turks in 1453.

Byzantine scholarship, theological writings apart, largely consisted of the continued study and teaching of the classical Greek authors and, of course, Homer, and of the grammar of classical Greek, from which the everyday language of most people was steadily diverging on the way to becoming the modern Greek language. The short *Téchnē* was reinforced by a large amount of commentaries (*schólia*), attempting to fill out its compressed style, and among them we find some valuable information and explanations not otherwise available. As the syntactic works of

Apollonius were lengthy and extensive, many summaries and *précis* of his writings were produced for educational use. Some of these, like some of their western Latin counterparts, were in question-and-answer catechistic form. It was this sort of scholarship, kept alive in Byzantium while the knowledge and the study of Greek fell almost to extinction in the early Middle Ages among western nations, that provided the teachers, the grammars, and the scholarly tradition which enabled Italy and then the rest of western Europe in the Renaissance rapidly to recreate the teaching of Greek in schools and universities as a major part of a liberal education.

Byzantine scholars belonged to a post-classical age. By general recognition the literature of their era never approached the standard of the classical epochs of Greece, in variety, spontaneity, or profundity. In the Byzantine period, theological controversies apart, literary studies were largely concentrated on the past, and in this respect linguistic scholarship was a proper product of the times. The descriptions, analyses, and explanations of the grammarians and the commentators formed part of a wider body of learning devoted to the study of earlier literary works. This was an age of dictionaries, glossaries, and commentaries, of working over past originals rather than of new creation.

The value of Byzantine linguistic and literary work is acknowledged as having been essential for the maintenance of a continuity of classical scholarship and as having provided for the preservation and copying of classical Greek texts for ultimate reproduction by western Renaissance printing houses. But the merits of original thought have generally been denied to Byzantium by historians, except in some matters of theology. It is true that in general Byzantine scholars and teachers were epitomizers, commentators, and preservers, rather than pioneers and developers; but in certain parts of Greek grammatical theory some of their leading men do appear to have reached fresh insights into such categories as nominal case and the semantic analysis of the verbal tense system.

Byzantine scholars continued the study of the Greek case system, and a semantic analysis of the cases by Maximus Planudes (c. 1260–1310), highly praised by Hjelmslev in his study of this category, was one of the linguistic insights carried back to Renaissance Europe from Byzantium at the end of the Middle Ages, and became influential in the development of theories of case in modern Europe.[93]

The essence of their analysis of the cases was the 'localist' theory, that maintains the proposition that the spatial or local relations of movement to, movement from, and location at or in are the fundamental and original meanings of the oblique cases and that the other more abstract meanings and grammatical functions are derived from these. In the analysis of verbal tenses a nearer approach to the two-dimensional Stoic system (p 34, above) seems to have been achieved while still within the accepted time reference parameter of the Aristotelian–Alexandrian tradition. In fairness it must be said that controversy still surrounds these assessments of Byzantine linguistic scholarship.[94]

It is not difficult to detect omissions and misrepresentations in that part of Greek grammar summarized in the *Téchnē* and in the later contributions of Apollonius Dyscolus and his successors. While this criticism may seem at first sight flattering to modern scholarship, it is much less appropriate than is some sympathetic reflection on the very great achievements of successive generations of Greek scholars in devising and systematizing a formal terminology for the description of the classical Greek language as it was written and read aloud (and they set their sights no higher), a terminology which, through the medium of translation and adaptation to Latin, became the foundation for nearly two thousand years of grammatical theory and the teaching and study of the Greek and Latin languages. From the resources of a language not previously required to embody precise metalinguistic statements the Greeks had hammered out, through stages that we are able in great part to retrace, a detailed and articulated technical vocabulary for grammatical description.

Retrospectively, it is easy to present this process as a uniform movement along a single track, as each generation adds its contribution to the increasing body of theory, method, and systematically described data. There is much to be said for this in broad outline, since successive scholars were each aware of their predecessors' work and reacted to it favourably or critically. But earlier stages were not all just superseded and forgotten. As we know, Stoic grammatical theory continued as part of Stoic philosophy, though it did not form part of the central tradition of Greek and then Latin linguistic study. In trying to identify main trends, we must not unwittingly impose a tidier pattern or sequence on events than is likely to have occurred in the actual succession of states of affairs, as many individuals each tried to make their contribution in the situation in which they found themselves or in which they found it congenial to work.[95] This, of course, applies no less in other fields of intellectual historiography.

The Greek triumph in intellectual civilization is to have done so much in so many fields; their work in logic, ethics, politics, rhetoric, and mathematics, to mention only some subjects, comes to mind at once. Their achievement in that part of linguistics in which they were strongest, namely grammatical theory and grammatical description, is strong enough to deserve and to sustain critical examination. It is also such as to inspire our gratitude and admiration.

FOR FURTHER CONSULTATION

H. ARENS, *Sprachwissenschaft: der Gang ihrer Entwicklung von der Antike bis zur Gegenwart*, Freiburg/Munich (second edition) 1969, 3–30.

M. BARATIN and F. DESBORDES, *L'analyse linguistique dans l' antiquité classique*, I, *Les théories*, Paris, 1981.

K. BARWICK, 'Probleme der stoischen Sprachlehre und Rhetorik', *Abhandlungen der sächsischen Akademie der Wissenschaften zu Leipzig, philologisch-historische Klasse* 49.3 (1957).

F. H. COLSON, 'The analogist and anomalist controversy', *Classical quarterly* 13 (1919), 24–36.

E. EGGER, *Apollonius Dyscole: essai sur l'histoire des théories grammaticales dans l'antiquité*, Paris, 1854.

H. KOLLER, 'Die Anfänge der griechischen Grammatik', *Glotta* 37 (1958), 5–40.

J. LALLOT (ed.), 'Etudes sur les grammairiens grecs', *Histoire epistémologie langage* 7.1 (1985).

A. A. LONG (ed.), *Problems in Stoicism*, London, 1971.

B. MATES, *Stoic logic*, Berkeley, 1953 (*UCP Phil.* 26).

M. POHLENZ, 'Die Begründung der abendländischen Sprachlehre durch die Stoa', *Nachrichten von der Gesellschaft der Wissenschaften zu Göttingen, philologisch-historische Klasse Fachgruppe* 1 *Altertumswissen-schaft*, N. F. 3.6 (1939).

J. RIST (ed.), *The Stoics*, Berkeley, 1978.

R. H. ROBINS, *Ancient and mediaeval grammatical theory in Europe*, London, 1951, chapter 1.
'The *Technē grammatikē* of Dionysius Thrax in its historical perspective', in P. SWIGGERS and W. VAN HOECHE (eds.), *Mots et parties du discours*, Leuven, 1986, 9–37.

J. E. SANDYS, *History of classical scholarship* (third edition), Cambridge, 1921, volume 1.

T. A. SEBEOK, *Historiography of linguistics*, 69–126.

H. STEINTHAL, *Geschichte der Sprachwissenschaft bei den Griechen und Römern* (second edition), Berlin, 1890.

D. J. TAYLOR (ed.), *The history of linguistics in the classical period*, Amsterdam, 1987 (= *Historiographica Linguistica* 13.2–3, but with different pagination).

A. TRAGLIA, 'La sistemazione grammaticale di Dionisio Trace', *Studi classici ed orientali* 15 (1956), 38–78.

K. VERSTEEGH, 'The Stoic verbal system', *Herwes* 108 (1980) 338–55.

NOTES

1. The earliest known writing system, at first pictorial, appears to be that of the Sumerians (c. 3000 B.C., in Mesopotamia). Some scholars suggest a derivation link between this script and ancient Egyptian and even Chinese, though this latter seems unlikely. The Sumerian script was at first used only in restricted contexts for administrative purposes, rather than for general and literary communication. It was later extended in the range of its uses. See further, D. DIRINGER, *The alphabet*, New York, 1968; I. J. GELB, *A study of writing*, Chicago, 1969; G. SAMPSON, *Writing systems*, Stanford, 1985.

2. See also G. MOUNIN, *Histoire de la linguistique*, Paris, 1970, 51–61; T. JACOBSEN, 'Very ancient linguistics: Babylonian grammatical texts', D. HYMES (ed.), *Studies in the history of linguistics: traditions and paradigms*, Bloomington, 1974, 41–62; J. A. BLACK, 'The Babylonian grammatical tradition: the first grammars of 'Sumerian', *TPS* 87 (1989), 75–99.

3. L. BLOOMFIELD, *Language*, London, 1935, 4.

4. HERODOTUS 8.144.2: τὸ Ἑλληνικόν, εον ὅμαιμόν τε καὶ ὁμόγλωσσον. On interpreters in antiquity, H.S. GEHMAN, *The interpreters of foreign languages among the ancients*, Lancaster, Pa, 1914.

5. C.D. BUCK, *Comparative grammar of Greek and Latin*, Chicago, 1933 68–78.

6. BUCK, op. cit., 68–74; *The Greek dialects*, Chicago, 1928, 16.

7. e.g. PLATO, *Theaetetus* 207 B, *Philebus* 17 B, 18 D.

8. DIOGENES LAERTIUS, *Vitae philosophorum* 3.25: πρωτος ἐθεώρησε τῆς γραμματικῆς τὴν δύναμιν.

9. W. D. ROSS: *Aristotle*, London, 1923, 116–17; C. SINGER, *A short history of science*, Oxford, 1941, 40–1.

10. DIOGENES 7.49: προηγεῖται ἡ φαντασία, εἶθ᾽ ἡ διάνοια ἐκλαλητικὴ ὑπάρχουσα, ὃ πάσχει ὑπὸ τῆς φαντασίας τοῦτο ἐκφέρει λόγῳ. id. 7.83: πάντα τὰ πράγματα διὰ τῆς ἐν λόγοις θεωρίας ὁρᾶσθαι. id. 7·55: της διαλεκτικης θεωριας συμφωνως δοκεῖ τοις πλείστοις ἀπὸ τοῦ περὶ φωνῆς ἐνάρχεσθαι τόπου.

11. DIOGENES 7.62 (τὸ σημαῖνον and τὸ σημαινόμενον); BARWICK, 1957, chapter 1; LONG, 1971, chapter 5; F. DE SAUSSURE, *Cours de linguistique générale* (fourth edition), Paris, 1949, 156–7.

12. STEINTHAL 1890, volume 1, 305–7; V. EGLI, 'Stoic syntax and semantics', TAYLOR, 1987, 107–32.

13. PLATO, *Cratylus*, 384 D. On this dialogue see further J. C. RIJLAARSDAM, *Platon über die Sprache: ein Kommentar zum Kratylos*, Utrecht, 1978.

14. ibid., 399 C, 414 C, 421 D, 423 B, 426 C–427 D.

15. ibid., 384 D.

16. *Lectures on the science of language*, London, 1862, lecture 9.

17. ARISTOTLE, *De interpretatione* 2: κατὰ συνθήκην, ὅτι φύσει τῶν ὀνομάτων οὐδέν ἐστιν (cp. 4).

18. ibid., 1: ἔστι μὲν οὖν τὰ ἐν τῇ φωνῇ τῶν ἐν τῇ ψυχῇ παθημάτων σύμβολα, καὶ τὰ γραφόμενα τῶν ἐν τῇ φωνῇ.

19. ORIGEN, *Contra Celsum* 1.24: ὡς νομίζουσιν οἱ ἀπὸ τῆς Στοᾶς φύσει [ἐστὶ τὰ ὀνόματα] μιμουμένων τῶν πρώτων φωνῶν τὰ πράγματα.

20. ibid., 1.24; BARWICK, 1957, chapter 4.

21. DIOGENES 7.192.

22. 'vix tanto hiatu digna esse videtur', J. CLASSEN, *De grammaticae Graecae primordiis*, Bonn, 1829, 80.

23. I. BEKKER, *Anecdota Graeca*, Berlin, 1816, volume 2, 629: ἀναλογίας ἐκλογισμός.

24. cp. COLSON, 1919.

25. SEXTUS EMPIRICUS, *Adversus grammaticos* 195; QUINTILIAN, *Institutio oratoria* 1.6.27.

26. SEXTUS, op. cit., 148–53.

27. STEINTHAL, 1890, volume 1, 360.

28. cp. ARISTOTLE, 1131 a 29, 1131 a 31, 1096 b 28, 1106 a 36.

29. DIOGENES 7.59; SANDYS, 1921, 149.

30. ἐτυμολογία ἐστὶν ἡ ἀνάπτυξις τῶν λέξεων δι' ἧς τὸ ἀληθὲς σαφηνιζεται, G. UHLIG, *Grammatici graeci*, volume 1.1, Leipzig, 1883, 14.

31. L. KUKENHEIM, *Contributions à l'histoire de la grammaire qrecque, latine, et hébraique à l'époque de la Renaissance*, Leiden, 1951, 80.

32. BEKKER, *Anecdota Graeca*, volume 2, 774–5.

33. PRISCIAN 1.2.4: Sicut enim illa (sc. elementa mundi) coeuntia omne perficiunt corpus, sic etiam haec (sc. elementa vocis) literalem vocem quasi corpus aliquod componunt.

34. *Cratylus* 424 C; *Theaetetus* 203 B; *Cratylus* 399 A–B.

35. DIOGENES 7.56; BEKKER, *Anecdota Graeca*, volume 2, 773.

36. DIOGENES 7.57.

37. cp. C. F. HOCKETT, 'Two models of grammatical description', *Word* 10 (1954), 210–34.

38. ARISTOTLE, *De sophisticis elenchis* 14.

39. ARISTOPHANES, *Clouds* 660–80.

40. DIOGENES 9.53–4. On Greek phonetic description, W. S. ALLEN, 'The Greek contribution to the history of phonetics', in R. E. ASHER and E. HENDERSON (eds.), *Towards a history of phonetics*, Edinburgh, 1981, 115–22.

41. *Cratylus* 399 B, 425 A; *Sophistes* 262 A-263 D.

42. *Rhetorica* 3.5, 3.12.

43. *De interpretatione* 2–3.

44. A. MEILLET, *Linguistique historique et linguistique générale*, Paris, 1948, 30.

45. *De interpretatione* 3–6.

46. op. cit. 3: ῥῆμα δέ ἐστι τὸ προσσημαῖνον χρόνον . . . καί ἐστιν ἀεί των καθ' ἑτέρου λεγομένων σημεῖον.

47. op. cit. 1; 10; cp. PLATO, *Cratylus* 399 B.

48. *De sophisticis elenchis* 14.

49. *De interpretatione* 2, 3; *Topica* 1.15, 5.7.

50. PLATO, *Protagoras* 342 E, 343 A–B.

51. *Analytica priora* 42 b, 30; *Analytica posteriora*, 94 a 12.

52. L. HJELMSLEV, *La catégorie des cas*, Aarhus, 1935, 1–70.

53. J. VON ARNIM, *Stoicorum veterum fragmenta*, Leipzig, 1905–24,
    volume 2, 206 a; DIOGENES 7.192; LONG, 1971, chapters 4 and 5;
    MATES, 1953, chapter 2; M. FREDE, 'Principles of Stoic grammar',
    RIST 1978, chapter 2. F.P. DINNEEN, 'On the Stoic contribution to
    grammatical theory', *Historiographia linguistica* 12 (1985), 149–64;
    H. E. BREKLE, *Einführung in die Geschichte der Sprachwissenschaft*,·
    Darmsteter, 1985, 44–67.

54. e.g. Dionysius of Halicarnassus, *De compositione verborum* 2.

55. DIOGENES 7.57–8; BEKKER, *Anecdota Graeca*, volume 2, 842; cp.
    BLOOMFIELD, *Language*, 205.

56. DIOGENES 7.64; STEINTHAL, 1890, volume 1, 299.

57. HJELMSLEV, *Cas*, 7.

58. BEKKER, *Anecdota Graeca*, volume 2, 890–1; STEINTHAL, 1890,
    volume 1, 307–17; BARWICK, 1957, 51–3.

59. BEKKER op. cit., 891–2. C. H. M. VERSTEEGH, 1980, 338–57, gives a
    recent concise review of the linguistic analysis of the Greek verbal
    system of tenses by the Stoics with critical appraisals of earlier in-
    terpretations and a comparison with Varro and the mainline Latin
    grammatical tradition in regard to the Latin verb.

60. The text of the *Téchnē* is given in BEKKER, op. cit., 627–43, and in
    G. UHLIG, *Grammatici Graeci* 2.1, Leipzig, 1883. Translations in
    French and in English are available in J. LALLOT, 'Denys le Thrace:
    Téchnē grammatikē', *Archives et documents de la Société d'histoire
    et d'épistémologie des sciences du langage* 6 (1985), 1–104 (with
    notes), and in A. KEMP, 'The *Technē grammatikē* of Dionysius Thrax:
    English translation with introduction and notes', TAYLOR, 1987, 169–
    89. The genuineness of the modern text was first effectively
    challenged by V. DI BENEDETTO, 'Dionisio Trace e la Techne a lui
    attribuita', *Annali della Scuola Normale Superiore di Pisa*, serie 2,
    27 (1958), 169–210, and 28 (1959), 87–118. For the progress of
    the controversy since then see J. PINBORG, 'Classical antiquity:
    Greece', SEBEOK, *Historiography of linguistics*, 69–126; A. WOUTERS,
    *The grammatical papyri from Graeco-Roman Egypt. Contributions
    to the study of the 'ars grammatica' in Antiquity*, Brussels, 1979;
    ROBINS, 1986, 9–11.

61. P. B. R. FORBES, 'Greek pioneers in philology and grammar', *Classi-
    cal review* 47 (1933), 112.

62. BEKKER, op. cit., 629: γραμματική ἐστιν ἐμπειρία τῶν παρὰ
    ποιηταῖς τε καὶ συγγραφεῦσιν ὡς ἐπὶ τὸ πολὺ λεγομένων. μέρη δὲ
    αὐτῆς εἰσὶν ἐξ· πρῶτον ἀνάγνωσις ἐντριβὴς κατὰ προσῳδίαν,
    δεύτερον ἐξήγησις κατὰ τοὺς ἐνυπάρχοντας ποιητικοὺς τρόπους,
    τρίτον γλωσσῶυ τε καὶ ἱστοριῶν πρόχειρος ἀπόδοσις, τέταρτον
    ἐτυμολογίας εὕρεσις, πέμπτον ἀναλογίας ἐκλογισμός, ἕκτον κρίσις
    ποιημάτων, ὃ δὴ κάλλιστόν ἐστι πάντων τῶν ἐν τῇ τέχνῃ. cp.
    APOLLONICES DYSCOLUS, *syntax* 1.1 (G. UHLIG, *Grammatici Graeci* 2.2,
    Leipzig, 1883, 3–4: . . . τὴν σύνταξιν . . . ἀναγκαιοτάτην οὖσαν
    ἐξήγησιν τῶν ποιημάτων.

63. BEKKER, op. cit., 656, 732.
64. cp. ROBINS, 'Theory-orientation versus data-orientation: a recurrent theme in linguistics,' *Historiographia linguistica* I (1973), 11–26.
65. e.g. PLATO, *Theaetetus* 201 E; ARISTOTLE, *Metaphysics* 983 b 12, 1014 a 26–9.
66. DIONYSIUS OF HALICARNASSUS, *De compositione verborum* 14, 1–2: ἀρχαὶ τῆς ἀνθρωπίνης καὶ ἐνάρθρου φωνῆς, αἱ μηκέτι δεχόμεναι διαίρεσιν.
67. BEKKER, op. cit., 774.
68. BUCK, *Comparative grammar*, § 89, 92; W. S. ALLEN, *Vox Graeca*, Cambridge, 1968, 66–7, 71–2.
69. BEKKER, op. cit., 804.
70. BEKKER, op. cit., 754–7; ALLEN, op. cit., 80–2.
71. λέξις ἐστὶ μέρος τοῦ κατὰ σύνταξιν λόγου ἐλάχιστον.
72. λέξεως σύνθεσις διάνοιαν αὐτοτελῆ δηλοῦσα.
73. BEKKER, op. cit., 676: ὁ Θρᾷξ Διονύσιος, ὁ περὶ τῶν ὀκτὼ μερῶν τοῦ λόγου διδάξας ἡμᾶς.
74. The *Téchnē* included the relative pronoun, ος, η, ö, in the class of *árthron*. The position of relative clauses normally following their antecedent noun and the similar morphology of the article and the relative pronoun allowed him to refer to this as a postposed article.
75. ὄνομά ἐστι μέρος λόγου πτωτικόν, σῶμα ἢ πρᾶγμα σημαῖνον.

    ῥῆμά ἐστι λέξις ἄπτωτος, ἐπιδεκτικὴ χρόνων τε καὶ προσώπων καὶ ἀριθμῶν, ἐνέργειαν ἢ πάθος παριστῶσα.

    μετοχή ἐστι λεξις μετέχουσα τῆς τῶν ῥημάτων καὶ τῆς τῶν ὀνομάτων ἰδιότητος.

    ἄρθρον ἐστὶ μέρος λόγου πτωικόν, προτασσόμενον καὶ ὑποτασσόμενον τῆς κλίσεως τῶν ὀνομάτων.

    ἀντωνυμία ἐστὶ λέξις ἀντὶ ὀνόματος παραλαμβανομένη, προσώπων ὡρισμένων δηλωτική.

    πρόθεσίς ἐστι λέξις προτιθεμένη πάντων τῶν τοῦ λόγου μερῶν ἔν τε συνθέσει καὶ συντάξει.

    ἐπίρρημά ἐστι μέρος λόγου ἄκλιτον, κατὰ ῥήματος λεγόμενον ἢ ἐπιλεγόμενον ῥήματι.

    σύνδεσμός ἐστι λέξις συνδέουσα διάνοιαν μετὰ τάξεως καὶ τὸ τῆς ἑρμηνείας κεχηνὸς πληροῦσα.
76. e.g., *De sophisticis elenchis* 168 b 28–31, *Topica* 117 a 7, 128 a 38, 131 a 27. The Latin grammarians translated *parepómena* by *accidentia*.
77. *De lingua Latina* 8.66–7.
78. BUCK, *Comparative grammar*, § 389.
79. A. HILGARD (ed.), *Grammatici Graeci* 1.3, Leipzig, 1901, 250.
80. PRISCIAN 11.1.1: 'Maximus auctor artis grammaticae'. The text of Apollonius's works is to be found in R. SCHNEIDER and G. UHLIG (eds.), *Grammatici Graeci* 2, 1–2, Leipzig, 1878, 1910. An English translation of Apollonius's four books on syntax is available in F. W. HOUSEHOLDER (tr.), *The Syntax of Apollonius Dyscolus*, Amsterdam, 1981.

81. e.g. *Syntax* 1.39 (*Gram. Graec.* 22, 35).

82. *De pronomine* 33 b; PRISCIAN 13.6.29, 13.6.31.

83. *De adverbio*, BEKKER, *Anecdota Graeca*, volume 2, 529; *Syntax* 1.39 (*Gram. Graec.* 2.2, 35) ἕκαστον αὐτῶν ἐξ ἰδίας ἐννόιας ἀνάγεται. *De pronomine* 85 a: οὐ φωναῖς μεμέρισται τὰ τοῦ λόγου μέρη, σημαινομένοις δε.

84. *Syntax* 1.36 (*Gram. Graec.* 2.2, 33) τὰ ὑπόλοιπα τῶν μερῶν τοῦ λόγου ἀνάγεται πρὸς τὴν τοῦ ῥήματος καὶ τοῦ ὀνόματος σύνταξιν.

85. ibid. 3.14–8 (*Gram. Graec.* 2.2, 395): ἡ ἐνέργεια ὡς πρὸς ὑποκείμενόν τι διαβιβάζεταί.

86. ibid. 3.14–18 (*Gram. Graec.* 2.2, 280, 282 –3).

87. ibid. 2. 43–7 (*Gram. Graec.* 2.2, 156–60).

88. ibid. 1.36 (*Gram. Graec.* 2.2, 33).

89. ibid. 1.55–6 (*Gram. Graec.* 2.2, 47–8) An alternative analysis of this sentence envisaged by Apollonius treats ταχὺ ελθὸν as a neuter adjectival phrase linked with παιδίον, 'a quick boy coming up helped us', with a different immediate constituent structure; cp. STEINTHAL 1890, volume 2, 342; HOUSEHOLDER, op. cit., 40.

90. ibid. 3.172 (*Gram. Graec.* 2.2, 418–19: τὸ ἐρᾶν ὁμολογεῖ τὸ προσδιατίθεσθαι ὑπὸ τοῦ ἐρωμένου. 'Being in love admits to being affected by one's beloved', and therefore the verb properly constructs with the genitive case, the case used of the agent in passive sentences.

91. BUCK, *Comparative grammar*, § 240; J. WRIGHT, *Comparative grammar of the Greek language*, London, 1912, § 326.

92. ROBINS, 1986, 18.

93. HJELMSLEV, *Cas*, 12. Maximus Planudes showed more originality of thought than is generally credited to Byzantine grammarians (Robins, 'The case theory of Maximus Planudes', *Proc. of the eleventh International Congress of Linguists*, Bologna, 1974, 107–11).

94. A full historical account and discussion of the 'localist' theory and of rival theories can be found in HJELMSLEV, *Cas*. For a contrary view see D. L. BLANK, 'Apollonius and Maximus on the order and meaning of the oblique cases', TAYLOR, 1987, 67–83. Several articles on both topics are printed in LALLOT, 1985, with bibliographic references to earlier publications. To these may be added ROBINS, 'Ex Oriente lux: a contribution of the Byzantine grammarians', S. AUROUX *et al.* (eds), *Matériaux pour une histoire des théories linguistiques*, Lille, 1984, 217–25, and 'Text and textual interpretation in ancient Greek linguistics', *Semiotica* 70 (1988), 331–44.

95. See D. J. TAYLOR, 'Rethinking the history of language science in classical antiquity', TAYLOR, 1987, 1–16, in which some revisions of the earlier accepted presentation of the course of the history of linguistics are proposed, with several of the questions raised being referred to in this chapter and in chapter 3.

Chapter 3

Rome

In passing from Greece to Rome we enter a very different world. One rightly speaks of the Greco-Roman era as a period of unified civilization around the Mediterranean area, but the respective roles of Greece and Rome were dissimilar and complementary. Without the other, the contribution of either to European civilization would have been less significant and less productive.

The Romans had for long enjoyed contact with Greek material culture and intellectual ideas, through the Greek settlements in the south of Italy; and they had learned writing from the western Greeks. But it was during the third and second centuries B.C. that the Greek world fell progressively within the control of Rome, by now the mistress of the whole of Italy. The expansion of Roman rule was almost complete by the Christian era, and the Roman Empire, as it now was, had achieved a relatively permanent position, which, with fairly small-scale changes in Britain and on the northern and eastern frontiers, remained free of serious wars for a further two hundred years. The second half of this period earned Gibbon's well-known encomium: 'If a man were called to fix the period in the history of the world during which the condition of the human race was most happy and prosperous, he would, without hesitation, name that which elapsed from the death of Domitian to the accession of Commodus' (i.e. A.D. 96–180).[1]

In taking over the Hellenistic world, the Romans brought within their sway the Jewish people and the land of the Old and New Testaments. The intellectual background of Greece and Judaea and the political unity and freedom of intercourse provided by Roman stability were the conditions in which Christianity arose and spread, to become in the fourth century A.D the state religion of the Roman Empire. To these three peoples, the Greeks, the Romans, and the Jews, modern Europe and much of the entire modern world owe the origins of their intellectual, moral, political and religious civilization.

From their earliest contacts the Romans cheerfully acknowledged the superior intellectual and artistic achievements of the Greeks. Linguistically this was reflected in the different common languages of the eastern and the western provinces. In the western half of the empire, where no contact had been made with a recognized civilization, Latin became the language of administration, business, law, learning, and social advancement. Ultimately spoken Latin (by no means identical with classical literary Latin) displaced the former languages of most of the western provinces, and became in the course of linguistic evolution the modern Romance, or neo-Latin, languages of contemporary Europe. In the east, however, already largely under Greek administration since the Hellenistic period, Greek retained the position it had already reached; Roman officials often learned and used Greek in the course of their duties, and Greek literature and philosophy were highly respected. Ultimately this linguistic division was politically recognized in the splitting of the Roman Empire into the Western and the Eastern Empires, with the new eastern capital at Constantinople (Byzantiium) enduring as the head of the Byzantine dominions, though with diminishing territory, up to the time of the western Renaissance.

The accepted view of the relation between Roman rule and Greek civilization was probably well represented in Vergil's famous summary of Rome's place and duty: let others (i.e. the Greeks) excel if they will in the arts, while Rome keeps the peace of the world.[2]

During the years in which Rome ruled the western civilized world, there must have been contacts between speakers of Latin and speakers of other languages at all levels and in all places. Interpreters must have been in great demand, and the teaching and learning of Latin (and, in the eastern provinces, of Greek) must have been a concern for all manner of persons both in private households and in organized schools. Translations were numerous. The first translation of the Old Testament into Greek (the Septuagint) was the work of Jewish scholars of the Hellenistic age, and from the third century B.C. Greek literature was systematically translated into Latin. So much did the prestige of Greek writing prevail, that Latin poetry abandoned its native metres and was composed during the classical period and after in metres learned from the Greek poets. This adaptation to Latin of Greek metres found its culmination in the magnificent hexameters of Vergil and the perfected elegiacs of Ovid. It is surprising that we know so little of the details of all this linguistic activity, and that so little writing on the various aspects of linguistic contacts is either preserved for us or known to have existed. The Romans were aware of multilingualism as an achievement. Aulus Gellius tells of the remarkable king Mithridates of Pontus (120–63 B.C), who was able to converse with any of his subjects, who fell into more than twenty different speech communities.[3]

In linguistic science the Roman experience was no exception to the general condition of their relations with Greek intellectual work. Roman linguistics was largely the application of Greek thought, Greek controversies, and Greek categories to the Latin language. The relatively similar basic structures of the two languages, together with the unity of civilization achieved in the Greco-Roman world, facilitated this metalinguistic transfer.

The introduction of linguistic studies into Rome is credited to one of those picturesque anecdotes that lighten the historian's narrative. Crates, a Stoic philosopher and grammarian, came to Rome on a political delegation in the middle of the second century B.C., and while sightseeing fell on an open drain and was detained in bed with a broken leg. He passed the time while recovering in giving lectures on literary themes to an appreciative audience.

It is probable that Crates as a Stoic introduced mainly Stoic doctrine in his teaching; but Greek thinkers and Greek learning in general entered the Roman world increasingly in this period, and by the time of Varro (116–27 B.C), both Alexandrian and Stoic opinions on language were known and discussed. Varro is the first serious Latin writer on linguistic questions of whom we have any records. He was a polymath, ranging in his interests through agriculture, senatorial procedure, and Roman antiquities. The number of his writings was celebrated by his contemporaries, and his *De lingua Latina*, wherein he expounded his linguistic opinions, comprised twenty-five volumes, of which books 5 to 10 and some fragments of the others survive.

One major feature of Varro's linguistic work is his lengthy exposition and formalization of the opposing views in the analogy-anomaly controversy (pp. 23–6, above), and a good deal of his description and analysis of Latin appears in his treatment of this problem. He is, in fact, one of the main sources for its details, and it may be argued that he misrepresented it as a matter of permanent academic attack and counter-attack, rather than as the more probable co-existence of opposite tendencies or attitudes.[4]

Varro's style has been criticized as unattractive, but on linguistic questions he was probably the most original of all the Latin scholars. He was much influenced by Stoic thought, including that of his own teacher Stilo; but he was equally familiar with Alexandrian doctrine, and a fragment purporting to preserve his definition of grammar, 'the systematic knowledge of the usage of the majority of poets, historians, and orators',[5] looks very much like a direct copy of Thrax's definition (p. 36, above.). On the other hand he appears to have used his Greek predecessors and contemporaries rather than merely to have applied them with the minimum of change to Latin, and his statements and conclusions are supported by argument and exposition, and by the independent investigation of earlier stages of the Latin language. He was much admired and quoted by later writers on linguistics, though in the main stream of linguistic theory his treatment of Latin grammar did not bring to bear the influence on the mediaeval successors to antiquity that more derivative scholars such as Priscian did, who set themselves to describe Latin within the framework already fixed for Greek by the *Téchnē* and the syntactic works of Apollonius.

In the evaluation of Varro's work on language we are hampered by the fact that only six of the twenty-five books of the *De lingua Latina* survive. We have his threefold division of linguistic studies, into etymology, morphology, and syntax,[6] and the material to judge the first and second.

Varro envisaged language developing from an original limited set of primal words, imposed on things so as to refer to them, and acting productively as the source of large numbers of other words through subsequent changes in letters, or in phonetic form (the two modes of description came to the same thing for him).[7] These letter changes take place in the course of years, and earlier forms, such as *duellum* for classical *bellum*, war, are cited as instances. At the same time meanings change, as, for example, the meaning of *hostis*, once 'stranger', but in Varro's time, and in classical and later Latin, 'enemy'.[8] These etymological statements are supported by modern scholarship, but a great deal of his etymology followed the same line and served the same ends as did Greek work in this field (pp. 26–7, above). *Anas*, duck, from *nāre*, to swim, *vítis*, vine, from *vís*, strength, and *cūra*, care, from *cor ūrere*, to burn the heart, are typical both of his work and of Latin etymological studies in general.[9]

A fundamental ignorance of linguistic history is seen in Varro's references to Greek. Similarities in word forms bearing comparable meanings in Latin and Greek were obvious. Some were the product of historical loans at various periods once the two communities had made indirect and then direct contacts; others were the joint descendants of earlier Indo-European forms whose existence can be inferred and whose shapes can to some extent be 'reconstructed' by the methods of comparative and historical linguistics. Two examples may be cited as illustrations: Greek *phérō* (φέρω) and Latin *ferō*, I carry, are both reflexes of the reconstructed Indo-European verb **bher-*. Latin *feretrum*, bier, is a direct loan from Greek *phéretron* (φέρετρον). But of this, Varro, like the rest of antiquity, had no conception. All such words were jointly regarded by him as direct loans from Greek, whose place in the immediate history of Latin was misrepresented and exaggerated as a result of the Romans' consciousness of their cultural debt to Greece, the fact that their alphabet was directly derived from one of the varieties of the Greek alphabet, and mythological associations of Greek heroes in the story of the founding of Rome.

In his conception of vocabulary growing from alterations made to the forms of primal words, Varro united two separate considerations, historical etymology and the synchronic formation of derivations and inflexions. Certain canonical members of paradigmatically associated word series were said to be primal, all the others resulting from 'declension' (*dēclīnātiō*), formal processes of change.[10] Derivational prefixes are given particular attention in book 6, chapter 38.

One must regret Varro's failure to distinguish these two dimensions of linguistic study, because, as with other linguists in antiquity, his synchronic descriptive observations were much more informative and perceptive than his attempts at historical etymology. As an example of an apparent awareness of the distinction, one may note his statement that, within Latin, *equitātus* cavalry, and *eques* (stem *equit-*), horseman, can be associated with and descriptively referred back to *equus*, horse, but that no further explanation on the same lines is possible for *equus*.[11] Within Latin it is primal, and any explanation of its form and its meaning involve diachronic research into earlier stages of the Indo-European family and cognate forms in languages other than Latin.

In the field of word form variations from a single root, both derivational and inflexional, Varro rehearsed the arguments for and against analogy and anomaly, citing Latin examples of regularity and of irregularity. Sensibly enough he concluded that both principles must be recognized and accepted in the word formations of a language and in the meanings associated with

them.[12] In discussing the limits of strict regularity in the formation
of words he noticed the pragmatic nature of language, with its
vocabulary more differentiated in culturally important areas than
in others. Thus *equus*, horse, and *equa*, mare, had separate forms
for the male and female animal because the sex difference was
important to the speakers, but *corvus*, raven, did not, because in
them the difference is not important to men; once this was true
of doves, formerly all designated by the feminine noun *columba*,
but since they were domesticated a separate, analogical, masculine form *columbus* was created.[13] Varro further recognized the
possibilities open to the individual, particularly in poetic diction,
of variations (anomalies) beyond those sanctioned by majority
usage, a conception not remote from the Saussurean interpretation of *langue* and *parole*.

One of Varro's most penetrating observations in this context
was the distinction between derivational and inflexional formation, a distinction not commonly made in antiquity. One of the
characteristic features of inflexions is their very great generality;
inflexional paradigms contain few omissions and are mostly the
same for all speakers of a single dialect or of an acknowledged
standard language. This part of morphology Varro called 'natural-
word form variation' (dēclinātiō nātūrālis), because, given a
word and its inflexional class, we can infer all its other forms.[14]
By contrast, synchronic derivations vary in use and acceptability
from person to person and from one word root to another (cp.
p. 25, above); from *ovis*, sheep, and *sūs*, pig, are formed *ovíle*,
sheepfold, and *suile*, pigsty, but *bovile* is not acceptable to Varro
from *bōs*, ox, although Cato is said to have used the form (the
normal Latin word for ox-stall was *būbíle*).[15] The facultative
and less ordered state of this part of morphology, which gives a
language much of its flexibility, was distinguished by Varro in his
use of the term 'spontaneous word form variation' (*dēclīnātiō
voluntāria*).

Varro showed similar originality in his proposed morphological
classification of Latin inflected words. His use in this of the morphological categories shows how he understood and made use of
his Greek sources without deliberately copying their conclusions.
He recognized, as they had done, case and tense as the primary
distinguishing categories of inflected words in the classical
languages, and set up a quadripartite system of four inflexionally
contrasting classes:

Those with case inflexion,	nouns (including adjectives),
those with tense inflexion,	verbs,

those with case and   participles,
   tense inflexion,
those with neither,   adverbs.

These four classes were further categorized by their syntactic and semantic functions: nouns named, verbs made statements, adverbs supported (i.e. constructed with verbs and were subordinated to them), and participles joined (they shared much of the morphology and syntax of verbs and nouns and were a major means of joining or embedding of one clause within another, e.g. *puer legit*, the boy is reading; *puerum vídí*, I saw the boy; *puerum legentem vídí*, I saw the boy reading.[16] In the passages dealing with these classes the adverbial examples are all morphologically derived forms like *doctē*, learnedly, and *lectē*, choicely. His definition would apply equally well to the underived and monomorphemic adverbs of Latin, like *mox*, soon, and *tunc*, then, but these are referred to elsewhere among the uninflected, invariable or 'barren' (*sterile*) words.[17] A full classification of the invariable words of Latin would require the distinction of syntactically defined subclasses such as the *Téchnē* used for Greek and the later Latin grammarians took over for Latin; but from his examples it seems clear that what was of prime interest to Varro was the range of grammatically different words that could be formed on a single common root (e.g. *legō*, I choose, I read, *lector*, reader, *legens*, reading, one who reads, and *lectē*, choicely). All of this research, along with his etymologies, was part of his quest for an account of the way in which the word stock of a language could have grown, during the relatively short time span that the ancient world allowed, to serve the needs of an advanced civilization.

In his treatment of the verbal category of tense, Varro displayed his sympathy with Stoic doctrine, in which two semantic functions were distinguished within the forms of the tense paradigms, time reference and aspect (pp. 33–4, above). In his analysis of the six indicative tenses, active and passive, the aspectual division, incomplete-complete, was the more fundamental for him, as each aspect regularly shared the same stem form, and in the passive voice the completive aspect tenses consisted of two words, though Varro claims that most people erroneously only considered the time reference dimension.[18]

Varro put the Latin 'perfect' tense forms *didicī*, etc., in the present completive place, corresponding to the place of the Greek perfect tense forms. In what we have or know of his writings he does not appear to have allowed for one of the major differences

Aspect	Time	past		present		future	
Active							
incomplete	*discēbam*	I was learning	*discō*	I learn		*discam*	I shall learn
complete	*didiceram*	I had learned	*didici*	I have learned		*didicerō*	I shall have learned
Passive							
incomplete	*amābar*	I was loved	*amor*	I am loved		*amābor*	I shall be loved
complete	*amātus eram*	I had been loved	*amātus sum*	I have been loved		*amātus erō*	I shall have been loved

(The Latin future perfect was in more common use than the corresponding Greek (Attic) future perfect.)

between the Greek and Latin tense paradigms, namely that in the Latin 'perfect' tense there was a syncretism of simple past meaning ('I did'), and perfect meaning ('I have done'), corresponding to the Greek aorist and perfect respectively. The Latin 'perfect' tense forms belong in both aspectual categories, a point clearly made later by Priscian in his exposition of a similar analysis of the Latin verbal tenses.[19]

If the difference in use and meaning between the Greek and Latin perfect tense forms seems to have escaped Varro's attention, the more obvious contrast between the five term case system of Greek and the six term system of Latin forced itself on him, as it did on anyone else who learned both languages. Latin formally distinguished an ablative case; 'by whom an action is performed' is the gloss given by Varro.[20] It shared a number of the meanings and syntactic functions of the Greek genitive and dative case forms. For this reason the ablative was called the 'Latin case' or the 'sixth case'.[21] Varro took the nominative forms as the canonical word forms, from which the oblique cases were developed, and, like his Greek predecessors, he contented himself with fixing on one typical meaning or relationship as definitive for each case (his apparent mistranslation of the Greek *aitiātikè ptôsis* by *cāsus accūsātivus* has already been mentioned, p. 40, above).

Varro was probably the most independent and original writer on linguistic topics among the Romans.[22] After him we can follow discussions of existing questions by several authors with no great claim our attention. The analogy-anomaly controversy gradually faded away. Priscian used *analogia* to mean the regular inflexion of inflected words, without mentioning *anōmalia*; the term *anōmalia*, (whence English *anomalous* = irregular, as a technical term sometimes used in grammar) appeared occasionally among the late grammarians.[23] In evaluating Varro's linguistic thought in so far as it is accessible through the texts that survive, we must bear in mind that to the best of our knowledge there were as yet no grammars or dictionaries of the Latin language in circulation.

Varro's ideas on the classification of Latin words have been noticed; but the word class system that was established in the Latin tradition enshrined in the works of Priscian and the late Latin grammarians was much closer to the one given in the *Téchnē*. The number of classes remained at eight, with one change. A class of words corresponding to the Greek (definite) article *ho, hē, tó,* the, did not exist in classical Latin; the definite articles of the Romance languages developed later from weakened forms of the demonstrative pronoun *ille, illa, illud,* that. The Greek relative pronoun was morphologically similar to the article and classed with it by the *Téchnē* and by Apollonius.[24] In Latin the relative pronoun, *quī, quae, quod,* who, which, was morphologically akin to the interrogative pronoun *quis, quid,* who?, which?, and both were classed together either with the noun or the pronoun class.[25]

In place of the article the Latin grammarians recognized the interjection as a separate word class, instead of treating it as a subclass of adverbs as the *Téchnē* and Apollonius had done.[26] Priscian regarded its separate status as common practice among Latin scholars, but the first writer who is known to have dealt with it in this way was Remmius Palaemon, a grammatical and literary scholar of the first century A.D., who defined it as having no statable meaning but indicating emotion.[27] Priscian laid more stress on its syntactic independence in sentence structure.

The literary critic and educationalist Quintilian (first century A.D.) was Palaemon's pupil; he wrote extensively on education, and in his *Institutio oratoria,* wherein he expounded his opinions, he dealt briefly with grammar, regarding it as a propaedeutic to the appreciation of literature in a liberal education, and defining it in terms similar to those used by Thorax at the beginning of the *Téchnē* (p. 36, above). In a matter of detail, Quintilian discussed the analysis of the Latin case system, a topic always prominent in the minds of Latin scholars who had studied Greek. He suggested isolating the instrumental use of the ablative (*gladiō,* with a sword) as a seventh case, since it has nothing in common semantically with the other meanings of the ablative.[28] Separate instrumental case forms are found in Sanskrit, and may be inferred for unitary Indo-European, though the Greeks and Romans knew nothing of this. It was (and is) common practice to name the cases by reference to one of their meanings (dative 'giving', ablative 'taking away', etc.), but their formal identity as members of a six term paradigm rested on their meaning, or more generally, their meanings, together with their syntactic functions being associated with a morphologically distinct form in at least some of the members of the case inflected word classes. Priscian saw this, and in view of the absence of any morphological feature distinguishing the instrumental use of the ablative case forms from their other uses, he reproved such an addition to the descriptive grammar of Latin as redundant (*supervacuum*).[29]

The work of Varro, Quintilian, and others during the classical age of Rome shows the process of absorption of Greek linguistic theory, controversies, and categories, in their application to the Latin language. But Latin linguistic scholarship is best known for the formalization of descriptive and didactic Latin grammar, to become the basis of all education in later antiquity and the Middle Ages and part of the traditional schooling of the modern world. The Latin grammars of the present day are the direct descendants of the compilations of the later Latin grammarians, as the most cursory examination of Priscian's *Insitutiones grammaticae* will show.

Priscian's grammar (*c.* A.D. 500), comprising eighteen books and running to nearly a thousand pages as published today may be taken as representative of their work. Quite a number of writers of Latin grammars, working in different parts of the Roman Empire, are known to us from the first century A.D. onward.[30] Of them Donatus (fourth century) and Priscian are the most familiar. Though they differ on several points of detail, on the whole all these grammarians set out and follow the same basic system of grammatical description. For the most part they show little originality, doing their best to apply the terminology and categories of the Greek grammarians to the Latin language. The Greek technical terms were given fixed translations with the nearest available Latin word: *ónoma, nōmen; antōnymiā, prōnōmen; sýndesmos, coniunctiō*, etc. In this procedure they had been encouraged by Didymus, a voluminous Alexandrian scholar of the second half of the first century B.C., who stated that every feature of Greek grammar could be found in Latin.[31] He followed the Stoic word class system which included the article and the personal pronouns in one class (p. 32 above), so that the absence of a word form corresponding to the Greek article did not upset his classification.[32] Among the Latin grammarians, Macrobius (c. A.D. 400) gave an account of the 'differences and likenesses' of the Greek and the Latin verb,[33] but it amounted to little more than a parallel listing of the forms, without any penetrating investigation of the verbal systems of the two languages.

The succession of Latin grammarians through whom the accepted grammatical description of the language was brought to completion and handed on to the Middle Ages spanned the first five centuries of the Christian era. This period covered the *pax Romana* and the unitary Greco-Roman civilization of the Mediterranean that lasted during the first two centuries, followed by the breaking of the imperial peace in the third century, and the final shattering in the fourth and fifth centuries of the western provinces, including Italy, by invasion from beyond the earlier frontiers of the empire. Historically these centuries witnessed two events of permanent significance in the life of the civilized world. In the first place, Christianity, which, from a secular standpoint, started as the religion of a small deviant sect of Jewish zealots, spread and extended its influence through the length and breadth of the empire, until, in the fourth century, after surviving repeated persecutions and attempts at its suppression, it was recognized as the official religion of the state by the Emperor Constantine early in the fourth century. Its subsequent dominance of European thought and of all branches of learning for the next thousand years was now assured, and neither doctrinal schisms nor heresies, nor the lapse of an emperor into apostasy could seriously check or halt its progress. As Christianity gained the upper hand and attracted to itself men of learning, the scholarship of the period shows the struggle between the old declining pagan standards of classical antiquity and the rising generations of Christian apologists, philosophers, and historians, interpreting and adapting the heritage of the past in the light of their own conceptions and requirements.

The second event was a less gradual one, the splitting of the Roman world into two halves, east and west. After a century of civil turmoil and barbarian pressure, Rome ceased under Diocletian (284–305) to be the administrative capital of the empire, and his later successor Constantine transferred his government to a new city, built on the old Byzantium and named Constantinople after him. By the end of the fourth century the empire was formally divided into an eastern and a western realm, each governed by its own emperor; the division roughly corresponded to the separation of the old Hellenized area conquered by Rome but remaining Greek in culture and language, and Italy and the provinces raised from barbarism by Roman influence and Roman letters. Constantinople, assailed from the west and from the east, continued for a thousand years as the head of the Eastern (Byzantine) Empire, until it fell to the Turks in 1453. During and after the break-up of the Western Empire, Rome endured as the capital city of the Roman Church, while Christianity in the east gradually evolved in other directions to become the Eastern Orthodox Church.

Culturally one sees as the years pass on from the so-called 'Silver Age' (late first century A.D.) a decline in literary values, a gradual exhaustion of older themes, and a loss of vigour in developing new ones. Save only in the rising Christian communities, scholarship was backward-looking, taking the form of erudition devoted to the acknowledged standards of the past. In the Latin west, as in the Greek east, this was an era of commentaries, epitomes, and dictionaries. The Latin grammarians, whose outlook was similar to that of the Alexandrian Greek scholars, like them directed their attention to the language of classical literature, for the study of which grammar served as the introduction and foundation. The changes taking place in the spoken and the non-literary written Latin around them aroused little interest; their works are liberally exemplified with texts, all drawn from the prose and verse writers of classical Latin and their anteclassical predecessors Plautus and Terence.

How different accepted written Latin was becoming can be seen by comparing the grammar and style of St Jerome's fourth-century translation of the Bible (the Vulgate), wherein several grammatical features of the Romance languages are anticipated, with the Latin preserved and described by the grammarians, one of whom, Donatus, second only to Priscian in reputation, was in fact St Jerome's teacher.

The nature and the achievement of the late Latin grammarians can best be appreciated through a consideration of the work of their greatest representative, Priscian, who taught Latin grammar in Constantinople at the beginning of the sixth century. Though he drew much from his Latin predecessors, his aim, like theirs, was to transfer as far as he could the grammatical system of the *Téchnē* and of Apollonius's writings to Latin. His admiration for Greek linguistic scholarship and his dependence on Apollonius and his son Herodian, in particular, 'the greatest authorities on grammar', are made clear in his introductory paragraphs and throughout his grammar.[34]

Priscian worked systematically through his subject, the description of the language of classical Latin literature. Pronunciation and syllable structure are covered by a description of the letters (*literae*), translating the Greek *grámmata* (γράμματα) defined as the smallest parts of articulate speech, of which the properties are *nōmen*, the name of the letter, *figūra*, its written shape, and *potestās*, its phonetic value. All this had already been set out for Greek (p. 28, above), and the phonetic descriptions of the letters as pronounced segments and of the syllable structures follow the terminology established by the Greek linguists. They provide partial evidence of the pronunciation of the Latin language.[35]

From phonetics Priscian passes to morphology, defining the word (*dictiō*) and the sentence (*ōrātiō*) in the same terms that the *Téchnē* had used, as the minimum unit of sentence structure and the expression of a complete thought, respectively.[36] As with the rest of western antiquity, Priscian's grammatical model is word and paradigm, and he expressly denied any linguistic significance to divisions, in what would now be called morphemic analysis, below the word.[37] On one of his rare entries into this field he misrepresented the morphemic composition of words containing the negative prefix *in-* (*indoctus*, untaught, etc.), by identifying it with the preposition *in*, in, into.[38] These two morphemes, *in-*, negative, and *in-*, the prefixal use of the preposition, are in fact in contrast in the two words *invīsus*, unseen, and *invīsus*, hated (literally, looked (askance) at).

After a brief review of earlier theories of Greek linguists, Priscian set out the classical system of eight word classes laid down by the *Téchnē* and Apollonius, with the omission of the article and the separate recognition of the interjection, already mentioned. Each class of words is defined, and described by reference to its relevant formal categories (accidents (*accidentia*), whence the later *accidence* for the morphology of a language), and all are copiously illustrated with examples from classical texts. All this takes up sixteen of the eighteen books, the last two being devoted to syntax. Priscian, writing in a Greek-speaking city, addressed himself to readers already knowing Greek, as Greek examples are widely used and comparisons with Greek are drawn at various points, and the last hundred pages (18.20.157 ff.) are wholly taken up with the comparison of different constructions in the two languages. Though Constantinople was a Greek city in a Greek area, Latin was declared the official language when the new city was founded as the capital of the Eastern Roman Empire; numbers of speakers of Greek as a first language must then have needed Latin teaching, though Latin was little known or used after the eighth century.

The eight parts of speech (word classes) in Priscian's grammar may be compared with those in Dionysius Thrax's *Téchnē* Reference to extant definitions in Apollonius and Priscian's expressed reliance on him allow us to infer that Priscian's definitions are substantially those of Apollonius, as is his statement that each separate class is known by its semantic content.[39]

nōmen (noun, including words now classed as adjectives): the property of the noun is to indicate a substance and a quality, and it assigns a common or a particular quality to every body or thing.[40]

verbum (verb): the property of a verb is to indicate an action or a being acted on; it has tense and mood forms, but is not case inflected.[41]

participium (participle): a class of words always derivationally referable to verbs, sharing the categories of verbs and nouns (tenses and cases), and therefore distinct from both.[42] This definition is in line with the Greek treatment of these words (p. 39, above).

prōnōmen (pronoun): the property of the pronoun is its substitutability for proper nouns and its specifiability as to person (first, second, or third)[43]; the limitation to proper nouns, at least as far as third person pronouns are concerned, contradicts the facts of Latin. Elsewhere Priscian repeats Apollonius's statement that a specific property of the pronoun is to indicate substance without quality,[44] a way of interpreting the lack of lexical restriction on the nouns which may be referred to anaphorically by pronouns.

adverbium (adverb): the property of the adverb is to be used in construction with a verb, to which it is syntactically and semantically subordinate.[45]

praepositiō (preposition): the property of the preposition is to be used as a separate word before case-inflected words and in composition before both case-inflected and non-case-inflected words.[46] Priscian, like the *Téchnē*, identified the first part of words like *prōconsul*, proconsul, and *intercurrere*, to mingle with, as prepositions.

interiectiō (interjection): a class of words syntactically independent of verbs, and indicating a feeling or a state of mind.[47]

coniunctiō (conjunction): the property of conjunctions is to join syntactically two or more members of any other word class, indicating a relationship between them.[48]

In reviewing Priscian's work as a whole, one notices that in the context in which he was writing and in the form in which he cast his description of Latin, no definition of grammar itself was found necessary. Where other late Latin grammarians defined the term, they did no more than abbreviate the definition given at the beginning of Thrax's *Téchnē*. It is clear that the place of grammar, and of linguistic studies in general, in education was the same as had been precisely and deliberately set out in the *Téchnē* and summarily repeated by Quintilian. Priscian's omission is an indication of the long continuity of the conditions and objectives taken for granted during these centuries.

Priscian organized the morphological description of the forms of nouns and verbs, and of the other inflected words, by setting up canonical or basic forms, in nouns the nominative singular and in verbs the first person singular present indicative active; from these he proceeded to the other forms by a series of letter changes, the letter being for him, as for the rest of western antiquity, both the minimal graphic unit and the minimal phonological unit. The steps involved in these changes bear little or no relation to morphemic analysis, but follow the lines required for stating the morphological rules in a word-based grammar, such as prevailed in antiquity.[49]

The accidents or categories in which Priscian classed the formally different word shapes of the inflected or variable words included both derivational and inflexional sets, Priscian following the practice of the Greeks in not distinguishing between them. Varro's important insight was disregarded. But Priscian was clearly informed on the theory of the establishment of categories and of the use of semantic labels to identify them. Verbs were defined by reference to action or being acted on, but he pointed out that on a deeper consideration ('*sī quis altius consīderet*') such a definition would require considerable qualification; and case names were taken, for the most part, from just one relatively frequent use among a number of uses applicable to the particular case named.[50] This is probably more prudent, if less exciting, than the insistent search for a common or basic meaning uniting all the semantic functions associated with each single set of morphologically identified case forms. The status of the six cases of Latin nouns is shown to rest, not on the actually different case forms of any one noun or one declension of nouns, but on semantic and syntactic functions systematically correlated with differences in morphological shape at some point in the declensional paradigms of the noun class as a whole; the many-one relations found in Latin (as in other languages) between forms and uses and between uses and forms are properly allowed for in the analysis.[51]

In describing the morphology of the Latin verb, Priscian

adopted the system set out in the *Téchnē* for the Greek verb
(pp. 40–1, above), distinguishing present, past, and future, with
fourfold semantic division of the past into imperfect, perfect,
plain past (aorist), and pluperfect, and recognizing the syncretism
of perfect and aorist meanings in the Latin perfect tense forms.[52]
Except for the recognition of the full grammatical status of the
Latin perfect tense forms, Priscian's analysis, based on that given
in the *Téchnē*, is manifestly inferior to the one set out by Varro
under Stoic influence. The distinction between incomplete and
complete aspect, correlating with differences in stem form, on
which Varro laid great stress, is concealed, although Priscian
recognized the morphological difference between the two stem
forms underlying the six tenses.[53] Strangely, Priscian seems to
have misunderstood the use and meaning of the Latin future
perfect, calling it the future subjunctive, though the first person
singular form by which he cited it (e.g. *scripserō*, I shall have
written) is precisely a form which differentiates its paradigm
from the perfect subjunctive paradigm (*scripserim*, I wrote) and,
indeed, from any subjunctive verb form, none of which show a
first person termination in -*ō*. This seems all the more surprising
because the corresponding forms in Greek, e.g. *tetýpsomai*
(τετύψομαι), I shall have been beaten, are correctly identified.[54]
Possibly his reason was that his Greek predecessors had excluded
the future perfect from their schematization of the tenses, in that
this tense was not much used in Greek, and was felt to be an At-
ticism (p. 34, above). A like dependence on the Greek categorial
framework probably led him to recognize both a subjunctive
mood (subordinating) and an optative mood (independent, expressing a wish) in the Latin verb, although Latin, unlike Greek,
nowhere distinguishes these two mood forms morphologically, as
Priscian in fact admits, thus confounding his earlier explicit
recognition of the status of a formal grammatical category
(pp. 61–2 above).[55]

Despite such apparent misrepresentations, due primarily to an
excessive trust in a point for point applicability of the *Téchnē* and
Apollonius's systematization of Greek to the Latin language,
Priscian's morphology is detailed, orderly, and in most places
definitive. His treatment of syntax in the last two books is much
less so, and a number of the organizing features that we find in
modern grammars of Latin are lacking in his account; they
were added by mediaeval and Renaissance scholars on to the
foundation of Priscianic morphology. Confidence in Priscian's
syntactic theory is hardly increased by reading his assertion that
the word order, most common in Latin, nominative case noun or

pronoun (subject) followed by verb is the natural one, because the substance is prior to the action it performs[56]; such are the dangers of philosophizing on an inadequate basis of empirical fact.

In the syntactic description of Latin, Priscian classified verbs on the same lines as had been worked out for Greek by the Greek grammarians, into active (transitive), passive, and neutral (intransitive), with due notice of the deponent verbs, passive in morphological form but active or intransitive in meaning and syntax and without corresponding passive tenses.[57] Transitive verbs are those colligating with an oblique case (*laudō tē*, I praise you, *noceō tibi*, I injure you, *egeō miserantis*, I need someone to pity me); and the absence of concord between oblique case forms and finite verbs is noted.[58] But the terms subject and object were not in use in Priscian's time as grammatical terms, though the use of *subiectum* to designate the logical subject of a proposition was common.

Priscian made mention of the ablative absolute construction, though the actual name of this construction is a later invention; he gave an account and examples of exactly this use of the ablative case: *mē vidente puerum cecīdīsti*, while I saw it you beat the boy, and *Augustō imperātōre Alexandria prōvincia facta est*, when Augustus was emperor Alexandria was made a province.[59]

Priscian had little to say on the systematic analysis of Latin syntactic structures. Like his model Apollonius (p. 43, above), he was strong on detailed exemplification but weak on theoretical syntax itself. The relation of subordination was recognized as the primary syntactic function of the relative pronoun, *quī, quae, quod*, and of similar words used to embed a verb or a whole clause within another clause.[60] The concept of subordination was employed in distinguishing nouns (and pronouns used in their place) and verbs from all other words, in that these latter were generally used only in syntactically subordinate relations to nouns or verbs, these two classes of word being able by themselves to constitute complete sentences of the favourite, productive, type in Latin.[61] But in the subclassification of the Latin conjunctions, the primary grammatical distinction between subordinating and coordinating conjunctions was left unmentioned, the coordinating *tamen*, however, being classed with the subordinating *quamquam* and *quamsī*, although.[62]

Once again it must be said that it is all too easy to exercise hindsight and to point out the errors and omissions of one's predecessors. It is both more fair and more profitable to realize the extent of Priscian's achievement in compiling his extensive, detailed, and comprehensive description of the Latin language of the classical authors, which was to serve as the basis of grammatical theory for eight centuries and as the foundation of Latin teaching up to the present day. Such additions and corrections, particularly in the field of syntax, as later generations needed to make could be incorporated in the frame of reference that Priscian had employed and expounded.

Any division of linguistics (or of any other science) into sharply differentiated periods is a misrepresentation of the gradual passage of discoveries, theories, and attitudes that characterizes the greater part of man's intellectual history. But it is reasonable to close an account of Roman linguistic scholarship with Priscian. In his detailed (if in places misguided) fitting of Greek theory and analysis to the Latin language he represents the culmination of the expressed intentions of most Roman scholars once Greek linguistic work had come to their notice. And this was wholly consonant with the general Roman attitude in intellectual and artistic fields towards 'captive Greece' who 'made captive her uncivilized captor and taught rustic Latium the finer arts'.[63]

Priscian's work is more than the end of an era; it is also the bridge between antiquity and the Middle Ages in linguistic scholarship. By far the most widely used grammar, Priscian's *Institutiones grammaticae* ran into hundreds of manuscripts, and formed the basis of mediaeval Latin grammar and the foundation of mediaeval linguistic philosophy, which must be considered in the next chapter. Priscian's grammar was the fruit of a long period of Greco-Roman unity. This unity had already been broken by the time he wrote, and in the centuries following, the Latin west was to be shattered beyond recognition. In the confusion of these times, the grammarians, their studies and their teaching, have been identified as one of the main defences of the classical heritage in the darkness of the Dark Ages.[64]

For Further Consultation

H. ARENS, *Sprachwissenschaft: der Gang ihrer Entwicklung von der Antike bis zur Gegenwart*, Freiburg/Munich (second edition), 1969, 30–4.

M. BARATIN and F. DESBORDES, *L'analyse linguistique dans l'antiquité classique*, I, *Les théories*, Paris, 1981.

R R. BOLGAR, *The classical heritage and its beneficiaries*, Cambridge, 1954.

J. COLLART *Varron grammairien latin*, Paris, 1954.

D. FEHLING, 'Varro und die grammatische Lehre von der Analogie und der Flexion', *Glotta* 35 (1956), 214–70, 36 (1958), 48–100.

H. NETTLESHIP, 'The study of grammar among the Romans in the first century A.D.', *Journal of philology* 15 (1886), 189–214.

R. H. ROBINS, *Ancient and mediaeval grammatical theory in Europe*, London, 1951, chapter 2.

J. E. SANDYS, *History of classical scholarship* (third edition), Cambridge, 1921, volume 1.

T. A. SEBEOK, *Historiography of linguistics*, 127–77.

H. STEINTHAL *Geschichte der Sprachwissenschaft bei den Griechen und Römern* (second edition), Berlin, 1890.

D. J. TAYLOR, *Declinatio: a study of the linguistic theory of Marcus Terentius Varro*. Amsterdam, 1975.

—— (ed.), *The history of linguistics in the classical period*, Amsterdam, 1987 (= *Historiographia linguistica* 13.2–3, but with different pagination).

Notes

1. E. GIBBON, *The decline and fall of the Roman Empire* (ed. J. B. BURY), London, 1909, volume 1, 85–6.

2. VERGIL, *Aeneid* 6, 851–3:
   Tu regere imperio populos, Romane, memento
   (hae tibi erunt artes), pacisque imponere morem,
   parcere subiectis et debellare superbos.

3. *Noctes Atticae* 17.17.2; H. S. GEHMAN, *The interpreters of foreign languages among the ancients*, Lancaster, Pa., 1914.

4. cp. FEHLING, 1956–58. On the possible preservation by Varro (De lingua Latina 8.68–9) of part of the analogy–anomaly argument among Greek scholars, Robins, 'Varro and the tactics of analogist grammarians', *Studies in Greek, Italic, and Indo-European linguistics* (ed. A. M. DAVIES and W. MEID), Innsbruck, 1976, 333–6. That this controversy was fairly widely current among educated Romans is evidenced by the interest said tolerance been taken in it by Julius Caesar, who himself wrote on analogy in language (GELLIUS, *Noctes Atticae* 1.10.4; 9.14.25; 19.8; SUETONIUS, *Caesar*, 56).

5. H. FUNAIOLI, *Grammaticorum Romanorum fragmenta*, Leipzig, 1907, 265: Ars grammatica scientia est eorum quae a poetis historicis oratoribusque dicuntur ex parte maiore.

6. *De lingua Latina* 8.1.

7. ibid. 8.5.

8. ibid. 5.3, 5.73.

9. ibid. 5.37, 5.78, 6.46.

10. ibid. 6.37–8, 8.3.

11. ibid. 7.4.

12. ibid. 9.3, 10.74.

13. ibid. 9.56.

14. ibid. 8.21–2, 9.35, 10.16.

15. ibid. 8.54; CHARISIUS, *Ars grammaticae* I (H. KEIL, Grammatici Latini I, Leipzig, 1857, 104).

16. VARRO, op. cit., 6.36, 8.44, 10.17.

17. ibid. 8.9–10.

18. ibid. 9.96–7, 10.48.

19. PRISCIAN 8.10.54.

20. VARRO, op. cit., 8.16.

21. ibid. 10.62.

22. On Varro's linguistic theory in relation to modern linguistics, cp. D. T. LANGENDOEN, 'A note on the linguistic theory of M. Terentius Varro', *Foundations of language* 2 (1966), 33–6; TAYLOR, 1975.

23. PRISCIAN, *Institutio de nomine pronomine et verbo* 38, *Institutiones grammaticae* 5.7.38; PROBUS, *Instituta artium* (H.KEIL, *Grammatici Latini*, Leipzig, 1864, volume 4), 48.

24. *Téchnē*, § 20 (I. BEKKER, *Anecdota Graeca* 2. Berlin, 1816, 640); APOLLONIUS DYSCOLUS, *Syntax* 1.43.

25. As noun, PRISCIAN 2.4.18, 2.6.30, 13.3.11; as pronoun, PROBUS, *Instituta* (KEIL, *Grammatici* 4), 133.

26. APOLLONIUS, *De adverbio*, BEKKER, *Anecdota Graeca* 2, 531.

27. CHARISIUS, *Ars grammaticae* 2.16 (KEIL, *Grammatici* I (1857), 238): Nihil docibile habent, significant tamen adfectum animi.

28. QUINTILIAN, *Institutio oratoria* 1.4.2–3, 1.4.26.

29. PRISCIAN 5.14.79.

30. Their works are published in the eight volumes of H. KEIL, *Grammatici Latini*, Leipzig, 1855–1923.

31. PRISCIAN 8.17.96.; *De figuris numerorum* 9.

32. PRISCIAN 11.1.1.

33. *De differentiis et societatibus Graeci Latinique verbi*, KEIL, *Grammatici* 5, Leipzig, 1923, 595–655.

34. 'Artis grammaticae maximi auctores', dedicatory preface 1–2, 6.1.1, 11.1.1.

35. 1.2.3, 1.3.7–8. On the pronunciation of Latin, W. S. ALLEN, *Vox Latina*, Cambridge, 1965.

36. 2.3.14: Dictio est pars minima orationis constructae; 2.4.15: Oratio est ordinatio dictionum congrua, sententiam perfectam demonstrans.

37. 2.3.14.

38. 17.16.104.

39. 2.4.17.

40. 2.4.18: Proprium est nominis substantiam et qualitatem significare; 2.5.22; Nomen est pars orationis, quae unicuique subiectorum corporum seu rerum communem vel propriam qualitatem distribuit.

41. 2.4.18: Proprium est verbi actionem sive passionem . . . significare; 8.1.1.: Verbum est pars orationis cum temporibus et modis, sine casu, agendi vel patiendi significativum.

42. 2.4.18: Participium iure separatur a verbo, quod et casus habet, quibus caret verbum, et genera ad similitudinem nominum, nec modos habet, quos continet verbum; 11.2.8: Participium est pars orationis, quae pro verbo accipitur, ex quo et derivatur naturaliter,

genus et casum habens ad similitudinem nominis et accidentia verbo absque discretione personarum et modorum.

The problems arising from the peculiar position of the participle among the word classes, under the classification system prevailing in antiquity, are discussed in 11.1.1.–11.2.8.

43. 2.4.18: Proprium est pronominis pro aliquo nomine proprio poni et certas significare personas; 12.1.1: Pronomen est pars orationis. quae pro nomine proprio uniuscuiusque accipitur personasque finitas recipit.

44. 13.6.29: Substantiam significat sine aliqua certa qualitate (cp. 13.6.31).

45. 2.4.20: Proprium est adverbii cum verbo poni nec sine eo perfectam significationem posse habere; 15.1.1: Adverbium est pars orationis indeclinabilis, cuius significatio verbis adicitur.

46. 2.4.20: Praepositionis proprium est separatim quidem per appositionem casualibus praeponi . . . coniunctim vero per compositionem tam cum habentibus casus quam cum non habentibus; 14.1.1: Est praepositio pars orationis indeclinabilis, quae praeponitur aliis partibus vel appositione vel compositione.

47. 15.7.40: Videtur affectum habere in se verbi et plenam motus animi significationem, etiamsi non addatur verbum, demonstrare.

48. 2.4.21: Proprium est coniunctionis diversa nomina vel quascumque dictiones casuales vel diversa verba vel adverbia coniungere; 16.1.1: Coniunctio est pars orationis indeclinabilis, coniunctiva aliarum partium orationis, quibus consignificat, vim vel ordinationem demonstrans.

49. For a modern version of such a statement of morphological rules cp. P. H. MATTHEWS, 'The inflectional component of a word-and-paradigm grammar', *Journal of linguistics* 1 (1965), 139–71.

50. 8.2.7; 5.13.73.

51. 17.25.182–6.

52. 8.8.38; 8.10.51–8.

53. 8.10.55.

54. 8.8.38.

55. 18.8.76; 18.10.79; 18.10.82.

56. 17.16.105–6.

57. 8.2.7–8; 8.3.14.

58. 17.15.93; 17.21.153–4.

59. 18.2.30.

60. 17.5.30.

61. 17.2.12–13

62. 16.1.1; 16.2.10.

63. HORACE, *Epistles* 2.1.156–7:
Graecia capta ferum victorem cepit et artes
Intulit agresti Latio.

64. F. LOT, *La fin du monde antique et le début du moyen âge*, Paris 1951, 189. Since Keil's edition of Priscian (*Grammatici* 2 (1885) xiii)) it has been the tradition that a thousand Priscian manuscripts were

known to have existed. H. BUTTENWIESER (*Speculum* 17 (1942), 50–5) reduces this figure to around 370; but this is impressive enough, when one bears in mind that before the invention of printing every manuscript represented an individual copy.

For the most recent enumeration of Priscianic manuscripts see M. PASSALACQUA, *I codici di Prisciano*, Rome, 1978.

Chapter 4

The Middle Ages

'The Middle Ages' is a term used to designate and characterize the period of European history between the breakdown of the Roman Empire as a unitary area of civilization and administration, and the sequence of events and cultural changes known as the Renaissance and generally taken as the opening phase of the modern world. Periodization of this sort is a descriptive convenience for the historian rather than a precise record of the facts; the 'decline and fall' of the Roman Empire, and the revival of learning, the rise of humanism and nationalism, religious reformation, and the other features collectively regarded as characterizing and constituting the Renaissance are not events that can be located at particular points in time; they summarize a multitude of events of historical significance and, perhaps of more importance, changes of attitude and of ways of behaving, that took place gradually and at different times in different places, but together served to mark off the European situation after them as recognizably and irreversibly altered from what had preceded. Any date taken symbolically as the start or as the finish of the Middle Ages must be arbitrary, and, if taken at all literally, misleading.

'Middle', of course, would have no meaning for anyone living in the mediaeval period; the term springs from the sense of Renaissance men that, among other achievements, they were again linking hands with the bright civilization and humanism of the classical era across the gulf of intervening darkness and barbarism.[1] In this sweeping generalization, people of the first years of modern Europe exaggerated the blackness of mediaeval times and undervalued the cultural and intellectual activities and products of the Middle Ages. But a decline there undoubtedly

was over a wide field of human life during the centuries immediately following the collapse of Rome.

The first six centuries following the dissolution of the Western
Roman Empire are often distinguished, as the 'Dark Ages', from
the later mediaeval period between about 1100 and the Renaissance, during which the flowering of mediaeval civilization
recovered much of the ground lost in the turmoil of earlier years.[2]
However, currently historians rightly pay tribute to the work of
early mediaeval scholars, not least for their part in the provision
of material for the teaching of Latin, during the Carolingian
years, in particular (early ninth century).

During this time the Eastern Empire fared better. Though its
territory was attacked from different sides and reduced in area,
a continuity of Greek thought and learning coexisted with the
spread of official Christianity, which gradually attained the status
of the separate Eastern Church. No sharp break in organized life
and civilization occurred such as was suffered by the west, and in
matters of scholarship, Greek philosophy and Greek literature
were never lost, and the ancient Greek authors were subjects of
continuous commentary and exegesis. Byzantine scholars wrote
explications and commentaries on the works of Dionysius Thrax
and of Apollonius Dyscolus, and research continued on the
theory of some grammatical categories (cp. pp. 45-6, above).

The Roman Empire in the west, already under pressure from
barbarian invasions over the frontiers that had been nearly stable
from Augustus (27 B.C.–A.D. 14) to Marcus Aurelius (161–
80), failed to stand the strain, and its territory passed into the
hands of various tribes, mostly Germanic. In 410 Rome suffered
the humiliation of being sacked by the Visigoths, and in 476 the
last of the emperors in the west, poor Romulus Augustulus, was
summarily deposed by a German mercenary, Odovacar, and Italy
passed seventeen years later into the Ostrogothic kingdom under
Theodoric.

The causes of the collapse of the empire of the 'eternal city'
have been the focus of earnest enquiry from the time when, with
the sack of Rome in his memory, Augustine sought for a Christian interpretation of secular history in *The city of God* (*Civitas
Dei*). Certainly from the end of the second century A.D. external
pressures on the frontiers were more severe than hitherto, and
certainly, too, one can point to grave weaknesses of character and
wrong decisions on the part of those called upon to face those
pressures. Civil fighting, invasions, and later wars between the
Eastern Empire and the successors to the western emperors
cumulatively caused an absolute fall in standards of life, security,

and liberal civilization such as had been enjoyed in the first two centuries of the Christian era. Two events may be thought symbolic: the fortification of Rome under Aurelian (270–5), and the destruction of the aqueducts supplying water to the city during the sixth century wars waged by Justinian in his attempts to reconquer the former territory of the old Roman Empire. These calamitous years were, probably, marked by no greater an amount of misdirection, shortsightedness, and obstinacy in the pursuit of impracticable and undesirable ends than that which disfigured the first half of the twentieth century; but our unhappy predecessors had not the uncovenanted advantages of modern technology to repair the results of wanton destruction.

But one must not overpaint the darkness. Many of the Germanic tribes had adopted Christianity, and were anxious to consider themselves part of the Roman Empire and indeed to defend their newly acquired territory against much more savage tribes, whose pressure had first impelled them across the imperial frontiers. The Latin of the western provinces survived every Germanic invader, whose speech left only a few lexical items in the modern Romance languages that are the descendants of the spoken Latin of those regions.

In the west, much of classical literature was irreparably lost; for some centuries the study and even the knowledge of Greek was greatly reduced, and in the Dark Ages much of Greek philosophy that was available was in the form of Latin translations of selected works. In the disturbance of the times and the collapse of pagan authority and standards, the Church grew in prestige as a refuge and as a patron of learning and education, possessing, in the Papacy and bishoprics, centres of secular power. The most formative literature of the period was Christian literature of various types, and with the closure of the philosophical schools of Athens by Justinian in 529, such learning as continued in both east and west was under clerical toleration or patronage and was often clerically inspired.

A great debt is owed for the preservation of a continuity of education and learning to the monasteries, abbeys, churches, and, later, universities, that were founded during the early Middle Ages. In institutions dominated by Christian clerics, pagan literature, that is to say the classical literature of antiquity, was bound to be suspect, and there are instances of deliberate hostility to these authors and the language in which they wrote, as contrasted with the later, more nearly colloquial, Latin of the Vulgate and of church usage. Already Jerome had experienced feelings of guilt at his too great interest in Cicero and the classics at the expense

of holy scripture, and Pope Gregory the Great (590–604)
declared his contempt for the rules of Donatus in application to
the language of divine inspiration; a French abbot of the ninth
century was careful to draw the examples he used in his lectures
on grammar from the scriptures to avoid clerical displeasure. But
in a number of places of learning ancient literature continued to
be studied, ancient manuscripts were copied and preserved, and
grammatical theory was taught.[3]

Latin remained the language of learning, and its authority was
increased by its use as the language of patristic literature and of
the services and the administration of the western (Roman)
Church). This alone ensured the language a high place, and
linguistic studies in the early years of the Middle Ages were
largely represented by studies in Latin grammar. Mediaeval education was built on the foundation of the 'Seven liberal arts';
grammar, dialectic (logic), and rhetoric formed the first part, or
trīvium, music, arithmetic, geometry, and astronomy the second
part, or quadrīvium. A jingle summarizes their functions:

> Gram loquitur; dia vēra docet; rhet verba colōrat;
> Mūs canit; ars numerat; ge ponderat; ast colit astra.[4]

The division into the trīvium and quadrīvium and these terms
were the work of Boethius (c. A.D. 500), a Roman scholar and
statesman, who among his many writings made a number of Latin
translations from the works of Aristotle, which formed a good
part of the restricted amount of Greek literature available in the
west in the early Middle Ages.

Grammar was thus the foundation of mediaeval scholarship,
both as a liberal art itself and as a necessity for reading and writing Latin correctly. All these studies were subordinate to
theology, the study of the Christian faith and Christian doctrine;
but as an example of the persistence of cultural themes, one can
trace the organization of the seven arts back into the classical
period. Varro is known to have written Disciplinae, an encyclopaedia on subjects of education, that included the seven arts,
together with medicine and architecture. This was the model for
Augustine's survey of the seven arts (in which he substituted
philosophy for astronomy), and around the same time Martianus
Capella (fifth century A.D.) wrote an account of the seven arts
in the form of an allegory of the marriage of Mercury and
Philologia, at which the seven bridesmaids were Grammar, Logic,
Rhetoric, Geometry, Arithmetic, Astronomy, and Music.
Capella's style has been found tedious, but the book became a

standard school text. Cassiodorus, who was one of those most responsible for organizing monastic life around the study and preservation of both classical and Christian literature, also set out the seven liberal arts in the course of his *Institutiones* (c. 550).[5]

Such was the context in which grammar was studied and taught in the first centuries after the collapse of the Western Roman Empire. The work itself was in the main practical and normative. In the years before 800 Donatus was the main authority; thereafter Priscian's work, with the aid of numerous commentaries, became the chief teaching resource. Further writing took the form of numerous commentaries and glosses; in other fields this linguistic scholarship was supported by etymological and lexicographical work such as is well known from the pen of Isidore of Seville (seventh century).

The historical importance of these works in the teaching of Latin and in the consequent preservation of the major cultural link with the classical past cannot be exaggerated. It has, however, been unjustifiably neglected in the historiography of linguistics, perhaps because of the great theoretical interest aroused by the philosophical grammarians of the late mediaeval scholastic age. In the earlier period much thought was given to the methods and the materials required for the successful teaching of Latin, particularly in and after the Carolingian period. It is known that Charlemagne, crowned Emperor by the Pope in 800, was shocked by the low standards attained in Latin by many of his clerics and that he gathered a number of grammar teachers into his court to set about a raising of educational levels. Alcuin of York was one of these scholars. In particular, provision had to be made for the needs of pupils whose mother tongue was of the Germanic family and who had to learn Latin from scratch, unlike the young people of Latin descent in the old Western Empire, who were being educated to maintain the classical standards of the language, late varieties of which they already spoke.[6]

Christianity has from its earliest days been conceived potentially as a world religion, and missionary activity has been held to be an important part of the work of the Church in most denominations. The contacts between Christians and non-Christians from the beginning involved linguistic work of a practical nature, and have through the course of history contributed significantly to the growth and development of linguistic science. St Jerome, responsible for the Latin translation of the Bible (the Vulgate), devoted one of his letters to a discussion of the theory of translation, justifying a rendering of sense for sense rather than of word for word.[7] Such knowledge as we have of the Gothic language comes to us almost wholly from the translation of parts of the New Testament into that language by Ulfilas in the fourth century; and the alphabet in use today for Russian and some other Slavic languages is the descendant of one devised in the ninth century by two Byzantine evangelists St Cyril and St Methodius of the Eastern Church and Empire, who adapted the Greek alphabet for the use of Christianized Slavs.

Though a good amount of Latin teaching must have gone on throughout the period of Rome's ascendancy, little is known of the methods. Christian missionary work and the founding of monasteries and churches in foreign lands gave a new impetus and inspiration to the teaching of Latin grammar, and the status enjoyed by the Roman Church in Christianized Europe, and by Latin, its official language, gave, equally, a desire to be taught.

In England Bede and Alcuin wrote grammars of Latin in the seventh and eighth centuries. An example of a specifically didactic grammar of Latin is Aelfric's *Latin grammar* and *Colloquium* (Latin conversation book), and his Latin–Old English glossary that accompanied it. These were composed around 1000 for English children speaking Old English (Anglo-Saxon). Aelfric was abbot of Eynsham in Oxfordshire; he wrote a practical manual addressed to schoolboys, and he based his prescription on the works of Priscian and Donatus. Rather significantly, though this was not the explicit purpose of his book, he told his readers that his book would be equally suitable as an introduction to (Old) English grammar.[8] Though he was aware of differences between the two languages, as in the matter of gender distribution between lexically equivalent nouns and the lack of exact correspondence between their two case systems,[9] he did not question or discuss the applicability of the Priscianic system to Old English, and as his was one of the first known grammars specifically directed at English-speaking learners, it may be taken as setting the seal on several centuries of Latin-inspired English grammar.

After the conversion of Ireland in the fifth century, Latin scholarship flourished to an important extent during the first millennium in centres of learning founded by the Church. Until the Scandinavian invasions of the ninth century, Ireland was in the forefront of Christian civilization, and Irish churchmen played an important part in the spread of Christianity and literacy on the continent of Europe. Latin grammar was studied in Ireland through the works of Donatus, Priscian, and Isidore, and this linguistic learning merged with the native bardic tradition to produce the grammatical and poetic teaching of the mediaeval bardic tracts, which indeed continued down to the seventeenth century. The technical terminology of Irish linguistic scholarship shows a combination of borrowing and adaptation of Latin terms with a parallel development of technical terms from native Irish words; this latter component included terminology devised to cover the features of the initial mutations, of great importance in the phonology and grammar of the Celtic languages, but not found in Latin (or elsewhere in Indo-European). A ninth-century manuscript of glosses on Priscian shows the partial assimilation of his terminology and descriptions into the Irish language; and the *Auraicept na nÉces* (the poets', or scholars', primer) parts of which probably go back to the seventh century, also exemplifies the mingling in Ireland of the Latin and the native linguistic traditions; this work was studied down to the eleventh and twelfth centuries.[10]

In the history of linguistic science, the second part of the Middle Ages, from around 1100 to the close of the period, is the more significant. This was the period of scholastic philosophy, in which linguistic studies had an important place and in which a very considerable amount of linguistic work was carried on. This same era is also marked by the flowering of mediaeval architecture (the so-called 'Gothic') and literature, and the founding of several of the earliest universities of Europe. The movements of whole populations had now ceased, and the ascendancy of the Roman Church, strengthened by the foundation of the Dominican and Franciscan Orders, provided a central authority which, despite controversies and antagonisms, united all men's cultural activities as part of the service of God, and subordinated all intellectual pursuits to the study of the faith.

Hitherto linguistic work had been almost wholly paedagogical in its aims and largely derivative in its doctrine, being applied to the teaching of Latin in accordance with the compilations of Donatus and Priscian. Such purely didactic work went on throughout the scholastic period. Several manuals of Latin grammar were published in verse, as an aid to the students' memory. One such is the *Doctrinale* of Alexander of Villedieu, written about 1200, and running to 2645 lines of rather barbarous hexameters.[11] It would seem that the Latin taught in the schools where this manual was in use was nearer the Latin serving as the mediaeval *lingua franca* of educated life than the language of the classical authors who had served Priscian as his material.

The *Doctrinale* is severely practical, and it remained a popular and prescribed textbook throughout the mediaeval period, and in some schools long afterwards, though in general it fell into the disfavour that mediaeval grammar of all sorts encountered in the renewed classicism of the Renaissance.[12]

Linguistic descriptions of other languages appeared during this period, serving the ends of literacy, popular literature, and educational standards. Irish work in this field has been noticed above; a Welsh grammar is known from the thirteenth century, and its source is said to go back to the tenth.[13] The high reputation of the Provençal Troubadour literature fostered a demand for grammatical information about the Provençal language, and from about 1240 several grammatical descriptions were written.[14]

One of the most striking examples of practical work in this period was the *First grammatical treatise*, by an unknown Icelandic scholar of the twelfth century, who showed a remarkable originality and independence of thought. The text takes its rather inappropriate title from the position it occupied in the original manuscript, and the author is in consequence identified simply as the 'First Grammarian'.[15] He was, in fact, primarily interested in spelling reform, in improving the use of an alphabet derived from the Latin alphabet for the writing of the Icelandic language of his day. He was well versed in the work of the Latin grammarians, notably in the work of Donatus; but it is in his treatment of orthographic problems that he displayed an understanding of the principles implicit in phonological analysis and in its application such as was rare in this period of the history of linguistics. Besides this, his observations on the pronunciation of the language, which are in themselves valuable evidence for this stage of Icelandic, show him to have been a phonetician beyond the rank of any known European contemporary.

His short text points to the inadequacies of the existing Icelandic alphabet then in use, and, some eight hundred years in advance, anticipates several parts of Prague phonological theory (pp. 224–7, below) and the exploitation of the phoneme concept to a remarkable extent. The Icelandic of his time maintained the potentiality of thirty-six distinctive vowel segments, nine vocalic qualities each of which could be long or short, nasalized or non-nasalized. He was able to order the nine qualities along the dimension open-close in reference to the values assigned to the Latin vowel letters *a, e, i, o* and *u*; and by marking length and nasality with diacritics (a superscript accent mark and dot, respectively) and leaving their absence unmarked, he kept graphically distinct the thirty-six vowels by the use of just eleven symbols, nine letters and two diacritics. These were required if the orthography was to give an adequate indication of the contrastive pronunciations.

Several consonants occurred as long or geminate in contrast with their short or single counterparts. He suggested writing the long consonants with a capital letter; thus *n* represents [n], and *N* represents [nn]. Conversely, he pointed out that phonetic differences that were dependent on their environment need not be marked separately; so the pronunciations [ð] and [θ], at the time both allophones of /θ/, were assigned the single letter þ, and the velar nasal [ŋ], an allophone of /n/, could be unambiguously indicated in the letter sequence *ng*.[16]

In addition to his advanced phonological theory, his discovery and demonstration procedures were quite modern. Phonemic distinctions were ascertained by controlled variation of a single segment in a constant frame, along such ordered series of words as *sár, sǫr, sér, sęr, sór, sør, súr, sýr*, and they were illustrated by sets of minimally different pairs of words whose difference in meaning depended on the difference of a single letter (one phoneme). The pairs are glossed by being worked into sentences, some of them revealing a racy sense of humour:

Eigi eru *ǫl ǫL* at einu
Not *all ales* are alike;

Mjǫk eru þeir menn *fràmèr*, er eigi skammask at taka mina konu *frà mér*.

Those men are *brazen*, who are not ashamed to take my wife *from me*. (The examples are given in the usual Old Norse spellings; only the examples being contrasted are written in the First Grammarian's reformed orthography.)

Whether in his theoretical exposition, his practical applications, or in the style in which he met imagined objections, the First Grammarian is a pleasure to read. Yet the fate of his *Treatise* is a sad one. Shortly after the twelfth century Iceland fared ill, through climatic changes and disease, and became much more sundered from European life and learning. The text remained unpublished until 1818, and after that it was largely unknown outside Scandinavia. Much of the ground it had covered so well was gone over again in the modern era by scholars who were then considered to be pioneers. One must not only have something worthwhile to say, if one is to have an assured place in history; one must also have an adequate cultural situation for it to become known and appreciated.

By far the most interesting and significant development in linguistics during the Middle Ages is the output of 'speculative grammars' or treatises *De modis significandi* ('on the modes of signifying') from a number of writers during the high period of scholastic philosophy (*c.* 1200–1350). Speculative grammar went far beyond the requirements of the teaching of Latin, and the writings in which it was expounded existed side by side with standard teaching manuals such as the *Doctrinale* of Alexander of Villedieu.

Speculative grammar is a definite and distinct stage in linguistic theory, and the different authors, or Modistae, as they are sometimes called, with reference to the key term *modí significandí* represent substantially the same theoretical point of view, and share the same conception of linguistic science, its objectives, and its place among other intellectual studies. There are, of course, numerous details of presentation in which they differ, as may be expected; a full study and appreciation of this period of linguistics would require proper notice of these differences, but in a historical survey of the subject attention may be concentrated on the broad outlines of the theory that was shared by all those working within it.

Speculative grammar was the product of the integration of the grammatical description of Latin as formulated by Priscian and Donatus into the system of scholastic philosophy. Scholasticism itself was the result of the integration of Aristotelian philosophy, at the hands of such thinkers as St Thomas Aquinas, into Catholic theology. Scholasticism was a system of thought reinforced by and reinforcing the Christian faith of the day, which could serve to unify within itself all branches and departments of human learning and in which the claims of reason and revelation could be harmonized. Probably not before and certainly never since, has the fabric of knowledge been so undivided at its heart.

The rise and growth of scholastic philosophy came about from a number of historical factors, apart from the emergence of men of first rate intellectual abilities and devotion. The greater tranquillity and settledness of the later Middle Ages have been mentioned. In addition, a knowledge of the Greek language, of Greek writers, and, above all, of Greek philosophy as set out by Aristotle became more readily available to the west from around the twelfth century. This increase of knowledge came from opposite ends of the Mediterranean world. The Crusades, though reflecting little credit on the western participants, resulted in more direct contacts between the Roman Church and the Eastern Empire, and the capture of Constantinople in 1204 stimulated interest in the Greek sources of Aristotelian philosophy (known earlier from Latin translations), and released a number of Greek manuscripts to the west. By the fourteenth century Greek was being regularly taught in a number of European universities. From Spain a considerable amount of Greek philosophical writing was reintroduced into the rest of western Europe through Arabic and Jewish translations and commentaries. During the Arab occupation of Spain, Toledo in particular was a centre of the translation of Arabic versions of Aristotle into Latin. Several of the scholastics knew and studied Aristotelian philosophy through Latin translations rather than in the original Greek, and the commentaries by Arabic scholars, of whom Averroes and Avicenna are the best known, contributed to their interpretation.

Earlier Christian philosophers had laid more weight on Plato and Platonic thought than on Aristotle, partly because Platonic theory was more readily available through the writings of the neo-Platonists of the third century and after. The works of Aristotle were not accepted without a struggle in all seats of learning, but the teaching of St Thomas was decisive in making him the dominant philosopher in mediaeval Christian thought.

In the context of scholasticism, the mere description of Latin, as laid down by Priscian and Donatus, was considered inadequate, however useful it might be paedagogically. This change in the conception of the proper objectives of higher level grammatical studies came about gradually, as did the terminology in which speculative grammar was set out. Commentators had already begun to go further than straightforward elucidation and exegesis, and the view was now expressed that Priscian had not delved deeply enough into his subject in merely describing the language, but should have investigated the underlying theory and the justification for the elements and categories that he employed. William of Conches (twelfth century) complained that Priscian had neglected to deal with the causal basis of the various parts of speech and their accidents.[17] Some of the charges against Priscian and the other Latin grammarians show an interesting resemblance to the charges of neglecting explanatory adequacy of theory in favour of mere observational adequacy of data recording, that are made today by generative grammarians against their more purely descriptive predecessors associated with Bloomfield and the dominant trends in linguistic work during the second quarter of the present century. From the twelfth century on, they provided the impetus that led to speculative grammar and to a theory of language set within the philosophy of the times. There was, too, a marked increase in the volume of grammatical research and study that was carried on.[18]

In the middle of the twelfth century Peter Helias wrote a commentary on Priscian in which he sought philosophical explanations for the rules of grammar laid down by him. The examination of Peter Helias's work in relation to a number of commentators preceding him suggests that he was not so much a pioneer in the application of logic to linguistic questions, but rather one of the first grammarians to bring some systematization into earlier rather unordered statements.[19] Thereafter the role of the philosopher in grammar was considered a major one; the theoretical basis of grammar, as distinct from its mere exposition to schoolboys, was the philosopher's province: 'It is not the grammarian but the philosopher who, carefully considering the specific nature of things, discovers grammar'; 'As is the fool to the wise man, so is a grammarian ignorant of logic to one skilled in logic'.[20]

From this attitude consistently arose the conception of an underlying universal grammar, a recurrent quest of theoretical linguists thereafter. Earlier grammarians had not made universalistic claims. They had no need to; their interest was confined first to Greek and then to Greek and Latin, two languages not ill served by the same set of classes and categories. In the Middle Ages Latin remained the only really necessary scholar's language, despite the later increase in men's knowledge of Greek and some study of Arabic and Hebrew. Roger Bacon, who himself wrote a grammar of Greek as well as one of the earliest speculative grammars, and who insisted on the importance of studying Arabic and Hebrew, could declare that grammar was one and the same in all languages in its substance, and that surface differences between them are merely accidental variations.[21] The unity of grammar, realized with superficial differences in different languages, was also compared to the unity of geometry irrespective of the different shapes and sizes of any actual diagrams.[22]

During the scholastic period certain linguistic topics were discussed by writers whose main concern was not linguistic science in the narrower sense. An important distinction was made explicit in semantics, subsequently to be treated under a number of different terms but always maintained as essential in some form. In the thirteenth century, Petrus Hispanus, later to be Pope John XXI, in the course of his *Summulae logicales* referred to the difference between *significātiō* and *suppositiō* as separate but related semantic properties of words.[23] *Significātiō* may be translated as the meaning of a word, and was defined as the relation between the sign or word and what it signified. By virtue of this meaning relation, a given sign may act as a substitute for, or be accepted in place of, a given thing, person, event, etc., or a set of such things; with nouns this is the relation of *suppositiō*. Thus because *homō*, man, means 'man', *homō* or *man* may stand for (*suppōnere*) Socrates, Guy Fawkes, or Harold Wilson. *Significātiō*

is prior to *suppositiō*, and when the *significātiōnē* or meanings of
more than one word are brought together in constructions their
suppositiō may be restricted by this. Thus *homō albus*, white
man, can only be accepted for men who are white, not for dark-
skinned men nor for white existents other than men. This basic
distinction comes up repeatedly, in somewhat different forms and
with different interpretations, in such binary oppositions as meaning and reference, connotation and denotation, and intension and
extension.

Some logicians and grammarians made a further distinction, involving the opposition of form and matter, that of formal
supposition and material supposition. In its formal supposition a
word stands for or is accepted for a thing, person, etc., in what
later logicians call object language or first order language; in
material supposition the word stands for itself, in a metalanguage
or second order language. These two types of supposition are
exemplified in *Peter is the Pope* and *'Peter' is a name*.

This same distinction between form and matter recurs at
various points in modistic speculative grammer. The difference
between *vox*, sound, and *dictiō*, word, treated by Priscian and,
in fact, going back to the Stoics, is expressed thus by Michel de
Marbais (thirteenth century): 'A word includes in itself its sound
as it were its matter and its meaning as its form.'[24]

Mediaeval modistic linguistics concentrated on grammar; the
fact that Latin was everywhere learned as a second language, and
pronounced with 'an accent' depending on the first language of
the individual and his community, may have been partly responsible for their lack of interest in phonetic detail. The modistae
excluded pronunciation from their field, but some writers of the
period mention certain features of mediaeval Latin wherein it had
changed from the standards of the classical grammarians, and a
number of independent treatises on phonetics are known.
Etymology in the Middle Ages continued on the lines already
known from antiquity.

The theory of the speculative grammarians involves a good deal
of new technical terminology, and in detail its exposition is a formidable task. To arrive at a full understanding of the theory and
the conceptual framework of these grammarians some of the
specialist literature must be read, along with at least one actual
modistic text. Fortunately there are now several books fulfilling
these requirements and modern editions of a number of texts.
Thomas of Erfurt's *Grammatica speculativa* (*c.* 1310), a relatively
late example of modistic theory (once wrongly attributed to Duns
Scotus) is available in an English translation side by side with the

Latin text. For further items the bibliography at the end of this chapter should be consulted together with the references[25] given in the notes. In essence, the grammar of Priscian and Donatus was presented as an accurate reflection of the constitution of reality and the powers of the human mind, on which it depended. Considering their universalistic pretensions, it is remarkable how the modistae preserved intact almost all the details of Priscian's Latin morphology, down to subdivisions of word classes quite obviously having reference only to Latin (for example the subclassification of proper nouns into *praenōmina,* forenames, *cognōmina,* surnames, and *agnōmina,* personal titles, all categories strictly limited to Latin onomastics).[26] In dealing with verbal tenses no attempt was made to go descriptively beyond Priscian's rather inadequate formulation or to take Varronian or Stoic theory into account. In these respects a certain naivety appears in the unquestioned descriptive basis of what is otherwise a logically thought-out and internally coherent system of philosophical grammar. It is also a testimony to the place and influence of Priscian in mediaeval linguistic thought.

In the modistic system, things possess as existents various properties or modes of being (*modī essendī*). The mind apprehends these by the active modes of understanding (*modī intelligendī actīvī*), to which there correspond the passive modes of understanding (*modī intelligendī passīvī*), the qualities of things as apprehended by the mind. In language the mind confers meanings on vocal sounds (*vōcēs*), whereby they become words (*dictiōnēs*), and the active modes of signification (*modī significandī actīvī*), in virtue of which they become parts of speech (*partēs orātiōnis*), and signify the qualities of things; these qualities are now represented by the passive modes of signification (*modi significandi passivi*), the qualities of things as signified by words.

Two *modī essendī* that were found in all things and underlay our entire apperception of the world and the constitution of our language were the *modus entis,* the property of permanence or persistence in time whereby things may be recognized as things, and the *modus esse,* the property of change and succession (also called the *modus fluxūs,* the *modus fierī,* and the *modus mōtūs*), whereby persistent things may be recognized as undergoing changes or other processes that involve temporal succession.[27]

One may represent the system diagrammatically:

modī essendī

modī intelligendī actīvī   *modī intelligendī passīvi*

modī significandī actīvī   *modī significandī passīvī.*

Again with reference to the distinction between form and matter, the *modī essendī*, the *modī intelligendī passīvī*, and the *modī significandī passīvī* differ formally, since they are on different levels, but they are the same materially, in that they all relate to the properties of things, as they are, as they are understood in the mind, and as they are expressed in language.[28]

The *modī significandī* are the key terms in the system. Every part of speech, or class of words, is distinguished by its representing reality through a particular mode or from some particular point of view; and every category applicable to any word class is itself a mode contributing its own semantic component. This system of description and the theory lying behind it may be illustrated and compared with the Dionysian and Priscianic systems by setting out the modistic definitions of the eight Priscianic word classes of Latin, as they were given by Thomas of Erfurt:

> *nōmen*: a part of speech signifying by means of the mode of an existent or of something with distinctive characteristics (this is said to be the equivalent of Priscian's definition involving substance and quality). The mode of an existent is the mode of stability and permanence.[29]
>
> *verbum*: a part of speech signifying through the mode of temporal process, detached from the substance (of which it is predicated).[30]
>
> *participium*: a part of speech signifying through the mode of temporal process, not separated from the substance (of which it is predicated).[31]
>
> *prōnōmen*: a part of speech signifying through the mode of an existent, without distinctive characteristics. The mode of existing without distinctive characteristics comes from the property or mode of being of primal matter (cp. pp. 42 and 66 above).[32]

The remaining, indeclinable, parts of speech were said to have fewer *modī significandī* involved with them and to be derived from fewer properties in things. An earlier modista, Michel de Marbais, had rather loosely compared them with the syncategorematic terms of the logicians.[33]

> *adverbium*: a part of speech signifying by the mode of being constructed with another part of speech that signifies through the mode of temporal process,[34] and further qualifying that mode but without other syntactic relationship.[35]
>
> *coniunctiō*: a part of speech signifying through the mode of joining two other terms.[36]

praepositiō: a part of speech signifying through the mode of syntactic construction with a case inflected word, linking and relating in to an action.[37]

interiectiō: a part of speech signifying through the mode of qualifying a verb or a participle, and indicating a feeling or an emotion.[38] The specific association of the interjection with verbs and particples seems to spring from its earlier inclusion in the adverb class by the Greek grammarians. Other modistae, such as Siger de Courtrai, did not restrict it in this way, and this accords more with Priscian's definition (p. 66, above) and with Latin usage.[39]

It is apparent that the formal aspects of earlier definitions have been replaced by the ascription of specific meaning categories, some of them shared by more than one word class; but each class is defined by a particular mode of signifying that distinguishes it from all the others. The declinable (inflected) word classes are defined by reference to the categories of scholastic philosophy, ultimately referable to Aristotle's categories of being; but in applying this terminology to the indeclinable word classes, the modistae treated *modus significandi* almost as the equivalent of syntactic function. While class meanings are more readily (if often roughly) ascribable to nouns and verbs, it is much less easy to do this for those classes of words normally found in subordinate positions within syntactic complexes (as were the Latin uninflected words), unless meaning is very much widened to include formal syntactic relations, as the Firthians do explicitly and the modistae did by implication.[40]

The scholastic interpretation of Aristotelian doctrine is apparent throughout modistic grammar. Priscian's grammatical description of Latin was readily adaptable to this, since Aristotelian influence was strongly felt in its source, the system set out in the *Téchnē*. Defining categories were designated *modī significandī essentiālēs*, and Priscian's *accidentia* became *modī significandī accidentālēs*, covering such categories as case and tense.

Although modistic theory was primarily focused on what one might call the morphosemantics of Priscian's Latin grammar, the ascription of a distinct and definite category of meaning to each formal difference exhibited by classes of words, it was in syntax that the speculative grammarians made the greatest innovations and the most significant developments. A number of the fundamental concepts of later syntactic theory can be assigned to this period of linguistic science. A thirteenth-century writer corrected the previous concentration on morphology by declaring that grammar is above all concerned with syntax; and it may be said that in the mediaeval speculative grammars there appeared for the first time in Europe since the Stoics, whose work on syntax can only be tentatively reconstructed, a definite and explicit theory of sentence structure.[41] Indeed, not only the theoretical modistae but also the writers of the later mediaeval practical manuals and teaching grammars, such as the *Doctrinale* of Alexander of Villedieu, made use of terms and concepts beyond those found in Donatus and Priscian, in particular that of government (*regimen*), in dealing with the syntax of nominal case forms.

Thomas of Erfurt's treatment of syntax may be briefly summarized as an example of modistic theory.[42]

An acceptable sentence (*sermō congruus et perfectus*) arises from four principles, comparable to the four Aristotelian causes:

material, the words as members of grammatical classes (*constructibilia*),

formal, their union in various constructions,

efficient, the grammatical relations between different parts of speech expressed in the inflexional forms (*modī significandī*), that are required by the construction and imposed by the speaker's mind,

final, the expression of a complete thought.[43]

Acceptability required three conditions to be satisfied: the word classes involved must be such as to constitute a syntactic construction (e.g. noun and verb), the words must exhibit appropriate inflexional categories (*modī significandī accidentālēs*), and the words as individual lexical items must be collocable (in the Firthian sense). *Cappa nigra,* black cap, is collocationally appropriate (*propria*), but *cappa categorica,* *categorical cap, though grammatically congruent (*congrua*), is inappropriate (*impropria*) since it involves an unacceptable collocation. A century earlier, and seven centuries before pseudo-sentences like *sincerity admires John* were made famous in discussion, a grammarian had pointed out the unacceptability of *lapis amat filium,* *the stone loves the boy, despite its formal correctness [44]; several centuries before that, and quite independently, Indian linguists had formulated the same distinction (p. 160, below).

The construction of noun and verb (*compositiō*) was taken as fundamental, as in earlier syntactic descriptions, and the terms *suppositum* and *appositum* (subject and predicate) were used to denote the syntactic functions of the two parts of the basic sen-

tence; the *modī significandī essentiālēs* of the noun and the verb
(*modus entis* and *modus esse,* respectively) are involved in the
interrelations of subject and predicate. The terms *suppositum* and
appositum were, of course, related to the *subiectum* and
praedicātum of the logicians, but they were, very properly, kept
distinct.

Other constructions were related either to the *suppositum* or
to the *appositum*, and the analysis of *Sōcratēs albus currit bene*,
white Socrates runs well, comprises a major structure of *suppositum* (*Sōcratēs*) and *appositum* (*currit*), with one subordinate
element related directly to each head, but only mediately to the
rest of the sentence. The specific use of *suppositum* and *appositum* as syntactic terms designating nouns and pronouns as the
subject and verbs as the predicates of declarative (indicative) sentences appears to have developed in the twelfth century in the
writings of Petrus Helias. Before then *suppositum* was used more
in the general sense of *suppositiō* found in Petrus Hispanus, as
what a noun stood for or referred to. A similar but non-technical
and non-theoretical usage is to be seen in Priscian's *Institutiones*.[45]

Earlier theory had distinguished the subject–verb construction
and the verb–object (oblique case) constructions, but the terms
suppositum and *appositum*, or any strictly syntactic terms, had
not been used to cause these abstract components of sentence
structure. The modistae went further, and analysed syntactic relations in terms of dependence and the termination (satisfaction)
of a dependence: 'One part of a construction stands to another
either as depending on it or as satisfying its dependence'[46]. With
various subdivisions, the relation of dependent to terminant was
used to characterize constructions such as the following:

Dependent	Terminant	
verb (*appositum*)	noun in nominative case (*suppositum*)	*Sōcratēs currit*
verb	noun in oblique case (object)	*legit librum*
adjective (*nōmen adiectīvum*)	noun	*Sōcratēs albus*
adverb	verb	*currit bene*
noun	noun in genitive case	*fīlius Sōcratis.*[47]

It will be seen that this relation does not coincide with the relation of dependent to head in modern syntax (cp. especially the

last example), nor with any single syntactic relation. Its main importance lies in the recognition of syntactic relations in sentence structures other than the surface relations of inflexional concord.

The relation of government (rection) between one word and another had already been identified by the time of Peter Helias,[48] who used *regere*, to govern, in denoting the relation of prepositions to oblique case nouns as well as the types of relation exemplified above in so far as case forms were involved. He is said to have defined this relation as 'causing a word to be put in the particular case in which it is put'.[49] Thomas of Erfurt did not use *regere* or morphologically associated words as technical terms; but in the sense in which *government* is mostly used today in the description of languages like Latin, in reference to the relation of prepositions to certain oblique case forms, he used the verb *dēservīre* to be subject to, an interesting example of two metaphors drawn from words of opposite literal meanings to bear precisely the same technical sense.[50] *Regere* and *regimen* were used by some modistae as well as by Alexander of Villedieu.

Dependency and its termination are also used to distinguish subordinate clauses and constructions from independent or main constructions. *Sī Sōcratēs currit*, if Socrates runs, is dependent, because the reader or hearer expects more before he accepts the sentence as complete, or the dependency terminated.[51]

Transitive and intransitive as categories of syntactic constructions make their appearance in modistic syntax. The terms were not used in the same sense in which they had been used of verbs by Priscian (following the terminology of Apollonius, pp. 42–3, above), and in which they are used today, but rather a general connection can be traced between them. The modistae apply the terms *constructiō intransitīva* and *constructiō transitīva* to certain syntactic relations between sentence components, or elements of sentence structure, that involve several different classes of words. In a noun–verb–noun sentence like *Sōcratēs legit librum*, Socrates reads a book, the relation between the first noun (*suppositum*) and the verb (*appositum*) is a *constructiō intransitīva*, as is the relation between the noun and the verb in a sentence like *Sōcratēs currit*, Socrates runs; and the relation between *legit* and *librum* is a *constructiō transitīva*, the verb *legit*, reads, acting as the pivot of the whole structure, with dependence on each noun (p. 92 above). The same distinction is made between adjective and noun in concord, *Sōcratēs albus*, white Socrates, a *constructiō intransitīva* and noun (including adjective) and an oblique case, *filius Sōcratis*, son of Socrates, *similis Sōcratī*, like Socrates, *constructiōnēs transitīvae*. The basis of the distinction is that intransitive

constructions need involve only one term in the grammatical
category of person, whereas transitive constructions necessarily
involve two (i.e. non-coreferential nouns or pronouns).[52] It is
noteworthy that the later mediaeval grammarians made explicit
use of word order in the identification of sentence components,
and that the word order assumed as normal was that common to
the Romance languages of today, noun verb noun, or subject
verb object, rather than the order noun noun verb (subject object
verb) characteristic of classical literary Latin.[53] In mediaeval
times, Latin of the type exemplified in scholastic writing was a
living mode of communication, even though it was everywhere
acquired as a second language.

The modistae followed Priscian's morphological description of
Latin very closely, but in relating the morphological categories
(*modī significandī* in their terminology) to the syntax of sentence
construction, they came to make an important distinction between categories (modes) of one word that were directly involved
with the categories of other words and those that were not. These
were designated *modī respectīvī,* modes involved in further syntactic relations, and *modi absolūtī,* modes not so involved.[54] Some
writers further defined the *modī respectīvī* as *principia construc-
tiōnis* (the bases of sentence structure). Thus the essential modes
of the noun and verb, the *modus entis* and the *modus esse* (p. 89,
above), make possible their relationship as *suppositum* and *appositum* in the sentence, and are therefore both *modī respectīvī.*
Likewise among the accidental modes (Priscian's *accidentia*),
case, gender, and mood are syntactically relevant categories
(*modī respectīvī*), but form (*figūra, schêma* in the *Téchnē*), simple
or compound (e.g. *dīves,* rich, *praedīves,* very rich), and type
(*species, eîdos* in the *Téchnē*), primary or derived (e.g. *calleō,* I
am hot, *callescō,* I become hot), are not, i.e. they are *modī
absolūtī.*

The modistae differ in detail on the distribution of particular
categories (modes) in these two classes, but broadly a distinction
was drawn on syntactic lines between what have been termed in
later formal grammar inflexional and derivational formations.
The modistic distinction bears some relation also to the distinction made by Varro between *dēclīnātiō nātūrālis* and *dēclīnātiō
voluntāria* (p. 58, above), though there is no evidence of an actual use of Varro's work by the modistae. Varro was concerned
with morphological regularity and irregularity; the modistae were
concerned with syntactic function. The partial correspondence between Varro's *dēclīnātiō voluntāria* and their *modī absolūtī,* and
between his *dēclīnātiō nātūrālis* and their *modī respectīvī* arises

from the fact that in Latin (as in many other languages) inflexional formations tend to be much more regular and systematic
than derivational formations.

The syntactic system worked out by the modistae enabled them
to arrive at a clearer picture of the essential function of certain
classes of word and in consequence to refine their definitions. The
distinction between noun and adjective assumed a position of
greater importance. In antiquity adjectives had been assigned to
a variety of subclasses of the *ōnoma/nōmen* class (pp. 39 and 66,
above). Peter Helias referred to a primary division of the *nōmen*
into *nōmen substantivum* and *nōmen adiectívum*, and Thomas of
Erfurt, in describing the *nōmen*, distinguished *nōmen substantivum* from *nōmen adiectívum* by their *modí essentiālēs* of syntactic
independence (*per sē stantis*) and of construction with a noun
(*adiacentis*).[55]

The verb and the participle share the *modus esse*, the category
of process in time; but the verb is grammatically distinct from the
noun, and in the minimal noun-verb, or *suppositum–appositum*
sentence it is one of the two polar terms. The participle, while
sharing in much of the syntax and semantics of the verb, including
time reference and construction with oblique case forms, can also,
with or without other words attached to it, itself act as a nominal
element in sentence structure. This distinction was marked by
referring to the verb as separated from the substance denoted by
the noun (*significans per modum esse distantis ā substantiā*), and
to the participle as not separated from this substance (*significans
per modum esse indistantis ā substantiā*)[56] In this way complex
sentences can be built up through participial subordination or embedding, as part of a theory of syntactic extension or recursion
which any theory of syntax must contain: from *Sōcratēs videt
puerum*, Socrates sees the boy, and *puer legit*, the boy is reading,
one can produce the more complex sentence *Sōcratēs videt
puerum legentem*, Socrates sees the boy reading; in *puer legit* the
verb *legit* with its own *modus esse* (*distantis*) is by the creation of
this sentence brought into union (*compositiō*) with the noun and
its *modus entis*; in the participial phrase of the complex sentence
this union has already been effected (*indistantis*) before the
further embedding under *videt*.

Similarly, the rather unsatisfactory definitions of the preposition by ancient grammarians were replaced by a succinct
statement of its function (in Latin), syntactically tied to a case
inflected word and relating this to a verb or participle (*ad
actum redūcens*). Thomas of Erfurt explicitly rejects the identification of bound morphemes in certain words as prepositions

along with the free prepositions, a confusion which had led Priscian into inaccuracy.[57]

The system of relations and categories outlined above is by no means the same as the system used today in traditional Latin grammar or in current theories formal grammar. But it shows a remarkable growth of syntactic insight and the development of terminology and theory, from which present-day linguists have found a great deal that is applicable and revealing in the formal analysis of the classical languages and of others. It can, in fact, be claimed that a definite and coherent theory of sentence structure and of syntactic analysis was achieved by the modistae, one that dealt with levels of structure deeper than those immediately involved with the morphological categories of the inflected words of Priscian's Latin grammar.

Writers of the speculative grammars did not have to concern themselves directly with the topic that received the greatest attention from mediaeval philosophers. This was the so-called 'question of universals'. While scarcely a linguistic problem except on the most liberal interpretation of the field and scope of linguistics, it was centred on one aspect of the relation between the use of language to talk about the world and the nature of the world in itself. The question primarily refers to the semantic status of the terms or words used to make general propositions, broadly speaking the sort of words that can occur as single predicates or right-hand members of subject–predicate propositions in Aristotelian logic, such as *Socrates is a man* and *man is rational*, and so on. Do such terms stand for real universals existing in their own right apart from and independent of the particular things or persons of which the terms are predicated? Or, do they exist as a common property or character within the particulars? Or, finally, are they no more than general or universal terms used by the speakers of a language, with no status apart from the language and the speaker? These questions, first promoted by Plato's theory of 'ideas' or ideal forms, were brought into particular prominence at the beginning of the mediaeval period by Boethius in his commentary on the writings of the neo-Platonist Porphyry; and various refinements and modifications of the three fundamental viewpoints on the problem were the subject of continuous debate during the whole of the Middle Ages (the question is still a living one, and likely to remain so, but it no longer holds the same central position in philosophical enquiry and controversy). The nominalist point of view, that universals are words or names only, with no real existence outside language, has been made famous by one of its exponents, William of Ockham (first half of the fourteenth century), to whom the saying 'entia nōn sunt multiplicanda praeter necessitātem' (entities are not to be increased in number beyond what is necessary) has been attributed, wrongly in the actual words used, but rightly in the doctrine.

The theory of language set out by the modistae, in terms of the *modī essendī, intelligendī,* and *significandī,* however, rests on a 'moderate realism', basically an Aristotelian view as interpreted by St Thomas Aquinas, and one of the tenets of Thomist philosophy. In this view, as far as human knowledge is concerned, universals are abstracted from real properties of particulars and then considered apart from them by the mind.[58] In modistic terms the mind abstracts the *modī essendī* from things, considers them as *modī intelligendī,* and language permits such abstractions to be communicated by means of the *modī significandī.*

The assumption was that all men carry out this process alike, and that despite superficial differences all languages communicate in the same way, or as the modistae put it, the *modī essendī,* the passive *modi intelligendī* and *significandī* are all the same materially. Thus it is that the now central question of linguistic theory, the nature of universal grammar and of linguistic universals in general, may be regarded as a bequest from the mediaeval scholastic grammarians (cp. p. 86, above).

At least superficially, this sort of view became harder to maintain when in later years wider linguistic experience and interests showed how very different languages are in their grammatical constitutions and in the semantic categories associated with their most important formal features. An almost diametrically opposite point of view was expressed in this century in what has come to be called the 'Whorf hypothesis', from the name of its most vigorous proponent; but the essence of the theory may be seen in the thought of Herder and Humboldt in the eighteenth and early nineteenth centuries and in Sapir, Whorf's teacher, in the twentieth (pp. 232–3, below).[59] In this hypothesis peoples whose languages and culture are widely separated from those of others must be allowed to live in partly different worlds, or in worlds differently conceived and structured from the 'standard average European' world of the classical European inheritance, and that these differences are in some respects correlated with the grammatical and semantic structure of their languages.

Expressed in modistic terminology the universalists stress the essential oneness of the *modī intelligendī* (reinforced in the Middle Ages by the assumption of a God-given faculty of reason implanted in the minds of human beings), from which were derived the *modī significandī* of grammatical structure. Their opponents would start from the very diverse sets of *modī significandī* manifested in different languages, at least on a 'surface' analysis of their grammatical forms and constructions, and would argue therefrom that human thinking and human understanding depend primarily on the use of one's first language, so that the *modī intelligendī* would themselves arise from the *modī significandī*, and that the *modī essendī* of the 'real world', so far as mankind can apprehend them, depend on the *modī intelligendī*. A position between these two extremes might be maintained by saying that the *modī intelligendī* probably differ from language community to language community, and that the traffic is not all in one direction; the *modī intelligendī* give rise to *modī significandī*, but are themselves influenced in the course of years by the *modī significandī* and the actual forms in which they are expressed. The discussion of linguistic universals and of universal grammar has been continued from differing standpoints and theoretical positions from the Middle Ages until the present day. This will be noticed in later chapters and is the subject of much current research and publication.

It is worth-while studying the work of the speculative grammarians, both to see how their linguistic thought arose from the intellectual context of their time, and to consider its relevance to current problems in the theory and the analysis of language. Apart from their contribution to the theory and the terminology of syntactic description, mentioned above, the modistae raised questions on the most important topics that concern our attempt to understand language and its place in human life and society. Moreover they not unfairly represent some aspects of the mediaeval achievement. They wrote in, and illustrated from, Latin, the international language of European culture during the Middle Ages; but they sought to give a universal validity to the rules exhibited in Latin grammar. Mediaeval scholars wished for a system of knowledge in which all branches and all disciplines would accept the same philosophical and religious principles; and after the confusion of the Dark Ages they endeavoured to establish firmly all sciences on true and stable foundations.

The demand that grammatical description should be integrated into philosophical theory brought about a great change in people's attitudes towards linguistic studies. Philosophy in its widest sense had been the cradle of linguistics and of the first speculation on language in ancient Greece; but since the emergence of the Alexandrian school represented in the *Téchnē,* whose standpoint remained dominant in Apollonius and his

Greek and Latin successors, the study of classical literature and the language and style of reputed poets and prose writers had been the accepted purpose and context of linguistic work. So much has this been an accepted and continuing tradition that after the explicit statement of the tasks and purposes of linguistics at the beginning of the *Tēchnē* (p. 36, above), later writers either repeated it summarily, confined themselves to such brief phrases as 'the knowledge of correct speaking and correct writing' (*scientia rectē loquendī rectē scrībendī*), or, as Priscian, felt it unnecessary to give any statement or definition to introduce their subject.[60] But the changed outlook of the later Middle Ages demanded explicit recognition in changed definitions of linguistic science. Siger de Courtrai wrote: 'Grammar is the science of language, and its field of study is the sentence and its modifications, its purpose being the expression of the concepts of the mind in well formed sentences.'[61]

Contemporaries were aware of this change in the definition and conception of the subject. Formerly grammar had been directed towards the *auctōrēs*, the writers of classical literature, now it was exclusively concerned with its place among the *artēs*, the seven liberal arts (p. 78, above), wherein pagan literature had no place unless, like the philosophical writings of Aristotle, it had been officially incorporated into accepted doctrine. The Latin of the speculative grammarians was by classical standards clumsy and inelegant; the forms employed were often unacceptable when considered in relation to the usage of classical Latin authors, and the philosophical theory adduced to justify the theory of modistic grammar was held by later critics of the period to be at best irrelevant and at worst pettifogging and obscurantist. In modern terms the modistae were theory orientated, and the adherents of classical literature and Priscian's grammar as it stood were data orientated, their data being literary texts and classical usage. The difference between the two attitudes is illustrated by the choice of examples; the linguists of antiquity and the late Latin grammarians used quotations from classical texts, Priscian being very free with his citations, but the modistae made up their examples almost formulaically, without regard to actual utterance or to situational plausibility; being only concerned with exemplifying a particular structure, they frequently produced sentences that could scarcely have occurred in any other context (the example quoted above, *Sōcratēs albus currit bene*, white Socrates runs well, is quite typical).

This sort of opposition between the *artēs* and the *auctōrēs* was not new in Christian Europe; something similar could be seen in

the heart-searching of St Jerome and others on whether they were
guilty of preferring Cicero to Holy Writ; but the rise of the modistic approach to grammar sharpened it and brought it into direct
contact with linguistic studies. We find this the subject of a well-
known allegory, the *Battle of the seven arts*, in which the *auctōrēs*,
classical authors from Homer onwards, are based on Orleans,
where classical scholarship and literature had remained
entrenched, and go out to do battle with the philosophers and
the personifications of the seven arts at Paris, one of the main
centres of logic and speculative grammar.[62] It is ironical that Priscian, who in method owed much to Aristotelian models and
whose Latin grammar was the foundation of mediaeval grammatical theory, is now, as champion of the *auctōrēs* from Orleans,
matched in allegorical combat with Aristotle, who had been made
responsible for the assumed logical basis of grammatical rules
and concepts and, as the inspiration of scholastic philosophy, had
become a leader of the *artēs*.

In the allegory the *artēs* win, but at the end of the story it is
prophesied that in time the true grammar of the classical texts
will return in triumph. This indeed happened, but as part of the
many and profound movements of thought that characterized the
intellectual and cultural side of the Renaissance, which was simul-
taneously the full-scale revival of classical learning and the birth
of the modern world.

For further consultation

ALEXANDER VILLADEI, *Doctrinale* (ed. D. REICHLING), Berlin, 1893
    (*Monumenta Germaniae paedagogica* 12).
H. ARENS, *Spachwissenschaft: der Gang ihrer Entwicklung von der Antike
    bis zur Gegenwart*, Freiburg/Munich (second edition) 1969, 35–61.
G. L. BURSILL-HALL, *Speculative grammars of the Middle Ages*, The
    Hague, 1971.
M. A. COVINGTON, *Syntactic theory in the high Middle Ages*, Cambridge,
    1984.
M. GRABMANN, *mittelalterliches geistesleben*, Munich, 1926, volume
    1, chapter 4.
E. HAUGEN (ed.), *First grammatical treatise*, London, 1972.
R. HUNT. 'Studies on Priscian in the eleventh and twelfth centuries',
    Mediaeval and renaissance studies 1(1941–3), 194–231, and 2(1950),
    1–56 (reprinted in HUNT, *The history of grammar in the Middle
    Ages*, 1980 (*Amsterdam studies in the theory and history of linguistic
    science*, Series III, volume 5)).
J. KOCH (ed.), *Artes liberales*, Leiden and Cologne, 1959.
E. F. K. KOERNER *et al.* (eds.), 'Studies in medieval linguistic thought', *His-
    toriographia linguistica* 7.1–2 (1980).

V. A. LAW, *The insular Latin grammarians*, Woodbridge, 1982.

L. J. PAETOW, *The battle of the seven arts*, Berkeley, 1914 (*Memoirs of the University of California* 4.1).

J. PINBORG, *Die Entwicklung der Sprachtheorie im Mittelalter*, Copenhagen, 1967.

——, *Logik und Semantik im Mittelalter*, Stuttgart, 1972.

H. ROOS, 'Die modi significandi des Martinus de Dacia', *Beiträge zur Geschichte der Philosophie und Theologie des Mittelalters* 37.2(1952).

I. ROSIER, *La grammaire spéculative des Modistes*, Lille, 1983.

J. E. SANDYS, *History of classical scholarship* (third edition), Cambridge, 1921, volume I.

T. A. SEBEOK, *Historiography of linguistics*, 179–230.

SIGERUS DE CORTRACO, *Summa modorum significandi, Sophismata* (ed. J. PINBORG), 1977 (*Amsterdam studies in the theory and history of linguistic science*, Series III, volume 14).

THOMAS OF ERFURT, *Grammatica speculativa* (ed. G. L. BURSILL-HALL), London, 1972.

C. THUROT, *Notices et extraits de divers manuscrits latins pour servir à l'histoire des doctrines grammaticales au moyen âge*, Paris, 1869 (reprinted Frankfurt am Main, 1964).

D. L. WAGUER (ed.), *The Seven Liberal Arts*, Bloomington, 1986.

M. DE WULF, *History of medieval philosophy* (tr. P. COFFEY), London, 1909.

J. ZUPITZA (ed.), *Aelfrics Grammatik und Glossar*, Berlin, 1880 (*Sammlung englischer Denkmäler* 1).

Notes

1. W. P. KER, *The Dark Ages*, London, 1904, chapter 1.
2. ibid., 1. For an account of the religious history of the early Middle Ages see J. HERRIN, *The formation of Christendom*, Oxford, 1987.
3. JEROME, *Epistulae* 22 c 30; GREGORY, *Epistulae* 5.53(*Gregorii I Papae registrum epistularum*, Berlin, 1891, volume 1, 357); *Histoire littéraire de la France*, Paris, 1738, volume 4, 445–6. An attractive survey of the co-existence of pagan and Christian literary studies is to be found in the now classic book, H. WADDELL, *The wandering scholars*, London, 1949, chapter 1.
4. SANDYS, 1921, 670 (Gram(mar) speaks; dia(lectic) teaches the truth; rhet(oric) adorns the words we use; mus(ic) sings; ar(ithmetic) counts; ge(ometry) measures; ast(ronomy) studies the stars).
5. AUGUSTINE, *Retractatio* 1.6. CASSIODORUS'S *Institutiones* consists of two books, 1, on Sacred literature, and 2, on Secular (classical) literature, in which latter the seven liberal arts are described in turn. There is an edition by R. A. B. MYNORS. *Cassiodori Senatoris institutiones*, Oxford, 1961, and an English translation by L. W. JONES, *An introduction to divine and human readings*, New York, 1946, where see also pp. 47–58, 'The influence of Cassiodorus on the culture of the Middle Ages'.

6. See further E. HOVDHAUGEN, *Foundations of western linguistics*, Oslo, 1982, chapter 5; V. A. LAW, 1982; id., 'Linguistics in the earlier Middle Ages: the Insular and Carolingian grammarians', *TPS* 1985, 171–93; id., 'Late Latin grammars in the early Middle Ages: a typological history', *Historiographia linguistica* 13(1986), 365–80. For teaching in the later period, V. A. LAW, 'Originality in the medieval normative tradition', T. BYNON and F. R. PALMER (eds), *Studies in the history of western linguistics*, Cambridge, 1986, 43–55; J. J. MURPHY, 'The teaching of Latin as a second language in the 12th century', *Historiographia linguistica* 7 (1980), 159–75; L. L. HOLTZ, *Donat et la tradition de l'enseignement grammatical: étude sur l'Ars Donati et sa diffusion (ive-ixe siècle) et édition critique*, Paris, 1981.

7. JEROME, *Epistulae* 57.

8. ZUPITZA, 1880, preface, lines 1–7.

9. ibid., 18–19, 22–4.

10. *Auraicept na n-Éces, The scholars' primer* (ed. G. CALDER), Edinburgh, 1917; B. Ó CUIV, 'Linguistic terminology in the mediaeval Irish bardic tracts', *TPS* 1965, 141–64; id. 'The linguistic training of the mediaeval Irish poet', *Celtica* 10 (1973), 114–40.

11. ALEXANDER VILLADEI, 1880.

12. ibid., lxxxix.

13. J. WILLIAMS AB ITHEL, *Dosparth edeyrn davod aur, or The ancient Welsh grammar*, London, 1856, xi.

14. A Provençal grammarian, Uc Faidit, wrote the *Donatz proensals* in the middle of the thirteenth century, to which a Latin translation was subsequently added, either by the author or by someone else (see J. H. MARSHALL (ed.), *The Donatz proensals of Uc Faidit*, London, 1969). The *Donatz* follows the tradition of Donatus and Priscian, assuming that this will be suitable for the Provençal language, occasionally noting obvious structural discrepancies – for example, that Provençal has no morphological differences corresponding to the six Latin cases, except for the distinction between the nominative and accusative singular in some nouns (cp. MARSHALL, op. cit., pp. 67–78, 92–3). A fourteenth-century book. *Las flors del gay saber* or *Leys d'amors* (*Les fleurs du gai savoir, Lois d'amour*, edited with parallel French translation by A. F. GATIEN-ARNOULT, *Monumens de la littérature romane* 1–4, 1841–9), combines a grammar of the language along the lines of Donatus along with instruction on the writing of Troubadour-style poetry, the recognition of infelicities, and general rules of verse composition. Cp. further V. A. LAW, 'Originality in the medieval normative tradition', in T. BYNON and F. R. PALMER (eds.), *Studies in the history of western linguistics*, Cambridge, 1986, 43–55

15. HAUGEN, 1972. On subsequent linguistic studies in Iceland, R. J. McCLEAN, 'The grammatical terminology of modern Icelandic', *Studia Germanica Gandensia* 4 (1962), 291–300.

16. HAUGEN, 1972, 19, 25–7, 31, 46–7.

17. 'Causes vero inventionis diversarum partium et diversorum acciden-tium . . . praetermittit' (ROOS, 1952, 93); THUROT, 1869, 17.

18. G. WALLERAND (ed.), *Les oeuvres de Siger de Courtrai*, Louvain, 1913 (*Les philosophes belges* 8), (36).

19. HUNT, 1941–3, 1950.

20. 'Non ergo grammaticus sed philosophus, proprias naturas rerum diligenter considerans . . . grammaticam invenit', THUROT, 1869, 124; ALBERTUS MAGNUS: 'Sicut se habet stultus ad sapientem, sic se habet grammaticus ignorans ad peritum in logica', ALEXANDER 1893, xi–xii.

21. GRABMANN, 1926, 118; ROGER BACON: 'Grammatica una et eadem est secundum substantiam in omnibus linguis, licet accidentaliter varietur', WALLERAND, *Oeuvres*, (43).

22. By Robert Kilwardby, THUROT, 1869, 127. PINBORG, 1967, 25 mentions the influence of Arabic scholars on the later mediaeval doctrine of universal grammar.

23. J. P. MULLALLY. *The Summulae logicales of Peter of Spain*, Notre Dame, 1945.

24. PRISCAN I.I.I., 2.3.14; p. 19, above; THUROT, 1869, 156; Dictio includit in se vocem tanquam sibi materiam et rationem significandi tanquam sibi formam.

25. On the authorship of Thomas of Erfurt's *Grammatica* see GRABMANN, 1926, 118–25.

    Probably the best two texts to study first are SIGERUS, 1977, and THOMAS, 1972; cp. also L. G. KELLY (ed.), *Pseudo-Albertus Magnus: quaestiones de modis significandi*, Amsterdam, 1977; K. REICHL (ed.), *Tractatus de grammatica*, Munich, 1976; ROOS, 1952. These editions all have extensive introductions; for those who read German the introduction in ROOS, 1952, is particularly useful.

    The following items are recommended for further reading: BUR-SILL-HALL, 1971; PINBORG, 1967; ROSIER, 1983; id., 'La notion de partie du discours dans la grammaire speculative', *Histoire épistémologie langage* 3.1 (1981), 49–62; L. G. KELLY, '*Modus significandi*, an interdisciplinary concept', *Historiographia linguistica* 6 (1979), 159–80. Of these references ROSIER, 1983, is especially clear and useful, and a very good summary of modistic theory will be found in M. A. COVINGTON, 'Grammatical theory in Middle Ages', in T. BYNON and F. R. PALMER (eds.), *Studies in the history of western linguistics*, Cambridge, 1986, 23–42.

26. THOMAS, 1972, chapter 13.

27. ibid., chapter 25; SIGERUS, 1977, 3.16.

28. THOMAS, 1972, chapter 4.

29. THOMAS, chapter 8, § 16: Nomen est pars orationis significans per modum entis vel determinatae apprehensionis; modus entis est modus habitus et permanentis.

30. ibid., chapter 25, § 48; Verbum est pars orationis significans per modum esse distantis a substantia.

31. ibid., chapter 33, § 65: Participium est pars orationis significans per modum esse indistantis a substantia.

32. ibid., chapter 21, § 37: Pronomen est pars orationis significans per modum entis et inderterminatae apprehensionis; § 36: modus indeteminatae apprehensionis oritur a proprietate, seu modo essendi materiae primae.

The precise relationship between *materia prima* and the *modus significandi* of the pronoun, as set out fully and explicitly by THOMAS OF ERFURT(1972, chapter 21, § 36), is illuminating on the integration of speculative grammar with scholastic metaphysics. The *modus indeterminatae apprehensionis* arises from the *modus essendi* of *materia prima*, not because it is just the function of pronouns to signify *materia prima*, but because from the indeterminate unformed nature of *materia prima* the mind grasps the essentially indeterminate reference of pronouns as compared with nouns (ex modo essendi reperto in materia prima intellectus movetur ad considerandum aliquam essentiam sic indeterminatam). This reinforces the expressed belief in the harmony holding between the world, human understanding, and human language, part of the unity of science characteristic of much mediaeval thinking.

33. THUROT, 1869, 188; THOMAS, 1972, chapter 44, § 86.

34. i.e. a verb or a participle.

35. THOMAS, 1972, chapter 36: Adverbium est pars orationis significans per modum adiacentis alteri quod per modum esse significat ipsum esse absolute determinans. For the use of *absolute*, see p. 94, above.

36. ibid., chapter 39, § 76: Coniunctio est pars orationis per modum coniungentis duo extrema significans.

37. ibid., chapter 41, § 81: Est praepositio pars orationis significans per modum adiacentis alteri casuali ipsum contrahens et ad actum reducens.

38. ibid., chapter 43: Interiectio est pars orationis significans per modum determinantis alterum quod est verbum vel participium, affectus vel motus animae repraesentans.

39. SIGERUS, 1977, 64.

40. cp. J. R. FIRTH, 'The technique of semantics', *TPS* 1935, 36–72.

41. THUROT, 1869, 213; ROBINS, 'Functional syntax in mediaeval Europe', *Historiographia linguistica* 7 (1980), 231–40; I. ROSIER, 1983, chapter 4; COVINGTON, 1984, chapter 4; C. H. KNEEPKENS., *Het indicium constructionis*, Nijmegen, 1987.

42. THOMAS, 1972, chapters 45–54.

43. ibid., chapter 45, § 89.

44. ibid., chapter 53, § lll; THUROT, 1869, 21.

45. See S. EBBESEN, 'Early supposition theory (12th–13th century)', *Histoire épistemologie langage* 3.1 (1981), 35–48; C. H. KNEEPKENS. "Suppositio" and "supponere" in twelfth-century grammar', J. JOLIVET and A. DE LIBERA (eds.), *Gilbert de Poitiers et ses contemporains*, Naples, 1987, 325–51.

46. THOMAS, 1972, chapter 45, § 89: Unum constructible est ad alterum dependens vel alterius dependentiam determinans. For a current version of dependency grammar, R. A. HUDSON, *Word grammar*, Oxford, 1984.

47. Socrates runs; he reads a book; white Socrates; he runs well; son of Socrates.
48. THUROT, 1869, 239–43.
49. ibid., 21: Conferre dictionem poni in tali casu, in quo ponitur. Thurot rejects its attribution to Peter Helias.
50. THOMAS, 1972, chapter 42, § 82.
51. ibid., chapter 54, § 118.
52. ibid., chapters 47–8. This may be an extension of Priscian's use of *transitio ab alia ad aliam personam* in reference to transitive verbs (13.5.26, 18.1.4).
53. THOMAS, 1972, chapter 47; I. ROSIER, 'Transitivité et ordre des mots chez les grammairiens médiévaux', S. AUROUX *et al.* (eds), *Matériaux pour une histoire des théories linguistiques*, Lille, 1984, 181–90.
54. ibid., chapter 7, § 14.
55. THUROT, 1869, 166; THOMAS, 1972, chapter 10, § 18.
56. THOMAS, 1972, chapter 25, § 48, chapter 33, § 65; cp. p. 89, above.,
57. ibid., chapter 42, § 83; cp. pp. 65–6, above.
58. THOMAS AQUINAS, Summa theologiae 1, q. 85, a. 1.
59. B. L. WHORF, *Four articles on metalinguistics*, Washington, 1950; J. B. CARROLL (ed.), *Language, thought and reality: selected writings of Benjamin Lee Whorf*, New York, 1956. The expression 'standard average European' is Whorf's; cp. E. SAPIR, 'The status of linguistics as a science, Lang, 5(1929), 207–14.
60. ROOS, 1952, 84–6.
61. SIGERUS, 1977, 1; Grammatica est sermocinalis scientia, sermonem et passiones eius in communi ad exprimendum principaliter mentis conceptus per sermonem coniugatum considerans.
62. PAETOW, 1914; SANDYS, 1921, 676–8; H. WADDELL, *The wandering scholars*, London, 1949, chapter 6.

Chapter 5

The Renaissance and after

The Renaissance is traditionally regarded as the birth of the modern world and of modern history, in so far as such inevitably arbitrary divisions of historical time can be meaningful. Most of the features that characterize contemporary history can be seen emerging at this time and continuing without a break up to the present day. Several of them had a direct effect on the directions taken by linguistic studies, and these must be noticed in this chapter.

One can identify the Renaissance, at first, as an Italian development spreading outwards, and especially northwards in Europe, from the fourteenth century. A separate and predominantly religious movement, the Reformation, belonging to the sixteenth century and centred on the German-speaking parts of Europe, led to the establishment of the varieties of the Protestant faith, at first as a fundamental break with Roman Catholicism and the Papal authority of the time and subsequently as one part of the major division of western European Christianity into Catholic and non-Catholic, with Protestantism taking various forms such as Lutheranism, Calvinism, Anglicanism, etc.

These two movements may be said to have initiated modern Europe, and because of the influence exerted for some time by Europe on the world as a whole they may also be seen as largely responsible for many of the characteristics of the modern world. In some respects the two movements favoured similar changes in public and private attitudes, and as far as linguistics is concerned we may draw attention to a number of concomitant developments: for example, the expansion of Europe overseas with the consequential vast and fairly sudden increase in European knowledge of non-European languages, sometimes of types and structures hitherto unknown and unsuspected. At the same time a much greater respect, and therefore more intensive work, was accorded to most of the vernacular languages of modern Europe. But perhaps the most important part of Renaissance scholarship was the completion of the revival, which had begun in Italy, of the study of classical Latin and classical Greek, not, as in the case of mediaeval Latin for international and learned communication and for philosophizing, but as the vehicles of splendid literatures and as the former languages of a mighty civilization, separate from and anterior to the Church, which Renaissance man was in the happy position of being able to recreate. This, in fact, is what gave rise to the term *Renaissance*, and to this period we may ascribe the establishment of classical literature and the ancient history of Greece and Rome (*literae humaniores*) as a central component, at least until recently, of European school and university education. In their different ways both the Renaissance and the Reformation fostered a respect for intellectual humanism, the focusing of attention on humankind and human nature as the central interest in science and art, the Renaissance by the importance it attached to the classics, the Reformation by its insistence on the accessibility of the Bible, in translation from the Latin if necessary, to all individual Christians as the key to the faith, in opposition to the erstwhile authority of the priesthood and the Papacy ('the spiritual priesthood of all believers').

As with any other great movements in intellectual, social, and artistic life, it is absurd to try to assign a specific date for the inception of these two creators of the modern world. One can, of course, draw attention to the dates of particular significant or symbolic events, such as the publication of Luther's ninety-five theses in 1517, but any such dates must be arbitrary and misleading in the unfolding of multifarious changes in thought and action necessarily spread over decades, if not centuries. However, if only as symbolic dates we may identify the years of two quite independent events relatively close to one another, which together betoken the end of one part of the Old World and the beginning of the New World.

In 1492 Columbus discovered the American continent, setting in motion the expansion of Europe over the whole globe, and in 1453 Constantinople, the capital of the Eastern Empire, the successor state of the former unified Roman Empire, finally fell to the Turks; thus was brought to an end the last survivor in the uninterrupted succession of the classical Roman Empire, and numbers of Greek scholars were impelled westward to Italy. Manuscripts of classical texts were brought from Constantinople by emigrants and were also actively sought out and carried home by Italian scholars visiting that city and some others. This was, however, only the culmination of a process already well established. In the preceding years Greek scholars had come to the west and begun the revival of Greek learning. At the end of the fourteenth century Manuel Chrysoloras, invited from Constantinople as a teacher of Greek, produced the first modern grammar of that language in the west.[1]

A heightened consciousness of the classical past and an enhanced vigour in the present engendered a tremendous vitality among leading men in all spheres of activity. Few scruples stood in the way of ambition whether good or bad; of the period it has been said that the only crime of which Renaissance man was not guilty was the destruction of ancient manuscripts.[2] From this era of history dates the conception of the 'Middle Ages', a dark and inglorious period lying between antiquity and the new age. The achievements of mediaeval Europe, which have been noticed in the preceding chapter as far as they concerned linguistic scholarship, were gravely underestimated by the men of the Renaissance. Even as late as the nineteenth century Froude could write in his mellifluous prose as he contemplated the end of the Middle Ages: 'A change was coming upon the world, the meaning and direction of which even still is hidden from us, a change from era to era. The paths trodden by the footsteps of ages were broken up; old things were passing away, and the faith and the life of ten centuries were dissolving like a dream. Chivalry was dying; the abbey and the castle were soon together to crumble into ruins; and all the forms, desires, beliefs, convictions of the old world were passing away, never to return. A new continent had arisen up beyond the western sea. The floor of heaven, inlaid with stars, had sunk back into an infinite abyss of immeasurable space; and the firm earth itself, unfixed from its foundations, was seen to be but a small atom in the awful vastness of the universe. In the fabric of habit in which they had so laboriously built for themselves, mankind were to remain no longer.'[3] Modern scholarship has done much to raise our estimation of the mediaeval period, and to soften the break between epochs that was formerly imposed. But changes there were, irreversible changes, and their effects were far-reaching.

One direct consequence of these changes as far as linguistics is concerned is that the strands of history become more numerous and more complicated. Hitherto it has been not unreasonable to follow the course of linguistic studies by attending to the study of the Greek language by Greek scholars and the later study of

Latin by Latin scholars, together with the theoretical developments built on the foundations of Latin grammar by the speculative grammarians. European work outside these confines was relatively small in extent and, with a few notable exceptions like the work of the 'First grammarian', largely derivative in character. This is no longer true after the end of the Middle Ages. Not only were linguistic horizons widened and the work of non-European linguists beginning to make its impact on the European tradition, but the living languages of Europe were from now on systematically studied, and new lines of linguistic thought, taken for granted today as part of general linguistics, made their appearance. The study of Greek and Latin grammar continued, and the further refinements and developments that carried it from the mediaeval period to modern teaching practice in the classical languages are a proper object of specialist study; but they can no more represent the course of the history of linguistics as a whole.

During the later Middle Ages Arabic and Hebrew had been studied in Europe, and in the University of Paris in the fourteenth century both languages were officially recognized. The Arabic language had been forceably brought to the notice of the Mediterranean peoples some centuries earlier, as a consequence of the rapid spread of Arab power and of the Islamic religion over much of the Near East, the north African coast, and the Iberian peninsula in the seventh and eighth centuries. Roger Bacon wrote a grammar of Hebrew and knew Arabic. Indeed, the necessity of some knowledge of Hebrew, as the language of the Old Testament, had been realized sporadically since the time of Jerome (345–420); but such studies had often been undertaken in a clandestine, half shamefaced manner, Christians fearing charges of associating with the enemies of the Church and Jews fearing the accusation of proselytizing.

Its biblical status had given Hebrew a place alongside Latin and Greek as a language worthy of attention. Isidore (seventh century) along with many others regarded it as the language of God and therefore the first language to be spoken on earth.[4] But with the loosening of clerical bonds during the Renaissance Hebrew was studied more widely and with greater penetration. Greek, Latin, and Hebrew were the three languages in the knowledge of which the *homo trilinguis* of the Renaissance prided himself.[5] A number of Hebrew grammars were written in Europe, in particular Reuchlin's *De rudimentis Hebraicis*.[6] Reuchlin, also a great classical scholar and one of the leaders of the Renaissance in Germany, drew the attention of western scholars to the radically different word class system in use by native Hebrew grammarians; noun, verb, and particle.[7] The former two are declinable and the particles indeclinable. Reuchlin matches the Hebrew grammatical tradition to the Latin tradition by subdividing the noun into noun, pronoun, and participle, and the particles into adverb, conjunction, preposition, and interjection; but he goes on at once to warn his readers that a great part of the categories ('accidents') and their associated theory that apply to the Latin word classes are inapplicable to Hebrew and so require no mention.[8] In 1529 N. Clénard's grammar of Hebrew became definitive for that language in western Europe.

In their increasing knowledge and understanding of Hebrew and their acquaintance with the work of native Hebrew linguists, western scholarship for the first time came into intellectual contact with a non-Indo-European language and a tradition of grammatical analysis not directly, if at all, derived from the Greco-Roman tradition.

Hebrew linguistic scholarship had its origin in the exegesis of the sacred literature of the Hebrew people, including the books of the *Old Testament*, but from the early Middle Ages it also developed under the influence of Arabic linguistic work.[9] This was due both to the structural similarities of these two Semitic languages and to the political power of the Arabs after the Islamic expansion over the Near East, north Africa, and Spain. Technical terms and categories were borrowed from Arabic linguists for the descriptive analysis of Hebrew. By the end of the twelfth century grammars of Hebrew were being written by Jews living in Spain and elsewhere for their coreligionists. Among these grammarians the Qimhi family are well known as the authors of linguistic treatises. Earlier, another Spanish Jew, Ibn Barun, had written a comparative study of the Arabic and Hebrew languages.[10]

Arabic linguistic studies, like Hebrew studies, took their inspiration from sacred literature, in the Arabs' case the Koran. As the sacred book of Islam, the word of God revealed to the prophet Muhammad, the Koran was the bond of unity over the entire extension of the Arab dominions and the wider Islamic faith, from the seventh century onward. The Arabic text of the Koran is a holy text and for ritual and official uses translations are not valid, and therefore non-Arab converts had to learn Arabic to read and understand it (as non-Arab members of the faith still do in Muslim schools in Malaysia and elsewhere). Like other sacred texts the book gave rise to a tradition of linguistic exegesis and commentary; there were, too, the needs of the bureaucracy in the training of administrators and officials in the recognized language of the Islamic Empire. The teaching of

Arabic in the Islamic world thus took up a position analogous to that of Latin in the Western Empire.

Some rivalry developed between different philological schools in the Arab world, and, particularly in the school of Basra, Aristotelian influence was felt as part of the wider impact made on Arabic learning by Greek philosophy and Greek science. Basra laid stress on the strict regularity and the systematic nature of language as a means of logical discourse about the world of phenomena; here it is possible that Aristotelian ideas on analogy made an impact (pp. 23–6, above). A group of linguistic scholars in Kūfa gave more importance to the diversity of language as it was actually found, including dialectal variations and textual occurrences as they were accepted; in some ways this school maintained 'anomalist' views. The extent, if any, of the influence of the *Téchnē* on Arab grammatical theory is disputed. The work had been translated into Armenian and Syriac early in the Christian era,[11] and may have been studied by the Arabs. But it is certain that Arabic linguists developed their own insights in the systematization of their language, and in no way imposed Greek models on it as the Latin grammarians had been led to do.[12]

Arabic grammatical scholarship reached its culmination at the end of the eighth century in the grammar of Sībawaih of Basra, significantly not an Arab himself but a Persian, thus witnessing to the perennial stimulus to linguistic research lying in culturally imposed language contacts. He was a pupil of Al-Khalīl, who had himself worked in metrical theory and lexicography. Sībawaih's work, known just as 'the book', *Al kitāb*, fixed in the main the grammatical description and teaching of the Arabic language from then on. Sibowaih, like the *Téchnē*, rested on the foundations laid by his predecessors. He set out the grammar of classical Arabic substantially as it is known today, recognizing three word classes, inflected noun and verb and uninflected particle. The description of the verbal inflexions was mostly based on the 'triliteral' roots, familiar in such examples as *k-t-b*, write, whence come *kataba*, he wrote, *kitāb*, book, etc. Arab lexicographers made these consonantal roots the basis of their dictionary entries.

Additionally Sibawaih achieved an independent phonetic description of the Arabic script. While not up to Indian standards (pp. 156–8, below) it was ahead of preceding and contemporary western phonetic science. He and other Arab grammarians were able to set out systematically the organs of speech and the mechanism of utterance, interpreting articulation as the interference with egressive air in various ways by different configurations of the vocal tract. The modes of interference were designated *maxraj*, literally 'outlet' by which the air made its exit; and working from back to front, from the throat to the lips and the nose, they were able to expound in explicit technical terminology the segmental sounds of the Arabic language. Features such as the velarized articulation of the 'emphatic' consonants and the velarization and palatalization of vowels in certain phonetic contexts were correctly identified. Their only serious observational failure lay in not diagnosing the mechanics of the voice-voiceless distinction in the consonants, though the division of them into two classes was treated as important and the consonants were correctly assigned to them. In view of this omission, Indian influence on the Arabs' phonetic work may be doubted, though it has been suggested. Certainly the articulatory basis of sound classification and the order of description, from the back to the front, agree with Indian practice, and the Arabs' achievement in this branch of linguistics was far more successful in terms of descriptive accuracy than that of the Greeks and Romans.[13]

Interest in the Arabic and Hebrew languages and the separate scholarly tradition in which they had been treated contributed to the loosening of the bonds that too exclusive an attention to Latin and Greek had imposed on linguistics hitherto. But it was by no means the only factor. It was reinforced by a powerful drive in the study of the vernacular languages of Europe as themselves worthy objects of intense scholarly effort. In this field too, no sharp dividing line can be drawn. During the mediaeval period vernacular grammars of Provençal and Catalan had been written, and the historical importance and the methodological merits of these grammars, which have been noticed in the preceding chapter (82) are only now being properly appreciated.[14] In Italy Dante, whom some regard as the prophet of the later Renaissance, had pleaded the case for the study of the spoken Romance dialects as against written Latin, and through his writings in the vernacular had done much to establish a variety of spoken Italian as the literary and later the official language of the peninsula. But the Renaissance itself saw the publication of many of the first grammars of European languages, thus inaugurating an application of linguistic science that has developed without interruption from then on.

The first known native grammars of Spanish and Italian appeared in the fifteenth century, and the first native French grammars at the beginning of the sixteenth. During the same period grammars were published of Polish and of Old Church Slavonic. The first printed grammar of English appeared in 1586.[15]

The conditions in which these grammars were written and studied were very different from those prevailing in earlier times. The rise of national states and of a commercial middle class within them, patriotic feeling, and the strengthening of central governments made for the recognition of a single variety of a territorial language as official; men felt it a duty to foster the use and the cultivation of their own national language. From the end of the fifteenth century Castilian Spanish was so treated in Spain, and Charles V broke with the universalist Latin tradition in addressing the Pope in Spanish.[16] The invention of printing diffused knowledge at a vastly increased rate, and the rise of a commercial middle class spread literate education through wider circles of society and encouraged the study of modern foreign languages. The economics of printing, moreover, made the recognition of one single variety of a language (the 'standard language') and a uniform spelling an urgent requirement. The publication of dictionaries, both unilingual and bilingual, accompanied the publication of grammars, and has gone on ever since. In England, because of the introduction of French as the language of the conquerors after the Norman invasion and its continued use by the upper classes for some centuries thereafter, a number of grammars and practical manuals of the French language were produced during the Middle Ages. But the systematic study and teaching of French in England can really be said to begin with the publication in 1530 of J. Palsgrave's *L'esclaircissement de la langue françoyse*, a work of more than a thousand pages, dealing with French orthography, pronunciation, and grammar, the last in very great detail.[17]

Secular and humanist needs were reinforced by the rise in status of the vernacular languages of Europe after the translation of the Bible into them, one aspect of the religious Reformation. Luther's German Bible was printed in 1534, and by this time the Scriptures had been translated into a number of western European languages. A widespread interest in the theory and the technique of translation is indicated by the Frenchman E. Dolet's brief essay on the subject.[18]

On the whole the written languages of the educated classes were made the centre of grammatical study. But written languages were also spoken, and written to be pronounced. The pronunciation of mediaeval Latin had been relatively unimportant and varied with the first language of the speaker, while the grammars mechanically reproduced the not very scientific phonetic descriptions of Priscian and the classical grammarians. The new grammars of modern languages paid great attention to the relations between spelling, now being standardized in printing, and pronunciation. Problems of orthography and of spelling reform took on a fresh significance, and, while the confusing equation of letter and spoken sound continued, phonemic inadequacies of existing spellings were noted and resented. Thus early Italian grammars show new letter signs to distinguish open and close *e* and *o* (/ɛ/ and /e/; /ɔ/ and /o/).[19]

The serious study of the neo-Latin (Romance) languages can be said to have been inaugurated by Dante's *De vulgari eloquentia* in the early fourteenth century, wherein he extolled the merits of spoken languages learned unconsciously in early childhood and contrasted them with written Latin consciously acquired as a second language at school through grammatical rules. In a celebrated passage Dante made a plea for the cultivation of a common Italian vernacular which should serve to unify the peninsula of Italy in the way that centralized royal courts did for other peoples.[20]

The relationship between the Romance languages and Latin provided what the ancient world had always lacked, a proper theoretical framework for dealing with language change. It might reasonably be argued that it was in these studies that historical linguistics, as we understand it today, finds its real beginning. The rediscovery of classical antiquity in all its glory as part of the revival of learning gave Renaissance man a historical perspective such as the Middle Ages had not had. The sound changes (expressed as changes of letters) by which Spanish, French, and Italian words could be historically related to the corresponding older Latin forms were systematically recorded and seriously studied; and, perhaps more significantly, the questions that arise from changes in grammatical systems were faced and answered. The Romance vernaculars were not just corrupted Latin, but languages of merit and standing, in their own right, historically related to Latin in interesting ways.[21]

The causes of this linguistic change were discussed, and writers referred to the factors of linguistic contacts and mixtures, and of the gradual independent changes that take place in the transmission of a spoken language from one generation to the next. Scholars recorded the origin of the Romance futures from Latin infinitives followed by forms of the verb *habēre*, to have, and the fact that the caseless nouns of the modern Romance languages had replaced the paradigms of separate case forms found in Latin. This latter change provoked an important reappraisal of the role of prepositional constructions. While most of the Romance prepositions can be formally matched with their corresponding

Latin originals, there is a marked difference between those whose syntactic and semantic uses broadly continue those of the Latin forms, as with Italian *in*, in, and *con*, with, and those like French *de* and Italian *di*, which on the whole correspond semantically to Latin oblique case inflexions, usually the genitive, without any preposition. In 1525 Pietro Bembo raised the question whether these latter were prepositions properly speaking or rather just case-signs, *segni di caso*;[22] and the matter was discussed by his contemporaries, one writer arguing that *di* in *padrone di casa*, master of the house, is a *segno di caso*, but that it is a preposition in *sono partito di casa*, I have left the house.[23] It is easy to say that historical and descriptive linguistics are not adequately distinguished here; but what is important is the beginning of the process of setting free the grammatical description and teaching of modern languages from categories imposed for no other reason than their relevance to Latin, a process to be seen at work also in the succession of grammars of English after the Renaissance, despite the lack in this case of a direct genetic relationship (p. 132–3, below). In like manner the Priscianic system of eight word classes was not left unquestioned. Systems of fewer and of more classes were proposed. Nebrija in his *Gramatica de la lengua castellana* (1492) set up ten.[24] However the definite separation of nouns and adjectives into distinct classes had to wait until the eighteenth century.

Among the Renaissance grammarians Pierre Ramée (Petrus Ramus, born *c.* 1515) is well known, and has been hailed as a precursor of modern structuralism.[25] More generally he is regarded as one of the thinkers who marked the transition from the mediaeval to the modern world. His educational reforms were widely influential in northern Europe, and with his celebrated rejection of Aristotle in his master's degree disputation ('*quaecumque ab Aristotele dicta essent commentitia esse*', 'everything Aristotle said is wrong') he went on to revivify the study of the liberal arts in Paris, formerly the stronghold of Aristotelianism and modistic grammar. He vigorously championed the humanistic teaching of the classical languages, through their literature rather than through scholastic Aristotelianism. After becoming involved in the religious strife of the times, he was murdered in the massacre of St. Bartholemew in 1572.[26]

Ramus wrote grammars of Greek, Latin, and French, and set down his theory of grammar in his *Scholae grammaticae*.[27] While in his grammar of French he made didactic use of references to Latin grammar, he showed a proper appreciation of each individual language. Rather than follow philosophical arguments on

grammar, which, he said, did not save the scholastics from bar-
barisms,[28] he stressed the need in the ancient languages to follow
the observed usage of the classical authors, and in the modern
languages the observed usage of native speakers. His grammatical
descriptions and classifications are formal in today's sense, relying
neither on semantics nor on the categories of logic but on the
relations between actual word forms.

Ramus's grammar of French contains one of the earliest treatments of the pronunciation of the language; and he took care also
to point to the differences between Latin as formerly spoken by
Latin-speakers and Latin as variously pronounced by those who
subjected it to their own phonological patterns after learning it
at school.[29] In Latin grammar he preserved the Priscianic eight
word classes, but in demanding purely formal criteria for their
identification he made inflexion for number and its absence the
basic division between them, contrasting nouns, pronouns, verbs,
and participles (which he regarded as nouns) with all the rest.[30]
This reliance on number as the principal category for grammatical
classification was influential; whereas case inflexion on which the
ancient grammarians had relied so much had largely disappeared
in the modern languages, number still remained as an inflexional
category. Ramus made use of the same distinction in his French
grammar,[31] and it was taken up after him by some writers of
English grammars (p. 133, below).

In his account of Latin morphology he reorganized the traditional system of declensions by making his basic criterion for
classification the parisyllabicity or imparisyllabicity of the case
forms of a noun or adjective (whether the different cases did or
did not substantially agree in the number of their syllables). Latin
verbs are distinguished primarily by whether their future tense is
formed with -b- (amābō, etc.) or not, thus largely corresponding
to the traditional first and second conjugations on the one hand
and the third and fourth on the other.[32] Interestingly Ramus
remarked that though Priscian and the other grammarians of
Latin did not make use of this classification themselves, they
none the less provided the material on which such a formal classification could be made.[33]

Ramus's syntax was also based on the distinction between
words with number inflexion and words without it, and was sys-
tematized by reference to the two categories of syntactic relation,
concord and government (in this he was indebted to mediaeval
grammatical theory).[34]

Contacts between European linguistic scholarship and the work
of Jewish and Arabic grammarians during the later Middle Ages

have been mentioned already. These were by no means the only non-European languages with which Europeans became acquainted in the Renaissance. Colonization of the New World and voyages of discovery round the globe, the establishment of trading stations and expatriate settlements, and the despatch of missionaries all played their part in awakening scholars to the hitherto undreamed wealth of linguistic diversity in the world. This process continued unchecked, and indeed is still in progress, with missions playing a leading part. Appropriately Firth referred to the linguistic aspect of the expansion of Europe as the 'discovery of Babel'.[35]

From the New World, the first grammar of an American-Indian language, Tarascan (Mexico), was published in 1558; thereafter grammars of Quechua (Peru), Nahuatl (Mexico) and Guarani (Brazil) were published in 1560, 1571, and 1640, respectively; in Europe a Basque grammar appeared in 1587 and the seventeenth century saw grammars of Japanese and Persian published.[36] Among the linguistic work done under the control of missionary activities, mention should be made of the achievements of Jesuit missionaries during the sixteenth, seventeenth, and eighteenth centuries and of the *Propaganda Fide* department of the Roman Church. India, south-east Asia, and the Far East were all visited, and several of the languages there encountered were first subjected to a roman transcription by Catholic missionaries for the translation of the Scriptures. The alphabets devised by these missionaries for some of the languages of India and Burma, and the phonetic observations accompanying them have been praised by linguists of the present century,[37] and the transcription made by Alexander de Rhodes for Vietnamese in 1651 is still, with minor alterations, the official writing system of Vietnam.

Some study of Sanskrit was undertaken, and isolated observations were made on certain apparent resemblances between that language and Italian, Greek, and Latin (p. 150, below).

Trade routes had linked China and the Roman Empire overland through central Asia, and the western world was dimly aware in antiquity of the Seres (far away to the east). Late in the thirteenth century Marco Polo had travelled through Asia as far as China and had studied a number of Asian languages during his residence. But prolonged direct contacts between European scholars and the Chinese really started with the arrival of traders and missionaries in the Far East. Francis Xavier had established Jesuit missions in China and Japan by the time of his death in 1552, and several members of these missions became masters of different varieties of Chinese. Of them Ricci is one of the best known.

Trigault, who translated Ricci's famous diary into Latin, recorded the salient differences between the Chinese languages and those of western Europe that strike the first year student of Chinese today: the almost complete lack of morphological paradigms such as had received so much attention in Latin and Greek and were seemingly essential to grammatical structure, the distinction of what would otherwise be lexical homophones by differences in pitch (tones), and the existence of a common written language (Chinese characters) readily intelligible to literate persons irrespective of the differences, amounting often to complete barriers to intercommunication, that existed between several of the varieties of spoken Chinese.[38]

China had developed an indigenous tradition of linguistic studies by the time western scholars made contact with the country and its languages. A character writing system, properly defined as the graphic representation of individual morphemes by separate symbols, had been in use since the middle of the second millennium B.C. and was of native origin, despite certain superficial similarities to character systems in other parts of the world. This mode of representing the language in writing, together with the isolating, analytic structure of Chinese grammar, determined the course taken by linguistic studies in Chinese civilization.

From the end of the sixteenth century the nature of the Chinese writing system was known in Europe and it played an important part in some directions of linguistic research (p. 127, below), besides making European scholars aware of the existence of a group of languages whose phonological, grammatical, and lexical organization differed markedly from those of languages with which earlier generations had been familiar. The first grammars of Chinese published in European languages, by Francisco Varo and by J. H. de Prémare, appeared at the beginning of the eighteenth century.[39]

The virtual absence of morphological paradigms in Chinese did not encourage early grammatical study, apart from some attention to the class of particles. A distinction was made between 'full words', those capable of standing alone and bearing an individual lexical gloss, and 'empty words' or particles, serving grammatical purposes within sentences containing full words but scarcely having a statable meaning in isolation. This passed through Prémare into general linguistic usage.[40] Full words were further divided into 'living words', verbs, and 'dead words', nouns. But the main linguistic efforts of the Chinese were turned on to lexicography and phonology.

Dictionaries were produced in China from the second century A.D. onward. As elsewhere the stimuli were the linguistic changes in the lexicon of the literary language. These made some characters obsolete and altered the meanings of others, thus increasing the difficulties of studying the ancient classics of Chinese literature. One of the earliest known Chinese dictionaries, the *Shuo wên* (*c.* A.D. 100), making use of the revised writing system that had been standardized three centuries earlier, arranged the characters in the manner employed ever since, by 'radicals', though the number of the 'radicals' has since been reduced. Each character is analysed into two components in lexicography, a 'radical', which in part correlates with the general meaning of some of the characters containing it, and the 'phonetic', which sometimes gives an indication of the pronunciation of the character, though semantic and phonetic changes have made these indications very patchy and at best only approximate. The 'radicals' are ordered serially starting with those containing one stroke, in ascending order of numbers of strokes; and the characters containing each 'radical' and so listed under it are likewise arranged in ascending order of numbers of strokes in the 'phonetic' (certain characters consist of 'radical' only; these come first in the lists).

Later dictionaries attempted to deal with the problem of indicating the pronunciation of characters, in view of phonetic changes that had taken place in the language since the classical literary era. This provided the matrix for the development of the phonological study of literary Chinese. The character represented the morpheme rather than the word, though in classical Chinese especially many words were mono-morphemic; and, broadly speaking, the morpheme was phonologically represented by a single syllable, falling within a limited number of possible syllable structures. There was no segmental representation of the components of the syllable in Chinese character writing, and the focus of Chinese phonological thinking was on the isolated monosyllable and on the means of indicating the pronunciation of characters that had become obsolete or had formerly had different phonetic values.

At first the only method available was the citation of a homonym of the character concerned, but from the third century A.D. onward the syllable was analysed into initial and final components, the final being taken as everything coming after the initial consonant, and including the tone. The pronunciation of a character could now be indicated by the citation of two other characters whose pronunciation was assumed to be known, the initial of the first and the final of the second giving the syllabic composition and so the pronunciation of the character in question. Thus the character read /ko/ with a rising tone followed by the character read /hwɛ/ with a level tone would indicate the pronunciation of a character read /kwɛ/ with a level tone.

By the time this technique was in use Buddhist missionaries were already active in China, and it is possible that even this limited phonological analysis of the syllable was inspired by acquaintance with an alien alphabetic script. Certainly it was with the aid of Buddhist monks that in A.D. 489 the Chinese tones were for the first time systematically defined as integral components of spoken syllables, although Chinese had been a tone language from time immemorial.[41]

The next advance in phonological analysis was directly influenced by Sanskrit linguistic studies (pp. 156–8 below). In the eleventh century the well-known rhyme tables set out the total of the occurrent syllables of literary Chinese, represented by characters, on a chart in which the vertical columns held the initials and the horizontal rows listed the finals, now further analysed so as to distinguish medial (post-initial) semivowels such as /-w-/, final vowel or vowel plus consonant, and the tone. This two-dimensional classification enabled Chinese scholars to distinguish, as the Stoics had already done in the west (p. 28 above), between non-occurrent but phonologically possible forms and forms excluded by the rules of Chinese syllable structure. Indian influence is marked in the ordering of the initials by their articulation; the plosives and nasals were arranged in groups of four by place and manner of articulation, /k/, /kh/, /g/, /ŋ/, /t/, /th/, /d/, /n/, etc., and articulatory terminology was used to differentiate them. These rhyme tables are of the greatest importance in the reconstruction of the spoken forms of Chinese syllables in this period of the language, but their historical significance lies in their evidence of the development under Sanskritic influence of a segmental analysis in the face of the tradition engendered by a morphemic-syllabic script, which had first suggested an analysis into initials and finals much more like Firthian prosodic phonology than segmental phonemics.[42]

Various modifications and elaborations were made in this system of phonological analysis during the mediaeval and modern periods of Chinese linguistic scholarship. The emphasis changed from the study of the language of classical literature to the contemporary colloquial northern Chinese of Peking, along with other varieties of spoken Chinese. In the seventeenth century Pan-lei, an excellent phonetician and dialectologist, travelled all over China studying the dialect variations of the different regions. But little of further general importance took place before

European scholarship began seriously to interest itself in the linguistic problems presented by the Chinese language (or languages), including the transcription of Chinese syllables in roman letters, an interest very much to the fore at the present time.

It has been seen how important a part was played by linguistic contacts from outside in the development of Chinese phonological analysis. But China herself was the source of a linguistic problem and of its solution, the adaptation of the Chinese character writing system to an unrelated language of very different structure.

The Japanese language is genetically unrelated to Chinese, but from the fifth century A.D. onward there was considerable contact between Japan and China, and the Japanese borrowed freely from Chinese literature and other aspects of Chinese culture, with large numbers of Chinese words being taken into the language. Writing was introduced from China, and the problem at once arose of adapting the characters that in Chinese represented unchanging monosyllables to the requirements of a language rich in agglutinative derivations and inflexions. At first the problem was solved by ignoring it; the agglutinated elements of words were left unrepresented and the characters were used as they would have been in Chinese sentences. Ultimately the situation still in use today was evolved, wherein the characters are used to represent invariable words and the constant root element of variable words, while the derivational and inflexional parts of word structures are written in the *kana* syllabary, a set of syllabic signs derived from bits of particular characters used for their phonetic value alone.

An intermediate stage, however, is worthy of notice. In this the character represented the root of the word, but other grammatical elements, as well as certain particles in close syntactic relationship with it, were indicated graphically by means of diacritical marks written at different positions round the character itself. Thus the verb *kasikom-*, to fear, would be represented by a particular character bearing a similar meaning in Chinese, and a small circle at its lower left hand corner would further indicate the word *kasikomite*, fearing, and a diagonal stroke at the top right-hand corner would indicate the word *kasikomi-tari*, (he, etc.) feared.[43] This orthographic system did not remain in use, but it is of interest in its similarity to certain linguistic speculations and experiments in Europe during the sixteenth and seventeenth centuries (p. 130, below).

To many thinking people in the first phase of the Renaissance in Europe, the revival of ancient learning and the new awareness

of the glories of the Greco-Roman classical world were probably
the most significant characteristics of the age. Indeed, the words
'Renaissance' and 'revival of learning' testify to this conception.
It is noticeable how numbers of early Renaissance writers quote
freely from classical sources to justify and illustrate their arguments, looking directly to antiquity, no longer under any taint of
paganism, but rather seen as a period of exalted humanism with
which Renaissance thinkers, in stressing the worth and dignity of
man in his own right, felt an intellectual and moral kinship. Such
men of the Renaissance considered themselves to be continuing
the work of ancient civilization. The classical texts available in
Europe were now approximately those available today, and the
study of ancient literature took on the forms recognizable in the
present age in the classical curricula of schools and universities.

The Greek and Latin classics were read for their own merits
and in the original languages, not by means of translations or
through the official interpretations of scholastic theologians. In the
Renaissance the conception may be said to have been formed of
the study of classical literature as the basis of a liberal education.

This changed attitude towards Latin and Greek had its effect
on the linguistic study of these languages, especially of Latin. The
emphasis was set on Latin as the language of Cicero and Vergil,
the language of the ancient world, not on mediaeval Latin as a
lingua franca of education and intellectual intercourse. Latin as
an elegant language enshrining a great literature was the proper
object of study. Scholarly works continued for some time to be
written in Latin, but the rise in status of European vernaculars
and the spread of secular learning in secular states fostered national languages as proper media for scholarly and scientific
publication.

Many of the technical advances in descriptive efficiency realized during the Middle Ages were retained, and in places
mediaeval didactic grammars like that of Alexander of Villedieu
continued in use; but the general conceptions of the speculative
grammarians were severely attacked by classically oriented grammarians of the Renaissance as being philosophically tedious,
educationally undesirable, and couched in a barbarous degeneration of the Latin language. The return to preeminence of the
auctōrēs foretold in the *Battle of the seven arts* had indeed come
to pass.[44]

Scholastic grammarians had done little more than copy
Priscian's account of Latin pronunciation, and the actual speaking
of Latin largely depended on the phonetics of the first language
of the persons concerned. This feature of Latin speaking con-

tinued as it still does today; but concern for what was considered to be the correct pronunciation, that is to say the pronunciation of the time of Cicero and the other golden age authors, was expressed in writings on the Latin language even if their practical effect on most pupils was, as it still is, relatively small.

Erasmus (1466–1536) wrote on the correct pronunciation of Latin and Greek, and his system of Greek pronunciations was accepted in northern Europe.[45] Among other observations on Latin, he established along with others that the Latin letters c and g represented velar articulations in all positions in classical Latin, although the currently spoken Romance languages with only a few exceptions (Illyrian and Sardinian) had sibilant or affricate pronunciations of these letters before front vowels. The orthographers, whose work on the phonetic interpretation of current spelling systems has already been noticed (p. 114, above), also turned their attention to this hitherto neglected aspect of classical scholarship in Europe.[46] In the writing of Latin, Ramus introduced the letters j and v to represent the semivowel pronunciations (in words such as jam (iam), now, and virtūs, virtue), as distinct from the vowel pronunciations [i] and [u]; u had previously been the cursive form of V. The two letters j and v were known for a time as the 'Ramist consonants'; one notices that v still survives but not j in the usual way of writing Latin.[47]

The teaching of Latin and Greek grammar gradually took on the form in which it is known today in the standard school textbooks. Essentially this process involved the incorporation of mediaeval syntactic notions into the morphological systematization of the late Latin grammarians, ultimately with further developments such as the final separation of the adjective from the noun class (though as late as Madvig's Latin grammar the terms 'noun substantive' and 'noun adjective' remained in use[48]), and the merging of the participle into the inflexions of the verb.

By the sixteenth century a reaction against exclusively literature-based grammars was seen in certain writers, notably J. C. Scaliger and Sanctius, who were again looking for a philosophical justification for grammatical rules. Scaliger's De causis linguae Latinae sought to renew, along earlier scholastic lines, the explanation of grammar by reference to Aristotelian philosophical concepts; he bitterly attacked Erasmus for showing an excessive devotion to Cicero as the only proper model for Latin prose.[49] Sanctius devoted much space in his Minerva seu de causis linguae Latinae to a logical theory of syntax.[50]

In England W. Lily's Latin grammar enjoyed the distinction of being officially prescribed for school use by King Henry VIII in

1540 (the official version, in fact, contained contributions from other contemporary grammarians as well).[51] Lily's grammar in the main follows the Priscianic system, with eight word classes or parts of speech. It is severely practical and didactic, and does not engage in linguistic or philosophical theory or speculation. A century later Bassett Jones published his *Essay on the rationality of the art of speaking*,[52] expressly as a supplement to Lily's grammar. He laid claim to the support both of Aristotle and of Francis Bacon, but his allegedly rational explanations of some grammatical facts are mostly either unoriginal or absurdly fanciful.

The effects on linguistic studies brought about by the rise of humanism, nationalism, and secular government, along with the overseas expansion of Europe, have been noticed. The Renaissance period was also the first age of printing in Europe (independently China had invented paper in the first century A.D. and block printing in the tenth). From then on literacy and the demand for education grew steadily, even though universal education was not achieved in Europe before the nineteenth century. Knowledge travelled faster and spread more widely. The study of foreign languages as well as that of the classical languages was immeasurably enlivened by the multiplicity and availability of printed texts, grammars, and dictionaries. These same factors made the exchange of knowledge and theoretical discussion between scholars in different lands much easier and more speedy, and as time went on some of the features of the present-day world of learning began to take shape. Learned societies, sometimes fostered by national governments, came into being as centres for scholarly debate and scientific research. In Britain the Royal Society was founded in 1660 and its early years were much concerned with linguistic research; and in France Cardinal Richelieu established the *Académie française* in 1635 to keep permanent watch and ward on the literary and linguistic standards of the French language. Learned and specialized journals, such as now play so great a part in the development of linguistics, and the other branches of knowledge, grew up around the societies and institutions, though this process was not fully achieved before the nineteenth and twentieth centuries.

It was seen in earlier chapters how the course of linguistic science in antiquity and the Middle Ages was in part determined by its involvement in controversies between opposing points of view on questions wider in extent than the study of language itself. In the sixteenth, seventeenth, and eighteenth centuries the philosophical world was characterized by the contrast between empiricism and rationalism, and the epistemological views embodied in each had their counterparts in the treatment of linguistic questions.

Empiricism had arisen as part of the challenge to the accepted ideas of mediaeval scholasticism. The rise of a modern scientific outlook ready to confound authority with observed fact and to remodel theory to incorporate newly discovered data was famously exemplified in the work of Galileo, Copernicus, and Kepler. Empiricism as a philosophical standpoint was a particularly British contribution; Francis Bacon had stressed the observational origin of all knowledge and the importance of induction as opposed to deduction, and Locke, Berkeley, and Hume wrote what are now the accepted expositions of this phase of philosophy.

The centrepiece of empiricism was the thesis that all human knowledge is derived externally from sense impressions and the operations of the mind upon them in abstraction and generalization. Its extreme form appears in Hume's total rejection of an *a priori* component of knowledge. Opposed to this in many ways was the rationalist position, expounded by Descartes and his followers. The rationalists sought for the certainty of knowledge not in the impressions of the senses, whose fallibility could never be wholly excluded, but in the irrefutable truths of human reason. In some respects the Cartesian position was the more traditional, but both schools of thought agreed in their reliance on mathematics and Newtonian science in place of scholastic Aristotelianism as the foundation of philosophical reasoning.

A celebrated aspect of the empiricist-rationalist distinction turned on the question of 'innate ideas'. Locke, Berkeley, and Hume denied the existence of any ideas implanted in the human mind prior to experience; the Cartesian rationalists regarded certain innate ideas as the basis of any certainty in our knowledge; these included the ideas of number and figure, and logical and mathematical conceptions. To some extent the two sides were nearer in fact than in terminology. Experience of the world and knowledge are not merely sense impressions, and the part played by the rationalist innate ideas corresponds somewhat to that of Locke's admitted 'operations of our minds within'. The question centrally at issue is the extent to which the human mind plays an active role in perception and in the acquisition of knowledge.[53]

During the sixteenth and seventeenth centuries a number of separate but related movements made their appearance in linguistic research, springing from the intellectual condition of the times. In them both rationalist and empiricist influences may be seen at work.

The recession of Latin as the only international language of learning and authority, the emergence of the European vernaculars into full recognition, and the new discoveries in the field of languages overseas all helped to create the feeling that it was in men's power to improve and even to create languages to suit the needs of the age.

Francis Bacon had deplored the unnecessary controversies caused by the inadequacies of existing languages, part of the 'idols of the market place', and envisaged a vast improvement based on the analogy of words with things, not just with one another. In distinguishing the descriptive grammar of a particular language from a philosophical or general grammar he seems to have had the idea of constructing an ideal language for the communication of knowledge from the best parts and features of a number of existing languages.[54] The invention of printing made standardized spellings more important, and, in turning attention to the relations between writing and pronunciation, aroused interest, since then perennial, in the problem of spelling reform. One gets the impression of numbers of scholars in England and on the continent working, partly in collaboration and partly in rivalry, on various aspects of language improvements and language planning.

The most radical proposal of the age was the invention of a new language for the advancement of learning and commerce throughout the civilized world. Latin as the erstwhile *lingua franca* was under challenge, and the extent of the world's linguistic Babel had been revealed; these projects of new universal languages were attempts at 'debabelization' or a restoration of the situation.[55] At this time people did not so much envisage a universal language like modern Esperanto created from the material of existing languages; rather, they had the bolder scheme of devising a system in which knowledge, thought, and ideas could be directly and universally expressed in symbols created for this purpose and for which pronunciations could be given. Leibniz (1646-1716) looked forward to the day when controversies would be resolved by the mere invitation to sit down and calculate by means of a newly devised universal symbolization of thought, free from the vagueness and uncertainties of natural languages. His *Specimen calculi universalis* anticipates some features of modern symbolic logic, though it is based on the Aristotelian syllogism.[56]

If such symbol systems were not to be hopelessly clumsy, human knowledge must be classified and reduced to an ordered conspectus. The inspiration that a universal language of this kind was practicable sprang from a number of sources: great faith in the power of human rationality, the classifications of the now rapidly expanding empirical sciences, the appreciation of the power of mathematical symbolism (Arabic numerals as written symbols with a pronunciation appeared in some projected languages[57]), and a misunderstanding of the nature of Chinese character writing, which had been known in Europe since the end of the sixteenth century.

Mathematics is a genuinely language-free mode of symbolization, though it has not got the semantic range or expressive power of a natural language (to speak of the 'language of mathematics' or 'mathematical language' is to use a metaphor, and the analogy should not be pressed too far). Chinese characters were at the time thought to be the direct representation of 'ideas' (*ideograph* is still a popular term for a Chinese character). This is not so; the written language of Chinese literature can be read and understood by educated speakers of mutually unintelligible varieties of spoken Chinese, but for all that it is a language like other languages, belonging to and evolved by a particular speech community or set of speech communities, and its characters represent morphemes, which can be given pronunciations, though different ones in different dialect areas. This written language has grammatical classes and grammatical rules as any other written language does, and cannot be understood or translated, except for very short and transparently obvious sentences, without a knowledge of the grammar. This was not grasped by sixteenth- and seventeenth-century Europe; the real study of the Chinese type of language began only later in the eighteenth and nineteenth centuries with the availability of grammars of Chinese written in European languages.

In the seventeenth century various people devised universal languages or 'real characters' as they were sometimes called. In France M. Mersenne, probably influenced by Descartes, suggested the creation of the best of all possible languages by which all men's thoughts could be put into the same words with brevity and clarity; anticipating Jespersen he recognized the rather general phonaesthetic associations of [i]-like vowels with thinness and littleness.[58] In England similar projects were advanced by such men as George Dalgarno, and Bishop John Wilkins, to whom Mersenne's work was known, and of these Wilkins's *Essay towards a real character and a philosophical language* is the most famous.[59] It was published with the support of the recently founded Royal Society, and is mentioned by Roget as one of the main inspirations of his *Thesaurus* nearly two hundred years later.[60]

Wilkins's project was nothing less than the creation of systematically worked out and universally applicable principles of a language, written and spoken, for communication between members of all nations of the world. The *Essay*, which runs to 454 pages, after criticizing the shortcomings of existing natural languages sets out what purports to be a complete schematization of human knowledge, including abstract relations, actions, processes, and logical concepts, natural genera and species of things animate and inanimate, and the physical and institutionalized relations between human beings in the family and in society.

All these classes and their subdivisions, and the various semantic relations and modifications involved with them are represented by written shapes, built into semantically self-sufficient and perspicuous 'real characters', each standing for an ideal word, translatable into or from the words of a natural language. A simple example may be given: 'father' is represented by the character ⌐, which consists of the basic sign ⌐ , for the genus 'economical' (interpersonal) relation, to which are added a right oblique line on the left, indicating the first subdivision, in the case of economical relations that of consanguinity, an upright line on the right indicating the second subdivision, in the case of consanguinity marking the relation of direct ascending, and a semi-circle above the middle of the character, indicating male. Should the character be used metaphorically, this can be specified by the addition of a short vertical line over the left end of the character: ⌐.

In order to provide a spoken form corresponding to each such character, Wilkins set out a system of universal phonetics, or of 'letters' standing for the major categories of articulation such as were said to be found in the known languages of the world. Each component of a character had its own syllable or single letter assigned to it, from which an equally perspicuous spoken word form could be built up. Thus in the spoken word for the character 'father', *Co* stands for economical relation, *b* and *a* for the two subdivisions, consanguinity and direct ascendant, respectively, giving *Coba*, parent, and the further addition of *ra* for male gives *Cobara* (probably [kobara]), father.

A universal grammar was proposed, consisting of word classes valid for all communicative needs. Syntactic rules were to be kept to a minimum, and the class membership and grammatical relations of words were to be indicated graphically by special signs affixed to or interposed between the characters, and phonetically by additions and modifications to the pronounced words.

In a final chapter Wilkins compared his 'philosophical language' with Latin as the nearest existing approach to a universal language, and the 'real character' aspect of it with Chinese character writing. He condemned the unnecessary lexical redundancy, grammatical complexity, and the irregularities of Latin, as contrasted with his own proposed language, and the formal complications of Chinese characters and their lack of semantic analysability and perspicuity, though he approved of the tendency to group characters for semantically related concepts under the same radical (p. 119, above).[61]

The efforts of men like Wilkins show how far linguistic theory and linguistic thought had moved since the Middle Ages. They also show a deep and subtle penetration into the way languages must in fact be naturally organized in order to fulfil the tasks successfully imposed on them. Nothing practical came of these suggestions for artificially constructed universal languages, and it is easy to perceive the naivety of Wilkins's attempts at the componential analysis and classifications of all human knowledge and experience. But the recent work of some generative grammarians in attempting to formalize the intuitive knowledge that native speakers have of the correct use of their language and the semantic interpretation of the words in it seems to proceed on somewhat similar lines, and has been described as an effort directed towards the 'atomization' of meaning.[62] The successful employment and understanding of the lexical resources of our native language is something that is performatively given to us while we are yet children, but the full explication of it seems still to be hidden from the wisest.

The notion of a universal thought structure possessed by mankind, or at least by all civilized mankind, basically independent of any particular language and therefore expressible in a universal language, was a conception perhaps natural to the rationalists. Similar attitudes towards the grammar of actual languages are found in the work of the rationalist Port Royal grammarians (pp. 136–7, below), and repeat in a different form the older universalism of the scholastic speculative grammarians. The interdependence of thought and language and the significance of linguistic as well as of cultural relativity were more readily appreciated in the climate of the later Romantic era.

Apart from the advancement of knowledge, the avoidance of sterile controversies, and the ease of communication between men of education in all lands, other considerations were in men's minds when they pondered the creation of universal languages: the facilitation of trade, the unity of the Protestant churches, and the science of cryptography. The possession of a new 'real character' serving Protestantism as Latin had once served the formerly universal Roman Church may have been only a minor factor; its extent is a matter for debate. During the English Civil War the codes and cyphers of each side attracted attention to certain structural features and frequencies of occurrence in the English language, and in 1641 Wilkins had written a work on secret communication.[63]

The cryptography of the time was intimately associated with another application of linguistics that flourished in England from the reign of Elizabeth I, the devising of systems of shorthand or 'characterie' as they were then called. Stenographic methods had been in use in ancient Rome, but like much else they appear to have been lost during the mediaeval period.

Modern shorthand, depending both on the use of phonetic symbols and on representations of particular words or word roots by specific outlines, may be traced back to British work in the sixteenth century. The name most associated with this is Timothy Bright, who worked out systems of shorthand employing both individual letter signs and character-like signs for words standing for classes of objects. Interest in shorthand and universal languages went together, and the same motives were adduced. Bright referred to the alleged ideographic nature of Chinese characters, independent of any particular language, and commended his system of 'characterie' as both a means of written communication and a device for preserving secrecy.[64]

In one respect Bright exploited a process very like that applied at one stage by the Japanese in their adaptation of the Chinese character script (p. 121, above). Grammatical additions or alterations to basic word forms, such as plurality in nouns, past tense in verbs, and comparison in adjectives, were indicated by marks, or 'pricks', on the right or left of the word sign itself. Some other grammatical forms were indicated by the use of a word sign to represent a homographic and homophonic morpheme, and by extension other semantically and grammatically related morphemes as well. Thus *friendship* was to be written with the *ship* sign below the *friend* sign, but below the *neighbour* sign this same *ship* sign stood for the *-hood* of *neighbourhood*.

One aspect of English empiricism in linguistic studies during the sixteenth and seventeenth centuries was the beginning of systematic phonetic description of the sounds of the English language, and of the formal analysis of English grammar, now that men felt free to challenge and modify the grammatical model enshrined in Priscian and Donatus.

Phonetic studies began seriously in England in the attention turned on spelling and its relation to pronunciation through the invention of printing and the diffusion of literacy, as on the continent. From the sixteenth to the eighteenth century work was carried on around phonetic questions under the titles of orthography and orthoepy (the term *phonetics* is first recorded in the nineteenth century); but the research was on what today would be called phonetics and phonology, and the empirical attitude in British philosophy from Francis Bacon to David Hume, as well as the nature of English spelling, fostered a tradition that has been given the title of 'the English school of phonetics'.[65] J. Hart, W. Bullokar, A. Hume, R. Robinson, C. Butler, J. Wallis, and W. Holder[66] are among those who wrote on English pronunciation in the sixteenth and seventeenth centuries, in some cases as part of a full-scale grammar of English. The formative influences of the times are shown by the fact that Wallis, besides his work on English, held the chair of geometry at Oxford University and was also a natural scientist. It is interesting to see, in addition to questions of spelling, modern objectives already in close association with phonetic studies, such as English language teaching for foreigners, teaching speech to the deaf, and the cultivation of standard English or 'the King's language'.[67]

The work of these orthographers and orthoepists has been much used in the reconstruction of the English pronunciation characteristics of their times[68]; in the history of linguistics their importance lies rather in the stage they had reached in phonetic theory and practice, and in the work they bequeathed to their better known nineteenth-century successors.

Among them W. Holder was perhaps the most successful. After some delay due to jealousy on the part of rivals such as Wallis, Holder's *Elements of speech* was published in 1669 by the Royal Society, of which he was a member. Holder was an observational phonetician and he achieved remarkable succinctness and accuracy in describing the articulation of speech sounds. He set down a general theory of pronunciation, referring consonantal differences to differences of 'appulse' between one organ and another, total in the case of stops and partial in fricatives and continuants; he referred vocalic differences to different degrees of aperture, with the further distinctions of front and back tongue raising and of lip rounding.[69] His conception of speech as 'determined by the alternation of appulse and aperture' has a very modern ring.

Holder came nearer than any other western scholar, before

contact was made with Indian phonetic work, to a correct articulatory diagnosis of the voice-voiceless distinction in consonants. His correct insight escaped the attention of his contemporaries and was left unremarked for over a century. He wrote, using 'voice' in its modern technical sense: 'The larynx both gives passage to the breath, and also, as often as we please, by the force of muscles, to bear the sides of the larynx stiff and near together, as the breath passeth through the rimula, makes a vibration of those cartilaginous bodies which forms that breath into a vocal sound or voice.' The excellence of his phonetic theory and the conciseness of his expression are shown in his summary statement on the nature of English vowels: 'The vowels are made by a free passage of breath vocalized through the cavity of the mouth, without any appulse of the organs; the said cavity's being differently shaped by the postures of the throat, tongue and lips . . . . Vowels . . . being differenced by the shape of the cavity of the mouth'.[70]

In the next century A. Tucker noted the prevalence of [ə] in English as a hesitation form and in the 'weak forms' of words unstressed in connected speech, forms almost wholly unmarked in orthographic writing.[71]

Problems of spelling in relation to pronunciation were the occasion for the invention of new typographical symbols for particular sorts of sound, and several of the phonetic symbols used today in the International Phonetic Alphabet were first suggested or invented during this period. Some writers went beyond English to suggest international alphabets, such work being often linked with systems of shorthand. F. Lodwick published an *Essay towards a universal alphabet* in the *Philosophical transactions* of the Royal Society in 1686, consisting of invented symbols systematically corresponding to articulatory differences; and Wilkins included in his *Essay* a sound chart which can be compared with early editions of the International Phonetic Alphabet, and an 'organic alphabet' with pictures of the articulation of eight vowels and twenty-six consonants, representing general phonetic categories, in which were shown the positions of the lips and, by a cut-away section, the positions of the tongue as well.[72]

The sixteenth and seventeenth centuries also saw the reworking of English grammar. Men started with the framework handed down from the late Latin grammarians and suggested by Aelfric as suitable for Old English as well as for Latin (p. 80, above); but the intellectual climate of the post-Renaissance world, a love of their own language, and English empiricist attitudes all encouraged them to test the categories against observation, and we can observe the different degrees to which this testing and re-appraisal took place in the allocation of words to word classes or parts of speech.

English grammarians of the sixteenth, seventeenth, and early eighteenth centuries usually started from the Latin system of the eight Priscianic classes enshrined in Lily's grammar, in that they either followed it or felt the need to express and justify their disagreements with it. Some, for example Bullokar,[73] set up the Latin system and assigned English words to each class. The English articles, *a(n)* and *the*, having no Latin counterpart were not given the status of a part of speech, but merely referred to as notes or signs set before nouns to identify them as nouns. Others treated the articles as a subclass of nouns adjective,[74] and Ben Jonson assigned them to a class of their own.[75]

A rearrangement of the Latin system in which the influence of Ramus may be seen is found in those grammarians such as A. Gill, who made number inflexion versus its absence a major binary distinction, setting off nouns and verbs from the rest, which he designated *dictiones consignificativae* in reference to their principal functions in subordinate relations with nouns and verbs, a distinction also made by the ancient grammarians (pp. 30, 42, above).[76] Butler linked nouns and verbs more closely in his system by regarding them both as having number and case inflexions; nominal case is illustrated by such forms as *man* and *man's*, and past tense and past participle inflexions (*loved*, *fallen*) are designated as oblique cases of the verb, the present tense form being the 'rect'.[77] This usage harks back to that of Aristotle.

Some other grammarians were influenced by Port Royal theories (p. 137, below) to divide the eight Latin classes according as they were held to denote objects of thought (noun, pronoun, participle, preposition, adverb (and article)), or manners of thought (verb, conjunction, interjection). This was applied to English by the writer (or writers) of a grammar attributed to J. Brightland,[78] though the systematization is not very clearly worked out.

More radically, Wilkins and C. Cooper distinguished two main classes, on semantic grounds, integrals and particles; Wilkins intended his system to be of universal applicability. Integrals were said to have a definite meaning of their own, while particles only consignify, relating or modifying the meanings of the integrals. Nouns and verbs are integrals; in Wilkins's systematization, which is more explicit and worked out as part of his philosophical grammar,[79] verbs are not given a separate class, but are regarded as nouns adjective (active, passive or neutral (intransitive)) always in association with or containing in their own form a copula (e.g. *lives*= *is living*; *hits*= *is hitting*). This analysis is similar to that of the Port Royal grammarians. Derived adverbs (from nouns adjective, like *badly*) are also integrals. The particle class is divided into essential (the copula verb, *to be*) and occasional; this latter group includes pronouns, articles, prepositions, non-derived adverbs, and conjunctions, and also modes and tenses (*can*, *may*, *will*, etc.). This treatment of the verbal auxiliaries, which Cooper follows for English, though inexplicitly,[80] bears some analogy with some analyses of English verbs current today.

The Latin tradition is seen in the retention of the adjective within the noun class, though formally this has less to commend it in English than in Latin, and in the preoccupation of most of the grammarians with the participle, treated either (purely traditionally) as a class in its own right, or as a noun adjective having particular derivational associations with the verb. Perhaps because Wilkins was framing a system of universal or philosophical grammar, applicable to English but not based simply on English, he was the most radical in revising the Priscianic–Lilyan tradition. Certainly he went further than his closest follower among grammarians of the English language, Cooper.

Grammars of English were written in great numbers from the sixteenth century up to the present day. Their main historical interest lies in the continuing process of testing and revising the grammatical framework handed down in the Latin-based system of description, in the light of actually observed English forms and structures. Such developments were not necessarily achieved in chronological order. Wallis (seventeenth century) was one of the most radical reformers of English descriptive grammar in his assertion that the language had only two tenses, present (*burn*) and past (*burned*), all other temporal and aspectual distinctions being effected by auxiliary verbs.[81]

Two early nineteenth-century grammars are well known, by Lindley Murray and by William Cobbett. Though they are similar, and fairly conservative, in theory and presentation, their social settings are interestingly dissimilar and reflect the different contexts in which English grammar has been and is taught and studied. Murray was an American citizen who settled in England after the War of Independence. Established near York, he wrote his celebrated *English grammar*, primarily with the needs of young students in mind. First published in 1795, it achieved very wide acceptance and ran into numerous reprintings during the first half of the nineteenth century. Somewhat conservative in theory, it may be taken as an example of a successful teaching grammar of English during this period. It is divided into four parts: Orthography, with an account of the various pronunciation values of the letters of the English alphabet, 'Etymology' (i.e., morphology, the parts of speech, their forms and inflexions), Syntax, and Prosody and punctuation. Prosody is divided into the rules of versification and the description of those features such as length, stress, pause, and intonation ('tone'), to which the term 'prosody' had been applied in antiquity (p. 44, above) in a manner in several ways anticipatory of its use by Firthians (pp. 246–7, below).

In his grammar Murray considered that three cases should be recognized in English nouns: nominative, genitive, and objective or accusative.[82] He argued this on the analogy of Latin, wherein despite the sameness of form between nominative and accusative in many nouns the cases were separately recognized. One does see in Murray the 'modern traditional' set of word classes for English: article, noun, adjective, pronoun, verb, adverb, preposition, conjunction, and interjection, with no suggestion of merging the adjective with the noun or of treating the participle as a separate word class.

Murray's style is clear and systematic, if rather unexciting and unoriginal. His concern for the general well-being of his young readers appears throughout his book. In the preface and in a final 'address to young students' he declares his wish to 'promote the cause of virtue as well as of learning', and the examples chosen display a gentle piety: *I will respect him, though he chide me; Duty and interest forbid vicious indulgences; Idleness produces want, vice, and misery*.[83] Quite apart from differences of theory, his choice of examples puts him and his work in a very different context from that of some modern writers who have favoured examples like *I'm going to get one for Bert*, and *All the people in the lab consider John a fool*.[84] Neither the one nor the other style is necessarily the better field for the exemplification of a grammatical description or a linguistic theory; one must hope that examples filled with puerile obscenities and political propaganda, such as disfigured some recent linguistic publications in the English-speaking world, will have proved a transient phase.

The repute of Murray's grammar may be seen in the prudence of Mrs. Jarley, the waxworks proprietor in Dickens's *Old Curiosity Shop*, when her audience was to comprise young ladies from select boarding schools, in 'altering the face and costume of Mr Grimaldi as clown to represent Mr Lindley Murray as he appeared when engaged in the composition of his English grammar'.

Though the theoretical framework and the categories employed
are very similar, the contemporary, less well-known, *Grammar of
the English language* by Cobbett, the radical politician (London,
1819), was conceived in quite a different setting. Written in the
form of a series of letters to his son James, it was 'intended . . .
more especially for the use of soldiers, sailors, apprentices, and
ploughboys'. A later edition includes 'six lessons intended to
prevent statesmen from using false grammar, and from writing
in an awkward manner', and contains a dedication to Queen
Caroline in which with radical eloquence Cobbett presses the case
for the literary education of the 'labouring classes': 'The nobles
and the hierarchy have long had the arrogance to style themselves
the pillars that support the throne. But, as your Majesty has now
clearly ascertained, Royalty has, in the hour of need, no efficient
supporters but the people.'

In doctrine so alike, in style so different, these two English
grammars embody two themes that had been prominent in the
teaching of English ever since the Renaissance had ushered in an
epoch of social mobility in English society: the careful maintenance of the linguistic standards appropriate to superior social
status, and the acquisition of such standards as a vital step in any
social advancement.

Just as empirical attitudes fostered descriptive phonetics and
the grammatical independence of different languages, so did the
rationalist movement make itself felt in the production of
philosophical grammars, especially those associated with the
French Port Royal schools. These religious and educational foundations were set up in 1637, and disbanded in 1661 owing to
political and religious strife[85]; but their influence was longer lasting in educational ideas, and their work in grammar can be seen
continuing in the *grammaires raisonnées* and 'general grammars'
of the eighteenth century. The Port Royal grammar was reprinted
as late as 1830.[86]

The rationalist grammars were in several ways the successors
of the mediaeval scholastic grammars. Though the educational
system of Port Royal included sound classical instruction, one or
two of its members declared a prejudice against the pagan literature of classical antiquity. Port Royal numbered among its
company writers on logic, and in their grammar the influence of
logic on linguistics was strongest. They expounded universal
grammar, but not in the same sense as either the universal
language planners or the mediaeval grammarians. Unlike the
language planners they were not inventing new systems of communication but expounding a general theory of grammar through
the medium of such languages as Latin and French. Unlike the

scholastics they asserted the claims of human reason above authority and they made Descartes rather than Aristotle the basis of their teaching. They did not seek a philosophical universalist explanation of all the details of Priscian's Latin grammar, ignoring other languages, but they did attempt to reveal the unity of grammar underlying the separate grammars of different languages in their role of communicating thought, itself comprising perception, judgment, and reasoning.

On the basis of this general grammar Port Royal scholars took the nine classical word classes, noun, article, pronoun, participle, preposition, adverb, verb, conjunction, and interjection, but redivided them semantically, the first six relating to 'the objects' of our thought and the last three to the 'form or manner' of our thought. The basic noun-verb dichotomy survived, but the repartition of the other classes around it was a different one. There was no attempt to follow the grammar of Donatus and Priscian as they had set it out, but a good deal of the tradition of Latin grammar was thought to underlie all languages and to find expression in various ways. Thus the six cases of Latin are, at least operationally, assumed in other languages,[87] though some of them were expressed by prepositions and word order in the 'vulgar languages' (i.e. modern European languages; the term is not pejorative); and Greek was said to have an ablative case always alike in form to the dative. This last statement is misleading; the translation equivalence of the Latin ablative is divided between the Greek dative and the Greek genitive. Collectively cases and prepositions were intended to express relations, but the two categories were kept theoretically distinct despite their common exponence in the 'vulgar languages', and the purely case-like usage of French *de* and *à* was contrasted with their genuinely prepositional functions, as had been done in earlier comparative studies of the classical and modern Romance languages (p. 115, above).[88]

Despite some similarities with the modistae and a like stress on the universal necessary features of all languages being variously manifested, there are striking differences in attitude. The universalist foundation envisaged by Port Royal was human reason and thought. The elaborate interrelations of the *modī essendī* of the external world and the *modī intelligendī* by which they were perceived and interpreted in the mind have no place in the Port Royal system, and the somewhat modistic explanation of the essential difference between noun and verb given by J. C. Scaliger, based on the categories of permanence and transience, was expressly criticized as both irrelevant and inadequate.[89]

Structural interpretations of the functions of certain classes of word may be noticed. Adverbs are no more than an abbreviation of a prepositional phrase (*sapienter*, wisely, = *cum sapientiā*, with wisdom). Verbs are properly words that 'signify affirmation' and, in other moods, desire, command, etc.[90] This returns the Port Royal grammarians to an analysis suggested by Aristotle[91] of all verbs other than the copula, to be, as logically and grammatically equivalent to this verb plus a participle, making *Peter lives* (*Peter is living*) structurally analogous with *Peter is a man*; the categories of intransitive and transitive (and active and passive) are said properly to belong not to the words commonly called verbs but just to the 'adjectival' element in them.[92]

This analysis, it should be noted, is not an alleged historical explanation, nor is it a surface description of verbal morphology, as Bopp was later to try to make it; it was the positing, in modern terms, at a deeper structural level, of elements that in actual sentences were represented conjointly with other elements.[93] The Port Royal grammarians might have claimed support from our wider knowledge today of languages in which virtually any root can be nominalized or verbalized by an appropriate affix, so that the distinction maintained in the surface grammar of European languages, at least, between *Peter is a man* and *Peter lives* disappears.[94]

The embedding or subordinating function of relative pronouns (Latin and French *qui*, etc., English *who*, *which*, etc.) is described in terms on which transformationalists lay stress as an anticipation of their own theories. A single proposition *the invisible God has created the visible world* is related to the more explicit form *God, who is invisible, has created the world, which is visible*, and, in a still more elementary representation, is said to unite the three propositions or judgments (underlying sentences), *God is invisible, God created the world* and, *the world is visible*, by including or embedding the first and the third in the 'principal and essential' second proposition as the matrix.[95] However, the Port Royal grammarians seem to have worked in other than purely formal terms, because the proposition *the valour of Achilles has been the cause of the taking of Troy* is said, unlike the other proposition, to be a simple one, no more than one judgment or affirmation. It is hard to follow this reasoning, as in transformational terms this latter sentence would be treated very similarly to the other.

The Port Royal grammarians made a genuine attempt to write a general grammar. Drawing examples from Latin, Greek, Hebrew, and modern European languages, they sought to refer them to alleged universal characteristics of language, underlying them. A wider knowledge of non-European languages does not appear to have interested them, or they might have revised their classical framework more radically. They envisaged general grammar as underlying the actual make-up of all languages, rather than as particularly exemplified in any one; but as scholarly patriots they took pride in the perspicuity, elegance, and beauty that they saw in the French language,[96] a testimony to the change in men's attitude to the European vernaculars wrought by the Renaissance.

Once the diversity of languages was properly accepted, and vernaculars were recognized as equally worthy of study and cultivation with the classical languages, linguistic scholars had to face the question of language universals. The ancient world had almost ignored the problem, being only interested in Greek and Latin; the scholastics had assumed that Latin as described and analysed by Priscian in fact represented the universal infrastructure of all languages; after the Renaissance, the empiricists stressed the individual variations of particular languages and the need to adjust categories and classes in the light of observation, while the rationalists still looked for what was common to all languages below surface differences. The whole question is still very much alive. Hjelmslev in his early *Principes de grammaire générale* demanded a universal *état abstrait* comprising the possibilities available to languages and differently realized in the *états concrets* of each particular one; failing this, linguistic theory would lapse into 'nihilism'.[97] The descriptives of what is now called the 'Bloomfieldian' epoch reduced the assumption of universals to a minimum and made the description of the observed forms paramount, by means of *ad hoc* categories and classes devised for each language independently and having little in common between different languages; Bloomfield declared that 'the only useful generalizations about languages are inductive generalizations'.[98] Likewise, Firthians spoke of general theory, but remained very cautious of general categories or universal grammar.[99] More recently Chomsky and the generative grammarians have reasserted, in terms strikingly similar to those both of the rationalist philosophical grammarians and of Hjelmslev in 1928, the importance of language universals, suggesting that in the deeper levels of linguistic structure languages will be found to share aspects of form that are a common human possession realized differently at the surface in different languages; indeed they claim that without this conception linguistics is doomed to confinement within a narrow empiricism and relative lack of significance and that, moreover, a basic universal grammar is the only satisfactory explanation of the ability of children to master their own first language, on the basis, largely, of exposure to sequences of random utterances.[100] In linguistics as in other realms of thought the old problems continue to present themselves, though in different ways to different generations.

The author of a later general grammar, Beauzée, expressed an attitude similar to that of the Port Royal scholars: grammar has two sorts of principles, those of universal validity arising from the nature of human thought, and those resulting from the arbitrary and mutable conventions that constitute the grammars of particular languages. The former, which are the objects of general grammar, are logically anterior to any given language and concern the very possibility and necessary conditions of the existence of any language.[101]

Though Beauzée's doctrine is in agreement with Port Royal, his grammatical system is somewhat different in its organization, and despite tributes to Descartes and Arnauld (a major Port Royal grammarian) in his preface, there are some explicit criticisms of certain Port Royal statements in the text. Beauzée's word classes are more modern in that the adjective is taken as a quite separate class, and the specific Port Royal bipartition of the classes is not mentioned. As in any general grammar, the classes must be defined in terms applicable to any language, and appeal is made to general semantic notions. Typical is the distinction between noun and pronoun on the one hand and verb and adjective on the other: nouns and pronouns express individual things, persons, and abstractions; adjectives and verbs express the qualities, states, and relations with which they are associated.[102] In some respects Beauzée, though a universalist, is less rigid. No attempt is made by him to impose a single system of cases on all languages, and the Port Royal scholars are reproved for insisting on their six cases in Greek in defiance of the forms actually observable in Greek nominal inflexions.[103]

The contrast between empiricism and rationalism in their relations with language study was reflected to some extent in the contrasts drawn between the investigation of languages from the outside on the basis of observed usage, whether of acknowledged writers or of socially accepted speakers, and research into human language from within, as part of man's endowment and as a manifestation of his rationality. The Italian Campanella (seventeenth century) distinguished these two types of grammatical study as *grammatica civilis* and *grammatica philosophica*. In the grammar of French the same rule was established by Vaugelas on the basis of the observation of good usage and of literary precedent, and explained by the Port Royal grammarians by reference to the exact significance of the sentences as understood by the hearer and intended by the speaker.[104]

During the period, and to some extent even in the later years of the Middle Ages, ways of thought about language began to emerge on topics which had either not been considered before or, if they had been, had fallen into terms that could not lead to any very useful conclusions. This has already been noticed in the beginnings of the historical linguistics of the Romance languages (pp. 114, above). Towards the end of the eighteenth century the historical approach to languages deepened and was enriched by new insights. Historical study was linked with typological comparison, and both found new and significant material in the languages then known to scholarship and in specially collected vocabularies and texts from previously unstudied fields.

From the end of the century the linguistic situation was quite transformed by one of the most important events in the history of linguistics, the full discovery of the language and scholarship of ancient Sanskritic India. But as the effects of this belong to the nineteenth and the twentieth centuries, it will be well to deal with them in subsequent chapters.

For further consultation

D. ABERCROMBIE, 'Forgotten phoneticians', *TPS* 1948, 1–34.

H. ARENS, *Sprachwissenschaft: der Gang ihrer Entwicklung von der Antike bis zur Gegenwart*, Freiburg/Munich (second edition), 1969, 62–80.

R. E. ASHER and E. HENDERSON (eds.), *Towards a history of phonetics*, Edinburgh, 1981.

W. BACHER, *Die Anfänge der hebräischen Grammatik*, Amsterdam, 1975 (first published 1895).

M. BAKALLA, *Arabic linguistics: an introduction and bibliography*, London, 1983.

R. R. BOLGAR, *The classical heritage and its benefactors*, Cambridge, 1954.

J. BURCKHARDT, *The civilization of the Renaissance in Italy* (first published in German, 1860, tr. S. G. C. Middlemore), London, 1944.

F. CADET, *Port Royal education* (tr. A. D. JONES), London, 1898.

R. DONZÉ, *La grammaire générale et raisonnée de Port-Royal*, Berne, 1967.

W. K. FERGUSON, *The Renaissance in historical thought*, Boston, 1948.

J. R. FIRTH, *The tongues of men*, London, 1937, chapters 5 and 6.

——, 'The English school of phonetics', *TPS* 1946, 92–132.

O. FUNKE, *Die Frühzeit der englischen Grammatik*, Berne, 1941.

F. P. GRAVES, *Peter Ramus and the educational reformation of the sixteenth century*, New York, 1912.

M. A. K. HALLIDAY, 'The origin and early development of Chinese phonological theory', R. E. ASHER and E. J. A. HENDERSON (ed.), *Towards a history of phonetics*, Edinburgh, 1981, 123–40.

D. HYMES (ed.), *Studies in the history of linguistics: traditions and paradigms*, Bloomington, 1974.

L. KUKENHEIM, *Contributions à l'histoire de la grammaire italienne, espagnole, et française à l'époque de la Renaissance*, Amsterdam, 1932.

——, *Contributions à l'histoire de la grammaire grecque, latine, et hébraique à l'epoque de la Renaissance*, Leiden, 1951.

——, *Esquisse historique de la linguistique française*, Leiden, 1962.

C. LANCELOT and A. ARNAULD, *Grammaire générale et raisonnée*, Paris, 1660 (reprinted Scolar Press, Menton, 1967).

I. MICHAEL, *English grammatical categories and the tradition to 1800*, Cambridge, 1970.

J. OWENS, *The foundations of grammar: an introduction to medieval Arabic grammatical theory*, Amsterdam, 1988.

G. A. PADLEY, *Grammatical theory in western Europe 1500–1700, the Latin tradition*, Cambridge, 1976.

——, *Grammatical theory in western Europe 1500–1700: Trends in vernacular grammar* I, Cambridge, 1985, II, 1988.

V. G. SALMON (ed.), *The study of language in seventeenth century England*, Amsterdam, 1979.

J. E. SANDYS, *History of classical scholarship* (third edition), Cambridge, 1921, volume 2.

T. A. SEBEOK, *Historiography of linguistics*, 231–382.

C. H. M. VERSTEEGH et al. (eds.) *The history of linguistics on the Near East*, Amsterdam, 1983.

E. VORLAT, *English grammatical theory 1586–1737*, Louvain, 1975.

Notes

1. SANDYS, 1921, 17–21. On the Renaissance see further BOLGAR, 1954, BURCKHARDT, 1944, and FERGUSON, 1948.

2. B. RUSSELL, *History of western philosophy*, London, 1946, 523.

3. J. A. FROUDE, *History of England from the fall of Wolsey to the defeat of the Spanish Armada*, London, 1875, volume 1, 61–2. On the historical concepts of the Middle Ages and the Renaissance in general, W. K. FERGUSON, *The Renaissance in historical thought*, Boston, 1948.

4. ORIGINES, 1.3.4.

5. KUKENHEIM, 1951, 88.

6. J. REUCHLIN, *De rudimentis Hebraicis*, Pforzheim, 1506; L. GEIGER, *J. Reuchlin*, Leipzig, 1871.

7. REUCHLIN, op. cit., 551.

8. ibid., 552, 585.

9. H. HIRSCHFELD, *Literary history of Hebrew grammarians and lexicographers*, London, 1926, 7. See further N. M. WALDMAN, 'The

Hebrew tradition', in SEBEOK, *Historiography*, 1285–1330. The classic work on Hebrew linguistics is BACHER, 1895. The 1975 edition brings the bibliography up to date.

10. P. WECHTER, *Ibn Barun's Arabic works on Hebrew grammar and lexicography*, Philadelphia, 1964. On linguistics in the Near East, VERSTEEGH *et al.*, 1983.

11. E. O. A. MERX, 'Historia artis grammaticae apud Syros', *Abhandlung für die Kunde des Morgenlandes* 9.2 (1889, Leipzig).

12. A. G. CHEJNE, *The Arabic language: its role in history*, Minneapolis, 1969; H. BLANC, 'Linguistics among the Arabs', SEBEOK, *Historiography*, 1265–83. For a positive view on Greek influence see C. H. M. VERSTEEGH, *Greek elements in Arabic linguistic thinking*, Leiden, 1977. As with the Greco-Roman analogy–anomaly controversy one must not overdo the idea of two quite separate and mutually exclusive sects. Rather, it was a matter of two opposing tendencies, focused to a considerable degree on the two places. See further OWENS, 1988, 8–15. OWENS, 1988, and H. E. BREKLE, *Einführung in die Geschichte der Sprachwissenschaft*, Darmstadt, 1985, chapter 5, provide good introductions to Arabic linguistic scholarship. BAKALLA, 1983, presents a comprehensive bibliography of linguistic studies in and on the Arabic language.

13. A. SCHAADE, *Sibawaihi's Lautlehre*, Leiden 1911 (several corrections are suggested by M. H. A. EL SARAAN, *A Critical study of the phonetic observations of the Arab grammarians* (Ph. D. thesis, University of London, 1951)). On Sibawaih's grammatical method, M. G. CARTER, 'An Arab grammarian of the eighth century', *JAOS* 93 (1973), 146–57. An example of an Arabic grammatical text, with translation and commentary, may be seen in M. G. CARTER (ed.), *Arab linguistics: an introductory classical text with translation and notes*, 1981 (*Amsterdam studies in the theory and history of linguistic science*, series 3, volume 24).

14. KUKENHEIM, 1932, 95.

15. J. H. ROWE, 'Sixteenth and seventeenth century grammars', in HYMES, 1974, 361–79. Vernacular grammar writing is dealt with fully in PADLEY, 1985 and 1988. See further A. AHLQVIST (ed.), 'Les premières grammaires des vernaculaires européens', *Histoire épistémologie langage* 9. 1 (1987); W. K. PERCIVAL, 'The grammatical tradition and the rise of the vernaculars', in SEBEOK, *Historiography*, 231–75. Useful collections of articles on the history of linguistic work in Italy, Spain, and Holland in and after the Renaissance are to be found in P. RAMAT *et al.* (eds.), *The history of linguistics in Italy*, 1986 (*Amsterdam studies in the theory and history of linguistic science*, series 3, volume 33); A. QUILIS and H.-J. NIEDEREHE (eds.), *The history of linguistics in Spain*, 1986 (ibid., volume 34; *The history of linguistics in the Low Countries*, 1988, (*Historiographia linguistica* 15. 1–2). ROBINS, 'The evolution of English grammar books since the Renaissance', in G. LEITNER (ed.), *The English reference grammar*, Tübingen, 1986, 292–306, gives a brief sketch of English grammar writing from 1586 to the

present day. For a historical survey of linguistic work on the German language, see W. BAHNER and W. NEUMANN (eds.), *Sprachwissenschaftliche Germanistik: ihre Herausbildung und Begründung*, Berlin, 1985.

16. KUKENHEIM, 1932, 205. cp. more generally, PERCIVAL, op. cit. (n. 15).

17. K. LAMBLEY, *The teaching and cultivation of the French language during Tudor and Stuart times*, Manchester, 1920; D. A. KIBBEE, 'John Palsgrave's Lesclaircissement de la langue françoyse', *Historiographia linguistica*, 12 (1985), 27–62.

18. *La manière de bien traduire d'une langue en aultre*, Paris, 1545. See further E. A. NIDA, *Toward a science of translating*, Leiden, 1964, chapter 2. The influence of Martin Luther in the Protestant parts of German-speaking Europe and the prestige of his German translation of the Bible are held largely responsible for the establishment of Luther's written German as the basis of standard German (cp. PADLEY, 1985, chapter 2.1, and 1988, chapter 4).

19. KUKENHEIM, 1932, 37–8.

20. Book 1, chapter 1; chapters 18–19. This work was not, in fact, actually published until the sixteenth century, in Latin and Italian. An English translation may be had in A. G. FERRERS HOWELL, 'Dante's treatise "De vulgari eloquentia"', London, 1890.

21. cp. R. A. HALL, 'Linguistic theory in the Italian Renaissance, *Language* 12 (1936), 96–107.

22. KUKENHEIM, 1932, 140. See further Padley, 1988, 100-5.

23. G. RUSCELLI, *Commentarii della lingua italiana*, Venice, 1581, 100.

24. KUKENHEIM, 1932, 98–9.

25. KUKENHEIM, 1962, 18; this is disputed by P. A. VERBURG, *Taal en functionaliteit*, Wageningen, 1952, 172–84.

26. GRAVES, 1912.

27. *Scholae grammaticae*, Frankfurt, 1595; *Gramere*, Paris, 1562.

28. *Scholae* 7–14, 95.

29. *Gramere* 10–11.

30. *Scholae* 95–6, 205–6.

31. *Gramere* 41.

32. *Scholae* 118, 223.

33. ibid. 118.

34. GRAVES, 1912, 130 (where see chart); more generally see PADLEY, 1976.

35. FIRTH, 1937, chapter 5.

36. ROWE, op. cit., in HYMES, 1974, 361–79.

37. e.g. FIRTH, 'Alphabets and phonology in India and Burma', *BSOS* 8 (1935-7), 517–46.

38. L. S. GALLAGHER, *The China that was*, Milwaukee, 1952, 42–8.

39. FRANCISCO VARO, *Arte de la lengua mandarina*, Canton, 1703; J. H. DE PRÉMARE, *Notitia linguae Sinicae*, Hongkong, 1893 (first published 1727).

40. PRÉMARE, op. cit., 36; J. VENDRYES, *Le langage*, Paris, 1921, 98–9.

41. LAI MING, *A history of Chinese literature*, London, 1964, 4; M. A. K.

HALLIDAY, 1981.

42. B. KARLGREN, *Philology and ancient China*, Oslo, 1926; R. A. D. FOR-
    REST, *The Chinese language*, London, 1948; HALLIDAY, 1981.

43. G. B. SANSOM, *An historical grammar of Japanese*, Oxford, 1928,
    chapter 1. For a brief account of linguistic work in China and Japan
    up to the present day, R. A. MILLER, 'The Far East', in SEBEOK, *His-
    toriography*, 1213–64.

44. M. GRABMANN, *Mittelalterliches Geistesleben*, Munich, 1926, volume
    I, 141–3. One may take note of the definition of grammar given
    by N. PEROTTI: 'Ars recte loquendi, recteque scribendi, scriptorum
    et poetarum lectionibus observata' (the art of correct speech and
    correct writing, found in the texts of prose writers and poets), very
    much in line with the classical definition handed down from
    Dionysius Thrax (p. 36) and with the classicizing spirit of Perotti's
    contemporary L. VALLA'S book, *De linguae Latinae elegantia*,
    Venice, 1471. See further PADLEY, 1976, chapter 1.

45. SANDYS, 1921, 127–32; ERASMUS, *De recta Latini Graecique sermonis
    pronuntiatione*, Basle, 1528. Research in this field has continued up
    to the present day; see W. S. ALLEN, *Vox Graeca*, Cambridge, 1974,
    and *Vox Latina*, Cambridge, 1978.

46. S. HAVERKAMP, *Sylloge altera scriptorum qui de linguae Graecae vera
    pronuntiatione commentarios reliquerunt*, Leiden, 1740, 124–5.

47. GRAVES, 1912, 124–5.

48. I. N. MADVIG, *Latin grammar* (tr. G. WOODS), Oxford, 1856, § 24.

49. Lyons, 1540; SANDYS, 1921, 129–30.

50. Salamanca, 1587. See further PADLEY, 1976, chapter 2; M. BREVA-
    CLARAMONTE, *Sanctius' theory of language*, 1983 (*Amsterdam studies
    in the theory and history of linguistic science*, Series III, volume
    27).

51. KUKENHEIM, 1951, 47; FUNKE, 1941, 49. In England, Sir Thomas
    Smith (1514–77) and Sir John Cheke (1514–57) strove to reform
    the pronunciation of classical Greek on the basis of Erasmus's
    teaching. This was ultimately successful, and in itself it stimulated
    orthographic and phonetic studies in this country (SANDYS, 1921,
    230–3; FIRTH, 1946, 100–1).

52. London, 1659.

53. J. LOCKE, *An essay concerning human understanding*, London, 1690,
    2.1.4; N. CHOMSKY, *Reflections on language*, London, 1976, chap-
    ter 1. See further R. I. AARON, *John Locke*, Oxford, 1937, chapter
    2.

54. J. M. ROBERTSON, *The philosophical works of Francis Bacon*, Lon-
    don, 1905, 119–20, 264, 523–4.

55. FIRTH, 1937, chapter 6; C. K. OGDEN, *Debabelization*, London, 1931.

56. C. J. GERHARDT (ed.), *Die philosophischen Schriften von Gottfried
    Wilhelm Leibniz*, Leipzig, 1931, volume 7, 200, 218–27: 'Sufficiet
    calamos in manus sumere sedereque ad abacos, et sibi mutuo
    . . . . . . dicere: calculemus'.

57. FIRTH, 1937, 72.

58. SALMON (ed.) *The works of Francis Lodwick*, London, 1972, 25, 90.

59. London, 1668. See further SALMON, 1979; SALMON, op. cit. in note 58; J. KNOWLSON, *Universal language schemes in England and France 1600–1800*, Toronto, 1975.

60. R. A. DUTCH (ed.), *Roget's Thesaurus*, London, 1962, XXXV.

61. WILKINS, *Essay*, 452.

62. J. J. KATZ and J. FODOR, 'The structure of a semantic theory', *Language* 39 (1963), 170–210; KATZ and P. M. POSTAL, *An integrated theory of linguistic descriptions*, Cambridge, Mass., 1964; D. W. BOLINGER, 'The atomization of meaning', *Language* 41 (1965), 555–73.

63. SALMON (ed.), *The works of Francis Lodwick*, London, 1972; WILKINS, *Mercury: or the swift and secret messenger*, London, 1641.

64. T. BRIGHT, *Characterie*, London, 1958 (first published 1558); W. J. CARLTON, *Timothy Bright*, London, 1911.

65. FIRTH, 1946.

66. B. DANIELSSON, *John Hart's works on English orthography and pronunciation*, Stockholm, 1955; FIRTH, 1946; E. J. DOBSON (ed.), *The phonetic writings of Robert Robinson*, 1957

67. FIRTH, 1946.

68. cp. E. J. DOBSON, *English pronunciation 1500–1700*, Oxford, 1957.

69. W. HOLDER, *Elements of speech*, London, 1669, 35-6, 80–90.

70. ibid., 23, 80.

71. ABERCROMBIE, 1948, 18–26.

72. WILKINS, *Essay*, 358, 378. See further FIRTH, 1937, chapter 6; id., 1946; ABERCROMBIE, 1948; V. G. SALMON, *The works of Francis Lodwick*, London 1972; ASHER and HENDERSON, 1981.

73. W. BULLOKAR, *Bref grammar for English*, London, 1586.

74. e. g. J. WALLIS, *Grammatica linguae Anglicanae*, Oxford, 1653, a work reprinted several times and much praised.

75. B. JONSON, *The English grammar*, London, 1640.

76. *Logonomia Anglicana*, London, 1621.

77. *The English grammar*, Oxford, 1634, chapter 3, § 3.

78. J. BRIGHTLAND, *A grammar of the English tongue*, London, 1711.

79. WILKINS, *Essay*, 298.

80. COOPER, *Grammatica linguae Anglicanae*, London, 1685.

81. J. A. KEMP (ed.), *John Wallis's Grammar of the English language*, London, 1972, 330–1. Further details in VORLAT, 1975, and FUNKE, 1941. For a brief historical survey of English grammar writing, see ROBINS, 'The evolution of English grammar books since the Renaissance', in G. LEITNER (ed.), *The English reference grammar*, Tübingen, 1986, 292–306. The close connection seen in this period between English scientific empiricism and the formal study of language is evident in the eighteenth century in the linguistic interest shown by the natural scientist J. Priestley (1733–1804), *The rudiments of English grammar*, London, 1761 (page vi: 'Grammar may be compared to a treatise of natural philosophy').

82. L. MURRAY, *English grammar* (thirty-fourth edition), York, 1821, 54-6.

83. ibid., 75, 127, 137.

84. FIRTH, 'Personality and language in society', *Sociological review* 42 (1950), 44; N. CHOMSKY, *Syntactic structures*, The Hague, 1957, 79.
85. CADET, 1898.
86. KUKENHEIM, 1962, 49. On the study of the grammars of the vernacular languages of continental Europe in and after the Renaissance, see PADLEY, 1985 and 1988.
87. LANCELOT and ARNAULD, 1660, 43–51.
88. LANCELOT and ARNAULD, 1660, 83. Such abstract cases may be compared but not, of course, identified, with the abstract cases in current Government and Binding theory (cp. G. C. HORROCKS, *Generative grammar*, London, 1987, 102–8.
89. ibid., 93–4; SCALIGER, *De causis linguae Latinae*, 137, 220.
90. LANCELOT and ARNAULD, 1660, 88–90.
91. *De interpretatione* 12; *Metaphysica* 1017 a 29.
92. LANCELOT and ARNAULD, 1660, 115.
93. cp. CHOMSKY, *Current issues in linguistic theory*, The Hague, 1964; id., *Aspects of the theory of syntax*, Cambridge, Mass., 1965. cp. p. 191, below.
94. e.g. E. SAPIR and M. SWADESH, *Nootka texts*, Philadelphia, 1939, 235–43.
95. LANCELOT and ARNAULD, 1660, 68; CHOMSKY, *Current issues*, 15–16.
96. LANCELOT and ARNAULD, 1660, 147.
97. L. HJELMSLEV, *Principes de grammaire générale*, Copenhagen, 1928, 15, 268.
98. L. BLOOMFIELD, *Language*, London, 1935, 20.
99. FIRTH, 'A synopsis of linguistic theory', *Studies in linguistic analysis* (Special volume of the Philological Society), Oxford, 1957, 21–2.
100. CHOMSKY, *Current issues*, chapters 1 and 5; id., *Aspects*, 117–18; *Reflections on language*, London, 1976, chapter 1; 'Principles and parameters in syntactic theory', N. HORNSTEIN and D. LIGHTFOOT (eds.), *Explanation in linguistics*, London, 1981, 32–75.
101. N. BEAUZÉE *Grammaire générale ou exposition raisonnée des éléments nécessaires du langage pour servir de fondement à l'étude de toutes les langues*, Paris, 1767 (reprinted, with introduction by B. E. BARTLETT, Stuttgart, 1974), ix-xi; B. E. BARTLETT, *Beauzée's grammaire générale*, The Hague, 1975.
102. BEAUZEE op. cit., volume 1, 403: 'Les noms et les pronoms expriment des êtres déterminés, au lieu que les adjectifs et les verbes expriment des êtres indéterminés'.
103. ibid., volume 2, 160.
104. PADLEY, 1976, 161–2; LANCELOT and ARNAULD, 1660, 75–83; C. VAUGELAS *Remarques sur la langue françoise*, Paris, 1670; cp. W. AYRES-BENNETT, 'Usage and reason in seventeenth century French grammar: a fresh look at Vangelas', H. AARSLEFF *et al* (eds.), *Papers in linguistics*, Amsterdam, 1987, 233–46.

Chapter 6

The eve of modern times

Both in general history and in the history of particular subjects the Renaissance is justifiably regarded as the beginning of the modern age. But the early nineteenth century saw a yet sharper turn towards the world to which we are now accustomed. Even in spite of the rapid changes during the present century, it requires less effort of the historical imagination to study the life and work of nineteenth-century people through their own lives and in their own context. Among the modern nation states of Europe, Germany and Italy achieved their independent existence during this century, and the patterns of industrial civilization spread over and transformed the predominantly agricultural life that had characterized Europe since antiquity.

Intellectually, too, the nineteenth century saw the emergence of modern conditions. New universities were founded in Europe and America, and the interplay of European and American scholarship, now so vital a force in education, only began seriously in this century. Popular education spread ever wider and the goal of universal literacy was for the first time made a practical proposition for governments. Learned societies and periodicals associated with them had already made their appearance, but many of those best known today in university libraries began publication in the nineteenth century, and improved communications made the exchange of articles and the systematic reviewing of books the dominant feature of academic life to which we are now accustomed.

In linguistics many of the scholars whose work was done in the nineteenth century are known to students well before they consciously delve into the history of the subject. Grimm, Whitney, Meyer-Lübke, Max Müller, Brugmann, and Sweet are just a few examples of nineteenth-century scholars who were partly responsible for shaping their branches of linguistics in the broad patterns still taught in present-day textbooks.

If any single year can, albeit artificially, be taken to mark the start of the contemporary world of linguistic science, it is the year 1786, just over a decade before the turn of the century. 1786 has been declared by a contemporary scholar to have initiated the first of the four really significant 'breakthroughs' in the modern development of linguistics up to the present day. In this year, as is now well known, Sir William Jones, a judge in the British court in India, read his famous paper to the Royal Asiatic Society in Calcutta, wherein he established beyond doubt the historical kinship of Sanskrit, the classical language of India, with Latin, Greek and the Germanic languages.

Jones's statement, though quoted in so many books already, should be set out here, because its effects in the circumstances of the time were so profound and far-reaching: 'The Sanskrit language, whatever be its antiquity, is of a wonderful structure; more perfect than the Greek, more copious than the Latin, and more exquisitely refined than either; yet bearing to both of them a stronger affinity, both in the roots of verbs and in the forms of grammar, than could possibly have been produced by accident; so strong indeed, that no philologer could examine all three without believing them to have sprung from some common source, which, perhaps, no longer exists. There is a similar reason, though not quite so forcible, for supposing that both the Gothic and the Celtic had the same origin with the Sanskrit.'[1]

What is vital about this event is not that it marked an absolute beginning to historical linguistics. Historical questions had been tackled before, and with some individual successes and insights; indeed, a special relationship between Sanskrit and some European languages, ancient and modern, had been surmised before Sir William Jones. But hitherto observations in these areas of linguistics had been in the main isolated and fragmentary. Historical significance characterizes events that can be seen to be linked in an enduring causal chain, whereby later participants start from the positions taken up by their predecessors. Such a state of affairs is observed in the development of grammatical theory and grammatical analysis in ancient Greece, and the same is true of the course of historical linguistics during the century following Jones's statement, during which it constituted the major branch of linguistic studies.

The progress of comparative and historical linguistics must be traced in its most significant theoretical aspects during the

nineteenth century; but the results of the introduction of serious
Sanskrit study into Europe, which followed the demonstration of
its historical relationships, were not confined to historical linguistics. Modern descriptive linguistics shows equally the effects of
contact with ancient India, even though in this case the full
realization took place much less immediately.

Roman Catholic missionaries had opened up the field of Indian
languages in earlier centuries (p. 117, above). The first known
reference to Sanskrit came at the end of the sixteenth century,
when the Italian Filippo Sassetti wrote home from India reporting
admiringly of the *lingua Sanscruta*, and pointing out a number of
resemblances between Sanskrit and Italian words. Subsequently
likenesses were noticed between Sanskrit and some European
languages by the German B. Schulze and the Frenchman Père
Coeurdoux[2]; but little came of these observations.

Jones's paper was not only of a more profound nature than pre-
vious pronouncements on Sanskrit by Europeans, but it came
propitiously on the eve of an awakening interest in Near Eastern
and Indian studies on the part of European scholars. The
Napoleonic wars were partly responsible, and during his supremacy
Napoleon deliberately encouraged French archaeological work in
Egypt and the Near East, inaugurating a long association of
French scholarship with the non-European languages of the
Mediterranean.

In Germany the brothers Friedrich and August von Schlegel
expressed themselves in similar terms on the need for Sanskrit
studies to be fostered and developed in the German universities.
In 1808, in the preface to his book *Uber die Sprache und Weisheit
der Indier*, Friedrich von Schlegel wrote of his hope to kindle
or at least to prepare the way for the love of Sanskrit studies in
Germany; and in 1819 August von Schlegel, appointed to a chair
in the newly founded University of Bonn (1818), declared that he
too would count himself fortunate if he could do something
towards establishing such studies in that country.[3] With
governmental support he achieved his object. In the expansion of
university education in Prussia after the wars chairs of Sanskrit
and of historical linguistics were set up and appointments made
to them under the influence of Wilhelm von Humboldt, who
served for a time as minister for public instruction in the Kingdom
of Prussia.

The first Sanskrit grammar in English was published early in
the nineteenth century, and from 1808 translations were made
into European languages of the classical Sanskrit literature of
India.

The linguistic study of Sanskrit by Europeans had a twofold effect; the comparison of Sanskrit with languages of Europe formed the first stage in the systematic growth of comparative and historical linguistics, and, additionally, in Sanskrit writings Europeans now came into contact with the independently developed tradition of linguistic scholarship in India, whose merits were acknowledged at once and whose influence on several branches of European linguistics was deep and lasting.

Linguistics in India goes back further than in western Europe, and has been maintained by a continuity of native scholarship ever since. It attained its classical period early in its history, and by the time Europeans became aware of it, Indian scholars had recognized definite schools and distinct doctrines, together with acknowledged texts and sources followed by successions of commentaries and exegesis.

Indian linguistics was not itself historical in orientation, though its roots lay in the changes languages undergo in the course of time. But the topics covered by modern descriptive linguistics: semantics, grammar, phonology, and phonetics, were all treated at length in the Indian tradition; and in phonetics and in certain aspects of grammar, Indian theory and practice was definitely in advance of anything achieved in Europe or elsewhere before contact had been made with Indian work. The stimulation afforded by Sanskritic linguistic scholarship carried by Buddhist monks into China has already been noticed (pp. 120, above). European scholars realized immediately that they had encountered a mass of linguistic literature in India of the greatest importance and stemming from an independent source, even though their interpretation and full appreciation of it was in part halting and delayed.

So far as we can tell, the original inspiration for linguistics in India was the need that was felt to preserve certain ritual and religious orally transmitted texts coming from the Vedic period (c. 1200–1000 B.C.), the oldest known stage of Sanskrit literature, from the effects of time and what was feared as dialectal contamination. The preservation without alteration of linguistic material handed down through the generations by oral transmission is an artificial process, an attempt to halt what is everywhere the natural outcome of linguistic continuity. Changes in pronunciation, grammar, and word meanings were observed in the rest of the language, and the dialectal divergences in the speech of different areas may have made even more apparent the special position of the Vedic texts, and, in a manner similar to the contrasts between Hellenistic Greek and classical literary

Greek, made necessary an apparatus of phonetic, grammatical, and semantic interpretation.

Such was the stimulus, but the response went far beyond these immediate needs; and, as a modern writer observes, 'a scientific curiosity, coupled with keen audition and an effective methodology, led to descriptions which must surely have transcended their original terms of reference'.[4]

In Greece we have preserved for us the stages through which linguistic scholarship passed virtually from its beginnings. In ancient India most of the linguistic literature that we have, and especially the best known piece of linguistic composition, Pāṇini's Sanskrit grammar, manifestly came at the end and as the culmination of a long line of previous work of which we have no direct knowledge. Pāṇini's grammar is known as the *Aṣṭādhyāyī*, or 'Eight books'; it is divided into eight main sections. It is not known whether its author wrote it down or put it together orally; its date, too, is uncertain, and it has variously been assigned to around 600 B.C. and 300 B.C. Clearly, however, linguistics in India must have been seriously under way well before the middle of the first millennium B.C.

Sanskrit Indian scholarship served as the model for the rest of India. It was the inspiration for the *Tolkāppiyam*, one of the earliest grammars of Tamil, a Dravidian language of central and south India (? second century B.C.), and for the native grammatical tradition of Tibet.[5]

Indian scholars covered virtually the whole field of synchronic linguistic studies, though their best known representative, Pāṇini, restricted his work to the intensive treatment of a limited range. In reviewing the Indian achievement as it was when it made its impact on European linguistics, it is legitimate to span several centuries together and to consider the work of Indian scholarship, divergent in time though united by the continuity of scholarly tradition, under three principal headings: general linguistic theory and semantics, phonetics and phonology, and descriptive grammar.

General linguistic theory was debated by Indian scholars as it was by scholars in the west, though before the end of the eighteenth century there was no contact between them. Language was considered against the background both of literary studies and of philosophical enquiry; and a number of the topics familiar to western scholarship and almost inevitable in a serious examination of language were also familiar to Indian linguists from early times.

Various questions involved in understanding the nature of word and sentence meaning were discussed from different points of view. Indian linguists considered the extent to which meanings could be regarded as a natural property of words, or the extent to which onomatopoeia could be taken as the model for describing the relationship between word and thing. As in the western nature-convention argument (pp. 21–2, above), men soon realized the very limited part that such a factor can play in language, and how much more typical of language is the arbitrary conventional relation between a form and its meaning.

Much thought was given to the variability and extensibility of word meanings, one of the major characteristics of language, enabling it to fulfil the unlimited requirements placed on it with its necessarily limited resources. Meanings were seen to be learned both from observation of the contexts of situation in which words were actually used in sentences and from direct statements by elders and teachers on particular words and their uses. While limits could hardly be set to actual usage, collocation often restricted the meaning range of a word by the exclusion of certain otherwise acceptable meanings of the word in isolation. Thus *dhenuḥ* which by itself could mean both 'mare' and 'cow', could only be taken as meaning 'cow' in such a collocation as *savatsa dhenuḥ*, cow with calf.[6] The almost unanswerable question was faced in India, as elsewhere, on the extent to which single word forms with multiple meanings should be regarded as polysemous words or as a number of different but homophonous words. Within this context much attention was paid to the relations between what was considered the primary meaning of a word, which was said to be understood first, and the various meanings arising from its metaphorical use (*lakṣaṇā*), both on everyday discourse and for particular literary effects.

While these were questions of great literary importance, the Indian logicians debated, again as did western logicians, whether words primarily denoted particulars, classes, or abstract universals, and how far word meanings were positive in identifying an object for what it was or negative in distinguishing it from the rest of reality. It was also realized that a word, e.g. *fire*, can stand for itself as well as for its primary denotation.

A question that is far from being solved today is that of the semantic relation between a sentence and its component words. Sentences are clearly more than the sum of their juxtaposed words, whether considered from the semantic or the grammatical point of view. The western tradition tended to concentrate on words as individual minimal meaning bearers and to regard the sentence as the product of word combinations in specific types of logical proposition. Plato and Aristotle mostly discussed meaning in relation to words as isolates, and Aristotle stressed the semantic minimality (in his view) and independence of the word as such (p. 31, above). Indian linguists debated the whole question of the primacy of the word as against that of the sentence. One set of thinkers maintained a view very like the general western attitude that the sentence is built up of words each contributing its meaning to the total meaning of the sentence. But an opposite view, particularly associated with Bhartṛhari, author of *Vākyapadīya* (*c.* seventh century A.D.), regarded the sentence as a single undivided utterance conveying its meaning 'in a flash', just as a picture is first perceived as a unity notwithstanding subsequent analysis into its component coloured shapes. Given the conception of the word unit, sentences can be identified as one-word sentences or as many-word sentences, but for the speaker and hearer they are primarily single sentence unities, words and word meanings being largely the creation of linguists and self-conscious speakers trying to analyse and classify sentence meanings in terms of smaller components. As an example of Bhartṛhari's attitude, the sentence *fetch a cuckoo from the woods* is not understood first as a sequence of words put together, because the full meaning of *fetch* in the sentence (i.e. the mode of fetching) is only grasped together with the meaning of *cuckoo*, and someone ignorant of the meaning of the word *cuckoo* is therefore to some extent ignorant of the meaning of the rest of the sentence.[7]

Such a view may be criticized, and it was, as extreme. It is echoed in Malinowski's dictum that 'isolated words are in fact only linguistic figments, the products of an advanced linguistic analysis',[8] and perhaps underestimates the psychological reality of the word as a viable unit for the native speaker as well as part of the linguist's analytical apparatus (the bound morpheme is probably a better example of an analytical creation, and it is noteworthy that *morpheme* is generally a technical term, or translated by a technical term, whereas words for *word* are found in a very large number of languages, both written and unwritten). It is, however, a necessary corrective against the typical western tendency to concentrate semantic enquiries on the word as a wholly independent unit only subsequently put into sentences.

This Indian appreciation of the semantic unity of the sentence is parallel to and may have been connected with their early appreciation of the phonological and phonetic differences between words as pronounced isolates and words pronounced in connected spoken sentences (*sandhi*, pp. 157–8, below).

An inevitable problem in any serious linguistic thought is the relation between the perceived utterances, spoken and written, of a language and the language itself, whether regarded from the point of view of what the speaker possesses as his linguistic competence or from that of what the linguist sets up as the system or systems of elements, categories, and rules underlying and accounting for the infinitely varied output of a living language. *Langue* and *parole, abstraction* and *exponent, emic* and *etic unit, form* and *substance*, are all examples of recent attempts to compass and express this relation. Indian linguists sought to express it in the theory of *sphoṭa*. This theory was formulated somewhat differently by different Indian scholars and has been much discussed. Essentially, in any linguistic element or constituent two aspects are distinguished, the actual event or individual realization (*dhvani*) and the unexpressed and permanent entity (*sphoṭa*) actualized by each occurrent *dhvani*. Sentence *sphoṭa*, word *sphoṭa*, and sound unit (*varṇa*) *sphoṭa* were all envisaged.

The *sphoṭa* of a sentence as a single meaningful symbol is realized or actualized by a succession of articulated sounds. At a lower level the word, in so far as it is a meaningful symbol in its own right, may be regarded as a unitary *sphoṭa* also actualized by a succession of sounds. But sounds do not function simply as audible disturbances of the air; a particular abstract and permanent unit of distinctive sound signalling capable of semantic differentiation is actualized by the multitude of slightly different prounciations each varying with the individual's voice, his style, and the physical situation in which he speaks. This last conception of the *varṇa sphoṭa* was especially associated with Patañjali (*c.* 150 B. C.). Bhartṛhari, on the other hand, in consonance with his theory of the primacy of the sentence, seems to have held the sentence *sphoṭa* to be the real *sphoṭa*. He, in fact, envisaged three levels in the realization of the sentence *sphoṭa* as a unitary meaningful symbol: the integral symbol itself, graphically and phonically ineffable, the sequential phonological pattern that expresses it, as normalized by the elimination of all individual variations (*prākṛta dhvani*), and the realization of this in the individual utterances of the sentence (*vaikṛta dhvani*). It would appear that the mediate stage would correspond to some interpretations of *varṇa sphoṭa*, and the entire scheme may be compared with the interlevel status accorded to phonology in relation to grammar and lexis on one side and to phonic utterance on the other by some linguists today.

A further development of the *dhvani-sphoṭa* relationship is seen in Ānandavardhana's theory of poetic language (*Dhvanyāloka*, ninth century A.D.) Just as the sounds reveal the meaningful entities themselves, so in poetry the chosen words and their literal meanings reveal further suggested senses and the beauty of the poem as a whole. Here one remarks a striking parallel with Hjelmslev's conception of stylistic analysis as the treatment of the content plane and the expression plane of a natural language in some specific usage as themselves together forming the expression plane of a higher order 'connotative semiotic'.[9]

Much of what has been briefly noticed in ancient Indian speculation on semantics and the theory of language strikes chords already familiar in the western tradition, though their approach is often rather different. What is most remarkable about Indian phonetic work is its manifest superiority in conception and execution as compared with anything produced in the west or elsewhere before the Indian contribution had become known there. In general one may say that Henry Sweet takes over where the Indian phonetic treatises leave off.[10] We have seen how Greek and Roman linguists made the major classifications of letters, as the representatives of speech sounds, in terms of their acoustic impressions. But at this stage in linguistics, prior to the technology and equipment needed for the scientific analysis of sound waves, articulatory description was the only possible frame for an accurate and systematic classification. And in view of the primacy and the observational accessibility of the speech organs in the act of phonation, articulation still remains fundamental in phonetic description, even though modern acoustic catergories may supplement and even supersede articulatory ones in phonological analysis.[11]

The Greeks and the Romans made articulatory features secondary in their phonetic descriptions; Arabic grammarians went further and achieved more in articulatory phonetics; but above all their contemporaries and successors before the nineteenth century were the ancient Indian phoneticians, whose work is preserved in a number of phonetic treatises which have been tentatively ascribed to the period 800–150 B.C.

Once their terminology is mastered or translated, the Indian phonetic writings on Sanskrit are, apart from relatively few points, easy to follow for the modern reader acquainted with phonetic theory and phonetic descriptions. As a result, more is known certainly about the pronunciation of the Sanskrit that they described (the ritual and sacred texts) than about any other ancient language. In certain matters their detailed statements can be readily interpreted today, whereas the nineteenth-century scholar W. D. Whitney, though he realized their worth and importance, was led to a too hasty dismissal of some of their reported observations.[12]

The place of phonetics was seen as the linking of grammar to utterance, and phonetic description was organized under three main headings, the processes of articulation, the segments (consonants and vowels), and the synthesis of the segments in phonological structures.

The articulatory organs were divided into intrabuccal and extrabuccal, extrabuccal being the glottis, the lungs, and the nasal cavity. These three are responsible for the distinctions of voice and voicelessness, aspiration and non-aspiration, and nasality and non-nasality, giving in the phonological system of Sanskrit a five term system at different articulatory positions, which may be exemplified by the bilabial series /b/, /p/, /bh/, /ph/, and /m/. Within the buccal cavity the articulatory organs are described from the back to the front, ending with the lips, and four degrees of stricture are distinguished: total buccal obstruction (stops and nasal consonants), fricative constriction, semivowel constriction, and absence of constriction, this last constituting vocalic articulation. The mechanism of articulation is described in terms of a stationary point of articulation (*sthāna*), for example the hard palate, and a moving articulator *(karaṇa)*, e.g. the tongue. This conception was extended to cover bilabial and glottal articulation, where it is scarcely plausible to regard one of the parts involved as stationary and the other as moving.

The correct diagnosis of the glottal activity in voicing is rightly regarded as one of the phonetic triumphs of the ancient Indians. The nearest approach to an accurate description in the west had been that of Holder in the seventeenth century (p. 132, above), which went unheeded at the time. The Indian linguists distinguished voice from voicelessness according as the glottis was closed or open in articulation, noticed the tendency for otherwise voiceless consonants to be voiced in intervocalic position (a common phonetic occurrence in a number of languages), and, against the nineteenth-century incredulity of Max Müller and Whitney, properly accounted for the production of voiced *h* ([ɦ]).[13]

Junction features and certain prosodic features of stretches of speech in connected utterance received careful attention. This is witnessed by the now universal technical use of the Sanskrit term *sandhi*, joining together, to denote the phonetic and phonological differences between disconnected words, morphemes, and the like, and the same elements combined into concatenated sequences. Indeed, as some Indian linguists asserted the priority of the sentence over the word as a meaningful unit, some of the phonetic treatises denied the word an independent phonetic existence outside or apart from the text; the breath group was the basic unit of phonetic description and word isolates were primarily paedagogical devices. Sanskrit orthography represented connected discourse, rather than successions of isolated words, such as was the practice of Greek and Latin orthography and is largely European orthographic practice today; but with some texts parallel versions were in use, a normal *sandhi*-marking text and a text written in word isolate forms, a *pada* (word) text.

The phonetics of word and morpheme juncture features associated with initiality and finality in the breath group, vowel length and syllable quantity, tone, and tempo were all described in precise detail. Vedic Sanskrit had three distinctive pitches, high, low, and falling (*udātta, anudātta, svarita*); these had disappeared by the Christian era.[14] Thanks to the Indian phonetic treatises we can compare Sanskrit with Ancient Greek, joint preservers of what was probably the tonal system of unitary Indo-European.

In their descriptive work it is clear that the Indian phoneticians operated within an intuitive conception of phonemic principles. The treatises do not discuss a concept like the phoneme as a theoretical abstraction, though some aspects of the *sphoṭa* theory may be seen to approach certain modern interpretations of the phoneme. They show themselves, however, well aware of certain phonetic differences which, being environmentally determined should be noted in a description but not assigned to separate distinctive sound units, for example the [φ] and [x] allophones of /h/ before labials and velars respectively; and in describing the high and low tones Patañjali pointed out that their distinctiveness rested on their relative not their absolute pitch levels.[15]

The Sanskrit alphabet or syllabary has been shown to have been devised on segmental phonemic lines, the only redundant symbol being the one standing for the palatal nasal consonant [ɲ(a)], since [ɲ] only occurs as an allophone of /n/ in juxtaposition with a palatal consonant.[16] And here this very redundancy of symbols arose from an equally sound phonological analysis which governed the usual arrangement of the alphabet, since [ɲ] stood to the palatal plosives in precisely the same phonetic relation as did the other nasal consonants, /ŋ/, /ɳ/, /n/, and /m/, to their corresponding plosive series.[17]

Worthy as the phonetic works of the ancient Indians are now seen to have been, it is for their grammatical theory and the grammatical analysis of their own language, Sanskrit, that Indian linguistic scholarship is best known today, and among Indian grammarians the name of Pāṇini stands out above all. Though his date is uncertain, quite definitely his is the earliest grammatical treatise extant on any Indo-European language, and the earliest scientific work in any Indo-European language, and in Bloomfield's words 'one of the greatest monuments of human intelligence'.[18] However, while it brings almost to perfection its avowed intentions in the field of Sanskrit grammar with which it deals, it is not what would ordinarily be called a complete grammar of the Sanskrit language. It would, perhaps, best be described in modern terms as a generative morphology of Sanskrit.

Pāṇini's grammar includes as its main component an exhaustive statement of the rules of word formation of Sanskrit. These rules are expressed in short statements, or aphorisms as they are often called, giving either definitions, or processes of word formation. Each is referred to as a *sūtra*, threads, a term also used of the ritual instructions in some of the earlier Vedic literature. There are also appendices giving a list of verbal roots, a list of similarly inflected nominal words, and a list of the sounds of Sanskrit. The rules, like the rules of today's generative grammarians, have to be applied in a set order; and apart from the completeness with which Pāṇini covers every aspect of Sanskrit word formation, those who have studied his work, whether in India or later in Europe, have been most struck by the ingenuity with which he achieved the extreme economy of his statements. This quest for economy was evidently part of the context of early Indian grammatical composition; a commentator remarked that the saving of half the length of a short vowel in framing a grammatical rule meant as much to a grammarian as the birth of a son.[19] This demand for economy may have been inspired primarily by the needs of oral recitation and commitment to memory, but it clearly became a canon of scholarly merit in its own right. It does, however, make the task of the reader enormously complicated; the *Aṣṭādhyāyī* is a grammarian's grammar, not a learner's or a teacher's manual (in this respect it is quite unlike the *Téchnē*). As Bloomfield observes, it is 'intelligible only with a commentary', and it has been the subject of continuous comment and explication ever since it was composed. Patañjali's *Mahābhāṣya* ('Great commentary') is the major Indian commentary, and most subsequent Indian work has been comment on comment.[20]

Though Pāṇini's composition is about as far removed as could be from one's conception of a teaching grammar, the teaching and presentation of Sanskrit today, as well as several important directions and features of descriptive linguistics can be traced back immediately to his genius.

Pāṇini's grammar is set in a context wherein the rest of the grammatical description of the language and its underlying theory

are implicit. The phonetic description of the language is equally
taken for granted; the set of sound units represented in the
Sanskrit alphabet, and listed in the *Aṣṭādhyāyī* is given without
further comment, though the sounds are ordered in sequences
that are both phonetically and morphologically relevant to his
grammatical rules. Actual phonetic statements in Pāṇini are very
few.

Indian linguists made use of four classes of words: nouns and
verbs (inflected), and prepositions and particles (uninflected).
The basic Indian theory of sentence structure required that for
words to constitute a sentence they must fulfil three requirements: they must have mutual expectancy as members of
appropriate grammatical classes in proper constructions, or they
would be no more than a lexical list devoid of further significance;
they must be semantically appropriate to one another, or we
would have to accept apparently grammatical non-sentences like
he wets it with fire, such as have, in fact, troubled linguists in
the east and the west throughout the history of linguistic thought
and still tease us today; and they must occur in temporal contiguity, or they could not be carried in the memory or understood
as a single utterance at all. The Sanskrit terms for these three
requirements were *ākāṅkṣā, yogyatā,* and *samnidhi*; they may be
compared to the somewhat corresponding Firthian relationships
of colligability and collocability of the elements and temporal
sequence of their actual exponents.[21]

In addtion to the phonological term *sandhi*, Indian grammatical
names for the different types of word compounding, a subject to
which they devoted considerable attention, have passed into
general currency. One may instance the terms *tatpurusha (tatpuruṣa)*, attributive compound (e.g. *doorknob, blackberry*), and
bahuvrihi (bahuvrīhi), exocentric compound (e.g. *turnkey,
humpback*).[22]

The verb, inflected for person, number, and tense, was taken
as the core of the sentence (in Sanskrit, as in Latin and Greek,
the verb could stand alone as a complete sentence). Other words
stood in specific relations to the verb, and of these the most
important were the nouns in their different case inflexions. Nouns
standing in different relations to the verb were designated by
the term *kāraka* (literally 'doing', 'acting'); the *kārakas* were
classified by the different types of relation between the action or
process referred to by the verb and the denotata of the nouns.
'Agent' and 'object' were two of them; but the *kārakas* are not
to be equated with cases, as normally understood; the Sanskrit
genitive in its most general use is not considered to express a

kāraka, because it relates nouns to nouns as its main grammatical function, not nouns to verbs. The exponents of *kārakas* included the case endings of case inflected words, but the same *kāraka* could be expressed in more than one formal structure.[23]

The rules of Sanskrit grammatical word formation, which form the bulk of Pāṇini's *Aṣṭādhayāyī*, are set in the general grammatical context sketched above. They are difficult to describe and exemplify without reference to the Sanskrit language. Bloomfield in an extended review gives a good summary of Pāṇini's method and of how a Pāṇinian description of the relevant parts of English grammar would appear and what it would accomplish.[24]

The generation of the word form *ábhavat*, he, she, it was (Latin *erat*), from the root *bhū-*, to be, passes through the following stages (the numbers refer to some of the relevant sūtras):[25]

bhū-a	3.1.2, 3.1.68.
bhū-a-t	1.4.99, 3.1.2, 3.2.111, 3.4.78, 3.4.100.
a-bhū-a-t	6.4.71, 6.1.158.
a-bho-a-t	7.3.84.
a-bhav-a-t	6.1.78.
ábhavat.	

Only the final representation is the form of a real word as pronounced in isolation; those preceding it illustrate the ordered application of rules, covering, of course, the formation of large numbers of words other than this one. The whole descriptive procedure may be compared with the stages by which the generative grammarians, more than two thousand years later, arrive at an actual form from underlying forms through successive representations of elements combined with each other in accordance with ordered rules.[26]

Pāṇini's descriptions involve the isolate identification of roots and affixes, which directly inspired the morpheme concept of present-day grammatical analysis. The study of Hebrew and Arabic had led later mediaeval Europe to recognize the abstract root as a constant that underlies inflexional paradigms, but the typical European model of grammatical description continued to be the one handed down by Dionysius Thrax and Priscian, a thorough-going word-and-paradigm one. Such a model, indeed, with its very obvious paedagogical advantages, continues strongly in use in language teaching, especially the teaching of ancient languages.

Formal variations among functionally equivalent elements, such as are handled under the modern concept of allomorphs of single morphemes, were dealt with by Pāṇini morphophonemically. He set up abstract basic forms, called *sthānin* ('having a place', 'original'), which by the rules of morphophonological change and internal *sandhi* were converted into the actual morphs of the resultant words; the formal replacements were called *ādeṣa* ('substitute'). General rules were given together with exceptions; in English the past tense formation of verbs with /-d/ would have been related to the environmentally determined variants such as /-t/ (*walked*) and /-id/ (*plodded*), with separate mention of individual irregularities like *run, ran*.[27] Bloomfield's *Menomini morphophonemics* has been regarded as Pāṇinian in method and inspiration.[28]

In the interests of the extreme economy of statement referred to earlier, Pāṇini's rules are set out in such a way that the repetition of a rule in relation to a subsequent rule in word formation is rendered unnecessary. Economy is further served by a number of special devices; the distinctive sound units listed by Pāṇini are arranged in a special order, bringing together those sounds jointly involved in the statement of certain rules. These sequences are further divided by the interposition of sound units used demarcatively, so that a succession of sounds can be abbreviated to the first sound and the marker following the last. Thus from the sequence *a i u (ṇ)*, *a i u* can be indicated by *aṇ*, and from *a i u (ṇ) ṛ ḷ e o (ṇ) ai au (c)*, *ac* can be used to mean 'all vowels' (*ṛ* and *ḷ* stand for vocalic *r* and *l*, respectively).[29] This type of abbreviation is extended to grammatical elements; *sup* refers to all nominal case endings and *tiṅ* to all verbal personal endings.

A rather famous example of Pāṇini's economy of verbiage is his final *sūtra* (8.4.68), which takes the form '*a a*', that is to say that *a* (which had been treated (e.g. in 6.1.101) as the qualitative equivalent of *ā*, so that the *sandhi* rule of vowel coalescence could be economically stated as *i-i=ī, u-u=ū, a-a=ā*) is in fact a closer, more central vowel sound.[30]

A descriptive device familiar to linguists today, zero representation of an element or category, is owed directly to Pāṇini. Apparently irregular forms may be made to appear more regular at the more abstract levels of representation and analysis by the assumption of a morpheme represented by a zero morph, i.e. with no overt exponent in the phonic material. Thus since most English noun plurals include an overt morph, usually a suffix, examples like *sheep* as a plural can be analysed as being /ʃiːp/-∅.

Pāṇini sets up as the minimal grammatical structure of a noun form the sequence root+stem suffix+inflexional suffix. In most noun forms each of these elements can be linked to actual phonetic segments as their exponents, but not in all nouns. Thus in -*bhājam*, sharing (accusative singular), -*bhāj*- represents the root, *bhaj*- and -*am* the final, inflexional suffix. Pāṇini's rules for such nouns specify a descriptively earlier segment *v* representing the stem-forming suffix (3.2.62), and a later rule deprives this *v* of overt representation, that is to say deletes it or represents it by zero (6.1.67).

Many different uses have been made of the zero concept in modern linguistics; some have protested against its excessive exploitation; but there are forms in many languages that are most economically analysed by means of a zero element. All of these uses derive from Pāṇini's first known application of this device; the most Pāṇinian example outside Sanskrit is de Saussure's analysis of Greek nominative case forms like *phlóx* (/phlóks/), flame, in which /phlóg-/ represents the root, /-s/ the nominative singular suffix, and the stem formative (as in *hīppos* (/hĩpp-ᴏ-s/), horse) is represented by a zero suffix (/phlóg-∅-s/).[31]

The impact of the work of Pānini and the other Indian linguists on Sanskrit studies in Europe from 1800 was deep and far-reaching. Two of the earliest Sanskrit grammars published in English, W. Carey's *Grammar of the Sungskrit language* (Serampore, 1806 and C Wilkins's *Grammar of the Sanskrita language* (London, 1808) pay tribute to the work of their Indian predecessors, which they had studied with the aid of living Sanskrit pundits in India.[32]

Concentration on the historical aspects of linguistic studies during the nineteenth century, itself the immediate result of the discovery by Europeans of the Sanskrit language and its relationships with the classical and modern languages of Europe, had the effect of delaying the full appreciation of Indian grammatical concepts and methods in descriptive work, but in phonetics the Indian insights were influential in the stimulation and development of both theory and practice throughout the century.

The study of Sanskrit was the prime incitement to early nineteenth-century comparative and historical work. But it came at a propitious time and to a Europe prepared for it. From Dante onward, through and after the Renaissance, various disconnected attempts had been made at linguistic history and at historically orientated comparisons between languages; but the bulk of linguistic scholarship, as has been seen in earlier chapters, had been directed at the description and analysis of languages, synchronic theory, paedagogy and other applications, and approaches to what can loosely be called the 'philosophy of language', general theories of the place and the working of language in human affairs.

During the eighteenth century, however, speculation was turn-

ing towards historical questions, enthusiastically though in a
rather unsystematic way. The origin of language, interpreted as
the search for man's 'first' or 'original' tongue while for ever
beyond the reach of any conceivable linguistic science, has always
fascinated linguistically minded people and in different forms has
been a focus of attention throughout recorded history. Psam-
metichus of Egypt's attempt to discover the 'oldest', i.e. the
original, language allegedly by recording an utterance (Phrygian
bekos, bread) from a child carefully brought up in a speechless
environment is a forerunner of other similar tales, told of other
personages and other languages.[33] But several linguistic thinkers
of the eighteenth century in different European countries asked
and tried to answer the question from a rather different viewpoint
at once more abstract and more amenable to scientific investigation: what lay between the beginnings of human language and its
obviously elaborate present form, and how the seeds of language
as it was known in historical times could have been sown in man's
prehistory. Men further sought historical explanations of the observed forms of words in accordance with supposedly universal
principles of linguistic development. While all this was far from
the systematic historical study of specific and determined families
of languages such as grew up in and dominated the next century,
it was nourished by the increasing knowledge, albeit often partial,
of newly discovered languages of the expanding world of
Eurpoean colonization, missions, and trade.

Attempts at seriously thought-out explanations of the origin
and development of language in mankind, considered as a single
species, united philosophers of the empiricist and rationalist per-
suasions characteristic of the eighteenth century and earlier with
those working well within the Romantic movement of its later
years and the turn of the century. This is not surprising, since it
is in language that men both communicate the collectively accumulated knowledge, argument, and principles of reasoning,
such as were held in so high esteem by men of the philosophical
Enlightenment, and, equally, give expression to the emotions and
individual sentiments on which the Romantics laid such stress.
Vernunftmensch, the man of reason, and *Gefühlsmensch*, the man
of feeling, realize themselves through the resources of their
language.

Half-way through the eighteenth century two French
philosophers discussed the origin and early development of
human speech. In 1746 E. B. de Condillac devoted the second
part of his *Essai sur l'origine des connoissances humaines*[34] to
language, and in 1755 Rousseau treated the same topic more

briefly in part of his *Discourse on the origin of inequality,* making favourable mention of Condillac's views.[35] A later work published posthumously in 1782 was his essay on the origin of languages.[36]

Condillac wrote within the intellectualist, rationalist-empiricist, tradition, relying a good deal on Locke's theory of knowledge, whereas Rousseau looked forward to the Romantic movement that was to follow; indeed, in many respects he can be said to have been one of its heralds. Their conceptions of the genesis of language were very similar. Language originated in deictic and imitative gestures and natural cries, but since gestures were less efficient as communicative signals the phonic element in human language became dominant, as specific sound sequences were semantically associated with existents and phenomena and as the power of human thought increased. Condillac envisaged a mixed stage in which spoken verb forms were accompanied by gestures indicating time reference, these latter subsequently replaced by vocal symbols uttered after the verb itself and finally agglutinated to it.[37] Rousseau suggested an almost deliberate agreement to make this substitution from gesture to speech on the lines of the social contract.[38]

Both Condillac and Rousseau considered that abstract vocabulary and grammatical complexity developed from an earlier individual concrete vocabulary with very few grammatical distinctions or constraints: and both regarded reliance on tonal contrasts in the manner of Chinese as a survival of a primitive feature, and likewise the attention paid to the intonation of declamatory speech in classical antiquity,[39] and both considered poetry to have sprung from chanting as the earliest literary form of language. On this, however, their different philosophical attitudes revealed themselves. Condillac dispassionately compared Latin and French oratory, and refused to express a value judgment as between the stylistic merits of Latin with its grammatically free word order and French with its more analytic structure and more fixed word order.[40] Rousseau on the other hand rejoiced in the supposed vivacity and passion of the earlier stages of human language, when poetry had not been chilled into reasoning, and before writing, unable to symbolize the stress and pitch differences and the vocal inflexions of speech, had substituted 'exactitude for expression' and enervated the liveliness of language itself: 'All written languages have to change their character and lose vigour in gaining clarity'.[41] Rousseau, who could dream of the noble savage uncorrupted by property and civil government, could also write of 'languages favourable to freedom; these are sonorous, prosodic, harmonious languages, which can be heard and understood from afar. Our languages are designed for the buzzing of the drawing room'.[42]

The widespread interest during the second half of the century in resolving problems concerning the origin of language is instanced by the prize offered by the Prussian Academy in 1769 for an essay answering the questions whether man could have evolved, unaided, language as it was known then, and if so how he went about it. This enquiry was in part a reaction against hitherto unsatisfactory statements and against the assertion of Süssmilch in 1754 that the complexity and perfect ordering of languages could only be explained as the direct gift of God to mankind, a view also expressed by Rousseau on divine guidance in the evolution of language, hinted at by Plato, and found in a number of traditional mythological accounts in the Old Testament and elsewhere.[43]

Herder's solution to the questions put by the Academy won him the prize and was published in 1772 as his *Abhandlung über den Ursprung der Sprache*.[44] It was written in great haste and with great feeling (he had, in fact, set down a few years before some of his opinions on language in a number of essays[45]). Probably few other academic prize compositions contain so many exclamation marks or exhibit so impassioned a rhetoric.

Herder asserted the inseparability of language and thought; language is the tool, the content, and the form of human thinking.[46] The close connection between thought and language had been a commonplace of philosophy since antiquity, but earlier writers from Aristotle to the modistae had taken for granted the hierarchic dependence of language on prior thinking and abstraction. Herder's assumption of the common origin and parallel development of both together through successive stages of growth and maturity was rather new; and he stated that, since language and thinking were interdependent, the thought patterns and the popular literature of different peoples could only properly be understood and studied through their own languages.[47] Such opinions had been expressed before. Indeed Condillac had insisted on the complementary and mutually supportive development processes of language and rationality in mankind's early history and in its present condition.[48] But at the beginning of the European and especially of the German Romantic era, and with the forces of European nationalism about to become a dominant theme of nineteenth-century politics, the assertion of the individuality of a nation's speech and its intimate bonds with national thought, national literature, and national solidarity was readily appreciated and initiated a continuing trend of linguistic theory. Sapir may be right in attributing much of Humboldt's distinctive thought on language to Herder's inspiration (cp. pp. 193–5), and if this is so both the adherents of Whorfian theories and the generative grammarians today can each trace some links back to this formative philosopher of language.[49]

Herder answered the question on the priority of language or of thought, by saying that since each depended on the other for its existence the two had a common origin and mankind had advanced in each by equal stages, developing a faculty uniquely possessed by man as distinct from all the rest of the animal kingdom. The first step was the abstraction and recognition of a recurrent entity with its own relatively constant and distinctive characteristics from the 'whole ocean of experience', and at the same time its designation by a vocal symbol. He assumed that hearing was the sense whose data were first isolated and named in this way, and the lamb was hailed as 'the bleeter' ('Ha! Du bist das Blöckende!'[50]). From the vocal symbolization of things by their auditory characteristics mankind moved outwards to the data provided by the other senses. Herder's arguments in support of the centrality of the auditory sense may endure little examination today as they stand, but the phonaesthetic component of so many vocabularies wherein visual and other features (littleness, spikiness, nearness, ect.) manifestly correlate with certain types of sound feature, lends some support to his hypothesis.[51] The first word stock was a 'simple vocabulary',[52] one largely confined to observable beings and events, and thereafter lexical diversity and grammatical differentiations grew with the accumulating treasure of men's thought.

This hypothetical reconstruction of the prehistory of speech, despite its obvious naiveties of expression, is as good as many other probings of events that lie beyond the reach of scientific observation. In particular it was a distinct advance on some earlier talk on the origin of language that had put the question in the form, how did language originate in man considered in all other respects as he was known at the time of asking and differing only by the lack of articulate speech.

Herder retained the traditional monogenetic theory of all languages, as of all cultures; and his theory suffered from the restricted time perspective allotted in the eighteenth century to man's existence on the earth, with a consequential attempt to see enduring characteristics of the early stages of language in alleged 'primitive languages' existing in the present. This carried with it such silly suggestions as that the verb enjoyed temporal priority of emergence among the word classes (in fact *word class* can have no meaning unless at least two classes are distinguished in a language); and Herder buttressed his assertion with the equally fallacious analogy with the child's use of language.[53]

It is less of a reproach to Herder, writing when he did, that he resorted to such arguments than to modern writers in whose speculations into the prehistory of speech these same outworn analogies still make their unmerited appearance.

Herder lay between the intellectualist and the Romantic movements and came under the influence of both; this gives great significance to his writings on history as well as those on language.[54] His own theory of the origin of language, though passionately expressed, was not out of key with intellectualist thinking. Interestingly, by the time the news reached him that he had won the prize for his essay, he had moved further towards the Romantics and was anything but happy with what he had written.[55]

A prominent representative of the universal philosophical theory of grammar in England during the eighteenth was James Harris, whose *Hermes or a philosophical enquiry concerning language and universal grammar* was published in 1751.[56] Harris's thought can be associated with the so-called Cambridge Platonists; while continental expositions of universal rationalist grammar based themselves in the main on Descartes. Harris, who was an Aristotelian scholar and very well read in ancient philosophy and literature, looked to Aristotle for the philosophical foundations of grammar. Like all universalists Harris had to distinguish between the individual structural differences of particular languages and 'those principles that are essential to them all'.[57] In his theory of word meaning he followed Aristotle closely; words are related to what they designate by convention and language is 'a system of articulate voices significant by compact'.[58] Sentence and word as universals are defined in Aristotelian terms as, respectively, a 'compound quantity of sound significant, of which certain parts are themselves also significant', and a 'sound significant, of which no part is itself significant'.[59]

Harris's system of grammar requires two 'principals', nouns (including pronouns) or 'substantives', 'significant of substances', and verbs or 'attributives', 'significant of attributes'.[60] Verbs include what are formally distinguishable as verbs proper, participles, and adjectives; this is very much in agreement with Plato and Aristotle on the *rhêma* (p. 31, above). Adverbs are a special type of attributives, being attributives of attributives, or second order attributives. Apart from the 'principals', languages distinguish two 'accessories', which lack independent meaning and may be compared to Aristotle's *sỳndesmoi* (except for Aristotle's inclusion of personal pronouns among them), divided into 'definitives' (articles and some pronominal words), which construct with a single word, and conjunctions (conjunctions and prepositions), which construct with two or more words.[61] Unlike the Greek grammarians, but following the Latin practice, Harris recognized interjections as a separate component of languages, though not a part of speech in the same way as the others.[62]

While basing his theory of universal grammar on Aristotelian doctrine, Harris was, unlike Aristotle, well aware of and interested in the surface differences between various languages; but just because the same function, as he considered it, was served by case inflexions in Latin and by prepositional phrases in English (*Brūtī, of Brutus*), one must look more deeply for the identification of those universal categories of grammar and relations which alone can give significance to the purely formal grammars of particular languages.[63]

In his theory of meaning Harris regarded the 'principal' words, that had independent meaning, as 'primarily, essentially and immediately' the symbols of general ideas, and only secondarily and via these general ideas the symbols of particular ideas.[64] He defended the concept of innate ideas against the prevalent English empiricist attitude, and along with his insistence on universal grammar he considered that the capacity of mankind to frame universal or general ideas, of which words were the signs, was certainly God-given.[65] As a philosopher he paid most attention to language as the means of expressing logical propositions; but while he linked his theory of language with Aristotle and with philosophical universalism, in a number of ways he looked forward to developments characteristic of the thought of the later eighteenth century. Indeed, his use of the Aristotelian distinction between matter and form (*hýlē* (ὕλη) *and eîdos* (εἶδος)) with reference to the phonic substance and the semantic function of speech foreshadows the important doctrine of *innere Sprachform* set out in the work of W. von Humboldt early in the nineteenth century.[66]

In stressing the importance of universals in the use of language, Harris agreed with Condillac as well as with Herder, who praised his work,[67] in linking the faculty of speech with the faculty of abstraction and the recognition of recurrent phenomena and persisting entities resembling one another. Condillac cited Locke in this part of his treatise; Locke attributed generality to ideas, though his more consistently empiricist successors, Berkeley and Hume, considered that generality could be properly predicted

only in terms, i.e. of words, not ideas.[68] With Herder, Harris
shared the recognition of the significance to be seen in the individual peculiarities of each language. Though he erected his
linguistic theory on underlying universals, as a philosophical
grammarian must, he laid more weight on the individuality of languages and their intimate connection with the history and life of
the people who speak them than some previous philosophical
grammarians had done, and in this he looked forward to the linguistic attitudes most characteristic of the Romantic movement.[69]
In an eloquent passage he enlarged and illustrated his theme
in his eulogy of the twin excellences of Greek thinkers and
writers and of the Greek language uniquely fitted to give them
expression.[70]

Harris's *Hermes* is somewhat better known than it might otherwise have been because it was the target for attack by Horne
Tooke. Tooke was a man of wide interests and involvements; he
wrote a number of political pamphlets, and played a leading part
in an appeal for subscriptions in aid of relatives of American
colonists killed by British troops at Lexington in 1775, for which
in the illiberal manner of authorities engaged in warfare King
George's justices fined him £200 and imprisoned him for a year
(he attributed his later gout to the poor quality of the claret available in the King's Bench prison). As Tooke was a natural rebel
and Harris occupied a position in what today would be called 'the
establishment', Harris was an obvious opponent,[71] and it happened that Tooke's thinking about language was violently
antagonistic to the tradition of philosophical grammar such as had
been expounded by Harris.

It was not difficult to fault Harris for his obscurity of language
in several places, and for apparent self-contradictions, as when,
struggling with the semantics of some of his 'accessories' (a problem on which linguistic theory is still unsettled), Harris declared
that conjunctions shared the attributes both of words having signification and of those having no signification of their own,[72] nor
to criticize his erection of an alleged universal system of grammar
on the basis of an inadequate factual knowledge of languages, as
when he allowed a place for prepositions, but not for postposi-
tions such as are found with comparable syntactic and semantic
functions in Hungarian and Turkish (and in several other major
languages not cited by Tooke).[73] Harris also opened his defences
to Tooke's onslaught when he declared that a 'distant analogy'
determined that the sun and moon are naturally assigned nouns
of masculine and feminine genders respectively, in defiance
or ignorance of the facts of the Germanic languages and of
Russian.[74]

Tooke's ideas on language are set out in a number of dialogues in which he gives himself a part, somewhat loosely and inconsequentially put together in dialogue form in *Epea pteroenta or the diversions of Purley*,[75] first published in two volumes in 1786 and 1805. Tooke's style is often pungent and racy; the following passage from a footnote (typically attacking Harris and seeking to explain away his undoubted estimation) may be cited as characteristic of the author and his writing, and of a period in English history when publicly uttered personal abuse was treated almost as an art form: 'For which [Harris's reputation] however I can easily account; not by supposing that its doctrine gave any more satisfaction to their minds who quoted it than to mine; but because, as judges shelter their knavery by precedents, so do scholars their ignorance by authority: and when they cannot reason, it is safer and less disgraceful to repeat that nonsense at second hand which they would be ashamed to give originally as their own.'[76]

Tooke's approach to grammar is partly in line with modern formal doctrines; gender for him is, as a grammatical category, primarily an exponent of syntactic constructions involving nominals in those languages wherein it appears.[77] This is because it was strongly empiricist in its methodology, owing much to the philosopher Locke, as Horne Tooke readily acknowledged. In this Lockean empiricist stance he certainly impressed his English contemporaries, especially in the natural sciences, and his political opinions pleased the radicals and the utilitarians. Such was his influence that a modern scholar has asserted that it was Horne Tooke who, for thirty years, 'kept England immune to the new philology', which was being so eagerly pursued in Germany and was to dominate European and American linguistic scholarship during the nineteenth century.[78]

His theory of language, as he expounded it, was a continuation of eighteenth-century opinions and research on the origin and development of human language as a general human capability and activity, following the same interests as those of Condillac and others, and in part repeating Condillac's thoughts on the gradual passage of independent naturalistic cries to the structured and highly organized languages, ancient and modern, with which we are familiar. In a flourish characteristic of his style he wrote: 'The dominion of speech is erected upon the downfall of interjections.' The objective of this evolutionary development was to enable us to communicate our thoughts with greater ease or 'dispatch' (a Lockean term).[79]

In the same vein he admitted only two essential parts of speech, the noun and the verb; every other word class was the result of 'abbreviation', by which languages were made to run more smoothly.[80] This argument was supported by his etymological examples, which are freely given in his book. Tooke's etymology, though historically oriented, is also of the eighteenth-century and earlier type, not the rigorously controlled language-family-specific formal-semantic etymology of the nineteenth-century comparative historical linguists, such as were being assembled at the time by August Pott, for example, for his *Etymologische Forschungen* and which were to become the acknowledged essential foundation for comparative historical linguistics (p. 189, below).

In Tooke's etymological justification for his theory of the development of language, adjectives and participles were just verbs used adjectivally ('adjectived') by position and syntax. English prepositions like *from* were to be etymologically derived from a recoverable, once existing, noun meaning 'origin'; and the first element in words like *beside* and *below* was 'merely the imperative *be*'.[81] Many more such unsustainable etymologies could be cited from his book.

Like others in the eighteenth century and afterwards, Tooke regarded inflexional and derivational elements in words as fragments of earlier independent words agglutinated to the root word. Again, some of his identifications are upheld by the scrutiny of later strictly controlled etymology, as with the English adjectival suffix *-ful* (*beautiful*, etc.), but others are certainly not, as when he derived Latin $\bar{\imath}b\bar{o}$, I shall go, from $\bar{\imath}$-, to go, plus *b-* (=Greek *boul-* (βουλ-), to wish) plus (*eg*)*o*, I, and *audiam*, I shall hear, from *audī(re)*, to hear, plus *am*(*ō*), I love (i.e. I want to hear)![82]

The view, also found in Condillac (p. 165, above) that morphological variation in word forms arises from the agglutination of independent words is borne out by historical evidence in a number of formations in languages. We can trace the coalescence, no doubt after the word order became fixed, of *dōnāre habeō* to *donnerai*, I shall give, in French, and similar forms in other Romance languages; and the suffixed articles of the Scandinavian languages and of Romanian are derived from earlier demonstrative pronouns occupying a position immediately after the nouns to which they referred (local late Latin *lupus ille*> Romanian *lupul*, the wolf). A sort of half-way stage can be seen today in the much more tightly bound and positionally fixed pronouns and negative elements in French verbal expressions as compared with their freely mobile antecedents in Latin. This is partly recognized orthographically in the hyphenation of such forms when occurring postverbally (e.g. *montrez-le-nous*, show it to us!, cp. Italian *mandatecelo*, send it to us!). But it is naively simplistic to suppose that all morphology can be ascribed to this process, and still more so to attempt to identify the independent originals of all the bound morphemes of contemporary or attested languages.

James Harris's linguistic work was highly valued by another eighteenth century British linguist, James Burnett (Lord Monboddo), a prominent figure in the literary and scientific life of Edinburgh, who wrote a six-volume treatise *Of the origin and progress of language*,[83] which included extensive accounts of the classical languages and some modern European languages and a discourse on literary style. Like Harris, Monboddo did not wish to deny divine intervention in the creation of so wonderful and complex a faculty as language,[84] but he turned his attention more towards its historical development than to the assertion of linguistic universals. He saw the intimate connexion between human society and human speech, but only envisaged a unilateral dependence between them, in that society may have existed for many ages before the invention of language, but this invention depended on the prior existence of society. He was quite prepared to admit the polygenesis of language, and though 'primitive languages' were said to lack facilities for abstract expressions, Monboddo asserted that man must have formed ideas of universals before he invented the words to symbolize them.[85] Herder's conception of the parallel origin and development of speaking and thinking is much more plausible.

Monboddo was among an unfortunately large number of linguists who have thought that the origin of language could be partly brought to light by the study of certain existing languages, seeking evidence of primitivity and the continuance of early characteristics in the languages of culturally primitive and illiterate peoples. These arguments that 'primitive languages' contain little abstract vocabulary and an inadequate grammatical organization are also seen in Herder, who knew and approved of Monboddo's work and saw the first volume translated into German in 1784.[86] They are also found in later writers, with less and less justification as linguistic descriptions of remote languages grew in numbers and in quality.

Monboddo's evidence of linguistic underdevelopment in the existence of one word expressions for a thing and its possessor was singularly unfortunate,[87] since he needed to look no further than Hungarian and Finnish among European languages to find precisely the same formation (Hungarian *lábam*, my foot, *virágunk*, our flower; Finnish *käteni*, my hand); and descriptive study of the languages of preliterates and culturally primitive people in no way bears out Monboddo's allegation that such languages are without the differentiation of word classes and syntactic rules.[88] His linguistic limitations are seen on the one hand in his dismissal of the language of the Chinese as 'exceedingly defective' and his assumption that in consequence they could not have made any progress in philosophy, and on the other in his statement that Sanskrit was 'formed . . . upon principles of philosophy, like Wilkins's artificial "real character"'.[89]

It is all too easy to find fault with eighteenth-century attempts at the historical study of language. What is noteworthy is that thinkers in different countries and with diverse backgrounds were drawn towards the history of language on the eve of a century wherein the history of languages, enlivened by a flash of light from the east, was to make unprecedented advances.

For further consultation

H. A. ARSLEFF, *From Locke to Saussure*, London, 1982.

——, *The study of language in England*, 1780–1860, Princeton, 1967 (second edition, London, 1983).

W. S. ALLEN, *Phonetics in ancient India*, London, 1953.

H. ARENS *Sprachwissenschaft: der Gang ihrer Entwicklung von der Antike bis zur Gegenwart*, Freiburg/Munich (second edition), 1969, 80–152.

S. K. BELVALKAR, *Systems of Sanskrit grammar*, Poona, 1915.

T. BENFEY, *Geschichte der Sprachwissenschaft und orientalischen Philologie in Deutschland*, Munich, 1869.

J. BROUGH, 'Theories of general linguistics in the Sanskrit grammarians', *TPS* 1951, 27–46.

——, 'Some Indian theories of meaning', *TPS* 1953, 161–76.

P. C. CHAKRAVARTI, *The philosophy of Sanskrit grammar*, Calcutta, 1930.

——, *The linguistic speculations of the Hindus*, Calcutta, 1933.

E. B. DE CONDILLAC, *Essai sur l'origine des connoissances humaines* (*Oeuvres de Condillac*, ed. G. LE ROY Paris, 1947, volume I, 1–118).

B. FADDEGON, *Studies on Pāṇini's grammar*, Amsterdam, 1936.

O. FUNKE, *Zur Sprachphilosophie des achtzehnten Jahrhunderts. James Harris's 'Hermes'* (*Studien zur Geschichte der Sprachphilosophie*, Berne, 1927, 5–48).

——, *Englische Sprachphilosophie im späteren 18 Jahrhundert*, Berne, 1934.

E. HEINTEL, *Johann Gottfried Herder: sprachphilosophische Schriften*, Hamburg, 1964.

J. G. HERDER, *Abhandlung über den Ursprung der Sprache* (*Herder's sämmtliche Werke*, (ed. B. SUPHAN), Berlin, 1891, volume 5, 1–156).

P. JULIARD, *The philosophies of language in eighteenth-century France*, The Hague, 1970.

B. LEIBIG, *Panini: ein Beitraag zur Kenntnis der indischen Literatur und Grammatik*, Leipzig, 1891.

V. N. MIŚRA, *The descriptive technique of Pānini: an introduction*, The Hague, 1966.

K. K. RAJA, *Indian theories of meaning*, Madras, 1963.

R. ROCHER, ''Agent' et 'object' chez Pānini', *JAOS* 84 (1964), 44–54.

J. J. ROUSSEAU, *Essai sur l'origine des langues (Oeuvres de J. J. Rousseau*, Paris, 1822, volume 13, 163–257).

E. SAPIR, 'Herder's 'Ursprung der Sprache'', *Modern Philology*, 5 (1907–8), 109–42.

T. A. SEBEOK, *Historiography of linguistics*, 3–67, 383–606.

J. F. STAAL, 'Sanskrit philosophy of language', *Current trends in linguistics* (ed. T. A. SEBEOK) 5 (1969), 499–531.

——, (ed.), *A reader on the Sanskrit grammarians*, Cambridge, Mass., 1972.

P. THIEME, 'Pāṇini and the pronunciation of Sanskrit', E. PULGRAM (ed.), *Studies presented to Joshua Whatmough*, The Hague, 1957, 263–70.

Notes

1. Quoted, *inter alia*, on J. E. SANDYS, *History of classical scholarship* (third edition), Cambridge, 1921, volume 2. 438–9; C. F. HOCKETT, 'sound change', *Language* 41 (1965), 185–204.

2. ARENS, 1969, 73; BENFEY, 1869, 336–8; L. KUKENHEIM, *Esquisse historique de la linguistique française*, Leiden, 1962, 31.

3. HEIDELBERG, 1808, ix: '. . . die Liebe für dieses Studium, wenigstens vorläufig. auch in Deutschland anzufachen.' In BENFEY, 1869, 380: 'Ich würde mich glücklich schatzen, wenn ich etwas dazu beitragen könnte, das Studium des Sanskrit in Deutschland einheimisch zu machen.'

4. ALLEN, 1953, 6.

5. R. A. MILLER, *Studies in the grammatical tradition in Tibet*, 1976 (*Amsterdam studies in the theory and history of linguistics* 6).

6. RAJA, 1963, 51.

7. BROUGH, 1953, 176–8.

8. B. MALINOWSKI, *Coral gardens and their magic*, London, 1935, volume 2, 11.

9. CHAKRAVARTI, 1930, 84–125, 1933, 42–7; BROUGH, 1951; L. HJELMSLEV, *Prolegomena to a theory of language* (tr. F. J. WHITFIELD), Baltimore, 1953, 73-6.

10. ALLEN, 1953, 7.

11. R. JAKOBSON, *Selected writings I: phonological studies*, The Hague, 1962, 438 and *passim*.

12. ALLEN, 1953, 5; ibid., 3–7, 90. Much of the scholarly writing on ancient Indian linguistics presupposes a considerable prior knowledge of Sanksrit, making it difficult of access to the linguist who is not also a Sanskritist. This is unfortunate; the linguistic treatises of the Indians and the theories, insights, and methodology

that they contain are an important part of any comprehensive historical view of the subject and they should be understood and appreciated by as many linguists as possible. In the case of the Indian phoneticians Allen's *Phonetics in ancient India* (1953) may be unhesitatingly recommended. Though the Sanskrit passages and technical terms are given, with full references to the sources and the technical literature, no knowledge of Sanskrit is required for the understanding of his account, from which an excellent picture of the achievement of the Indians in phonetics and phonology can be grasped.

13. ibid., 35.

14. T. BURROW, *The Sanskrit language*, London, 1955, 114.

15. ALLEN, 1953, 50, 89.

16. M. B. EMENEAU, 'The nasal phonemes of Sanskrit', *Language*, 22 (1946), 86–93.

17. Details in ALLEN, 1953. The development of /ɲ/ as a phoneme in some Middle Indian dialects may have been a contributory factor (EMENEAU, op. cit., 90–2); L. RENOU, 'Pāṇini', *Current trends in linguistics* 5 (1969), 481–98.

18. L. BLOOMFIELD, *Language*, London, 1935, 11; P. THIEME, *Pāṇini and the Vedas*, Allahabad, 1935, ix.

19. B. SHEFTS, Grammatical method in *Pāṇini*, New Haven, 1961, ix.

20. *Language* 5 (1920), 270. It is difficult without a thorough knowledge of Sanskrit to manage an adequate appreciation of Pāṇini's grammatical exposition, even though translations into European languages have been available for some time, such as O. BÖHTLINGK, *Pāṇini's Grammatik, herausgegeben, übersetzt, erlautert und mit verschiedenen Indices versehen* (1887, reprinted Hildesheim, 1964), and L. RENOU, *La grammaire de Pāṇini traduite du sanskrit avec des extraits des commentaires indigènes* (Paris, 1966). For English readers the most useful translation now is S. M. KATRE, *Aṣṭādhyāyī of Pāṇini* (Austin, 1987), with a brief introductory essay, roman transliterations of each *sūtra* with English translations. See also M. Winternitz, *A history of Indian literature* (tr. S. KETKAR), Calcutta, 1927, 40–6.

21. BROUGH, 1953, 162–3; J. R. FIRTH, 'Synopsis of linguistic theory', *Studies in linguistic analysis* (Special volume of the Philological Society, Oxford, 1957), 17; see further B. K. MATILAL, 'Indian theorists on the nature of the sentence', *Foundations of language* 2 (1966), 377–93; cp. p. 91, above.

22. CHAKRAVARTI, 1930, chapter 8; BLOOMFIELD, *Language*, 235. The Sanskrit terms themselves exemplify the categories that they refer to: *tatpuruṣa*, his-servant; *bahuvrīhi*, (possessing) much-rice.

23. ROCHER, 1964. The concept of *kāraka* is more akin to the abstract underlying cases proposed by C. J. FILLMORE, 'The case for case', *Universals in linguistic theory*, New York, 1968 1–88, and as used by J. M. ANDERSON, *On case grammar: prolegomena to a theory of grammatical relations*, Cambridge, 1977, and by the generative grammarians in Government and Binding theory (cp. G. C. HOR-

ROCKS, *Generative grammar*, London, 1987, 102–8. It must not be assumed, of course, that the Indian grammarians and the modern linguists just cited are all expounding the same theory; they are, however, operating with similar conceptual frameworks to explicate roughly the same aspects of syntactic relationships.

24. *Language* 5 (1929), 267–76.
25. BUISKOOL, 1939, 12–13.
26. N. CHOMSKY and M. HALLE, *The sound pattern of English*, New York, 1968, 220. cp. STAAL 1969.
27. cp. BLOOMFIELD, *Language* 5 (1929), 272–4.
28. *TCLP* 8 (1939), 105–15; ALLEN, 'Zero and Pānini', *Indian linguistics* 16 (1955), 106–13 (122).
29. The sounds used as demarcative symbols are bracketed.
30. ALLEN, 1953, 58, suggests an appropriate translation: 'a = [ə]'.
31. ALLEN, 'Zero and Pānini'; F. DE SAUSSURE, *Cours de linguistique générale* (fourth edition), Paris, 1949, 255–6; H. A. GLEASON, *Introduction to descriptive linguistics*, revised edition, New York, 1961, 76; W. HAAS, 'Zero in linguistic analysis', *Studies in linguistic analysis*, 33–53.
32. BENFEY, 1869, 383, called Wilkins 'the father of European Sanskrit studies'.
33. HERODOTUS 2.2.
34. CONDILLAC, 1947, 1–118.
35. F. C. GREEN (ed.), *Discours sur l'origine et les fondements de l'inégalité parmis les hommes*, Cambridge, 1941 (reference to Condillac, pages 41–2).
36. ROUSSEAU, 1822.
37. CONDILLAC, 1947, 84. A set of essays on Condillac's linguistic thought is published in J. SGARD *et al* (eds.), *Condillac et les problèmes du langage*, Geneva /Paris, 1982. Informed discussion on the conditions and the stage in which human speech may have begun and developed continues today, in some respects on lines remarkably similar to Condillac's ideas on the subject. cp. S. R. HARNAD *et al.* (eds), *Origin and evolution of language and speech*, *Annals of the New York Academy of Sciences*, vol. 280 (1976).
38. *Discours*, 45.
39. CONDILLAC, 1947, 64–9.
40. ibid., 69, 94.
41. ROUSSEAU, 1822, chapters 5 and 7.
42. ibid., 255: 'langues favorables à la liberté; ce sont les langues sonores, prosodiques, harmonieuses, dont on distingue le discours de fort loin. Les nôtres sont faites pour le bourdonnement des divans'.
43. J. P. SÜSSMILCH, *Versuch eines Beweises dass die erste Sprache ihren Ursprung nicht vom Menschen sondern allein vom Schöpfer erhalten habe*, Berlin, 1766; ROUSSEAU, *Discours*, 48–9; PLATO, *Cratylus* 397 C. 425 D; ALLEN, 'Ancient ideas on the origin and development of language', *TPS* 1948, 35–60.
44. HERDER, 1891.
45. *Herder's sämmtliche Werke*, ed. B. SUPHAN, Berlin, 1877, volume 2.

46. *Werke* 2, 24–6.
47. ibid., 26–8.
48. e.g. CONDILLAC, 1947, 61, 98–104, and in *Cours d'études pour l'instruction du Prince de Parme*, *Oeuvres* volume 1, 403. See further H. AARSLEFF, 'The tradition of Condillac', in AARSLEFF, 1982, 146–209.
49. SAPIR, 1907–8, 141; CHOMSKY, *Current issues*, 17–21, *Aspects of the theory of syntax*, Cambridge, Mass., 1965, 4, 8–9, 51.
50. HERDER, 1891, 34–5. ibid., 36.
51. ibid., 64–7; O. JESPERSEN, *Language*, London, 1922, chapter 20; FIRTH, *Speech*, London, 1930, chapter 6.
52. HERDER, 1891, 82–9.
53. ibid., 52–4, 134.
54. F. MCEACHRAN, *The life and philosophy of Johann Gottfried Herder*, Oxford, 1939, 32, and *passim*; R. G. COLLINGWOOD, *The idea of history*, Oxford, 1946, 86–93.
55. SAPIR, 1907–8, 137–8. A useful translation of ROUSSEAUS *Essai sur l'origine des langues* and of HERDER's *Abhandluing über den Ursprung der Sprache* is available in J. H. MORAN and A. GODE (tr.), *On the origin of language*, Chicago, 1966.
56. Pagination from the third edition, London, 1771.
57. HARRIS, op. cit., 7, 11.
58. ibid., 314–15, 328–9; ARISTOTLE, *De interpretatione*, 2, 4 (p. 22, above).
59. HARRIS, op. cit., 19–20.
60. ibid., 23–6, 192–3, 291–2.
61. ibid., 30–31.
62. ibid., 289–90.
63. ibid., 25–6.
64. ibid., 347–9.
65. ibid., 350–402.
66. ibid., 315; pp. 193–4, below.
67. *Werke* 15, Berlin, 1888, 181–2.
68. CONDILLAC, 1947, 89–91, J. LOCKE, *An essay concerning human understanding*, London, 1690, 2.11.9, 4.7.9.
69. HARRIS, op. cit., 409–11; FUNKE, 1934, 8–18.
70. HARRIS, op. cit., 419–24.
71. J. HORNE TOOKE, *Epea pteroenta or the diversions of Purley*, volume 1, London, 1829, 71.
72. HARRIS, op. cit., 259; TOOKE, op. cit., 112.
73. TOOKE, op. cit., 271–5.
74. HARRIS, op. cit., 45; TOOKE, op. cit., 53.
75. ἔπεα πτερόεντα, 'winged words', a stock phrase in Homer.
76. TOOKE, op. cit., 121.
77. ibid., 54.
78. TOOKE, op. cit., chapter 2; AARSLEFF, 1983, 70–4, 88–90. It was also said that knowledge of German was a rare accomplishment in late

eighteenth- and early nineteenth-century England (AARSLEFF, op. cit., 220–1). But see also A. BEYER, *Deutsche Einflüsse an die englische Sprachwissenschaft im 19. Jahrhundert*, Göppingen, 1981. A fairly lonely voice raised against Tooke at the time was J. FEARN'S *Anti-Tooke; or an analysis of the principles and structures of language, exemplified in the English tongue*, London, 1824–7 (reprinted in *Grammatica universalis*, 7.1, 7.2 (ed. H. E. BREKLE), Stuttgart 1972; cp. BREKLE, *Einführung in die Geschichte der Sprachwissenschaft*, Darmstadt, 1985, 153–70).

79. TOOKE, op.cit., 61; LOCKE, *Essay concerning human understanding*, 3.6.32.
80. TOOKE, op. cit., chapter 3.
81. TOOKE, op. cit., 377–83, volume 2, 469; cp. AARSLEFF, 1983, chapter 2.
82. TOOKE, op. cit., volume 2, 431–2.
83. Edinburgh, 1773–92 (reference to HARRIS, volume 1, 8).
84. ibid., volume 1, 191–2.
85. ibid., volume 1, 196–7, 302, 395–400.
86. R. HAYM, *Herder*, Berlin, 1880–5, volume 2, 224.
87. MONBODDO, op. cit., volume 1, 364–5.
88. ibid., volume 1, 370.
89. ibid., volume 2, 432–3, 481.

Chapter 7

Comparative and historical linguistics in the nineteenth century

It is a commonplace in linguistics to say that the nineteenth century was the era of the comparative and historical study of languages, more especially of the Indo-European languages. This is broadly justified, but it does not mean either that no historical research based on the comparison of languages was undertaken before that time or that all other aspects of linguistics were neglected during the nineteenth century. It is, however, the case that this century saw the development of modern conceptions, theoretical and methodological, of comparative and historical linguistics, and the greatest concentration of scholarly effort and scholarly ability in linguistics was devoted to this aspect of the subject rather than to others. As late as 1922, O. Jespersen, who did as much as many to foster synchronic, descriptive, linguistics, could write in the still prevailing nineteenth-century climate of opinion that linguistics was mainly a historical study[1]; and some of the most stimulating ideas on language structure suggested at the start of the century were applied first to a primarily historical view of language.

One can rightly speak of pre-nineteenth-century historical work on languages as sporadic, not because it necessarily lacked insight or an appreciation of what was involved, but because people's suggestions and researches remained largely in isolation, and since they were not taken up and developed by a continuous succession of scholars, each new thinker had little to build on or to react to. This was not so after 1800, when one is brought face to face with a remarkable continuity of scholarship focused on a specialized field of theory and practice, in which generations of men, mostly Germans or scholars from other countries trained in

Germany, built up their subject on the basis of what had been done by their predecessors or earlier contemporaries. They might start from where those before them had left off, or they might react against what they had considered errors of fact or misdirections of theory; but the sense of continuity of achievement, leading to a culmination, though not, of course, a stopping point, towards the end of the century, must be regarded both as a tribute to the scholarship of the time and as an inspiration to those looking back today on this remarkable century of successful endeavour.

Work on the historical relations of particular groups of languages by European writers may be said to have begun with Dante (1265–1321), though the relationship of Icelandic and English by virtue of resemblances in word forms had been asserted in the twelfth century by the brilliant 'First Grammarian' (pp. 82–3 above). Dante's *De vulgari eloquentia* has already been mentioned in connection with the post-mediaeval rise in status of the European vernacular languages (p. 114, above); this same work gives an account of the genesis of dialect differences and thence of different languages from a single source language as the result of the passage of time and the geographical dispersion of speakers.[2] Dante recognized three properly European language families: Germanic in the north, Latin in the south, and Greek occupying part of Europe and adjacent Asia.[3] He divided the contemporary Latin area into three distinct vernacular languages all descended from the Latin preserved by the grammarians; this common descent was shown by the considerable numbers of words that each shared with the others and which could be referred to a single Latin word.

As diagnostic marks of his language divisions Dante used a method seen again in J. J. Scaliger (pp. 182–3, below) and enshrined as a labelling device in the much later binary division of Indo-European into the *centum* and *satem* groups. He chose a single word meaning and noted its expression in different languages; thus the Germanic languages reply in the affirmative with 'iò' (*ja*, etc.), and the three Latin-derived languages use 'si' (Latin *sīc*) in Italy, 'oc' (Latin *hoc*) in southern France, and 'oil' (Latin *hoc ille*) in northern France (*hoc ille*, he (does) this, had become generalized as the affirmative reply to a question in this area[4]). From this division spring the names of the main linguistic regions of France, *Langue d'oc* (Provençal) in the south and *Langue d'oil* in the north.

Within these language areas Dante was keenly aware of dialectal differences, and in subsequent chapters he explores the possibility and desirability of a cultivated standard Italian for the whole peninsula and gives a most detailed and well exemplified survey of the Italian dialects, together with aesthetic judgments pronounced on them, in which none is rated perfect but the local Tuscan and Roman dialects of this day are dismissed with contempt.[5]

All this detailed classification is set within the conception of linguistic differentiation in the world having arisen in the way described in the story of the Tower of Babel (Genesis II), Hebrew being the first language spoken on earth before the building of the Tower, the language spoken by Adam as the gift of God.[6]

The monogenesis of all languages and the ascription of the status of the original or oldest language to Hebrew was a generally held idea during the first centuries of the Christian era, when science had to be reconciled with the literally interpreted creation story of Genesis. It may be compared with the early efforts of geologists and zoologists to fit their observations into the apparent chronology and sequence of events given in the Old Testament.[7] The monogenesis of all languages in Hebrew continued to be accepted for several centuries and, perhaps more important theoretically, when it was challenged, it was challenged by the submission of a rival language as the surviving original or 'oldest language'. The fact that Latin, the parent of the Romance languages, also survived as a written language in use during the period before the Renaissance, and as the spoken language of Roman Catholic church services and as a *lingua franca* for educated persons, may have made the conception of a more general surviving linguistic ancestor more plausible. Notorious in this sort of challenge was Goropius Becanus, who in a marvellous series of etymologies argued that the 'first' language, 'Cimmerian', survived in Dutch-Flemish[8]; but he was not the only one.

Alternative models of the historical relations of languages were not lacking during the period from Dante to Sir William Jones (early studies in the history of the Romance languages by Renaissance scholars have been noticed above, pp. 114–5); it was just that they were not taken up and developed by their contemporaries. J. J. Scaliger (1540–1609), son of J. C. Scaliger (p. 123, above), a scholar of wide and varied learning, dispensed with two fallacious dogmas that distorted the historical dimension of language study, the supposed linear historical relation between Greek and Latin, whereby Latin was thought to be directly descended from a dialect of Greek with some alien admixtures (cp. p. 57, above), and the alleged origin of all languages in Hebrew. Scaliger recognized eleven language families, four major and seven minor ones, covering the continent of Europe, within which the member languages were genetically related but between which no relationship could be established. These families agree broadly with modern groupings in so far as their member languages are concerned, but comprise what are now recognized as subfamilies of separate larger families, among them Indo-European and Finno-Ugrian.

The families which Scaliger conceived as the products of earlier single languages, on the model of Latin and the Romance languages, he designated *Muttersprachen* or *Matrices linguae* (mother tongues). The four major families in his eleven correspond to the present-day Romance, Greek, Germanic, and Slavic groups within Indo-European. Working on the basis of lexical similarities between members of a family, he named each family by reference to the words for 'God', which showed obvious likenesses in form within each but not with the words in the other three. Thus he wrote of *Deus* languages, *Theós* languages, *Godt* languages, and *Boge* languages, respectively. In view of his insight and its results one must regret that he did not look further into word forms exhibiting rather obvious similarities across the four families, before denying any relationship between them either lexical or grammatical.[9]

Further attempts at a classification of the languages of the world known to contemporary Europeans and studies in the comparative method itself were made by seventeenth-century scholars, and towards the end of the seventeenth century a more developed model of historical relationship between languages was put forward by two Swedish scholars. G. Stiernhielm (who continued to regard Hebrew as the source of all languages), in his edition of the Gothic Bible, set side by side the inflexions of Latin *habēre* and Gothic *haban* (to have), and despite the noncognation of the roots, of which he was unaware, he could argue from the personal endings that the two languages were closely related descendants of a single ancestor.[10] In a public lecture, A. Jäger spoke of an ancient language spreading, as the result of migrations, over Europe and part of Asia and producing thereby 'daughter' languages which in turn produced the languages known today as Persian, Greek, the Romance languages, the Slavic languages, Celtic, Gothic and the Germanic languages, while no trace of the original mother tongue survived.[11]

Nearly a century after Scaliger, Leibniz (1646–1716) turned his attention to historical linguistics in the course of his better known philosophical speculations and discussions of synchronic linguistic questions (p. 126, above). Leibniz saw no reason to discount a monogenetic theory of the world's languages, but he did not seek their origin in any actually living or attested language, and he firmly placed Hebrew within the Arabic family. Leibniz went to the opposite extreme from Scaliger; like Scaliger's, his smaller groups correspond with those made today, and Leibniz was one of the first to posit historical relations between Finnish and Hungarian, but he went further and on the basis of alleged common word 'roots' he set up two major divisions of the original language, Japhetic or Kelto-Scythian (a term used also by others) and Aramaic, covering respectively the languages of the north, including all Europe, and the languages of the south; thus he could link his system of relations between languages with the Biblical story of the sons of Noah (Genesis 10).[12]

Leibniz indicated some of the principles by which historical linguistic research is fruitfully undertaken. He pointed to the evidence in place names and river names of the earlier distribution of languages over areas from which they had later receded either through the expulsion of the speakers or the replacement of the language after the arrival of new-comers; Leibniz refers to the Basque language, now confined to a corner of the Franco-Spanish border country in the western Pyrenees, whose extension over a larger area in the Iberial peninsula is attested in this way.[13]

In view of the importance of etymological study in historical linguistics, Leibniz pressed for the preparation of grammars and dictionaries of the languages of the world, linguistic atlases, and a universal roman-based alphabet into which the non-roman scripts of languages could be transliterated. In particular he tried to encourage the rulers of Russia to begin surveying the many non-European languages of their territory and the collection of word lists and standard texts from them. Mention may be made here also of J. Ludolf, 1624–1704, writer of Amharic and Ethiopic grammars, who in correspondence with Leibniz stressed the need for morphological as well as lexical evidence for establishing historical relationships.[14]

The systematic gathering of material that was going to serve in the comparative study of languages had been going on as a notable feature of the centuries after the Renaissance when the European world was expanding so rapidly. Word lists and language surveys, interlingual dictionaries, and texts, usually those forming part of Christian worship and in particular the Lord's Prayer, were laboriously prepared and published, more especially in the eighteenth century. Two such surveys went under the title *Mithridates,* is deference to the polyglot monarch of ancient Pontus) (p. 55, above), the first by the Swiss C. Gesner in

1555, the second on the eve of the new era of historical studies in 1806 and 1817 by J. C. Adelung.[15]

Adelung's exposition stands typically on the borders between the older unsystematized periods of speculation and collection and the later epoch of the organization of genetically related families. His groupings were those of geographical propinquity, which he invested with historical significance, thus associating Greek and Latin in one closely united family. However, writing when he did, he included Sanskrit among the languages of India, and like Jones before him, he pointed to the unmistakable evidence in Sanskrit of its historical connection with the major languages of Europe.[16]

Catherine II's linguistic interests in her Russian dominions resulted in the publication in 1786–9 of comparative word lists from two hundred languages; these were compiled by the German P. S. Pallas, who saw his work in a wider context, since he entitled it *The comparative vocabularies of the languages of the whole world*.[17] Pallas's work was reviewed by C. J. Kraus in 1787, in an essay covering the important fields in which comparative linguistics must look for its advances: phonetics, semantics, grammatical structure, and the geographical location and distribution of languages.[18] By virtue both of its date and of its very real merits, this essay can still be read as an introduction to the study of comparative and historical linguistics.

Much of the gathering of diverse language material that took place in the eighteenth century must appear today rather haphazard and unformed by any comprehensive or directing theory, just as the rather general theories on the origin and development of language put out in the same period, which were noticed in the preceding chapter, seem to be largely empty speculation in the absence of adequate data from actual languages. But both these separate trends take their place in the stream of history, contingently but fortunately occurring in the years just prior to the seminal discovery of the relations between Sanskrit and the major languages of Europe, which in the favourable academic circumstances of the early nineteenth century was the stimulus to the integration of theory and data in an era of continuous progress.

During the eighteenth century, and, in fact, since the Renaissance, serious thought and factual investigations had continued on the historical relations between languages and on the historical or genetic families that could be discovered and established on these grounds. The main interest had lain in the comparison of vocabularies and structures of modern European languages with those of Latin, and in the obvious historical connection, whatever precisely it might be, between Latin and the Romance languages.

These historical investigations were accompanied, especially in the eighteenth century, by serious examination of the possible origin and development of human speech and language as such, again with reference both to vocabulary and to grammatical structure. Etymology, the historical study of items of vocabulary, and linguistic typology, as it is called today, were subjects of systematic exposition in articles in the French *Encyclopédie*, published in the second half of the eighteenth century, and a forerunner of nineteenth- and twentieth-century typology was established by the *Encyclopédistes* in their basic distinction between two opposing types or typological tendencies, *langues analytiques* and *langues transpositives*, broadly those, respectively, like several modern European languages that, with relatively little morphological features, rely on word order, supposedly the natural order of thought, and those like Latin and ancient Greek, possessing an extensive morphology, which could therefore indulge in much more variation in word order without affecting the grammar of their sentences. These writers also looked at the passage in time between one type and the other.[19]

It must be stressed, however, that though these fields of research were in general historically oriented they were not systematically distinguished. The *Encyclopédistes* refused to regard French as a direct descendant of Latin, because its grammatical structure, 'le génie principal de langue', was so different from that of French; French was instead considered to be the modern continuation of a much earlier Celtic language which, during the period of Roman rule, had incorporated very many Latin words.[20] And in this regard Sir William Jones, often thought of as a precursor of nineteenth-century established historical doctrine, on the strength of his famous paragraph eulogizing Sanskrit and propounding its historical kinship with most of the European languages (p. 149, above), was a man of the eighteenth century. In the quoted paragraph he relies on two proofs of common origin, etymology in the 'roots of verbs' and structure in the 'forms of grammar', and in another discourse he makes it clear that of the two he accords precedence to 'the similar grammatical arrangement' of languages being considered as genetically connected. Moreover, on the historical relation between modern Hindi and Sanskrit he is as firm in his judgment as were the *Encyclopédistes* on the relations between French and Latin; the discrepancies between the syntactic structures of the languages rule out a relation of descent, despite the fact of 'five in six words of Hindi being derived from Sanskrit'. But the indeterminacy of the methodology of the time is well illustrated by the quite opposite interpretation of the same facts only two years later by Halhed, who stated that, despite their structural differences, the etymological evidence was an irrefutable proof of the Sanskritic source of the language: 'It is indubitably derived from the Shanscrit. . . the same sounds are almost constantly applied in both languages to represent the same ideas . . . the inflexions . . . and the modes of grammatical regimen are widely different.'

An examination of the relevant literature of the seventeenth and eighteenth centuries shows how variously typological comparison and etymological correspondences were exploited and defended in the classification of languages into historical families. It was the achievement of the nineteenth century to separate clearly typology and etymology and to appreciate the proper role of each.[21]

In large part, linguistics in the nineteenth century was concentrated on the historical study of the Indo-European languages wherein most of the advances and refinements in method and theory took place. This period of linguistics was almost the preserve of German scholarship, and those working in it from other countries were either trained in Germany, like the American W. D. Whitney, or were German expatriates like Max Müller at Oxford. As was seen above, the European discovery of Sanskrit was the primary source of this development, and a number of the early scholars in historical linguistics were themselves Sanskritists, such as the brothers A. W. and F. Schlegel (1767–1845 and 1772–1829), F. Bopp (1791–1867), and A. F. Pott (1802–87).

In 1808 F. Schlegel published his treatise *On the language and the learning of the Indians* wherein he stressed the importance of studying the 'inner structures' of languages (i.e. their morphology) for the light that could be shed on their genetic relationships,[22] and it appears that the term *vergleichende Grammatik* ('comparative grammar', still a frequently used title for comparative and historical linguistics) was originated by Schlegel. It was indeed the comparison of the inflexional and derivational morphology of Sanskrit and the other Indo-European languages, especially Latin and Greek, on which the early comparatists concentrated. One may note the title of Bopp's publication of 1816, *On the conjugation system of Sanskrit, in comparison with that of Greek, Latin, Persian, and German,* and more significantly the title of T. Benfey's later account of the first half of the nineteenth century's work, *The history of linguistics and Oriental philology in Germany*. In the high tide of German nationalism, three years after the Prussian needle-gun had defeated the forces of Austria at Königgrätz and two years before the founding of the German Empire after the Franco-Prussian war, Benfey could write that the early workers in this field belonged among 'the brightest stars of the German intellectual heaven', and that the company of distinguished men who had contributed to the development of this branch of learning were almost exclusively the sons of the fatherland.[23]

Admitting the justice of this claim, one should none the less point out that two pioneering works on linguistic relationship through the comparative study of inflexions had been made outside Indo-European by non-German scholars at the end of the preceding century. In 1770 P. Sajnovics published his *Proof that the languages of the Hungarians and the Lapps are one and the same,* and in 1799 S. Gyármathi proved the historical kinship of Hungarian and Finnish.[24]

Four of the scholars best known in the linguistic science of the early nineteenth century are the Dane R. Rask (1787–1832) and the Germans J. Grimm (1785–1863), F. Bopp (1791–1867), and W. von Humboldt (1767–1835), and it is with Rask and Grimm that the comparative and historical study of the Indo-European family can be properly said to begin. The term *indogermanisch* (Indogermanic) appears first in 1823 and was used by Pott in 1833; in English *Indo-European* is cited from 1814.

It is often said, and justifiably said, that Rask, Grimm, and Bopp were the founders of scientific historical linguistics. Rask wrote the first systematic grammars of Old Norse and Old English[25]; and Grimm's *Deutsche Grammatik* (*Germanic* rather than *German grammar*)[26] is hailed as the start of Germanic linguistics. The now universal terms *strong* and *weak*, of inflexions (*stark* and *schwach*), *Ablaut* (vowel gradation), and *Umlaut* (vowel change ascribable to earlier environmental conditions), are all technical terms invented by Grimm; and though the existence of different sets of sound changes in the histories of individual languages had been asserted by A. Turgot in his article on etymology in the French *Encyclopaedia* in 1756,[27] it was Rask who first brought order into etymological relationships by setting out systematic comparisons of word forms, matching a sound in one language with a sound in another exemplified in numbers of different words. He wrote: 'If there is found between two languages agreement in the forms of indispensable words to such an extent that rules of letter changes can be discovered for passing from one to the other, then there is a basic relationship between these languages.'[28] The correspondences now known under the title of 'Grimm's law' were in fact first stated and illustrated by Rask in the work just quoted.

'Grimm's law' first appeared in the second edition of his *Deutsche Grammatik* (1822), after he had read Rask's work, in a long section on 'letters' (*von den Buchstaben*). With hindsight we see the importance in history of Grimm's formulation as the first of the sound laws that were to form the structure and support of Indo-European and of other language families. It remains the best known of all sets of sound correspondences within Indo-European, essentially embracing relations between consonant classes of three articulatory places and three types of release in the Germanic languages as compared with other Indo-European languages. These relations were set out by Grimm in Greek, Gothic, and Old High German; they needed later supplementation by Verner's law to account for the differential results of the place of the primitive word accent, and the traditional circularity with which the correspondences are set out, and Grimm's use of *Kreislauf* (rotation) to describe the successive changes from the pre-Germanic stage represented by Greek through Gothic to Old High German depended on the thoroughly unphonetic identification of aspirated plosives such as $[p^h]$, $[t^h]$, $[k^h]$, with the corresponding fricatives [f], [θ], [x] (or [h]), an identification surely only possible when the study of sound change was still undertaken as the study of letters. But though the terminology of 'letter changes' and some of its confusion persisted with Rask and Grimm, their work marks a very definite advance on the hitherto rather indiscriminate assumptions on the possibilities of substituting one sound (letter) for another in the history of languages (in his third edition (1840) Grimm retitled the section '*von den Lauten*' (on sounds)). Detailed exemplifications from specific languages, in relation to specific language families, and the later systematic study of etymologies such as Pott set out in his *Etymological investigations in the field of the Indogermanic languages*,[29] now began to replace the generalized *a priori* assumptions of eighteenth-century thinkers on the origin and development of language with mutually reinforcing sets of lexical correspondences between particular sets of words and morphemes in particular groups of languages, rather as a century later the descriptions of more and more languages were to constitute a necessary observational check and corrective to the speculations of the seventeenth- and eighteenth-century 'universal grammarians'.

One should, however, try to see the work of these early comparative and historical linguists in their contemporary context as well, not merely as they can be fitted into our own subsequent picture of the development of linguistics. The very term 'Grimm's law' is an anachronism; he did not make technical use of the word *law* to describe what he referred to as sound shift (*Lautverschiebung*); and in a much quoted passage he remarked: 'The sound shift is a general tendency; it is not followed in every case'.[30] Grimm and Bopp were very much the children of their own age, inspired by the historicism and nationalism characteristic of the Romantic era in which they lived and with which they were in sympathy. A. W. Schlegel was the German translator of Shakespeare, thereafter regarded as part of German literature (*'unser Shakespeare'*) and considered in spirit very much in tune with the *Sturm und Drang* (storm and stress) and Romantic movements in German life and letters. Grimm worked with his brother Wilhelm in collecting the German folktales that formed the basis of 'Grimm's fairy tales', known and loved by children the world over. This work along with Jacob Grimm's Germanic language studies belong to the general upsurge of national pride in the German language that began in the early eighteenth century, when Leibniz proposed the compilation of a dictionary of all the varieties of German,[31] and saw such a remarkable flowering in German literature from then on.

Grimm applied the ideas of Herder (p. 166–8, above) on the close relationship between a nation and its language to the historical dimension of language, seeing, indeed, in the sound shift to which he gave his name an early assertion of independence on the part of the ancestors of the German peoples,[32] nationalistic interpretations of linguistic phenomena carried still further by W. Scherer two generations later.[33]

Linguistic conceptions of the eighteenth century formed much of the setting for early nineteenth-century work. Rask's *Investigation* was an essay awarded a prize by the Danish Academy of Science for research into the source from which the ancient Scandinavian language could most surely be derived,[34] though he refused to recognize this 'source' in any extant or attested actual language. Bopp saw as the main purpose of his *Conjugation system* the reconstruction of the original grammatical structure of the language whose gradual disintegration had produced the attested languages of the Indo-European family.[35] Linguistic change was conceived as the breakdown of an original integral language state,[36] and Sanskrit was considered at this time to be, not indeed the original language of the family, but the nearest to it in morphological structure. In a striking metaphor Meillet declared that in his quest for the original state of the Indo-European language Bopp was led to discover the principles of comparative grammar as Christopher Columbus discovered America in his search for a new route to India.[37] In his later *Comparative grammar* Bopp declared his aims to be a comparative description of the languages concerned, an investigation of the laws governing them, and the origin of their inflexional forms.[38]

Both the use of comparison as the clue to earlier history and the conception of change as degeneration from primitive integrity were common property of the scientific thought of the time.[39] In analysing the inflexional forms of languages of the Indo-European family Bopp kept alive two other eighteenth-century ideas. He tended to regard inflexions as the result of earlier affixation of formerly separate auxiliary words, a mode of etymologizing already favoured by Horne Tooke (p. 172, above). Thus he analysed the Gothic weak preterites like *sōkidēdun* (they searched) as containing an original verb 'to do', and Latin futures and imperfects in -*b*- (*amābō*, I shall love, *amābam*, I was loving, etc.) as derived from the root *bhū*-, to be (in *fui*, I was, etc.). As was noticed earlier such processes of word formation do take place, and some of Bopp's etymologies are accepted; but his generalizing of the process to the extent of analysing Latin *amāris*, you are loved, from **amāsis*, as having an element -*s*- cognate with the flexive pronoun *s(ē)*, and Greek sigmatic aorists and futures like *elūsa* and *lūsō*, I loosed, I shall loose, as containing part of the verb 'to be' (Greek *es*-, Sanskrit *as*-) is pressing *a priori* theory against what the facts warrant. Bopp also, in fact, assumed that formal exponents of root (attribute), copula (predication), and person (subject) would be found in inflected verbal forms as a general rule, citing a plausible Latin example *possum*, I am able, and some untenable examples such as *amāvī*, I loved, in which he identified the -*v*- with the root *bhū*-, to be.[40] While much of his etymology on these lines is impossible, his aim can be seen as that of giving formal expression to the logical analysis of verbs current among the Port Royal grammarians and some others in earlier centuries.[41]

However, for all that has been said in the preceding paragraph, the linguists whose work and thought we have been following in the last few pages were all scholars belonging in spirit to the early nineteenth century, who thought along lines that became institutionalized and dominant during the rest of that century. But we must now take note of a man whose life stradled the two centuries (1767–1835) and whose thinking on language and on the important place of language in human life belongs firmly in the eighteenth century, Wilhelm von Humboldt.

Over a long period in his professional life he wrote voluminously on various topics in linguistics and on various languages. In so far as we can discover a general theme running through his writing, it would seem to be his concern to explicate the infinitely creative aspect of language, both grammatical and lexical, by which the necessarily finite resources available to each speaker can be made to respond to all the needs that as an individual and as a member of a nation or a speech community he may encounter.

It was this concern for the creative aspect of language that led him to define language as an *energeia*, a capacity in the speaker–hearer, not as an *ergon*, the fixed and dead description of the grammarian. It was this that led him further to the concept of linguistic form, *innere Sprachform*, which determined the phonetic, grammatical, and lexical structure of each language and to his now famous, though not actually original, tripartite typology of languages, as each strives for inner perfection as the means for the expression of the individual's and the nation's spirit.

In this postulated striving for improvement and perfection on the part of language, to some extent a linguistic application of Hegelian thought, Humboldt joined others of his age in their eulogies of Sanskrit as a magnificent example of inflectional structure. He was fully alive to the importance of Sanskrit and to the now developing Indo-European comparative-historical linguistics. This is witnessed by his securing the appointment of Bopp to the University of Berlin (p. 150, above). But he made clear that his own interests turned on language in general in the eighteenth-century manner, rather than on the methodological concentration that necessarily came to accompany nineteenth-century work.[42]

Wilhelm von Humboldt was one of the profoundest and most original thinkers on general linguistic questions in the nineteenth century, and one wonders whether, if his style had been less diffuse and his ideas more worked out and exemplified than they were, and his voluminous works were better known and more widely read, he would not be accorded a position comparable to that given to de Saussure as one of the founders of modern linguistic thought. He was one of the few early nineteenth-century linguists not concentrating predominantly on history. He did not, in fact, sharply distinguish the two aspects of linguistics, synchrony and diachrony, and he drew on his own knowledge and on what he read in Bopp and others to seek answers to the questions he raised of an essentially general linguistic kind.

Humboldt, brother of the geographer and ethnographer A. von Humboldt, played an important part in the public affairs of Prussia, was a widely travelled person, and had a knowledge of a number of languages, western and oriental, together with some acquaintance with a few American-Indian languages. He published a quantity of writings, on language and languages, of which the most important is *The variety of human language structure,* first published posthumously as a lengthy introduction to his description of the ancient Kawi language of Java.[43] It was hailed by Bloomfield a century later as 'the first great book on general linguistics'.

Humboldt's theory of language lays stress on the creative linguistic ability inherent in every speaker's brain or mind. A language is to be identified with the living capability by which speakers produce and understand utterances, not with the observed products of the acts of speaking and writing; in his words it is a creative ability (*energeia, Tätigkeit, Erzeugung*), not a mere product (*ergon, Werk, Erzeugtes*).[44] Still less should a language be identified with the dead products of the grammarian's analysis. The capacity for language is an essential part of the human mind; otherwise language could not have originated just environmentally; and by the nature of this capacity languages can be changed and adapted as circumstances require, and only so can the central fact (and mystery!) of language be explained: that speakers can make infinite use of the finite linguistic resources available to them at any time. Therefore no matter how much one analyses and describes a language, something of its essential nature remains unsaid, a point that perhaps linguists of today who look to Humboldt for part of their theory should heed.[45]

Though the capacity for language is universal, Humboldt follows the lines of Herder's thought in asserting the individuality of each different language as a peculiar property of the nation or the group who speak it (here the nineteenth-century nationalist arguments based on linguistic identification are prominent). The articulatory basis of speaking is common to all men, but sound only serves as the passive material for the formal constitution or structure of the language (*innere Sprachform*).[46] Humboldt's *innere Sprachform* is the semantic and grammatical structure of a language, embodying elements, patterns and rules imposed on the raw material of speech. In part it is common to all men, being involved in man's intellectual equipment; but in part also the separate *Sprachform* of each language constitutes its formal identity and difference from all other languages. This organizing principle of each language governs its syllable structures, its grammar, and its lexicon, the distinction between the latter two being of paedagogical significance only.[47] The latest potentialities of each language's *innere Sprachform* are the field of its literary artists, and, more important, the language and thought of a people are inseparable. Humboldt carries further Herder's conception of the parallel development of thought and language: 'a people's speech is their spirit, and their spirit is their speech'.[48]

Every language is a product of its past, and some languages show a greater advance than others as instruments and models of thinking. Typically of the time, he declared Sanskrit to be the best developed language of any that were known.[49] Thinking and perception are only made definite and communicable through a language, thought and language being interdependent and inseparable; words are not individual labels or names, but at the same time they both denote something and put it in a distinct category of thought.[50] The words of every language are organized in a systematic whole, so much so that the utterance of a single word presupposes the whole of the language as a semantic and grammatical structure; only loans from foreign languages can constitute extrasystemic isolates.[51] Differences between languages, therefore, turn not merely on the different speech sounds used by them, but involve differences in the speakers' interpretation and understanding of the world they live in (*Weltansicht*).[52]

The influence of this mode of thinking about language was not felt immediately. It has been pointed out that while he cites his contemporaries freely they do not appear to have made great use of his ideas.[53] But a number of lines can be traced from him to later nineteenth- and twentieth-century work. H. Steinthal (his pupil) and W. Wundt drew on him in their development of linguistic psychology and national psychology (*Völkerpsychologie*), and the aesthetic and idealistic school developed his teaching on the individuality, creativity, and artistic potentiality of every language. More recently there have appeared various 'neo-Humboldtian' trends in European linguistics, particularly associated with the work of L. Weisgerber on German, and the relevance of Humboldt's views to Whorfian theories in America needs no elaboration. A direct line has been traced in American linguistics from Humboldt through D. G. Brinton (who translated some of his publications), F. Boas, and E. Sapir to B. L. Whorf, with particular reference to work on the languages of native America.[54]

It is in the present time, with generative linguists' interest in the infinite creativity of language and the widespread general concern for typological studies, that Humboldt's thoughts about language have come fully into their own. Much attention has been paid to some probable philosophical sources for his ideas on language. He was well read in classical and modern European philosophy, and he lived in the period when German philosophy, most famously represented in the 'idealism' of Kant and Hegel, was coming to be regarded as the predominant philosophical influence in Europe as a whole.

One may also see how Kantian theory was itself influential in Humboldt's thinking. Kant's theory of perception involved sensations produced by the external world being ordered by categories or 'intuitions' (*Anschauungen*) imposed by the mind, notably those of space, time and causality. This was a universal philosophical theory; Humboldt adapted it relativistically and linguistically by making the *innere Sprachform* of each language responsible for the ordering and categorizing of the data of experience, so that speakers of different languages live partly in different worlds and have different systems of thinking. One notes the use by Humboldt of the three verbal nouns *Anschauen* *Denken*, and *Fühlen* (perception, thinking, and feeling) in connection with the operation of language.[55]

Possibly Humboldt is best known in linguistics for popularizing a tripartite language typology, isolating, agglutinative, and flexional, according to the predominant structure of the word as a grammatical unit.[56] This, however, was common ground to a number of contemporaries. F. Schlegel divided languages into those making grammatical use of internal changes of word form and those employing serially ordered elements; commenting on this A. W. Schlegel set up the three classes of isolating, affixing, and inflecting languages, a system presented somewhat differently by Bopp.[57]

Ideas about the typological development of language had been put forward in the eighteenth century (p. 186, above), and Humboldt conceived his scheme as historically relevant, although primarily a matter of synchronic classification. In his *Origin of grammatical forms and their influence on the development of thought* (1822) he traced the passage of languages from bare reference to objects, through the agglutination of auxiliary meaningful elements, to true inflexion as seen in Latin, Greek, and Sanskrit; but in *The variety of human language structure* (1836) the typology is one of description and grading. The two typological poles are Chinese and Sanskrit, the purest analytic or isolating language and the purest flexional language respectively, all others, including the agglutinative languages ('hybrids') being ranged between them.[58]

Humboldt recognized the value and the potentialities of any language structure, but his preference was for flexional languages, those languages whose grammatical word form variations involve either internal root changes or affixes bonded into the word by morphophonemic alternations of the constituent morphemes (to use later terminology) so that the formal unity of the word is reinforced.[59] At the other typological extreme, his attitude to Chinese is peculiar; like so many others at the time (and later) he regarded Chinese as devoid of formal grammatical classes or distinctions, but just for that reason having its own particular excellence as a language. He envisaged the growth and development of inflexions in the formative stage of a language, followed by their gradual decline in favour of a more analytical type of structure such as is seen in English. Chinese, however, had preserved its original isolating structure through its great linguistic conservatism, and Humboldt fancifully pointed out that should a form of Sanskrit have developed devoid of all its former inflexions, it would be quite different in grammatical structure from Chinese which had never had any (in fact, some Sinologists today consider that the state in which Chinese is known to us now is the result of the loss of an earlier inflexional system).[60]

In a separate section Humboldt divided sentence structures into three types also: those, as in Chinese, with no overt grammatical links between words, those like Sanskrit wherein word forms signal grammatical relations, and the type evinced by some American-Indian languages in which the essential structure of the sentence is incorporated into a single word (incorporating or polysynthetic languages). In neither of these typologies, of word form or of sentence form, was any one type wholly exclusive of features appropriate to the others. Confusion results if the two typologies are combined into one, making incorporation a fourth term in the word form typology, where it merely cross-cuts inflexion an agglutination.[61]

In the mid-nineteenth century perhaps the most influential and historically important figure in linguistics was A. Schleicher (1821–68). In his relatively short life he wrote a number of works on historical linguistics and linguistic theory, of which the best known is his *Compendium of the comparative grammar of the Indogermanic languages.*[62] The title is significant; comparative and historical linguistics in the Indo-European field was now considered a fit subject for systematic presentation in a handbook setting out the position so far achieved. Schleicher's own development in the theory of historical linguistics is shown in the subtitle: *Outline of a phonology and morphology of the Indogermanic parent language.* It had been the achievement of the early nineteenth century to work out the conception of historically related families of languages, each containing a definite number of members, derived from an ancestor no longer extant (instead of looking among known languages for the 'oldest' or the 'original'). Schleicher turned his attention to the nature and forms of this hypothetical ancestor and the genetic relationships linking it with its known descendants.

Schleicher had learned a number of European languages in his youth. He made something like a field study of Lithuanian, and his *Handbook of the Lithuanian language* was the first and is still a good scientific description of that language.[63] His interests embraced philosophy (of the Hegelian variety) and natural science, in particular botany, as well as linguistics. The *Stammbaumtheorie* or genealogical tree model, by which he set out the relations between the parent language and the known Indo-European languages, owes something to the methods of botanical classification by species and groups in the Linnaean system, but it may well have been partly inspired by the comparative method of reconstructing the genealogy of manuscripts expounded by F. Ritschl, one of his teachers.[64]

Extant languages were grouped together, by the possession of distinctive shared characteristics (lexical correspondences and the results of sound changes), into subfamilies, Germanic, Italo-Celtic, etc., for each of which a parent *Grundsprache* (common language) was assumed (like the known spoken Latin as the parent of the Romance language), and all of these were traced back to a single *Ursprache* (original language) possessing the characteristics shared by them all. This common ancestor of the Indo-European languages could be reconstructed by the comparison of the attested corresponding forms in the various sub-families, and the whole system of the languages in their historical relations was set out in the tree diagram.[65] Such reconstructed forms were, of course, different from known forms (and from inferred forms in a partially known language, as in the (different) reconstruction of a fragmentary inscription), and Schleicher initiated the practice of distinguishing them with an asterisk (whence the later term 'starred forms'); but he still felt sufficient confidence in his reconstructions actually to publish a fable composed in the *Ursprache*, just as one might today compose a passage in a dead language, a venture for which later writers have enjoyed criticizing him.[66]

The *Stammbaumtheorie*, as Schleicher's genealogical model is often called, represents an important development in Indo-

European historical linguistics, and in historical linguistic theory in general. It provides one means of displaying the members of a linguistic family, and reading from the inferred ancestor downwards one gets some picture of the history and the historical relations of the individual languages. It is, however, open to certain objections, objections which do not require its abandonment but only a sensible interpretation of its inevitably metaphorical representation of the facts. Languages do not sharply split at a given point in time corresponding to the division of a line in the tree; the splitting process begins subdialectally and proceeds through increasing dialectal divergence until the assumption of two or more distinct languages is warranted. This is a lengthy and a gradual process, and the point at which each stage is reached must remain arbitrary. Moreover, as long as geographical contiguity permits linguistic contacts between speakers, different dialects and even different languages can continue to influence one another (in this respect the development of a language family and that of a botanical family are quite different processes, although both can be represented by a tree diagram). This last point was appreciated by Schleicher's successors, including his pupil J. Schmidt, who recognized that certain sets of features were uniquely but differently shared by different groups of languages within Indo-European, thus invalidating the single splits of the *Stammbaumtheorie*. Schmidt supplemented this rather than replaced it, by his *Wellentheorie,* or theory of waves of innovations, linguistic changess including sound changes, that spread over a given area from dialect to dialect or even from language to language as long as linguistic contacts remained.[67]

Schleicher's model serves best as a literal representation of linguistic history, when language diffusion takes place over distances that involve the near total severance of the speakers, such, for example, as took place in the historical period with the Dutch settlers in South Africa and in certain isolated Spanish-speaking communities in the Latin New World.

The other major objection to a quite literal interpretation of the tree model is that it suggests that dialectal divisions are the most recent feature of linguistic history, since dialects occur at the end points of the tree. Only exceptionally, as in the case of ancient Greek, do we have an adequate knowledge of the dialect situation in dead languages; and the *Ursprache* and intermediate common languages are set up precisely on what is assumed to have been common in each to all the speakers. But all our knowledge of the conditions of language leads us to believe that dialect division was at least as pronounced in early days as it was later (probably more so), and indeed certain sets of correspondences within the Indo-European languages seem to demand the recognition of certain dialectal isoglosses already established within the *Ursprache* during the supposed period of unity. In so far as a strictly literal interpretation can be placed on the model, it should be read upwards as part of the historical linguist's method rather than downward as an accurate picture of historical events.

One important feature of the *Stammbaumtheorie* is that Sanskrit now began to assume its proper position in the family. Schleicher assigned it a place like any other language, in the 'Arian' (Indo-Iranian) group, though he assumed that the Sanskrit vowel system /a/, /i/, /u/ (the /e/ and /o/ of classical Sanskrit were later derivatives of diphthongs[68]) was also the original Indo-European vowel system; triadic systems of any kind may have appealed to his Hegelian upbringing. Subsequent study has shown that the Sanskrit language had undergone changes, since the separation of its branch from the original unitary state, at least to the same extent as the other Indo-European languages.

In the form in which Schleicher set them down neither the tree diagram nor the forms of the *Ursprache* have remained unaltered; further study by Indo-European specialists altered both the grouping of languages within the branches of the tree, the forms of the reconstructions, and the phonological inventory ascribed to the *Ursprache*. Even between 1861 and 1891 G. von der Gabelentz could say that this reconstructed language had suffered great changes in its forms,[69] and the twentieth-century discovery of the relatedness of Hittite to the Indo-European languages further altered the picture. These topics and the detailed research into the different groups of languages within Indo-European that was pursued during this period are matters for the history of Indo-European comparative linguistics rather than for the course of general linguistics as a whole.[70]

Schleicher's theory of linguistic history, whatever its original inspiration may have been, was in line with current ideas on evolution in the first half of the nineteenth century, with their teleological implication of a progression towards a goal of structural perfection. In his later years, after reading the German translation of Darwin's *Origin of species*, which presented the classic survivalist evolution rather than teleological evolution, Schleicher none the less considered that what he had already written on the history and prehistory of languages was broadly in line with Darwin's own thinking. In 1863 he published a short treatise on *Darwinian theory and linguistics*.[71] He regarded himself as a natural scientist and his subject, language, as one of the natural organisms of the world, to be treated by the methods of natural science, one moreover that independently of its speakers' will or consciousness has its periods of growth, maturity, and decline.[72] It was to biology that he looked in his quest for a scientific model for historical linguistics. Such ideas were current already, though less elaborated; F. Schlegel had likened comparative grammar to comparative anatomy, and Bopp had written that languages should be regarded as natural organic objects that grow according to definite laws, go through the phases of development, and in the end perish.[73] Schleicher maintained that Darwin's theory as worked out for the animal and vegetable kingdoms was generally appropriate for linguistic history, and that the diffusion of different languages over the earth's surface and their contacts and conflicts could be likened to the struggle for existence in the world of living things, in which the Indo-European languages were victorious![74]

Schleicher's biological approach to language governed both his theory of the *Ursprache* and his treatment of linguistic typology. He regarded the three current language types, isolating, agglutinating, and inflexional, as representing historical stages in the growth of languages to their highest point of organization. This conviction was expressed more than once in his statements that coexisting linguistic structural types represented the products of successive historical developments in the same way that successively evolved fishes, reptiles, birds, and mammals are represented today by coexistent species in our biological world.[75]

In this way Schleicher incorporated into a general theory of linguistic history both the eighteenth-century and Humboldtian ideas about linguistic types and current nineteenth-century work on the comparative-historical study of language families. The three major types, which for Humboldt had represented a general progress in the full realization of the potential power of language (its *Vollkommenheit*), were now brought into the time frame of the prehistory and history of Indo-European and other actual language families. Schleicher located the period of language growth in prehistory as far as the Indo-European family was concerned, with the unitary *Ursprache* as reconstructed by him representing the mature undamaged stage, subsequent historical developments being part of the decline.[76] This could in some degree be supported by the more flexional structure of the ancient classical languages as compared with their later descendants; but one notices from Grimm on a definite admiration for flexional morphology, more especially in its 'purest' manifestation by *Ablaut* as being the best mode of grammatical exponence. National feeling may subconsciously have had some influence; *Ablaut* is an important formative process in Germanic languages, and more fully exploited in German than, for example, in English (cp. the inflexional and derivational use of vowel gradation in such a word series as *sprechen*, to speak, *sprach*, spoke, *gesprochen*, spoken, *sprich*, speak!, *Gespräch*, conversation, *Spruch*, saying, proverb, *Sprüche* (plural)).

Grimm had written earlier of the 'strong' (*Ablaut*-using) inflexions of the Germanic languages as a potent and characteristic feature of this group, though *Ablaut* is, in fact, found in many languages of otherwise quite different composition.[77] As regards historical decline, Schleicher was very hard on English; referring to the changes undergone by the language since its separation from the others, he wrote that they show how quickly the language of a people important in history and in literary history can decline.[78]

The major linguistic controversy in the last quarter of the century was concerned with what is now referred to as the neogrammarian or *Junggrammatiker* doctrine. In treating this as part of the history of linguistics, which one should do, one is already within the bounds of contemporary history. Neogrammarian principles and their implications are, or ought to be, part of any teaching course in general linguistics, and expositions of them are to be found in serious textbooks on the subject.[79]

This, of course, is very far from saying that the neogrammarian standpoint is understood and taught today in the precise way in which its protagonists understood and defined it. As an important and challenging event, its formulation evoked a considerable and an immediate reaction, and, of more significance, stimulated a number of different lines of research and thinking in direct response to what had been said. Much of our linguistic theory, in particular our theory of historical linguistics, would not bear the form it bears today but for its direct dependence on the neogrammarian or *Junggrammatiker* doctrine. In treating this as linguistic scene, and 'we are all neogrammarians now'.

In surveying the neogrammarian epoch in a history of linguistics we must endeavour to see it both in its setting when neogrammarian principles were first propounded in a reaction to what had been said and done before, and in its setting as part of subsequent linguistic theory; in other words, we want to understand both how the neogrammarians interpreted their work and how linguists today find it profitable to interpret and use it.

The neogrammarians no less than Schleicher strove to ground their work on comparative-historical linguistics within the natural sciences. But whereas Schleicher had turned to biology, the neogrammarians looked to the exact physical sciences of inanimate nature such as geology and physics as their models.

The essence of their theory was summarily set forth in 1878 in a programmatic article in a journal founded by its two major proponents, H. Osthoff and K. Brugmann, in which the following statements were made: All sound changes, as mechanical processes, take place according to laws that admit no exceptions (*ausnahmslose Lautgesetze*) within the same dialect and within a given period of time, and the same sound will in the same environment always develop in the same way; but analogical creations and reformations of specific words as lexical or grammatical entities are equally a universal component of linguistic change at all periods of history and prehistory.[80]

Similar views had been expressed by different scholars in the preceding years; it fell to Osthoff and Brugmann formally to declare them as indispensable to historical linguistics and cheerfully to accept as official the title 'neogrammarian' (*Junggrammatiker*), originally a politically inspired nickname given to a group of young scholars in Leipzig, where they worked.

The conception of the sound law had been late in developing; Grimm and Bopp explicitly admitted exceptions, and Schleicher, despite an emphasis on regularity, allowed apparently irregular developments to pass as etymological evidence. The neogrammarians saw plainly the methodological requirements of comparative-historical linguistics as it had been practised in the past half century. A few really significant papers appeared in the years 1876–8 and marked the inception of the neogrammarian programme.[81] It was now clear that the existence of comparative and historical linguistics as a science rested on the assumption of regularity of sound change. The history of a language is traced through recorded variations in the forms and meanings of its words, and languages are proved to be related by reason of their possession of words bearing formal and semantic correspondences to each other such as cannot be attributed to mere chance or to recent borrowing. If sound change were not regular, if word forms were subject to random, inexplicable, and unmotivated variation in the course of time, such arguments would lose their validity and linguistic relations could be established historically only by extra-linguistic evidence such as is provided in the Romance field of languages descended from Latin.

The advance of scientific work without the explicit formulation of the theory on which its validity rests is no unusual occurrence in the history of science. The implications of nineteenth-century comparative and historical linguistics were stated in 1876 by A. Leskien: 'If one admits optional, contingent, and unconnected changes, one is basically stating that the object of one's research, language, is not amenable to scientific recognition.'[82] Others had spoken to similar effect though less explicitly; Verner, in his exposition of what is now known as 'Verner's law', showed that a large number of the apparent exceptions to the Germanic sound shift as formulated by Grimm could be systematically explained by reference to the position of the word accent in the earlier stages of the Indo-European family (e.g. Sanskrit (at the period when the I-E accent survived) bhrátā, Gothic brōpar, brother, but pitá, fadar, father); significantly he entitled his article 'An exception to the first sound shift', and wrote: 'There must be a rule for exceptions to a rule; the only question is to discover it.' The further implication of the theory was that systematic correspondences between sounds in languages demonstrate their relatedness, not merely the special case of similarity in actual phonetic shape; this was later clearly stated by A. Meillet.[83]

Grimm and his contemporaries lay under the influence of the Romantic movement; Schleicher saw his work within the context of biology and later of Darwinian theory; the neogrammarians wished to make historical linguistics an exact science in line with those natural sciences which had made such striking advances in the nineteenth century, notably geology. Nineteenth-century scientists held strongly to the universality of natural laws, realistically conceived; the uniformity of nature was a current dogma.[84] In this vein Osthoff wrote of sound laws proceeding by blind necessity, independently of the individual's will[85]; nevertheless, language was not a supra-individual organic entity with its own growth and life, as the earlier Humboldt and Schleicher and the later de Saussure (under Durkheimian influence) asserted; it simply had its existence in the individuals composing a speech community, and linguistic changes were changes in individuals' speech habits. In the interests of what they held to be a scientific outlook, the neogrammarians set their faces against the a priori and speculative conceptions of such predecessors as Schleicher with his distinction of a prehistoric period of growth and a historic period of decline. Except for the nature of the evidence, they argued that there was no difference between these periods as far as linguistic changes were concerned. Indeed, they drew attention away from the Ursprache as a supposed prehistoric reality to the data available in written records and in the spoken dialects of the present day; and from the neogrammarians stems the conception of Indo-European forms as formulae rather than as actual words or morphs. In a rather brutally expressed paragraph, Osthoff and Brugmann attacked any speculation beyond what the facts strictly warranted: 'Only that comparative linguist who forsakes the hypothesis-laden atmosphere of the workshop in which Indo-Germanic root-forms are forged, and comes out into the clear light of tangible present-day actuality in order to obtain from this source information which vague theory cannot ever afford him, can arrive at a correct presentation of the life and the transformations of linguistic forms.'[86]

Not for the last time in our science were data-orientation and theory-orientation to be brought into personal opposition. The neogrammarians concerned themselves with data and with laws governing the data drawing on the sciences of physiology (in phonetics) and psychology to cover the domains of sound change and analogical reformation or resistance. Such down-to-earth movements are a continual necessity in a science, but the neogrammarian abandonment of unprofitable speculation in favour of the meticulous attention to detail was bought at the cost of the temporary neglect of much that was fecund in the work of earlier linguists. The structural conception of language suggested by Humboldt, especially in his theory of *innere Sprachform* found no place in their work, and the areas of linguistics lying outside the immediate concern of the neogrammarians were generally treated from a historical point of view. H. Paul's *Principles of the history of language* (1880) exemplifies this (chapter 4), and more strikingly so does M. Bréal's *Essay on semantics* (1897),) although he may claim credit in history for introducing into linguistics the now universally used term 'semantics' (sémantique).[87] Perhaps it was in reaction to this onesided influence on linguistic studies exercised by the historicism of the period culminating in the neogrammarian school, dominant at the end of the century, that some twentieth-century structuralists and descriptivists have seemed never to tire of contemptuous references to the 'neogrammarian rut' and to 'neogrammarian atomism'.

Certainly the school, despite the opposition it aroused, became dominant, as it deserved to. The books of Bopp and Schleicher were replaced by the formidable *Outline of the comparative grammar of the Indogermanic languages* of Brugmann and Delbrück (Delbrück being responsible for the syntactic sections). Paul's *Principles* expounded neogrammarian theory, declaring that a scientific treatment of language must be a historical treatment, while W. Meyer-Lübke applied the theory to the field of the Romance languages.[88] In England J. Wright, and in France A. Meillet were both trained in neogrammarian linguistics; and so

LINGUISTICS IN THE NINETEENTH CENTURY

were the founders of American linguistics, F. Boas, E. Sapir, and L. Bloomfield. Bloomfield's work on the comparative and histori-cal study of the Algonkian family of American-Indian languages brilliantly applies the theory and methods, together with Bloomfield's descriptive abilities, to an entirely distinct and remote language family.[89]

As has recently been pointed out,[90] the neogrammarians mark one of the really significant stages in the history of linguistics in the past two centuries. Their influence was threefold: in the en-couragement given by their approach to linguistic science, in the immediate reactions of those shocked by them, and in the reac-tions of later generations.

Two fields that the neogrammarians saw to be very relevant to historical linguistics as they wished it to be pursued were phonetics and dialectology. Descriptive phonetics, whose history in Europe goes back at least to the Renaissance (pp. 131–2, above), had its own line of development in the nineteenth cen-tury, which it will be convenient to review in the next chapter. It received powerful reinforcement from the neogrammarian em-phasis on living languages and on the inadequacy of the letters of dead languages in giving information on their actual pronun-ciations. Never again could there be an excuse for confusing written letter with spoken sound. E. Sievers's *Principles of phonetics* (1876) bears the further explanatory title *Introduction to the study of the sounds of the Indogermanic languages*.[91]

The spoken dialects of Europe had been a focus of linguistic attention since the Romantic movement sanctified everything con-nected with 'the people', but the neogrammarians made them a vital field for scientific investigation in the light they could shed on linguistic change, since they represented the latest stage in the diversification of the Indo-European family.[92] Dialect studies, dialect surveys, and the publication of dialect atlases began in earnest during this period, even though some of the strongest op-ponents of neogrammarian doctrine were found among the dialectologists.

The challenging way in which the neogrammarians propounded their principles, although they were largely the tacit implications of the century's previous work, threw more weight on the study of loan words and on linguistic borrowing as a universal feature of the history of languages, and on analogy as an ever present tendency. Both these factors had been recognized before in lin-guistics, the existence of loan words since antiquity; and in ancient Greek synchronic grammatical theory, analogy, the regularity of the corresponding forms of grammatical paradigms had been picked out as one of the principles by which language was directed. But they had enjoyed less prominence in historical linguistics hitherto, before the need had been clearly seen of accounting for apparent breaches of sound laws; in 1868 W. Scherer had stressed the importance of analogical reformation, but his term 'false analogy' showed the secondary place assigned to this aspect of linguistic change.[93]

These developments were all envisaged and intended. But critical and hostile responses were immediate. These were expressed in terms of existing theory and existing knowledge whereas later reactions resulted from a re-examination of the neogrammarian position in the light of advances made in general linguistic theory and in descriptive techniques.

Criticism took a number of forms. The personal resentment caused among some older scholars by what seemed to them unnecessarily harsh expressions on the part of newcomers (Osthoff and Brugmann had been born in 1847 and 1849, respectively) is understandable and needs no historical discussion (the discourtesy of the young is a recurrent complaint in scholarship as in other fields of life). Some took the line that neogrammarian principles were nothing new, but just a statement of what comparative and historical linguist were doing anyway. This in a sense was fair enough. The neogrammarians were largely drawing out what had been implied by the very practice of the subject and distinguishing it from unnecessary and fallacious assumptions. This in itself was a service, as is any stocktaking in scientific theory and methodology. Moreover, in making explicit the principles on which the science rested, they went a long way towards ensuring that muddled and undisciplined thinking should not accept unsound arguments and false etymological connections.

However, the most important and radical arguments against the neogrammarian position as first set out by Osthoff and Brugmann and their colleagues came from specialists in a branch of linguistics that they had been at pains to encourage, the study of living dialects. The detailed examination of the working of language in relatively small communities closely investigated in the field showed how complex were the phenomena collectively covered by the terms 'dialect split' and 'dialect borrowing'. The more narrowly a language was scrutinized, the more it was seen that geographical dialect divisions are in constant fluctuation and far from clear-cut, as more gross and superficial descriptions imply. The number of relatively coincidental isoglosses required to delimit a dialect must itself be arbitrary, and if one presses differences in detail at all levels, including pronunciation, to their logical limits, then the dialect becomes the idiolect.

Moreover, temporal limits are as hazy as geographical limits. Sound changes, like any other linguistic changes, must begin and cease within some temporal limits as well as extending over certain geographical areas; but the detailed study of actual dialect situations shows that these limits tolerate certain words changing before certain others when the same sounds are involved, and that dialect interpenetration across major isogloss lines may upset the universal application of a sound shift in a particular region. Dialect maps such as the one given in Bloomfield's *Language*, page 328, show the result of catching a linguistic change in progress and descriptively freezing it.

One is not at the end of linguistic variation after pressing geographical divisions down to the idiolect. Most speech communities are cross-cut with social divisions in part manifested in differences of speech habits, as folk-linguistic attitudes to 'correct speech' bear witness; and many individuals carry in their linguistic competence more than one different social and often more than one different regional dialect, to be used in different circumstances; and these differences, in so far as they relate to pronunciation, may be the result of the operation or non-operation of a particular sound change.

Dialect division, rather crudely conceived, and analogical reformation or conservatism were the two factors envisaged by the neogrammarians as apparently running counter to the universality of sound laws. But the minute examination of dialect differences revealed other considerations that were relevant in etymological research, affecting not categories of sounds as such but particular words as individual lexical items. Word forms may be deflected from their expected regular phonetic development by homonymic clash, excessive reduction in length, nearness to or coincidence with taboo-words, popular or false etymologies, loans from a neighbouring dialect for prestige, and by other factors. Such events are necessarily individual and highly variable in their incidence; they are explicable given knowledge of the circumstances (which of course is often not given, especially in earlier periods of a language), but they are not predictable.

It is, therefore, significant that much of the more serious criticism of the neogrammarian assertion of universality came from specialists in dialectology and what has been called linguistic geography. In particular one may cite H. Schuchardt, who included in his works an article 'On sound laws: against the neogrammarians', and J. Gilliéron, responsible for the linguistic atlas of France and numerous studies of individual French etymologies, including his best known *Genealogy of the words for the bee*.[94]

A further development of detailed dialectal research took the form of 'word and thing' (*Wörter und Sachen*) studies, in which the history and geographical distribution of items of material culture (agricultural implements, cultivated plants, etc.) and their associated vocabulary were minutely investigated. Schuchardt was much concerned with this, and so was R. Meringer, responsible for founding in 1909 a journal, *Wörter und Sachen*, expressly devoted to this field.

Gilliéron is to be credited with the doctrine, at first sight utterly opposed to that of the neogrammarians, that 'every word has its own history'. But the two positions are not really so incompatible. Changes in the pronunciation of words involve two things: the transmission from generation to generation of articulatory habits rests on the learning in childhood of sets of sounds heard first in certain words but, once mastered, used without effort in any number of words; but for various reasons, not by any means all understood, changes take place in the course of successive transmission between the generations, and the recurrence of a relatively small number of sounds in the virtually limitless vocabulary of a language makes for the universality of sound changes. But words are also learned as whole lexical units, and any hesitation, individual change, or other peculiarity in the pronunciation of such a unit is also learned, and may be retained and propagated in later generations or within people's speech during their lifetime. Every word has its individual history in its semantics, grammar, and pronunciation. In most cases its phonetic evolution can be described by reference to the phonetic evolution of the sounds occurring in it, but in certain cases its pronounced form must be explained by reference to particular circumstances lying along its own particular history. The neogrammarians stressed phonetic uniformity; Gilliéron and his disciples stressed etymological individuality.

The neogrammarians had said that language had no existence apart from the speakers. A group of linguists known as the idealistic or aesthetic school emphasized the importance of the individual speaker in the origination and diffusion of linguistic change of all kinds. The leader of this group was K. Vossler, of Munich, who drew his ideas on the nature of language from Humboldt and, more immediately, from the Italian philosopher B. Croce, with whom he was in intimate friendship for half a century.

It is interesting to notice that these linguists were just as historically orientated as the dominant neogrammarians; but they conceived the history of languages in a rather different way. Like

Humboldt, Vossler stressed the individual and creative aspect of man's linguistic competence. All linguistic change begins with innovations in individual speech habits, and those that are going to give rise to some alteration in the language do so by being imitated by others and thus diffusing themselves. This would probably not be contradicted by the neogrammarians, but the idealists insisted on the conscious role of the individual in the process rather than on 'blind necessity'. Croce laid great importance on aesthetic intuition as a guide in all aspects of man's life, even though one may be unaware of it at the time. The recognized artist only carries further what every human being does all the time.[95]

Language is primarily personal self-expression, the idealists maintained, and linguistic change is the conscious work of individuals perhaps also reflecting national feelings; aesthetic considerations are dominant in the stimulation of innovations. Certain individuals, through their social position or literary reputation, are better placed to initiate changes that others will take up and diffuse through a language, and the importance of great authors in the development of a language, like Dante in Italian, must not be underestimated. In this regard the idealists reproached the neogrammarians for their excessive concentration on the mechanical and pedestrian aspects of language, a charge that L. Spitzer, himself very much in sympathy with Vossler, was later to make against the descriptive linguistics of the Bloomfieldian era.[96] But the idealists, in themselves concentrating on literate languages, overstressed the literary and aesthetic element in the development of languages, and the element of conscious choice in what is for most speakers most of the time simply unreflective social activity learned in childhood and subsequently taken for granted. And in no part of language is its structure and working taken more for granted than in its actual pronunciation, just that aspect on which the neogrammarians focused their attention. Nevertheless the idealistic school did well to remind us of the creative and conscious factors in some areas of linguistic change and of the part the individual can sometimes deliberately play therein.

Certain of the principles of the idealist-aesthetic linguists, combined with detailed dialectological studies, gave rise in Italy to the so-called 'neo-linguistic' school, which has made one of its main concerns the processes by which innovations are diffused over geographical areas (whence the term 'areal linguistics', sometimes used of the work of this school) and the historical inferences that can be drawn from the contrasting developments in central as against peripheral areas, which latter are likely to preserve archaic features the longest.[97]

The neogrammarians stimulated fruitful lines of linguistic research by the shock that the vigorous exposition of their views caused in the learned world of the time. As a result of the reconsideration to which the whole question of historical relationship among languages was subjected, their tenets may be seen today to have been somewhat modified but not at all superseded. Their conception of sound laws operating on languages by 'blind necessity' is as undesirable a reification as were the mythical periods of growth, maturity, and decline favoured by earlier scholars. The exceptionlessness of sound laws should be considered not so much a factual statement (though research has shown that it is borne out by the facts) as a methodological requirement. The linguist sets himself not to accept finally an etymology which appears to break correspondences of sounds established in other words in the language or languages involved, until he is able to explain the seeming deviance in some reasonable manner, whether, as in Verner's Law, through a refinement of the previous formulation of the sound changes, or in relation to one particular etymology alone. In such individual researches he is prepared to see the working of psychological, sociological, and aesthetic factors counteracting the physically or physiologically *blinde Naturnotwendigkeit* of the early neogrammarian formulation. The point, however, is this: such a justifiable or attested factor must be available for any such apparent exception to the uniformity of sound changes to be scientifically acceptable. While we certainly will not be able to account for all apparent exceptions and cannot, in the absence of omniscience, absolutely deny the occurrence of 'sporadic sound change', on which the opponents of the neogrammarians laid so much weight, we are bound, as long as comparative and historical linguistics is to remain, in the widest sense of the term, scientific, to reject such unsupported etymologies from any arguments in favour of a genetic relation between languages.

The opposition so far surveyed, together with the research and development for which it was partly responsible, sprang from the stage reached by linguistic scholarship at the time of the neogrammarians. Later reactions, from the standpoint of synchronic and structural linguistics, may conveniently be considered in the next chapter. Meanwhile it is worth reflecting on the results of nineteenth-century comparative and historical linguistics. From the isolated and undeveloped, though sometimes inspired, insights of earlier years, scholars in the nineteenth century worked out a model in terms of which the history of languages could be presented, and a method whereby research could be conducted. Though largely confined to the Indo-European family, which reached a definitive state during this period, their work provided a pattern which, despite some valid criticism, has been fruitfully applied to language families the world over, including some, such as the Algonkian family already mentioned, that had no written records of earlier epochs. By any standards this was a mighty achievement, and one that can be largely attributed to the linguistic scholarship of the German universities, one component of the renown that they rightly enjoyed in this century.

For Further Consultation

H. ARENS, *Sprachwissenschaft: der Gang ihrer Entwicklung von der Antike bis zur Gegenwart*, Freiburg/Munich (second edition) 1969, 155–399.

T. BENFEY, *Geschichte der Sprachwissenschaft und orientalischen Philologie in Deutschland*, Munich, 1869.

G. BONFANTE, 'Ideas on the kinship of the European languages from 1200 to 1800', *Calhiers d'histoire mondiale*, 1953–4, 679–99.

K. BRUGMANN and B. DELBRÜCK, *Grundriss der vergleichenden Grammatik der indogermanischen Sprachen*, Strassburg, 1886–1900.

K. BRUGMANN, *Kurze vergleichende Grammatik der indogermanischen Sprachen*, Strassburg, 1904.

H. H. CHRISTMANN (ed.) *Sprachwissenschaft des 19. Jahrhunderts*, Darmstadt, 1977.

D. DROIXHE (ed.), *Genèse du comparatisme indo-europeérne'*, *Histoire épistémologie language* 6.2 (1984).

H. M. HOENIGSWALD, 'On the history of the comparative method', *Anthropological linguistics* 5 (1963), 1–11.

W. VON HUMBOLDT, *Uber die Verschiedenheit des menschlichen Sprachbaues*, Berlin, 1836 (reprinted Darmstadt, 1949); tr. G. C. BUCK and F. A. RAVEN, *Linguistic variability and intellectual development*, Coral Gables, 1971.

—— *GESAMMETTE SCHRIFTEN*, Berlin, 1903–36

I. IORDAN, *An introduction to Romance linguistics* (tr. J. ORR), London, 1937 (revised edition, R. Posner, Oxford, 1970).

M. IVIĆ, *Trends in linguistics*, The Hague, 1965, chapters 1–12.

K. R. JANKOWSKY, *The neogrammarians*, The Hague, 1972.

O. JESPERSEN, *Language*, London, 1922, chapters 2–4

A. JOLY, (ed.) *La linguistique génétique: histoire et théories*, Lille, 1988.

L. KUKENHEIM, *Esquisse historique de la linguistique française*, Leiden, 1962.

W. P. LEHMANN (ed.), *A reader in nineteenth century historical Indo-european linguistics*, Bloomington, 1967.

M. LEROY, *Les grands courants de la linguistique moderne*, Brussels and Paris, 1963, 15–60.

M. L. MANCHESTER, *The philosophical foundations of Humboldt's linguistic doctrines*, Amsterdam, 1985.

A. MEILLET, *Introduction à l'étude comparative des langues indo-européennes*, Paris, 1922, Appendix 1.

H. PEDERSEN, *Linguistic science in the nineteenth century* (tr. J. W. SPARGO), Cambridge, Mass, 1931 (paperback, *The discovery of language*, Bloomington, 1962).

T. A. SEBEOK (ed.), *Portraits of linguists: a biographical source book for the history of western linguistics* 1746–1963, Bloomington and London, 1966.

——, *Historiography of linguistics*, 607–716.

J. T. WATERMAN, *Perspectives in linguistics*, Chicago, 1963, 18–60.

Notes

11. JESPERSEN, 1922. 7. cp. H. PAUL, *Prinzipien der Sprachgeschichte*, Halle, 1920, 20–1.

2. Book 1, chapter 9. See further G. BONFANTE, 'Ideas on the kinship of the European languages from A.D. 1200 to 1800', *Cahiers d'histoire mondiale* 1 (1953–4), 679–99; Robins, 'The history of language classification', *Current trends in linguistics* (ed. T. A. SEBEOK), 11 (1973), 3–41.

3. Book 1, chapter 8.

4. E. BOURCIEZ, *Eléments de linguistique romane*, Paris 1946, § 320 c.

5. Book 1, chapters 10–16.

6. Book 1, chapters 4 and 6.

7. cp. J. C. GREENE, *The death of Adam*, New York, 1961, 62–3, 235

8. *Origines Antwerpianae*, Antwerp, 1569.

9. 'Matricum vero inter se nulla cognatio est, neque in verbis neque in analogia', *Diatriba de Europaeorum linguis* (*Opscula varia*, Paris, 1610, 119–22).

10. Stockholm, 1671, (glossary) 78–9.

11. *De lingua vetustissima Europae*, Stockholm, 1686.

12. G. W. VON LEIBNIZ, *Neue Abhandlungen*, Frankfurt, 1961, volume 2, 20–1; ARENS, 1969, 94–104.

13. C. I. GERHARDT (ed.), *Die philosophischen Schriften von* G. F. *Leibniz*, Berlin 1882, volume 5, 263–4 Further, S. von der Scnburg, *Leibniz als Sprachforscher*, Frankfurt, 1973.

14. ARENS, 1969, 102, 105–6.

15. Zurich, 1555; Berlin 1806 and 1817.

16. ADELUNG, *Mithridates*, volume 1, 149–150. Catherine also sought the help of King Charles III of Spain for information on native American languages (C. L. DE TOVAR, 'J. C. Mutis on American languages'; *Historiographia linguistica* 11 (1984) 213–29)

17. *Linguarum totius orbis vocabularia comparativa*, St. Petersburg, 1786–9.

18. ARENS 1969, 136–46. For a survey of early work in comparative linguistics, see BONFANTE, 1953–4.

19. ROBINS, 'The history of language classification', in T. A. SEBEOK (ed.), *Current trends in linguistics* II (1973), 3–41 (see p. 14).

20. ROBINS, 'The life and work of Sir William Jones', *TPS* 1987, 11; ibid., 10; ibid., 12.

21. cp. G. J. METCALF, 'The Indo-European hypothesis in the sixteenth and seventeenth centuries', in DELL HYMES (ed.), *Studies in the history of linguistics*, Bloomington, 1974, 233–57; H. HOENIGSWALD, 'Etymology against grammar in the early 19th century', in DROIXE, 1984, 95–100; J. C. MULLER, 'Saumaise, Monboddo, Adelung: vers la grammaire comparée', in S. AUROUX *et al.* (eds), *Matériaux pour une histoire des théories linguistiques*, Lille, 1984, 389–96. On the classification of the American-Indian languages P. S. Duponceau in the early years of the nineteenth century was particularly clear in this respect; his and other American work is documented by M. R. HAAS in 'Grammar or lexicon? The American Indian side of the question from Duponceau to Powell', *IJAL* 35 (1969), 239–55.

22. *Über die Sprache und Weisheit der Indier*, Heidelberg, 1801. An English translation of parts of this text in Lehmann, 1967, 21–8. SCHLEGEL, *Über die Sprache*, 28.

23. *Über das Conjugationssystem der Sanskritsprache in Vergleichung mit jenem der griechischen, lateinischen, persischen, und germanischen Sprache*, Frankfurt, 1816; English translation of parts, Lehmann, 1967, 38–45.
BENFEY, 1869.
'. . . gehören zu den gläzendsten Gestirnen des deutschen Geisteshimmels'; 'Die Genossenschaft ausgezeichneter Männer, welche zur Entwickelung dieser Wissenschaft beigetragen haben, sind fast ausnahmslos Söhne unsres Vaterlandes', BENFEY, op. cit., 15.

24. *Demonstratio idioma ungarorum et Lapponum idem esse*, Copenhagen, 1770; *Affinitas linguae Hungaricae cum linguis Fennicae originis grammatice demonstrata*, Göttingen, 1799.

25. *Vejledning til det islandske eller gamle nordiske sprog*, Copenhagen, 1811; *A grammar of the Anglo-Saxon tongue* (tr. B. THORPE), Copenhagen, 1830.

26. Göttingen, 1819–37.

27. M. E. DAIRE (ed.), *Oeuvres de Turgot*, Paris, 1844, volume 2, 724–52.

28. *Undersøgelse om det gamle nordiske eller islandske sprogs oprindelse*, Copenhagen, 1818 (L. HJELMSLEV, *Ausgewählte Abhandlungen*, Cpenhagen, 1932, volume 1, 49–51); English translation of parts, Lehmann, 1967, 29–37.

29. A. F. POTT, *Etymologische Forschungen auf dem Gebiete der indogermanischen Sprachen*, Lemgo, 1833–6.

30. 'Die Lautverschiebung erfolgt in der Masse, tut sich aber im einzelnen niemals rein ab', *Deutsche Grammatik* (second edition), Berlin, 1870, volume 1, 503.

31. *Unvorgreifliche Gedanken betreffend die Ausübung und Verbes-serung der deutschen Sprache (Quellen und Forschungen zur Sprach-und Culturgeschichte* 23 (1877), 44–92).

32. *Geschichte der deutschen Sprache* (fourth edition), Leipzig, 1880, volume 1, 292.

33. W. SCHERER, *Zur Geschichte der deutschen Sprache*, Berlin, 1868. On these aspects of Grimm's work see V. WYSS, *Die wilde Philologie: Jacob Grimm und der Historismus*, Munich, 1979

34. PEDERSEN, 1931, 248–9.

35. *Conjugationssystem*, 8–11.

36. cp. RASK, *Undersøgelse* (HJELMSLEV, *Ausgewählte Abhandlungen*, volume 1, 48–9.

37. MEILLET, 1922, 458.

38. *Vergleichende Grammatik des Sanskrit, Zend, Griechischen, Lateinischen, Litauischen, Gotischen, und Deutschen*, Berlin, 1833, iii.

39. cp. COUNT DE BUFFON (1707–88), *Natural history* (tr. W. SMELLIE), London, 1785, volume 3, 216, volume 8, 62–3; J. F. BLUMENBACH (1752–1840), *A manual of the elements of natural history* (tr. R. T. GORE), London, 1825.

40. *Conjugationssystem*, 96, 151, 99, cp. 148; *Analytic comparison of the Sanskrit, Greek, Latin, and Teutonic languages* (1820, reprinted in *Internationale Zeitschrift für allgemeine Sprachwissenschaft* 4 (1889), 14–60), 23, 46–7, 53–6, 58.

41. cp. P. A. VERBURG, 'The background to the linguistic conceptions of Bopp', *Lingua* 2 (1950), 438–68.

42. cp. P. R. SWEET, *Wilhelm von Humboldt, a biography*, Columbus, 1980, volume 2, 394–5.

43. HUMBOLDT, 1949. L. BLOOMFIELD, *Language*, London, 1935, 18

44. HUMBOLDT, op. cit., 43–4.

45. 'Die Sprache muss von endlichen Mitteln einen unendlichen Gebrauch machen', ibid., 103. cp. N. CHOMSKY, *Current issues in lin-guistic theory*, the Hague, 1964, 17–21.

46. HUMBOLDT, op. cit., 89–98, 269.

47. ibid., 48.

48. 'Ihre Sprache is ihr Geist und ihr Geist ihre Sprache', ibid., 41.

49. ibid., 92; 291.

50. ibid., 115.

51. W. *von Humbolt*, 190, 3–36 volume 4 (1905), 14, volume 3 (1904), 295.

52. HUMBOLDT, 1949, 26.

53. ARENS, 1969, 205–6.

54. W. WUNDT, *Völkerpsychologie*, Leipzig, 1905–6; IORDON, 1937, ch. 2; W. BUMANN, *Die Sprachtheorie Heymann Steinthals*, Meisenheim, 1965; L. WEISGERBER, *Von den Kräften der deutschen Sprache*, volumes 1–4, Düsseldorf, 1949–50; id., *Das Menschheitsgesetz der Sprache*, Heidelberg, 1964; H. BASILUS, 'Neo Humboldtian ethnolinguistics', *Word* 8 (1952), 95–105; J. B. CARROLL, *Language, thought and reality: select writings of Benjamin*

Lee Whorf, New York, 1956; D. HYMES, 'Notes towards a history of linguistic anthropology', *Anthropological linguistics* 5 (1963), 59–103; T. BYNON, 'Leo Weisgerber's four stages in linguistic analysis', *Man* n.s. 1 (1966), 468–83; R. L. BROWN, *Wilhelm von Humboldt's conception of linguistic relativity*, The Hague, 1967.

55. HUMBOLDT, 1949, 90. E. CASSIRER, 'Die Kantischen Element in Wilhelm von Humboldts Sprachphilosophie', *Fertschrift P. Hensel*, Greiz, 1923, 105–27; U. V. SLAGLE, 'The Kantian influence on Humboldt's linguistic thought', *Historiographia linguistica* (1974), 341–50; MANCHESTER, 1985; L. FORMIGARI, 'De l'idéalisme dans les théories du langage: histoire d'une transition', *Histoire epistémologie langage* 10 (1988), 59–80.

56 HUMBOLDT, 1949, 114–26.

57. BENFEY, 1869, 366–7; BOPP, *Vergleichende Grammatik*, S 108.

58. HUMBOLDT, *Über das Entstehen der grammatischen Formen und ihren Einfluss auf die Ideenentwickelung*, 1822 (STEINTHAL, 1883, 67–101); HUMBOLDT, 1949, 204, 124.

59. MANCHESTER, 1985, chapter 7.

60. HUMBOLDT, op. cit., 292–3, 169, 258; B. KARLGREN, 'Le protochinois, langue flexionnelle', *Journal asiatique* 15 1920), 205–32. As recently as 1937 it was thought worthwhile writing an article under the title 'Has the Chinese language parts of speech?', *TPS* 1937, 99–119 (W. SIMON).

61. HUMBOLDT, 1949, 151–65; cp. C. E. BAZELL, *Linguistic typology*, London, 1958, 17–18.

62. *Compendium der vergleichenden Grammatik der indogermanischen Sprachen; kurzer Abriss einer Laut- und Formenlehre der indogermanischen Ursprache*, Weimar, 1861 (pagination from 4th edn., 1876).

63. *Handbuch der litauischen Sprache*, Prague, 1856–7.

64. HOENIGSWALD, 1963.

65. *Compendium*, 7; fuller version, *Die darwinsche Theorie und die Sprachwissenschaft* (second edition), Weimar, 1873, ad fin.

66. Text in JEPERSEN, 1922, 81–2.

67. J. SCHMIDT, *Die Vermandschaftsverhältnisse der indogermanischen Sprachen*, Weimar, 1872; cp. L. BLOOMFIELD, *Language*, London, 1935, 314–19.

68. W. S. ALLEN, *Phonetics in ancient India*, London, 1953, 62–4.

69 G. VON DER GABELENTZ, *Die Sprachwissenschaft* (second edition), Leipzig, 1901, 170.

70. Brief details and references in PEDERSEN, 1931, esp. chapter 7.

71. *Die darwinsche Theorie und die Sprachwissenschaft*, Weimar, 1863 (second edition, 1873); J. P. MAHER, 'More on the history of the comparative method: the tradition of Darwinism in August Schleicher's work', *Anthropological linguistics* 8.3 (1966), 1–12. SCHLEICHER, *Die Sprachen Europas (Linguistische Untersuchungen 2)* Bonn, 1850 (edited with introductory essay by E. F. K. Koerner. Amsterdam, 1983.

72. *Compendium*, 1–3; *Sprachvergleichende (linguistische) Untersuchun-*

gen, Bonn, 1848–1850, volume 2, 21; *Darwinsche Theorie*, 6–7; *Die deutsche Sprache* (second edition), Stuttgart, 1869, 37, 47.

73. *Über die Sprache*, 28; *Vocalismus oder Sprachvergleichende Kritiken*, Berlin, 1836, 1; 'Die Sprachen sind als organische Naturkörper anzusehen, die nach bestimmten Gesetzen sich bilden, ein inneres Lebensprinzip in sich tragend sich entwickeln, und nach und nach absterben.'

74. 'Das was Darwin für die Arten der Tiere und Pflanzen geltend macht, gilt nun aber auch, wenigstens in seinen hauptsächlichsten Zügen, für die Organismen der Sprachen', *Darwinsche Theorie*, 13; op. cit., 31–2.

75. *Sprachvergleichende Untersuchungen* 1. 4–5: 'was in der systematischen Betrachtung neben einander erscheint, das tritt in der Geschichte nach einander, auf' cp. op. cit., 2.9; T. BYRON. 'August Schleicher', in T. BYNON and F. R. PALMER, *Studies in the history of Western linguistics*, Cambridge, 1986, 133.

76. *Compendium* 4; *Sprachvergleichende (linguistiche) Untersuchungen*, 2, 10–20.

77. *Deutsches Wörterbuch*, Leipzig, 1919, volume 10.2.1., 876.

78. *Sprachvergleichende (linguistische) Untersuchungen* 2, 231: '. . . . wie schnell die Sprache eines geschchtlich und litterargeschichtlich bedeutenden Volkes herabsinken kann.'

79. e.g. L. BLOOMFIELD, *Language*, London, 1935, chapter 18, 20, 21; L. R. PALMER, *Introduction to modern linguistics*, London, 1936, chapters 3, 4, 7.

80. H. OSTHOFF and K. BRUGMANN, *Morphologische Untersuchungen* 1 (1878), iii–xx; English translation, Lehmann, 1967, 197–209.

81. Grimm, see n. 30; BOPP, *Vocalismus* 15: 'Auch suche man in Sprachen keine Gesetze die festeren Widerstand leisten als die Ufer der Flüsse und Meere'; SCHLEICHER, *Compendium* 489–90; Quite rightly in 1978, the centenary of the neogrammarian manifesto published by Osthoff and Brugmann, the Philological Society devoted its *Transactions* for the year to a retrospective examination of the theory and the practice of the neogrammarians. See also A. M. DAVIES, 'Karl Brugmann and late nineteenth-century linguistics', and H. M. HOENIGSWALD, 'Nineteenth-century linguistics on itself', in T. R. PALMER (eds.), *Studies in the history of western linguistics*, Cambridge, 1986, 150–71 and 172–88.

82. A. LESKIEN, *Declination im Slawisch-Litauischen und Germanischen*, Leipzig, 1876, xxviii: 'Lässt man beliebige, zufällige, unter einander in keinen Zusammenhang zu bringende Abweichungen zu, so erklärt man im Grunde damit, dass das Objekt der Untersuchungen, die Sprache, der wissenschaftlichen Erkenntnis nicht zugänglich ist'.

83. 'Eine Ausnahme der ersten Lautverschiebung', *Zeitschrift für vergleichende Sprachforschung* 23 (1877), 97–130 (101): 'Es muss eine Regel für die Unregelmässigkeit dasein; es gilt nur, diese ausfindig zu machen'; English tr., Lehmann, 1967, 132–63; MEILLET, 1922, 470–1.

84. H. W. B. JOSEPH, *An introduction to logic*, Oxford, 1916, chapter 19; T. C. CHRISTY, *Uniformitarianism in linguistics*, Amsterdam, 1983. It may be noted that one of W. D. Whitney's brothers was a professor of geology.

85. *Das Verbum in der Nominalkomposition*, Jena, 1878, 326: 'Die Lautgesetze der Sprachen geradezu blind, mit blinder Naturnotwendigkeit wirken.'

86. *Morphologische Untersuchungen* 1, ix–x: 'Nur derjenige vergleichende Sprachforscher, welcher aus dem hypothesentrüben Dunstkreis der Werkstätte in der man die indogermanischen Grundformen schmiedet, einmal heraustritt in die klare Luft der greifbaren Wirklichkeit und Gegenwart, um hier sich Belehrung zu holen über das, was ihn die graue Theorie nimmer erkennen lässt . . . nur der kann zu einer richtigen Vorstellung von der Lebens- und Umbildungsweise der Sprachformen gelangen.'

87. H. PAUL, *Prinzipien der Sprachgeschichte* (fifth edition), Halle, 1920 (tr. H. A. STRONG, *Principles of the history of language*, London, 1891), chapter 4; M. BRÉAL, *Essai de sémantique*, Paris, 1897, (tr. H. CUST, *Semantics: studies in the science of meaning*, London, 1900).

88. BRUGMANN and DELBRÜCK, 1886–1900; PAUL, op. cit., 20–2; W. MEYER-LÜBKE, *Grammatik der romanischen Sprachen*, Leipzig, 1890–1902.

89. H. HOIJER (ed.), *Linguistic structures of naive America*, New York, 1946, 85–129; C. F. HOCKETT, 'Implications of Bloomfield's Algonquian studies', *Language* 24 (1948), 117–31.

90. HOCKETT, 'Sound change', *Language* 41 (1965), 185–204.

91. *Grundzüge der Lautphysiologie: zur Einführung in das Studium der Lautlehre der indogermanischen Sprachen*, Leipzig, 1876.

92. OSTHOFF and BRUGMANN, *Morphologische Untersuchungen* 1, viii–ix.

93. *Zur Geschichte der deutschen Sprache*, Berlin 1868.

94. *Über die Lautgesetze: gegen die Junggrammatiker* 1885 (reprinted in L. SPITZER (ed.), *Hugo Schuchardt-Brevier*, Halle, 1928, 51–87); *Généalogie des mots qui designent l'abeille*, Paris, 1918.

95. K. VOSSLER, *Positivismus und Idealismus in der Sprachwissenschaft*, Heidelberg, 1904; B. CROCE, *Esterica come scienza dell' espressione e linguistica generale*, 1901 (ninth edition, Bari, 1950), 18: 'Anche niente più che una differenza quantitativa possiamo ammettere nel determinare il significato della parola *genio, genio artistico*, dal non-genio dall'uomo comune'; M. LEROY, 'Benedetto Croce et les études linguistiques', *Revue internationale de philosophie*, 7 (1953), 342–62.

96. 'Why does language change?', *Modern language quarterly* 4 (1943). 413–31; reply by BLOOMFIELD, *Language* 20 (1944), 45–55.

97. M. BARTOLI, *Introduzione alla neolinguistica*, Geneva, 1925; G. BONFANTE, 'The neolinguistic position', *Language* 23 (1947), 344–75.

Chapter 8

Linguistics in the present century

Centuries are a most arbitrary mode of historical periodization. But in cases where certain tendencies are concentrated in given centuries they may have some mnemonic value. Through a number of historical events and previous trends in linguistics, the nineteenth century was dominated by historical studies; but in tracing some of the developments that arose directly from the work of the neogrammarians we were led across into the twentieth; and likewise, in following up the genesis of present-day theories and attitudes, we shall be looking back into the nineteenth and preceding centuries, not merely for the antecedents of the scholars involved and the teaching that they received, but for specific movements of thought more closely connected with the present age than with the predominant concerns of the nineteenth century.

The nineteenth-century background, within which the early twentieth-century scholars grew up, has already been considered, and in it at least three major strands can be distinguished: the continuing tradition of grammatical and other linguistic work carried on by European scholars in different ways since antiquity, the progressive appreciation of Indian linguistic scholarship, especially in phonetics and phonology, and the assimilation of linguistic science, specifically as a historically orientated science, to certain general nineteenth-century attitudes, comparatism, evolutionism, and the positivism of the natural sciences.

In attempting to pick out the lines on which linguistics has moved and is moving in the present century, one is dealing with 'contemporary history'. The historical attitude is the same, but the material differs in being more plentiful and less easily formalized. On the one hand, one is concerned with persons and theories already familiar in elementary introductions to linguistics to a greater extent than with some nineteenth-century work and to a far greater extent than with the work of earlier periods; and on the other hand, the very nearness of the scene makes the discernment of definite directions and movements, and of relatively permanent 'schools', more difficult. The traveller, in lifting his eyes to survey the more distant scene whence he has passed, can view the plains, mountains, rivers, and forests that make up and characterize the terrain; but when he looks just about him, hillocks, pebbles, trees, and small streams often present no clearly outstanding picture of how the landscape will appear from a greater distance. Moreover, past scholars and their works are subject to the rough justice, and perhaps sometimes to the rough injustice, of their contemporaries and immediate successors in regard to what is found worthy of mention and development; and not all is preserved, particularly from earlier periods. It has been said that of the world's scientists most are alive today; and this is true of linguistic scientists, in view of the immense and so far unchecked expansion of linguistic studies in the world's universities. Anything like a full account of significant work in linguistics today and in the recent past, even on a scale comparable to that possible in antiquity and the Middle Ages, would be grossly disproportionate in length; and abbreviated mention would come to little more than an exercise in academic name-dropping. In this chapter the intention is broadly to survey some of the recent and current linguistic developments in their historical relationship with one another, rather than to give even a summary account of each where this is readily available in textbooks.[1]

The principal and most obvious contrast between the last two centuries has been the rapid rise of descriptive linguistics, as opposed to historical linguistics, to its present position of predominance. Significantly, the key figure in the change from nineteenth- to twentieth-century attitudes was the Swiss linguist Ferdinand de Saussure, who, after studying in Leipzig with members of the neogrammarian school, first made himself known to scholarship through an important contribution to Indo-European comparative linguistics.[2] Though he published little himself, de Saussure's lectures on linguistics in the early twentieth century so impressed some of his pupils in Paris and Geneva that in 1916 they published his *Cours de linguistique générale* as far as they could reconstruct it from their own and others' lecture notes and such materials as survived in de Saussure's hand.[3] In the history of linguistics, de Saussure is largely known and studied through what his pupils recollected of him.

De Saussure drew on a restricted range of languages, mostly the familiar languages of Europe; but his influence on twentieth-century linguistics, which he could be said to have inaugurated, is unsurpassed. The publication of the *Cours* has been likened to a 'Copernican revolution' in the subject.[4] A number of ideas on language and the study of language very much in sympathy with those of de Saussure had, in fact, been expressed nearly a century before by von Humboldt (pp. 193–5, above); the extent to which de Saussure was directly influenced by Humboldt is uncertain, though a connection has been suggested.[5] Humboldt's general linguistic theory attracted less immediate attention because at the time historical studies were in the ascendant; de Saussure's teaching came in an age when the drive of comparative and historical linguistic theory had temporarily reached an acceptable resting place in the tenets of the neogrammarians.

Historically, de Saussure's ideas may be put under three heads. Firstly, he formalized and made explicit, what earlier linguists had either assumed or ignored, the two fundamental and indispensable dimensions of linguistic study: synchronic, in which languages are treated as self-contained systems of communication at any particular time, and diachronic, in which the changers to which languages are subject in the course of time are treated historically. It was de Saussure's achievement to distinguish these two dimensions or axes of linguistics, synchronic or descriptive, and diachronic or historical, as each involving its own methods and principles and each essential in any adequate course of linguistic study or linguistic instruction. The lectures embodied in the *Cours* must be seen as a major factor in the development of descriptive linguistic studies in this century.

Secondly, he distinguished the linguistic competence of the speaker and the actual phenomena or data of linguistics (utterances), as *langue* and *parole* (like so many others, these Saussurean terms have passed untranslated into international currency). While *parole* constitutes the immediately accessible data, the linguist's proper object is the *langue* of each community, the lexicon, grammar, and phonology implanted in each individual by his upbringing in society and on the basis of which he speaks and understands his language. Much influenced by the sociological theory of Emile Durkheim, de Saussure perhaps exaggerated the suprapersonal reality of *langue* over and above the individual, more especially as he recognized that changes in *langue* proceed from changes made by individuals in their *parole*, while he yet declared that *langue* is not subject to the individual's power of change.[6]

Thirdly, de Saussure showed that any *langue* must be envisaged and described synchronically as a system of interrelated elements, lexical, grammatical, and phonological, and not as an aggregate of self-sufficient entities (which he compared to a mere nomenclature[7]). Linguistic terms are to be defined relatively to each other, not absolutely. This is the theory expressed in his statement that a *langue* is *forme, non substance*, and illustrated with his well-known metaphors of chessmen and trains, identified and known by their place in the whole system, of the game or the railway network, and not by their actual substantial composition.[8] In a language these interrelations lie on each of the two fundamental dimensions of synchronic linguistic structure, syntagmatic, in line with the succession of utterance, and paradigmatic (associative), in systems of contrastive elements or categories.[9]

This statement of the structural approach to language underlies virtually the whole of modern linguistics, and justifies de Saussure's claim on the independence of linguistics as a subject of study in its own right.[10] Whatever the different interpretations placed on the exact meaning of 'structuralism', few linguists would now disclaim structural thinking in their work.

Hjelmslev's glossematics may be regarded as the Saussurean emphasis on form as against substance in the 'content plane' (semantics and grammar) and in the 'expression plane' (phonology), and on the definition of form as the interrelations of elements, both carried to their logical extremes; that is to say, content analysis must be independent of extra-linguistic existential criteria, and expression analysis (phonology) must be independent of (assumed extra-linguistic) phonetic criteria. Relations between elements, not the elements themselves, are the object of a science, and only by keeping this strictly to the fore can the Saussurean ideal of an autonomous linguistics, not dependent on any other discipline, be realized. The two planes are each regarded as analysable into ultimate constituents (e.g. *mare* into /m/, /ɛ/, /ə/, or *m, a, r, e*, on the plane of expression, and into 'horse', 'female', 'singular', on the plane of content). They are not isomorphous, as no connection can be drawn between the individual phonemes or letters and the minimal elements of content; but both planes are to be analysed in an analogous way, and each is co-ordinate and equivalent in a language system. It is precisely this claim to equivalence between the two planes that others have found difficult to accept, since differences in expression are independently observable in a language and belong to a strictly circumscribed field, whereas differences in semantic content (which is limitless) are only revealed through differences in expression in a language.[11]

Elsewhere in linguistics, the structural study of meanings as depending in part on the co-presence in a language of numbers of related lexical terms in semantic fields represents the working out of ideas brought into prominence by de Saussure.[12]

But the most immediate and historically one of the most important effects of de Saussure's structural theory of language was in the realm of phonology, where it coincided remarkably with the tentative position reached about the same time in phonetics as the result of the work of nineteenth-century phoneticians.

Phonetics, with its allied activities and applications in shorthand, language teaching, and spelling reform, had received considerable attention in England from the Renaissance onwards; and the general stimulus to phonetic studies from the discovery of Indian phonetic work at the end of the eighteenth century has been mentioned in chapter 6.[13] Sir William Jones himself expressed and aroused great interest in the problems of the phonetic transcription of languages such as Sanskrit, Persian, and Arabic, which had a long tradition of literacy in systems of writing other than roman letters. His 'Dissertation on the orthography of Asiatick words in roman letters' praised the phonological appropriateness of the Devanagari syllabary and of the Arabic script to the disadvantage of English alphabetic spelling. Unlike most of his contemporaries he clearly distinguished between letter and sound, and he vigorously protested against the paedagogical reference to 'five vowels' in English.[14]

Sir William Jones's phonetic work was studied carefully in England by A. J. Ellis, who collaborated with Sir Isaac Pitman on alphabetic reform; and English interest in the physiology of speech led to the publication of C. R. Lepsius's *Standard alphabet*,[15] a cooperative product of English and continental scholarship, setting out the possible vowel and consonant sound types classified by their articulation, represented by distinctive symbols, and illustrated from a number of different languages. This was followed in 1889 by the revised International Phonetic Alphabet of what was later designated the International Phonetic Association. This alphabet, the 'IPA', has been kept continuously in print subject to periodic revision in arrangement, symbolization, and terminology.

Through the emigration of the remarkable Bell family, this same interest resulted in the invention of the telephone in the United States, where the name of the youngest Bell (Alexander Graham, 1847–1922) is commemorated in the Bell Telephone Company of America. He, like his father, Alexander Melville (1819–1905) and his grandfather, Alexander (1790–1865), worked on speech training and remedial applications of phonetics. A M. Bell was the inventor of a system of 'visible speech', on the lines of earlier attempts (p. 132, above), wherein each separate process of articulation received its own graphic notation. This system was adopted, with some corrections and modifications by Sweet in his *Primer of phonetics*.[16]

Henry Sweet (1845–1912) was one of the leaders in the study of phonetics and of Old, Middle, and New (modern) English in Great Britain in the second half of the nineteenth century. He was temperamentally inclined towards the synchronic, descriptive aspects of linguistics, in part by his rather intense nationalism and his hostility towards the dominant historical linguistic scholarship which he rightly associated with Germany. As it happened, in the perversity of human affairs, recognition for being the outstanding scholar that he was came more readily abroad, and notably in Germany, than in this country, where his outspokenly critical bearing, suspiciousness, and, in later years, his justified resentment prevented him from ever attaining professorial rank in a British university.[17]

During the nineteenth century, phonetic work drew on the progress of the allied fields of physiology and acoustics, and experimental investigations were an accepted part of phonetic research by the end of the century. The applications of phonetics in spelling reform and in language teaching were regarded as playing a major part in current efforts towards the extension of education and the cause of social progress in general.[18]

Up to the time of Sweet, phoneticians had concerned themselves with spelling reform, including the devising of additional alphabetic symbols, and with universal phonetic symbol systems. In the latter half of the century it became evident that with the increase in phonetic sophistication every orthography, however much it was reformed, would omit many observable phonetic differences, and that any narrow transcription that came anywhere near the unattainable goal of 'one sound, one symbol' would be too hopelessly complicated for practical use in the writing of a language. The approach to this dilemma can be seen in Sweet's early writing. In his *Handbook of phonetics* (1877) he drew the distinction between sounds whose differences depend in the language on their phonetic environment and are therefore non-distinctive, and sounds which may by themselves establish two words as lexically separate items. Virtually the same phonetic difference may be distinctive in one language and non-distinctive in another; and only the distinctive sound differences need separate notation in a broad transcription system for a particular language.[19] Since the relatively few distinctive sounds in a language could be readily transcribed with roman letters plus a few others, Sweet coined the term *broad romic*, as against narrow transcriptions, which needed many more and more diverse symbols.

Sweet did not use the term *phoneme*, though the concept clearly underlies his work. The explicit terminological distinction between sound or phone and phoneme was the work of a Polish scholar teaching in Russia, Baudouin de Courtenay, who made technical use of the Russian word *fonema*. His theory of the phoneme was published in 1893, but he had probably arrived at it rather earlier, around the same time as Sweet, though there was no contact between them then.[20]

It was not, however, before the second decade of the twentieth century, after the teaching of de Saussure had begun to make its impact, that the term *phoneme* gained wide currency, soon thereafter to become a linguistic universal. De Saussure had used the French word *phonème*, though generally in the sense of speech sound as a phonetic occurrence; but his structural theory of language in its application to phonology quite clearly formulated the concept of phonemic distinctiveness as its centrepiece.

Daniel Jones made it the basis of 'broad' versus 'narrow' transcription (terms previously used by Sweet) in his *Outline of English phonetics*, first published in 1918. During the twenties its status as a linguistic unit, or as a class of sounds, was debated and it was variously held to be a psychological entity, a physiological entity, a transcendental entity, and just a mere descriptive invention.[21] But the first really significant development in the evolution of the theory of the phoneme was the work of the Prague school in the twenties and thirties.

The Prague school was a group of Czech and other scholars, including Roman Jakobson, doctrinally centred round Prince Nikolai Trubetzkoy, a professor in Vienna 1923–38, Vilem Mathesius, and Roman Jakobson, which held regular meetings and published the *Travaux du cercle linguistique de Prague*. Their main interest lay in phonological theory, and the most important work associated with the school was Trubetzkoy's *Grundzüge der Phonologie* (principles of phonology), on which he was working up to his death.[22]

Trubetzkoy and the Prague phonologists applied Saussurean theory to the elaboration of the phoneme concept. Speech sounds belonged to *parole*, the phoneme belonged to *langue*. In studying languages as systems of internally related elements, Prague scholars did not treat the phoneme as a mere class of sounds or as a transcriptional device, but as a complex phonological unit realized by the sounds of speech. The relation of realization (representation or implementation) between units at one level and those at another level is fundamental to Prague theory. Each phoneme was composed by a number of separate distinctive or 'pertinent' features, which alone characterized it as a linguistic entity; and each distinctive feature stood in a definite opposition to its absence or to another feature in at least one other phoneme in the language. Phonological systems were classed in various ways according to the features distinguishing their component phonemes; thus English /p/, /b/, /t/, /d/, and /k/, /g/ formed oppositions of voicelessness and voice at each articulatory position, while ancient Greek had a three term plosive system

$$/p/ \qquad /t/ \qquad /k/$$

$$/p^h/ \quad /b/ \quad /t^h/ \quad /d/ \quad /k^h/ \quad /g/$$

involving the oppositions of voice and its absence and aspiration and its absence.[23]

The analysis of speech sounds into their component articulation features was not new, but the analysis of the unitary phonemes of the phonological level, that were realized by speech sounds, into ordered sets of specific contrasts between a smaller number of distinctive features was a definite advance in phonological theory and descriptive method.

Moreover this analysis below the phoneme revealed the complexity of phonological systems. Phonemes were seen not to be all members of one undifferentiated set of contrastive units in a language, but to enter into different systems of relations in different positions. /p/, /b/, /t/, /d/, and /k/, /g/ contrast as voiceless and voiced initially, medially, and finally in English words, but after initial /s/ the voice–voiceless contrast is non-operative or 'neutralized', as only one plosive can occur at each point of articulation. The same contrast is neutralized in German in word final position, where only voiceless plosives in the plosive class are found. This more refined analysis of phonological contrast was expressed by setting up 'archiphonemes', comprising just the features still distinctive in these positions of neutralization (i.e. bilabiality, etc. and plosion).

Similar processes of analysis were applied to features other than the consonant and vowel segments with which phonological theory had begun, the so-called prosodic (non-segmental) features of syllables, such as length, stress, and pitch (including intonation), an extension of descriptive phonology having important implications for the future. An equally significant move included

in phonological analysis the syntagmatic functions of certain
sound units and sound features as demarcators of syllable and
word boundaries in addition to their paradigmatic function in constituting distinct phonemes. In this syntagmatic, demarcative role
they were referred to as *Grenzsignale* or *signes oristiques* (boundary markers).[24]

The phoneme concept had originated in the search for the
theory of broad transcription. As the result of the work of the
Prague school it became one of the fundamental elements of linguistic theory as a whole, and of the scientific description and
analysis of languages.

While the main efforts of the Prague school were directed to
the explication of the phoneme concept and the development of
phonological theory, its members made a number of contributions
to other areas of linguistics, including the more peripheral topics
such as stylistics. Several syntactic studies were published, and
the comparative syntactic typology of Czech and other Slavic languages is strongly represented in the work of Czech linguists since
1945.[25] In morphology, Jakobson's study of the Russian case
system and his attempt to abstract from it a basic semantic content for each case represents an application of the same analytic
procedures as were being applied in phonology to the description
of grammatical categories.[26]

The linguistic theory worked out, with phonological analysis
principally in mind, by Trubetzkoy and his associates of the
Prague school led to a number of very important developments.
The analysis of linguistic units in terms of sets of distinctive features, already extended to morphology by Jakobson, has been
further applied to grammatical analysis in general and is now
central in much transformational-generative grammar (p. 252
below)[27] though the essential fluidity and indeterminacy of lexical
meanings in many, perhaps most, words in natural languages
makes it unlikely that anything like a total semantic analysis can
be acheived by these means alone.[28] This type of analysis has been
extended to semantics, in the hope that it may help to formalize
the apparently limitless range of semantic functions or meanings
carried by lexical items in languages. Obvious places for its application are restricted lexical sub-systems of terms in culturally
delimited areas, such as kinship vocabularies. In English, for example, 'aunt' can be analysed into 'kin', 'first degree ascending
generation', 'first degree collaterality' and 'female', contrasting
with 'uncle' by the feature of sex difference. Several attempts
have been made to extend this sort of componential schematization to other and wider areas of the lexicons of languages.

In phonetics and phonology, distinctive feature analysis made striking advances in alliance with instrumental and acoustic studies of speech transmission. This development has been particularly associated with R. Jakobson, one of the original Prague circle, who relatively early in his career decided that more light would be shed on some phonological questions by considering the distinctive features composing phonemes from the acoustic and from the hearer's point of view rather than from the articulatory or the speaker's position. In this approach, Jakobson drew on the findings of earlier acousticians such an H. von Helmholtz and C. Stumpf for the basic triangles

$$/i/ \quad /u/ \qquad /t/ \quad /p/$$
$$\text{and}$$
$$/a/ \qquad /k/$$

wherein acuteness and gravity are contrasted horizontally, and diffuseness and compactness are contrasted vertically, as acoustic features resulting from differences in the configurations of the vocal tract.[29]

Under pressure of war Jakobson moved to the United States, and in collaboration with scholars working with such equipment as the sound spectrograph he analysed the inherent distinctiveness of the phonemes of all languages into combinations of up to twelve binary contrasts of acoustic features, defined in terms of the distribution of energy at different frequencies ('formants') in their sound waves, rather than directly in relation to their articulations.[30] In this type of analysis, phonological systems are set out on a matrix of feature oppositions, the phonemes participating in more than one binary contrast in relation to the other phonemes of the language. This is displayed in Jakobson's and Lotz's diagram of the phonemic system of French. Feature analysis, in which segmental units are taken theoretically as no more than sets of simultaneous distinctive features, has provided one mode of stating the phonological link between the output of the syntactic component and the transcribed utterance in transformational-generative grammar (p. 252 below).[31]

In historical linguistics, the phoneme theory, especially in its Prague interpretation, led to a significant development of the neogrammarian position (pp. 202–3 above). The neogrammarian achievement had been to formalize and to make explicit the concept of the sound law, and it was with sounds as individual phonetic segments that they were concerned. When sound change was reconsidered in the light of the phoneme theory, by which the sounds of languages were understood as forming interrelated systems of contrasts, attention was paid to the evolution of phonological systems rather than to the changes of individual and supposedly independent sounds. This approach could be and was made from two different directions. Firstly, the end product of a sound change was a different phonological system, unless the change related merely to phonetic difference within the limits of an existing set of contrasts. In an eight vowel system with four front and four back vowel phonemes, the merger of two back vowels (say [ɔ]>[o]) entails the loss of the contrast of /ɔ/ and /o/, and an asymmetrical system of four front and three back vowel phonemes results. Jakobson traces the sequence in Latvian of /k/ and /g/ developing fronted allophones before the front vowels /i/ and /e/ ([ts] and [dz]), and these becoming separate phonemes, /ts/ and /dz/, contrasting with /k/ and /g/, after /ai/ had been monophthongized to /i/; Fourquet has re-examined and reinterpreted the Germanic sound changes comprising 'Grimm's Law' in terms of the evolution of systems rather than of the changes of particular sounds, and has sought to explain the historical phenomena as the maintenance of phonological oppositions under the pressure of successive general changes in the force of articulation on the part of speakers.[32]

Secondly, sound change can be considered not as regards its systemic effect, but from the viewpoint of its systemic causation. The neogrammarians had played very safe over the question of the causes of sound change, and Bloomfield followed them in declaring: 'The causes of sound-change are unknown.'[33] The occasion for sound change has always been seen in the conditions in which speech is transmitted as a socially learned capability from one generation to another; but quite certainly the causes are multiple and complex. External factors such as language contacts, bilingualism, the effects of substrates in the superimposition of an alien language upon a speech community, and the influence of writing systems must all be acknowledged. But a significant cause of sound changes is to be found within the phonological systems of languages themselves.

Strangely enough, de Saussure, for all his emphasis on the importance of the structural conception of language in synchronic linguistics, went so far as to deny explicitly any diachronic relevance of structure.[34] But two factors are constantly at work within phonological systems. The economy of effort produced by the multiple use of each feature contrast that has been once mastered tends towards the maintenance and the generation of symmetry in phoneme systems (/p/, /t/, /k/, /d/, /g/ requires as many contrasting articulation features as the fuller and more symmetrical system /p/, /t/, /k/, /b/, /d/, /g/); but the physiological asymmetry of the vocal tract interferes with the achievement of permanent symmetry (for example, in the matter of distinctive degrees of tongue height in vowel phonemes, there is more latitude for keeping the front vowels apart than for the back vowels). A. Martinet cites as an illustration the fronting of /u/ in Azores Portuguese, whereby the exploitation of the front-back contrast (acoustically acute-grave) in the close rounded vowel phoneme releases more space for the ready maintenance of phonemic contrast between the remaining back vowels, /a/, /ɔ/, and /o/.[35]

Researches on these lines, and the broadening of the theory of historical linguistics to embrace their results do not invalidate the neogrammarian insistence on the regularity of sound change as the basis of historical linguistics; but they do bring to historical linguistics further important insights and more powerful means of investigation.

During the nineteenth century, Russian linguists were in touch with general European developments, and the phoneme concept was apparently arrived at independently by eastern and western scholars at about the same time (p. 224 above). Trubetzkoy was Russian by birth and education, and hád worked on some of the vernacular languages of the Russian empire before leaving the country after the first world war. The Bolshevik revolution brought with it a sharp break with the linguistic scholarship of the rest of the world, and during the twenties, thirties, and forties, although phonological work went on and with it the study of the phoneme theory, Soviet linguistics was dominated by the eccentric dogmatisms of N. J. Marr (1864–1934).

Marr, himself half Georgian by birth and from his early youth gifted with remarkable language learning ability, turned his attention first, like some other Russian scholars, to Georgian and the rest of the Caucasian languages. In investigating the history of the Caucasian languages he gradually evolved his own theory (or theories) of linguistic history. Rejecting the accepted Indo-European theory, he drew his ideas from eighteenth-century beliefs in the gestural origin of language and from middle nineteenth-century opinion on linguistic typology as an indication of stages of progressive linguistic development. The 'Japhetic' languages, a term he used to cover the languages of the Caucasus, represented a stage in the evolution of language through which some other languages had already passed. Languages were historically related, not in linguistic families, but by the different evolutionary 'layers' of structure deposited from continual mixtures and combinations. Languages were not national, but class phenomena, and were part of the superstructure whose changes corresponded to changes in the economic base of the speakers' social organization; here he claimed the theoretical alliance of Marrism and Marxism.

Claiming to explain not only linguistic history but also linguistic prehistory by his theory, Marr soon transcended merely observational statements, and declared that the words of all languages could be traced back to four primitive elements: [sal], [ber], [jon], and [roʃ]. Such unsupported theorizing enjoyed official patronage, and several other Russian scholars found it prudent to uphold and even eulogize Marr's pronouncements, until 1950 when suddenly Stalin ordained the rejection of the whole Marrist edifice, pointing out, among other things, that language was not dependent on economic organization since the same Russian language served both pre-revolutionary capitalism and post-revolutionary communism, a statement of the obvious not apparently made before. Stalin's intervention both ended the long reign of Marrist theory and drew the world's attention to it.[36] Since then, with the post-war expansion of international cooperation in linguistic studies, Russian linguists have started to work in closer contact with those of the rest of western Europe and America, and current western developments are being keenly and fruitfully debated. In general linguistics particular attention is paid to lexicography, which is accorded the status of a component of linguistics along with phonology and grammar, rather than being merely a part of the description of languages. In comparative and historical linguistics, Slavic studies, suppressed under the eccentricities of Marr, have seen very considerable development. There is good hope that these tendencies will continue, and that Marrism will be remembered only as a sterile aberration, an awful warning of the extent to which modern tyranny can keep fantasy enthroned in defiance of fact. In particular within the context of traditional Indo-European studies we must take notice of a potentially far-reaching revision of opinions on the homeland, the dispersion and the structure of the Indo-European languages as a result of proposals by the Soviet scholars Gamkrelidze and Ivanov.[37]

Soon after the publications of de Saussure's *Cours*, other books were published in Europe dealing wholly or principally with synchronic linguistics, for example, O. Jespersen's *Language*, A. Gardiner's *Theory of speech and language*, K. Bühler's *Sprachtheorie*, and two important books written by Hjelmslev before the full working out of his glossematic theory, *Principes de grammaire générale* and *La catégorie des cas*.[38] At the same time certain trends in philosophical thought were bringing logicians into closer contact with the problems of linguistic analysis.[39] The inauguration of a series of international congresses of linguists in 1928 is further illustration of the growth of interest in general linguistic research.

However, it was in America that linguistics, and in particular descriptive linguistics, received most recognition in universities during the 1920s; and the course of American linguistics in the interwar decades exercised a profound and lasting effect on the development of linguistic studies and linguistic thinking throughout the world. In 1924 the Linguistic Society of America was constituted, with the periodical *Language* as its annual publication.

Three outstanding scholars set American linguistics on its course, Franz Boas, Edward Sapir, and Leonard Bloomfield. Boas was the eldest and he taught several American linguists of the next generation. Bloomfield is quoted as referring to him as 'the teacher in one or another sense of us all', and he paid generous tribute to his work for American linguistics in his obituary.[40]

These three men were not detached from their antecedents. Boas and Sapir were born in Europe, and Bloomfield studied neogrammarian historical linguistics under Leskien and Brugmann (1913–14). They were familiar with the work of the earlier American historical linguist and Sanskritist W. D. Whitney, himself much influenced by nineteenth-century European thought. Boas's and Sapir's basic attitude to language in its intimate bonds with the whole way of life and way of thought of its speakers can in great part be traced back to Humboldtian ideas (pp. 194–5 above). Noticeably in his writing on phonemic theory and procedure, Sapir espoused the psychological view of the phoneme, stressing the correspondence between the linguist's abstraction and the native speaker's reactions and intuitions on his language.[41]

American linguistics at this formative time. American theory was conditioned by the rigorous positivism of the behaviourist or mechanist psychologists. This influence was especially strong in Bloomfield, who in writing his standard textbook, *Language* (first published in 1933), drastically revised his earlier *Introduction to linguistic science* (London and New York, 1914), to bring its theoretical basis in line with the mechanist outlook of such behaviourists as A. P. Weiss, wherein statements about human activity and experience must be wholly expressed in terms relating, at least potentially, to phenomena observable in space and time by any and every observer. Bloomfield's 'talking to oneself or thinking' and 'mental images, feelings and the like are merely popular terms for various bodily movements' are typical of this attitude.[42]

On the practical side, the anthropological interest of Boas and Sapir were reflected in the close collaboration and association of anthropology and linguistics in American universities. Anthropologists and linguists faced a joint challenge in the vast field of the almost wholly preliterate American-Indian languages, scattered, often in small and dwindling communities, over so much of the United States and Canada. Since colonial days, missionaries, traders, and enthusiastic amateurs had compiled dictionaries and grammars of a number of these languages, and in 1891 J. W. Powell published the first full-scale classification of them.[43] Boas concentrated his work on these languages, and in addition to several descriptive studies he edited and in part wrote the *Handbook of American-Indian languages*.[44] Its *Introduction*, by Boas, is still an excellent introduction to descriptive linguistics.

Some American linguists made these languages their prime concern, extending their scope to include the languages of Central and South America (where Spanish and Portuguese missionaries and others had done work in earlier centuries); and many others prepared a descriptive account of one native American language in the course of their career, often as a doctoral thesis. The languages chosen had in most cases had little previous scholarship expended on them, and the field worker was learning the language at the same time as he was analysing it, a situation quite unlike that prevailing in earlier studies of most European languages. He was cast upon his own resources, and had himself to decide on and justify every statement and classification he made. This was, and still is, a most valuable part of a training in linguistics. One can contrast the amount of work done by the 'Bloomfieldian' linguists on American-Indian languages with the early development of transformational-generative linguistics carried out largely in English or in familiar European languages.

Sapir and Bloomfield stood in contrast, and they complemented each other in their approaches to their subject. Bloomfield was rigorously scientific, in the light of his own, mechanist, interpretation of science, concentrating on methodology and on formal analysis. Sapir, by contrast, ranged widely through and around his subject, exploring its relations with literature, music, anthropology, and psychology, and expressing views on language, like those of Boas, that were reminiscent of

Humboldt and were later developed by Whorf, both of whom insisted on the pervasive influence of language on human life. A glance through his *Selected writings* shows how wide was the scope of his scholarship, and a comparison of his *Language* with Bloomfield's *Language* gives a fair picture of the differences in their approaches to their subject.[45]

Because of the status of his book *Language* as a students' textbook (though it is much more than that) and his deliberate concentration on methodology, Bloomfield's interpretation of linguistics predominated in the attitude and outlook of most American linguistics during the thirties and forties. Much of the work done in these years was conceived by the scholars involved in it as the articulation or development of some of the ideas or suggestions expressed by Bloomfield; and the ensuing period has now come to be known as the 'Bloomfieldian era', although it cannot be said that every one of its characteristics can be directly traced back to Bloomfield's teaching.

Every scholar is an individual, and 'schools' and 'periods' are abstractions doing doubtful justice to the work and the workers actually compromised in them. But in a survey such as this, 'Bloomfieldian linguistics' can reasonably be treated as a unity; and because, during this period (1933–57), linguistics as an autonomous discipline became more firmly established and more widely represented in universities of the United States than elsewhere, Bloomfieldian influences were felt over the whole learned world in linguistic studies.

American linguists concentrated their attention on formal analysis by means of objectively describable operations and concepts, as Bloomfield had insisted that one should. The two fundamental units of description were the phoneme, successively extended to include all phonologically distinctive phonetic phenomena (p. 235, below), and the morpheme, the minimal unit of grammatical structure. The distinction between speech sound and phoneme was generally interpreted as that between member and class, with *phone* and *allophone* used to denote speech sounds. Grammatical analysis modelled itself on the already established phonological method, using *morph*, *allomorph*, and *morpheme* in the same way.[46]

It may fairly be said that phonology was the pace-maker in the Bloomfieldian era, as far as descriptive theory and methodology were concerned. By far the strongest impulse to a revision of theory and of its associated concepts came from progress in phonetic observation and phonological analysis. The Prague school and the earlier Firthians in fact devoted most of their attention to the phonological level of language; Jones concerned himself wholly with phonology and phonetics; and in America phonemic theory advanced further in its chosen direction than grammatical theory, and the grammatical theory of the time, with its especial interest in morphemic analysis, followed in the wake of progress in phonemics. In a comment on Hockett's *Manual of phonology* (1955), published towards the end of the period, one can read the well justified remark that a comparable manual of grammar could not as yet be envisaged.[47]

Though Bloomfield had devoted some attention to the formal definition of the word as a grammatical unit, later American linguists placed less weight on it in grammatical description. Sentence structure was set out in terms of immediate constituent analysis, in which the morphemes were linked together in trees, representing constructions of ascending size and complexity (such an analysis was implicit in the 'parsing and analysis' of traditional paedagogy, and was partially involved in Jespersen's theory of ranks). Bloomfield made a basic distinction between endocentric and exocentric constructions, according to whether the construction was or was not itself broadly similar syntactically to any of its own immediate constituents, and later generations formalized a preference for binary divisions within constituents.[48]

The generally favoured model of statement, in phonology and in grammar, was that of distribution. Some linguists of the period were characterized as 'distributionalists', and linguistic description was held by them to be the statement of the distributional relations of phonemes in phoneme sequences and of morphemes in morpheme groups and constituents. Thus Z. S. Harris, whose *Methods in structural linguistics* may be regarded as the development of certain aspects of Bloomfieldianism to their extremes, could write that linguistic procedures were directed at a 'twice-made application of two major steps: the setting up of elements, and the statement of the distribution of these elements relative to each other' more generally in recent years the terms *structuralism* and *structuralist* have been used restrictedly to refer to linguistic analysis modelled on Bloomfield's thinking.[49]

In such procedures the traditional distinction between syntax and morphology tended to be somewhat downgraded in importance; and also, in the interests of purely distributional statement, 'process' terminology (wherein forms are said to be related in terms of processes such as vowel change (*Ablaut*) or consonant alternation) was as far as possible avoided. Quite illegitimately, descriptive process was sometimes allegedly confounded with historical process, and therefore disliked in synchronic linguistics.[50]

The relation of the two levels, grammar (morphemics) and phonology (phonemics) was the province of morphophonemics, the link between the two principal aspects of formal linguistic analysis (Prague linguists had used *morphophonology* in a similar sense). It was first conceived as a relation of composition; morphemes were said to be composed or to consist of phonemes. This relationship is hard to maintain in the face of allomorphic variation in which different, and sometimes wholly different, phoneme sequences are morphemically equivalent, and later writers generally interpreted the relation between phoneme and morpheme as one of representation: phonemes compose morphs, and thereby represent the morpheme as a class.[51]

The two levels were considered to be hierarchically ordered in that morphemic analysis presupposed phonemic analysis, but not *vice versa*. The doctrine of the 'separation of levels', though not found as such in Bloomfield, was pressed by some linguists, G. L. Trager, for example, to such lengths that no grammatical statement of any kind could be legitimately used in phonemic analysis, and, conversely, grammatical analysis could only begin when phonemic analysis had been completed in a language. The deliberate abandonment of such 'grammatical prerequisites' as grammatical word boundaries laid a great, and some would say an intolerable, weight on the juncture phonemes delimiting phonemic words (wordlike sequences of phonemes juncturally definable).[52] A phonemic transcription, given the statement of the allophones of all the phonemes of a language, must, on this view be unambiguously and directly readable (excepting only for free variation among allophones), and, conversely, any uttered text must have one, and only one, phonemic transcription. This theoretical demand was later referred to as the requirement of 'biuniqueness'. D. Jones's limitation of phonemic analysis to phonetic phenomena within word boundaries was criticized as inadequate just because of its lack of biuniqueness, which, in fact, is now rejected by Chomsky.[53]

Grammatical statement in purely distributional terms, framed comparably to sequential phonemic statement, put a premium, in terms of case of analysis, on languages and parts of languages in which successive morphemes could be matched in one-to-one relations with successive phonemes or phoneme groups, and the less allomorphic variation among the bound forms (internal *sandhi*) the better. In English, words like *baked* and *cats* were more easily analysable morphemically than *took* and *mice*, and sometimes zero morphs were set up to provide a theoretical sequence when the word shape did not provide one: *took* was analysed as /tuk/

+ ∅,/tuk/ being an allomorph of /teik/, and ∅ being an allomorph of the past tense suffix, like /-d/, /-t/, -id/, etc.; and *mice* was analysed as /mais/ +∅,/ mais/ being an allomorph of /maws/ and ∅ an allomorph of the plural suffix, like /-s/, /-z/, /-iz/, /-ən/, etc.[54] Distributionalist typological evaluation would therefore seem to rate highest the agglutinative languages rather than the flexional languages, which involve much internal *sandhi*, *Ablaut*, and similar formations, so prized by nineteenth-century typologists (pp. 195, 200–1, above).

'Bloomfieldian' linguistics as it ultimately developed is presented in a number of textbooks produced towards the end of this period in the history of the subject: C. F. Hockett's *Course in modern linguistics*, H. A. Gleason's *Introduction to descriptive linguistics*, and A. A. Hill's *Introduction to linguistic structures*.[55] The period is surveyed historically through selected texts in M. Joos's *Readings in linguistics*, and various aspects of it are covered in some of the contributions to *Trends in European and American linguistics* 1930–1960.[56]

A turning point in linguistics in this century is generally attached to the year 1957, when Chomsky's *Syntactic structures* was first published, effectively introducing the linguistic public, firstly in America, then in the rest of the English-speaking world, and ultimately the whole world of linguistic scholarship, to what was called transformational-generative grammar. With the benefit of more than thirty years' hindsight it is possible to discern some major lines in the vast outpouring of linguistic publications of all sorts.

The two foremost movements in linguistics over the middle and later years of this century can be identified with Leonard Bloomfield on the one hand and, on the other, with those linguists who, for one reason or another, opposed part or all of his doctrine and methods. Of these latter, Chomsky and the generative grammarians are by no means the only representatives, but they are by far the most prominent, the most numerous, and deservedly the best known. In a historical treatment of this century's work in linguistics it is more appropriate to endeavour to place the leading scholars and schools in the larger context of Bloomfieldian, 'structuralist' linguistics and the various reactions to it, than it would be to try to give a summary account of the various competing theories and methods, an effort more appropriate to a general introductory textbook to the subject.[57]

The emotionally felt obligation shared by all the participants has been and remains that of conceiving and developing linguistics as a science, so that human language could share, or could be studied in a science that shared, the general progress that was made in the nineteenth and twentieth centuries by the natural and the social sciences. We have seen how in the nineteenth century the study of language was largely equated with its historical study, 'comparative grammar' or comparative-historical linguistics. This was part of Bloomfield's training and early scholarship. As a graduate and doctoral student he read Germanic linguistic studies, and he spent two early years working under Leskien and Brugmann in Leipzig, just before the first world war. Dedicated to the scientific treatment of language, he declared that Grimm's *Deutsche Grammatik* was 'the first great scientific linguistic work of the world'.[58] Bloomfield's own ambition, and in his own terms his achievement, were to subject descriptive linguistics to a comparably rigorous scientific treatment. His conception of science and of scientific methodology was set out through the whole of his major work *Language*, in several shorter publications, and in his *Linguistic aspects of science*.[59]

The problem, of course, was and remains the question: What criteria of science are applicable to linguistics as a science? For Bloomfield there was no doubt; science was empiricism interpreted and practised very strictly. His empiricist method was reductionist, deliberately concentrating on those aspects of language which could be exhaustively treated on empiricist lines as he understood them: 'Science shall deal only with events that are accessible in their time and place to any and all observers or only with events that are placed in coordinates of time and space.' Applied to the human sciences this led him to espouse behaviourism, and this was the precept that he handed on to his disciples, and which by and large they endeavoured to observe and to explicate. Effectively it involved the concentration on phonetics, phonological analysis, and formal grammar with an emphasis on morphology, all fields in which analysis could be based on publicly observable phenomena, speech as uttered, heard, and recorded, and words and texts as spoken or written. Its strengths were and remain solid, and in their own terms they are unchallengeable. The data are public and publicly checkable, and the methods are explicitly set out and followed. Indeed, it is noticeable how many textbooks and basic articles from the years 1940 to 1956 combine theoretical exposition with prescriptions for successful analysis, often of field notes gathered under field conditions in the investigation of languages–for example, those of native America, for the first time, prescribing the so-called 'discovery procedures'.[60]

Semantics, the study of linguistic meaning, is just that aspect of linguistics least amenable to scientific treatment as thus interpreted on rigorously empiricist lines. Apart from some restricted technical vocabulary–for example, that of chemistry–anything like a full analysis of what is meant by a word or by a sentence form to a native speaker must involve a vast and indeterminate amount of extralinguistics knowledge and the recognition of many private perceptions, feelings, thoughts, emotions, hopes, and fears, etc., which necessarily have to remain private, directly accessible to oneself and only inferable in others by what they may say about them or by their general behaviour. This is the explanation of Bloomfield's pessimistic observation in *Language*: 'The statement of meanings is the weak point in language study', and for his rather laboured glossing of perfectly recognizable commonsense words like *hungry* and *thirsty* by paraphrases referring to phenomena actually or potentially public and accessible to all observers: 'She was hungry; that is, some of her muscles were contracting, and some fluids were being secreted, especially in her stomach', and 'She was also thirsty: her tongue and her throat were dry'.[61]

Bloomfield's dismissive pronouncement on the possibilities of semantic analysis on the same scale of rigour that he required on the formal side of language encouraged almost a generation of linguists to neglect the pursuit of semantic studies in any depth, and even to exclude them from the main concern of the linguist.[62] Such was not Bloomfield's intention, and he resented publicly the suggestion that he or any other significant group of linguists ignored meaning or sought to study language without taking meaning into account.[63] What he claimed was that semantic analysis could not hope to come anywhere near the scientific precision open to the formal analysis of linguistic data as observed and recorded, that any such analysis of meanings would require a vast knowledge outside that of linguistics itself, and that meanings, real or supposed, could not properly be used as criteria in analytic procedures for just these reasons. Pushed to precision, the analysis and therefore the criteria break down. Examples are easy to find: the question whether a sunset is a thing, a state, or a process in time can be debated indefinitely; the status of a field of grain as a singularity or a collectivity is likewise indeterminate. But the distributional facts, *this is a fine sunset, the wheat is doing well*, and *the oats are doing well* are formally decisive in the analysis of English *sunset* as a noun and of *wheat* and *oats* as singular and plural nouns, respectively. And such is quite clear to any English speaker, whether or not he is able to distinguish the two sorts of grain seen growing in the fields.

Bloomfield, then, was a scientist; a scientist as he understood the demands of science: the linguist should handle what he could best handle within his science, relying on a set of publicly observable operations directed at publicly observable data. This was the *persona* he deliberately put forward as a scientist, but it was not his own private *persona* at all. It is clear that as a man he was as sensitive, as artistic, as appreciative of literature, and generally as cultivated as anyone, and probably more so than most.

His own reading was in no way restricted by his methodological constraints. He pronounced Humboldt's *Verschiedenheit* (p. 193, above) to be 'the first great book on general linguistics', though neither the book nor its author were at all confined within what Bloomfield held as the canons of scientific acceptability.[64]

In the years 1940 to the present time the greater part of linguistic theory and practice may be regarded as either the continuation of what had been, or was considered to have been, his teaching, or as reactions in different directions against it. We should consider in turn the major post-Bloomfieldian theories, but what is important historically is to see how they all in their own way are aimed at widening the scope of linguistic science and, thereby, freeing it from at least some of Bloomfield's restrictions and enriching it without invalidating its essentially scientific basis. The general theme was that Bloomfield had excluded more than was either necessary or desirable from the scientific study of language.

However, while it is true that all linguistic theorists in recent years, apart, of course, from those who continue to work on Bloomfieldian lines, agree on rejecting or surmounting some, at least, of his self-imposed constraints, it has been Chomsky who has most openly and explicitly challenged the whole philosophical basis of the Bloomfieldian canon of science as far as linguistics is concerned.

Bloomfield's conception of science was strongly empiricist. Chomsky proclaims his rationalist interpretation of science, at least as far as the science of language is concerned. This takes two forms of thinking about language, diametrically opposed to those of the Bloomfieldians. In the first place, Chomsky and those following his general approach are looking at language 'from the inside', at the 'competence' of the native speaker to use and to understand his own language. Empiricists, true to their principles, have to look on language 'from the outside', as the natural sciences have to, and involve themselves exclusively with the publicly available phenomena of speech and writing. An extreme example of devotion to this duty is seen in the deliberate decision of C. C. Fries to write his account of formal English grammar exclusively on the basis of extensive recordings of English converstions without any reference to his own knowledge and use of the language.[65]

The Chomskyan 'insider' viewpoint permits him recourse to necessarily personal, private, and individual perceptions and reactions, known directly to the speaker–hearer (including, of course, the linguist studying his own language), and only indirectly inferred in others from their speech or other behaviour: (un)acceptability, paraphrase, equivalence, well- and ill-formedness, speakers' own judgments on semantic differences and nuances and their assessments of the contextual appropriateness of vocabulary and sentence forms; in general, such essentially introspective evidence can be accepted at its face value from oneself and from others. On such an interpretation, language is itself a key to the partial understanding of the human mind or brain, a view shared under different conditions by the ancient Stoics (pp. 18–19, above), and on more than one occasion Chomsky has declared his view of linguistics as a branch of cognitive psychology.[66]

In the second place, the human mind or brain is not the *tabula rasa*, the empty receptacle of the empiricists, just waiting for impressions and data to impinge on it from outside. Rationalists regard the brain as genetically endowed with a rich and fairly detailed programme for receiving, interpreting, storing, and using the random information supplied by the senses. This is the equivalent of the 'innate ideas' of the classical seventeenth-century Cartesian rationalists (p. 125, above). In this light, first language learning is the processing by the child's brain of the random experience of speech that it encounters, whether directly spoken to it or uttered in its presence. This is done through a rather tightly constrained system of 'possible grammars' within which the data must be accommodated, stored, and understood.[67]

So Chomskyan generative linguists envisage first language acquisition as a special activity and capability, unlike most other forms of learning, and dependent on a particular genetically given component in the mind or brain, the Language Acquisition Device (LAD), specifically an aspect of universal grammar. In the light of this, first language acquisition, achieved almost unnoticed by all normal children and without formal teaching, is definitely distinguished from later second language learning and the further study of one's first language at school, which are consciously undertaken work that requires teaching by others, or at least deliberate self-teaching. Empiricists, on the other hand, regard first language learning as much more akin to other forms of learning and based on pattern recognition through sentence repetitions with variations in vocabulary, grammatical categories, etc.[68]

It was Bloomfield's emphasis on the detailed formal analysis of different languages that determined his view of language universals or universal grammar as a purely inductive exercise to be pursued only on the basis of accumulated data from large numbers of languages, much larger indeed than had so far been achieved. Hence, his rather dismissive treatment of the topic as contrasted with the Chomskyan assignment of universal grammar as the central hypothesis for the understanding of language structure and the ability of us all to acquire or 'internalize' such a complex, delicate, and rich system of rules from exposure over a few years to a very much limited and random body of data.[69]

In recent years a somewhat divergent development of Bloomfieldian immediate constituent analysis in grammar has been developed by K. L. Pike and his associates; it has mostly been exemplified in studies of Central and South American languages, in which these linguists have become predominantly interested. This system of analysis, which grew out of a more general theory of human behaviour suggested by Pike, is known as tagmemics, since the tagmeme is its fundamental grammatical unit. It is noteworthy that it is among tagmemicists, with their predominant interests in the field study of native American languages, that discovery procedures are still a matter of prime concern.[70] The tagmeme unites in a single unit a function in a larger structure and a class of items fulfilling that function; it is defined as 'the correlation of a grammatical function or slot with a class of mutually substitutable items occurring in that slot'.[71] 'Subject manifested or filled by noun', 'predicate manifested or filled by verb', and 'object manifested or filled by noun phrase' are all tagmemes. Such tagmemes compose larger structures like clauses and sentences, and sentences are analysed, not into successions of (usually binary) immediate constituents, but into strings of collateral constituents (whence the title 'string constituent analysis' is also used of this approach). The subject and object nouns or noun phrases are related equipollently to the verb in many tagmemic analyses, whereas by the usual immediate constituent and transformational-generative analysis the object noun is itself part of the verbal group.

In identifying tagmemes, semantic function as well as syntactic function is taken into account, as long as an identifiable class meaning can be associated with a definite class of formal items as 'fillers', so that 'subject', 'location', 'time', 'qualifier', and the like may all constitute tagmemic slots or functions. In thus employing semantics diagnostically, and in severely modifying immediate constituent structures in syntax, tagmemics marks its major divergences from 'Bloomfieldian' grammatical analysis. Its positing of a unit comprising both function (slot) and class of items (filler) performing that function seems to be most useful in dealing with languages in which a diversity of formally different classes may perform the same function (e.g. where the morphologically different classes of noun, adjective and verb can all be predicates), or, conversely, in which the same class may perform diverse functions in the sentence (e.g. nouns as subjects, modifiers, or objects). Where a single class of items fills a single slot, there is redundancy in expressing this by means of a complex unit.[72]

In several respects tagmemic theory and practice represent the closest continuation of Bloomfieldian linguistics in the post-Bloomfieldian world. Their concentration on languages hitherto unanalysed or inadequately analysed leads tagmemicists to maintain the 'structuralist' interest in discovery procedures, and among current schools of linguistics their adherents have been responsible for more field manuals than any others. In their descriptive techniques their incorporation as primitives of such abstract semantic terms as subject, location, qualifier, beneficiary, etc., from which some at least of the 'structuralists' would have kept themselves clear as extralinguistic and nonformal concepts, has been summed up by Longacre as 'a reaffirmation of function in a structuralist context'.[73]

Interestingly in one respect, despite their methodological and theoretical nearness to Bloomfield, the tagmemicists differ markedly from him in their practical interest in language work for Christian evangelistic purposes and for Bible translating, thus following the tradition begun by Ulfilas, Cyril and Methodius, and the Propaganda Fide department of the Roman Church (p. 117, above). Bloomfield was atheistical or at least agnostic as far as religion was concerned. There may be a lesson here, too, for those who try to derive political principles from the facts of human language.

Chronologically, one of the first challenges to Bloomfieldian 'structuralism' came in the work of J. R. Firth in England and a group of linguists working with him in the University of London during the 1940s and 1950s. Firth's attentions were primarily directed to phonology on the one hand and to semantics on the other. Apart from some isolated observations, he had little to say on syntax and morphology, and these levels of linguistic analysis were taken up after his death by Halliday, whose general system of description has been conceived as the continuation and development of Firth's ideas as he would have pursued them, had he lived to see them to completion (pp. 244–5 below).

Synchronic linguistic studies in Great Britain were initially concentrated on phonetics and phonology. Sweet's teaching was taken up and extended by D. Jones, whose *Outline of English phonetics*, first published in 1914, and *English pronouncing dictionary*, first published in 1917, are known and used all over the world, having carried the study and practice of 'received pronunciation' (RP) far beyond the relatively narrow geographical and social confines in which it characterizes the pronunciation of a native dialect.

More general linguistic questions were treated in Gardiner's *Theory of speech and language* (1932); but distinctive linguistic theory and the recognition of general linguistics as an academic subject in Great Britain owe most to J. R. Firth, Professor of General Linguistics in the University of London from 1944 to 1956, the first holder of a title in linguistics in this country. Firth devoted much of his attention to phonology, in which he put forward the theory of prosodic analysis (pp. 246–8, below). This was conceived within his general theory, which may be called the contextual theory of language.

Like American linguists, Firth drew on the work and thought of anthropologists, in his case particularly that of B. Malinowski, who, faced with the task of translating native words and sentences in ethnographic texts from the Trobriand Islands into comprehensible English, developed his theory of context of situation, whereby the meanings of utterances (taken as the primary data) and their component words and phrases were referred to their various functions in the particular situational contexts in which they were used.[74]

Firth extended this approach to language by treating all linguistic description as the statement of meaning, thereby stretching the application of the equation 'meaning is function in context' to cover grammatical and phonological analysis. The statement, for example, of the syntactic uses of a case form in a language such as Latin is the statement of its function in various grammatical contexts, and the statement of the phonological contrasts and the sequential possibilities of a consonant such as [b] or [n] in English is the statement of its function in various phonological contexts and in the context of the phonological system of the language.[75]

Meaning in the ordinary sense of the relation between language and the world of experience was handled in terms of the semantic functions of words, phrases, and sentences in different contexts of situation, of a more abstract nature than Malinowski's actual observed particulars, and providing a framework of categories, including reference and denotation,[76] by which utterances and their parts could be related to the relevant features and events in the external world. Firth stressed the parallelism between the internal, formal, contexts of grammar and phonology and the external contexts of situation, thus justifying his otherwise paradoxical extension of the use of the term *meaning*. It may be said that the basic differences between formal and semantic analysis were underestimated by Firth[77] but the move in semantics away from the entification of meanings simply as what is 'stood for' or referred to (since with many words no such referent is readily available), towards the interpretation of meaning as function (how words and combinations of words are used) was a most valuable one.

In his decision to do what Firth had never done, to present an explicit account of his theory of language and of linguistic analysis, Halliday, his former pupil, has set out in successive publications since 1961 to give a full, coherent, and exemplified account of Firth's theory, as he understands it, including a theory of morphology and syntax, which Firth had done little more than touch on.

Firth's conception of context of situation as the means of making statements of meaning and of phonology as the link between grammar and phonetics, is formalized in the following schematic diagram of descriptive linguistics:[78]

phonetics		linguistics		
substance	←→	form	←→	situation
phonic substance	phonology	grammar (closed system)	context	extralinguistic features
graphic substance	orthography	lexis (open system)		

The diagram on this page sets out M. A. K. Halliday's conception of linguistics as an organized and articulated science. It has, not surprisingly, changed and developed since its initial presentation in 1961,[79] but the picture there given remains substantially as it was.

Halliday's linguistic theory, as he has repeatedly made clear, is intended to follow up and build upon Firth's conception of linguistics, and to do for Firthian linguistics what Firth himself never in fact achieved, to present in its terms a full-scale theory of language and of linguistic analysis. The extent to which Halliday has succeeded in this aim remains a matter of debate, but his linguistic theory, especially in its current form, has attracted very considerable attention.

In its early stages the theory went under the self-explanatory name of 'neo-Firthian linguistics'; it was also designated 'scale and category grammar', this latter title being taken from the set of seven basic elements, three scales and four categories, of the theory as expounded in 1961.[80] Currently Halliday's theory is referred to as 'systemic grammar' or 'systemic linguistics', since the grammar of a language (in the widest sense of 'grammar') is envisaged as a highly complex and delicate set of systems of options, some sequentially ordered, some simultaneous, through which one must (figuratively) move in framing an utterance and in terms of which as a hearer one must interpret an utterance.

These interrelated networks of choices (the term *network* is Halliday's) are presumed to have taken the form they have, in all languages, in order that speakers and hearers can make use of their language to meet their requirements as determined by the general human situation and by their own particular culture. In his way Halliday, like Firth, links his linguistics with Malinowski's anthropology, and professes, as the central objective of his theory of language, to help answer the question: 'Why is language as it is?'[81]

In the analysis of linguistics form itself, Firth, like most British linguists of his time, was much more concerned with phonology than with grammar. Linguistic form was envisaged by him as sets of abstractions, as the lexical, grammatical, and phonological levels, referable to actual features and occurrences of phonic data serving as their several exponents. At each level the elements and categories abstracted were related to each other along the two Saussurean dimensions in syntagmatic structures and paradigmatic systems (Firth specialized the terms *structure* and *system* to refer respectively to these two dimensions of intralinguistic relationship); consonant–vowel–consonant and preposition-noun were typical structures, while the syllable initial plosives of a language or its nominal cases constituted systems of contrasting elements or categories. The levels were weakly hierarchic, in that phonological abstractions could serve mediately as exponents of grammatical abstractions while themselves having phonetic exponents in the phonic data, though exponency could also be taken directly as the relation between grammatical or lexical abstractions and the phonic data.[82]

The most distinctive aspect of Firth's linguistic work was prosodic phonology, the outlines of which were first presented programmatically in 1948, and developed in applications to a number of languages in the decade following.[83]

Firth's prosodoic phonology should be considered along with other systems of phonology that were evolved in the 1940s as responses to the challenge that phonology, as a part of descriptive linguistics, faced during the 1930s. Phonetics, an observational and descriptive science, aided by more and more sophisticated instruments ('experimental phonetics'), was now capable of distinguishing and recording phonetic phenomena involved in speech with a greater degree of accuracy than hitherto, and was bringing into the field of its precision features such as stress and the pitch levels and movements involved in intonation, together with the sound differences and their associated articulations that related to the transitions between syllables, words, and other stretches within whole utterances. Such phonetic phenomena had been noticed by Sweet, under the title of 'synthesis' (as contrasted with 'analysis', the description of consonants and vowels considered as separate sequential segments)[84] but in the interval they had been somewhat neglected in phonological theory. In part they provided the material for the *Grenzsignale* of the Prague school (pp. 225–6 above).

In one respect, prosodic theory made the most radical break with existing theory. Firth insisted on the separation of the requirements of transcription from the structure of an adequate phonological theory. Twaddell had, indeed, suggested such a divorce earlier, but with little effect on the phonological theory of the time. For Firth the phoneme as a theoretical unit had its value in the devising and justifying of economical broad transcriptions; the full display of the functional inter relations of sound features in utterance required a different set of terms and a different mode of analysis.[85] Since Firth was a strong adherent of the view that analytic concepts exist only within the descriptive system of the linguist and not in the language itself, such a coexistence of separate conceptual systems serving different purposes presented no difficulties for him.

Prosodic analysis involves two types of basic element:

phonematic units and prosodies. Each of these is set up in relation to some phonetic feature (or group of features) serving as
its exponent in the actual uttered speech material. Phonematic
units are consonants and vowels, and are serially ordered as segments; but any phonological structure (e.g. syllable, or syllable
group) may include one or more prosodies. Prosodies are assigned to definite structures, not to places between phonematic
units, and are set up to handle syntagmatic relations between certain phonetic features. Broadly, phonetic features are allotted to
prosodies rather than to phonematic units, if they either extend
over the whole or the major part of a structure, or are positionally restricted in it and thus serve to delimit or demarcate it. As
examples, the tones in Siamese (Thai) are treated as syllable
prosodies by the first criterion, and plosion in this language, being
confined to syllable initial position, is regarded as a syllable (part)
prosody by the second criterion[86]. Comparable examples of
prosodies of words, as phonological units, are vowel harmony
restrictions (usually accompanied by related differences in the
consonantal articulations) in languages like Turkish and Hungarian, and stress confined to a fixed place in the word and thus
serving to delimit its boundaries.

It will be seen that Firth's prosodies, and the prosodies of
analyses that followed this theory, in part deal with the same
phenomena as the *Grenzsignale of* Prague and the suprasegmental phonemes of the American phonemicists. There are, however,
a number of differences. Any type of phonetic feature that can
be shown to be syntagmatically involved with more than a single
segment can be treated as the exponent of a prosody; American
suprasegmental phonemes, other than junctures, were generally
limited to stress, length, and pitch, features not involving a basic
difference in the shape of the sound waves.[87] In prosodic analysis
no such restrictions apply, and some phonetic material that in
other systems of analysis would be part of some consonant or
vowel phonemes may be assigned to prosodies (e.g. retroflexion
in Sanskrit and some modern Indian languages, and palatal and
non-palatal articulation in some varieties of Chinese[88]), and for
the same reason the exponents of some phonematic units may
comprise fewer phonetic features than would belong to the
nearest corresponding phonemes in a phonemic analysis.

With transcriptional needs no longer a prime consideration, a
monosystemic set of analytic elements is not necessary. Prosodic
analysis is prepared to set up different systems of phonematic
units and prosodies at different places in structures where this
significantly facilitates the analysis. Thus syllable initial con-

sonants may well form a different system from syllable final consonants, with no identification of the members of one system with the members of another, even though certain phonetic features (exponents) may be shared between them. Moreover, unlike the 'Bloomfieldians', but like transformational-generative linguists (p. 252, below), prosodic phonologists see phonology as the link between grammar and the actual utterance, or, more abstractly, between grammar and phonetics; and grammatical categories and structures are properly relevant to phonological statement wherever a phonetic feature or phonetic features can be associated with them as exponents.[89] From this come the recognition of word and sentence prosodies, as well as syllable prosodies, and also the possibility of phonological systems different in certain respects for words of one class in a language and words of another class. The last two respects in which prosodic analysis differs from transcriptionally orientated phonemic analysis gave rise to the term *polysystemic* with reference to prosodic phonology. The outcome of a prosodic analysis is not a readable transcription, but a diagrammatic representation of the interrelations of elements and features in a stretch of utterance, that can be put into connection with its grammatical structure.[90]

The recently formulated theories of autosegmental and metrical phonology, recognizing different 'tiers' of phonological features over and above segments and segmental features can be regarded in several ways as a revival or a continuation of Firth theory of prosodies.[91]

A general theory of linguistic analysis that derives some of its characteristics from Prague theory is 'stratificational grammar', propounded by S. M. Lamb (*grammar* being used in its widest sense to cover formal analysis as a whole, as in transformational usage, pp. 250–1, below).[92] Different levels or strata are posited within language structure for the analysis of sentences: for example, sememic, wherein the distinctive meaning units of the language are set out in a network of relations (e.g. 'tiger', 'catch', 'male', 'human', 'agent', 'goal', and 'past'); lexemic, wherein the distinctive lexical units *man, catch -ed, tiger*, etc. are linked together in a sentence structure; morphemic, wherein morphemes appear in a successive string; and phonemic, and wherein simultaneous bundles of distinctive features make up a string of phonemic units (*the man caught the tiger*), setting out the passage from intended meaning to serially ordered and phonetically ordered form.

The levels are hierarchically related to each other and linked together by the relation of representation or realization, in that the lexemic level represents the sememic and is represented by the morphemic, which in turn is represented by the distinctive features of the lowest structural level, the phonemic. The nature of representation varies from simple, when one unit of a higher level is represented by one unit at the next lower level, to such complex representations as neutralization (two or more units not structurally distinguished in representation), composite representation (one units represented by more than one lower level unit, as in multiple allomorphic representation of a morpheme), zero representation, portmanteau representation, etc.

This theory reacted against the dominant linearity of 'Bloomfieldian' distributionalism, by displaying the different types of structural relation that may be involved in linguistic analysis, and the number of different ways in which a structure at one level may be related to (realized in, or represented by) a structure at another level. Stratificational linguistics embodies an organization whereby the speaker-hearer's processing and his reception of meanings (thoughts, perceptions, states of affairs, etc.) through speech can be explicated. Making meanings to be expressed the starting point of the stratificational apparatus, it is clearly psychological in orientation, and a possible link with some actual neurological processes in the brain, at least for one writer in this school, has not been excluded.[93]

While it can be maintained that the greater part of developments in linguistic descriptive theory and method since the 1950s has been concerned with reactions, of one sort or another, to what were felt to be unnecessary restrictions imposed by the Bloomfieldian 'structuralist' conception of a scientific stance in the subject, what can now be seen as the start of the most radical and influential movement in linguistic theory and practice may be located in 1957, when Chomsky's *Syntactic structures* was published, inaugurating transformational-generative linguistics, so named from the principal distinctive method and orientation of the work taken in hand.

The general philosophical stance in the matter of linguistics as a science taken by Chomsky and his adherents has been considered above (pp. 239–41). The actual theory, or theories, that have arisen from his insights and his teaching and publication have occupied many of the most active and insightful brains in linguistics over the last thirty years. Since the publication of *Syntactic structures* in 1957, Chomskyan linguistics, while broadly maintaining the general rationalist stance already discussed, has passed through a number of phases, survived and responded to a number of controversies, and radically changed its emphasis on description and analysis, as is indicated by its succession of popular titles: *transformational grammar, transformational-generative grammar,* and *generative grammar* (or *linguistics*).

A distinctive aspect of *Syntactic structures* was the use of formalized transformational relations, in the form of rules, to describe the differences between sentences of various types, illustrated from English but applicable in principle to all languages. Negative sentences, interrogative sentences, and passive sentences were all treated as transforms of a more basic 'kernel' sentence type represented by positive declarative sentences (i.e. various transformational rules derived sentences like *John does not appreciate music, does John appreciate music?, what music does John appreciate?,* and *music is appreciated by John* from a sentence like *John appreciates music*).

Transformational relations between sentences of different syntactic structures had been incorporated in an otherwise basically 'Bloomfieldian' type of linguistic description by Harris in two articles in 1952 and 1957[94]; and it may be pointed out that Chomsky was Harris's pupil. In 1957 Chomsky put forward a set of transformational rules in order to make available a more powerful grammar than, in his opinion, the immediate constituent or distributional ('phrase structure') model unaided allowed for. In this, it should be noted, Chomsky was reintroducing in a more explicitly formalized way concepts and relationships which had been part of traditional European language teaching all through its history. The term 'grammatical rule' is familiar to anyone who has learned a second language at school; it had been self-consciously dropped from 'Bloomfieldian' linguistics in order to avoid any suggestion of normative or prescriptive bias getting in the way of objective description. 'Structuralist' analysis had set its sights explicitly on the identification of 'elements' and their distributional relations with each other (p. 234, above). Some American reviewers of *Syntactic structures* made much of this apparently revolutionary break with the immediate past, when a 'grammar of rules' was put in the place of a 'grammar of lists', but European reviewers paid more attention to the continuity of Chomsky's grammar with the older European tradition, especially in relation to second language teaching, and it must be stressed that this is an aspect of his work on which Chomsky himself lays considerable emphasis.[95]

Syntactic structures was concerned almost exclusively with syntax and morphology (transformational-generative linguists generally use the term 'grammar' in a wide sense to include phonology, and they tend to treat morphology as a subset of syntactic rules). We can now see the years 1964 and 1965 as marking a major development in which transformational-generative theory was required to include semantics and phonology within its compass. Thus Katz and Postal wrote in 1964 : 'A linguistic description of a natural language is an attempt to reveal the nature of a fluent speaker's mastery of that language.'[96] Further appeals to linguistic intuitions or practical knowledge of the language are, ideally, unnecessary and illegitimate, because all such intuitions should have been made explicit and incorporated into the description of the language.

The aim set by such linguists to their work is higher than that explicitly set by any previous group of linguists. It amounts to nothing less than presenting in a description of a language everything that is implied by the linguistic competence of a native speaker. Their objectives of the transformationalists are to be attained by framing linguistic descriptions in terms of rules that embody the creative capacity of a native speaker to produce and to understand an infinite number of sentences (all and only the grammatical sentences of the language), most of which he has never uttered or heard before, through the availability of recursive rules and other devices in the formalized grammars of languages.

It is in the infinitely creative aspect of the native speaker's knowledge of his language that Chomsky and other transformational-generative linguists distinguish their conception of competence from what they consider the more static Saussurean conception of *langue,* and by which they contrast the creativity of generative linguistics from the more limited taxonomic objective of the 'Bloomfieldians', an objective that the Bloomfieldian generation certainly did not abjure.[97] Their insistence on the fact that their data, though a finite corpus, was a fair sample of the language would have enabled them to claim that they also made provision for the infinite creativity of a natural language, though they certainly gave less prominence to such concepts as syntactic recursion and lexical innovation.[98]

In 1965 *Aspects of the theory of syntax* represented the phase in transformational-generative theory when, as we now know, it was for the last time possible to maintain a basic unity within it; semantics and phonology were now incorporated into the descriptive system as they had not been in *Syntactic structures.* The attractive conception of a relatively abstract deep structure providing through its semantic interpretation for the meaning of the sentence, and through a succession of transformations generating the surface structure without any change in meaning being effected by them, and of surface structure being the input to the phonological rules, whose output was the uttered sentence, was rather rashly given the title of the 'standard theory'; and over the years since 1965 there has been broad agreement among generative linguists on the place and the form of phonology within grammatical description and gramatical theory. In other respects it did not long remain unchallenged, and today the various products of the original Chomskyan impulse furnish a theoretical diversity which appears unlikely to yield to any single version of the theory in the foreseeable future.

Broadly, phonology comprises a set of later rules converting syntactic surface structures into uttered or transcribed sequences of phones. This agrees with the Firthian role for phonology; but, of course, it lies in direct contradiction to the biunique refinements of 'structuralist' phonemics (p. 248, above). Since 1959, when M. Halle published his *Sound pattern of Russian*,[99] the phonological rules have generally been framed in terms of Prague School distinctive features. For a decade the acoustically designated features set out by Jakobson (p. 227, above) were the features used, but in 1968 Chomsky and Halle gave their reasons for a return to an articulatory set, not, to be sure, those of Trubetzkoy and the early Prague School, but one none the less based primarily on the shapes and movements of the articulatory organs involved in their production.[100] The concept of the distinctive feature, first formalized by Trubetzkoy and the early Prague School, has proved to be one of the most significant and enduring analytic concepts in linguistics, and distinctive feature theory is still being actively researched and developed. If any one concept holds the key to an understanding of the vicissitudes of linguistic theory in the present century it is this.

Distinctive features in phonology are, of course, a universal set from which languages make different selections in different permitted combinations. The analogy of phonological features with features at other levels, together with the rationalistic universalist leanings of most transformational-generative linguists (pp. 240-1, above) has given encouragement to a renewed search for language universals in other components of a grammar.[101] It is generally agreed that at the level of syntax significant universals will be found in deep structure or its counterpart in other versions of the theory. Interestingly, the 'Bloomfieldians', who so much stressed the individual differences between languages, concentrated all their formal analysis on what would now be called surface structures, just where transformational-generative linguists are readiest to recognize the main field for linguistic diversity.

Transformations had always been among the means serving the

attainment of the end, a generative account of what is involved in the competence of a native speaker; but *Aspects* saw the beginning of a process that has proceeded relentlessly since then: the reduction in the numbers and the role of transformations. Negation was marked in deep structure by an abstract element NEG, triggering particular surface representations instead of being a meaningful transformation in its own right. Subsequently, nominal derivatives of verbs like *arrival, departure, ignorance*, and so on, were detached from gerund forms (*arriving, departing, ignoring*, ets.) on various syntactic and semantic grounds, assigned directly to the lexicon along with underived words, and appropriately marked grammatically.[102] In its most recent from Chomsky's generative grammar retains only one highly constrained transformation rule, 'Move α', i.e. 'move what can be moved within the limits prescribed by the rest of the system'.

An example of the richness of the grammatical system now assumed by the generative grammarians to be innate and universal, though differently articulated in different languages, is to be seen in the current Government and Binding theory (GB for short). This takes its name from the two most important subcomponents or subtheories of the total grammar, which itself is considered to embody seven such subtheories. Very broadly, government deals with the assignment of specific grammatical roles to words and word groups (and can therefore be regarded as an extension of the classical notion of government or reaction (p. 93), above, and binding specifies the conditions under which pronouns and some other words are or are not coreferentially interpreted (as in *he admires him* and *he admires himself*).

Another version of generative grammar, Generalized Phrase Structure Grammar (GPSG), has dispensed with transformations altogether, relying on phrase structure rules in an enriched phrase structure component to achieve the required exhaustive grammatical descriptions. A comparable abandonment of transformational rules is also to be seen in the theory generally known as Lexical Functional Grammar (LFG).[103]

The incorporation of a semantic theory in one form or another within tranformational-generative linguistics is just one facet of the much greater interest in semantics on the part of almost all linguists in recent years, and it is in marked contrast to accepted American practice, at least, in the preceding 'Bloomfieldian' era (p. 238, above). For a time it was thought by some that, as in stratificational grammar, one could start with atomic semantic concepts, combining them by rules into lexical items (words, famously: *cause – become – not – alive → kill*). Various difficulties

encountered on the way have more or less led to the abandonment of this version of the theory.[104] Linguistic studies of
meaning have been extended to include much that would be considered by some as falling outside the realm of semantics and into
that of pragmatics, though it is hard to draw an agreed dividing
line between the two, and in terms of Firth's contextual theory
(pp. 243–4, above) the distinction had little significance. Social
and circumstantial presuppositions, conversational conventions,
the nature of 'speech acts', and differences in focus and emphasis
connected with word order, on all of which there is now a considerable body of writing, are manifestations of this trend in
present-day linguistics, which is by no means confined to those
working within transformational-generative theory. Indeed much
current concern with text linguistics, speech acts, semantic
relevance theory, and sociolinguistics in general may be fairly
regarded as far-reaching developments of topics and lines of research in large part put forward programmatically a generation
ago by J. R. Firth in his concept of the context of situation
(p. 243, above).[105]

Transformational-generative linguistics started as part of
synchronic, descriptive, linguistics, and this is still its primary interest. But the conception of a grammar as a set of ordered rules
has led to a reconsideration of historical linguistics, at least as far
as the representation of linguistic change is concerned. In 1966
R. D. King wrote the first textbook on historical linguistics along
these lines, in which changes in a language are considered as
changes in a subset of the rules, or in the order of the application
of the rules, that constitute its grammar (in the wide sense of that
term).

The possible parallelism in generative grammatical theory between the descriptive ordering of some phonological rules and the
historical sequence of actual sound changes is not the only impulse behind the vigorous pursuit of historical linguistics today.
With the neogrammarian understanding of 'sound laws' still behind them, historical linguists have had reinforcement in their
interest and their methods from the development of dialects
studies, recently with special reference to the various urban
dialects of large cities and from sociolinguistic studies in general,
wherein one may see a source of diachronic change in synchronic
heterogeneity.[106]

Interventions by Chomsky in the study of the history of linguistics have arisen from his conviction that much of his approach to
language is, basically, a more formalized development of traditional European practice (and, one might add, of Sanskritic

Indian practice, (p. 161) above). All this has not been without sharp controversy; it has certainly increased current interest in the history of the subject.[107]

The historian must leave his narrative when he reaches the contemporary situation, but history does not thereupon stand still. He tries to understand and to interpret the past, and to see the present as its product; but his efforts do not justify him in setting himself up as a prophet. However, some comprehension and appreciation of the history of linguistic science will enable him to study future movements and controversies with a greater sympathy, tolerance, and insight. To relate one's immediate interests to the trials and the achievements of fellow workers in past ages should lead to more balanced judgments and less intemperate enthusiasms. This may further justify the selection of the generativist school to close a survey of the history of linguistics, since several of its members look both to the new discoveries that their theory enables them to make and to the links that it has with the linguistic enquiries of earlier generations. Language is perhaps the most specifically human of mankind's faculties. In striving towards the understanding and knowledge of language, man has throughout his intellectual history been seeking more fully to attain self-knowledge, and to obey the injunction that faced the visitor to Apollo's temple at Delphi,[108] the centre of the ancient Greek world, where our civilization finds its source: ΓΝΩΘΙ ΣΕΑΥΤΟΝ.

For Further Consultation

H. ARENS, *Sprachwissenschaft: der Gang ihrer Entwicklung von der Antike bis zur Gegenwart*, Freiburg/Munich (second edition) 1969, 403–739.

L. BLOOMFIELD, *Language*, London, 1935.

N. CHOMSKY, *Syntactic structures*, The Hague, 1957.

—, *Current issues in linguistic theory*, The Hague, 1964.

—, *Aspects of the theory of syntax*, Cambridge, Mass., 1965.

— and M. HALLE, *The sound pattern of English*, New York, 1968.

J. R. FIRTH, 'The English school of phonetics', *TPS* 1946, 92–132.

—, *Papers in linguistics 1934–1951*, Oxford, 1957.

Z. S. HARRIS, *Methods in structural linguistics*, Chicago, 1951.

E. J. A. HENDERSON (ed.), *The indispensable foundation: a selection from the writings of Henry Sweet*, London, 1971.

L. HJELMSLEV, *Prolegomena to a theory of language* (tr. F. J. WHITFIELD), Baltimore, 1953 (first published in Danish, 1943).

G. C. HORROCKS, *Generative grammar*, London, 1987.

M. IVIĆ, *Trends in linguistics*, The Hague, 1965, 69–242.

R. JAKOBSON, *Selected writings I: phonological studies*, The Hague, 1962.

D. JONES, *An outline of English phonetics* (sixth edition), London, 1947.

———, *The phoneme: its nature and use*, Cambridge, 1950

———, 'History and meaning of the term "phoneme"', *Maître phonétique* July to December 1951, supplement.

M. JOOS (ed.), *Readings in linguistics*, New York, 1958.

M. LEROY, *Les grands courants de la linguistique moderne*, Brussels and Paris, 1963, part 3; English translation, Berkeley, 1967, chapter 7.

B. MALMBERG, *New trends in linguistics* (tr E. CARNEY), Stockholm, 1964.

C. MAHRMANN, A. SOMMERFELT. and J. WHATMOUGH (eds.), *Trends in European and American linguistics 1930–1960*, Utrecht, 1961.

C. MOHRMANN, F. NORMAN, and A. SOMMERFELT (eds.), *Trends in modern linguistics*, Utrecht, 1963.

F. J NEWMEIER, *Linguistic theory in America*, New York, 1986.

———, (ed), *Linguistic, theory: Foundations (Linguistics: the Cambridge survey)*, 1988.

F. R. PALMER (ed.), *Prosodic analysis*, London, 1970.

E. SAPIR, *Language*, New York, 1921.

———, *Selected writings* (ed. D. G. MANDELBAUM), Berkeley, 1951

F. DE SAUSSURE, *Cours de linguistique générale* (fourth edition), Paris, 1949.

T. A. SEBEOK (ed.), *Portraits of linguists: a biographical source book for the history of western linguistics 1746–1963*, Bloomington and London, 1966.

———, *Historiography of linguistics*, 717–1209.

N. S. TRUBETZKOY, *Grundzüge der Phonologie*, TCLP 7 (1939) (translated by J. CANTINEAU, *Principes de Phonologie*, Paris, 1949. English translation by C. A. M. BALTAXE, Berkeley and Los Angeles, 1969).

J. VACHEK, *The linguistic school of Prague*, Bloomington, 1966.

C. L. WRENN, 'Henry Sweet', *TPS* 1946, 177–201.

Studies in linguistic analysis (various authors), special volume of the Philological Society, Oxford, 1957.

History of linguistics (articles by various authors), *Anthropological linguistics* 5.1 (1963).

Notes

1. Further details on prominent scholars and their work may be found in IVIĆ, 1965, LEROY, 1963, and MALMBERG, 1964, which are devoted to nineteenth- and twentieth-century linguistics, surveyed from a historical point of view.

2. *Mémoire sur le systè me primitif des voyelles dans les langues indoeuropéennes*, Leipzig, 1879.

3. DE SAUSSURE, 1949, preface to first edition: for more details, R. GODEL, *Les source manuscrites du Cours de linguistique générale de F. de Saussure*, Paris, 1957 (ed.) R. ENGLER, *Ferdinand de Saussure, cours de linguistique générale* (edition critque), Wiesbaden, 1967. Further E. F. K. KOERNER, *Ferdinand de Saussure, origin and development of his linguistic theory in western studies of language*, Braunschweig, 1973; J. CULLER, *Saussure*, London, 1982.

4. P. A. VERBURG, *Lingua* 2 (1950), 441.

5. J. T. WATERMAN, *Perspectives in linguistics*, Chicago, 1963, 67.

6. E. DURKHEIM, *Les règles de la méthode sociologique* (eleventh edition), Paris, 1950; DE SAUSSURE, 1949, 31, 37, 138; cp. the judicious comments of SAPIR, 'Do we need a superorganic?', *American anthropologist* n.s. 19 (1917) 441–7.

7. DE SAUSSURE, 1949, 34, 97.

8. ibid., 151–4, 157, 169.

9. ibid., part 2, chapter 5; de Saussure used the term *associatif*, but since it was first suggested by Hjelmslev (*Acts of the fourth international congress of linguists*, Copenhagen, 1936, 140–51), *paradigmatic* has become the more generally current word.

10. DE SAUSSURE, 1949, 317.

11. Glossematics, the title chosen by Hjelmslev for this theory of language and linguistic analysis, was a highly theoretical and personal version of de Saussure's structural linguistics carried to its logical extreme. Because of its difficulties and the somewhat idiosyncratic nature of the terminology in which it has been expressed by Hjelmslev and others, it has not attracted all the attention that it probably deserves. For further details the following writings may be consulted: HJELMSLEV, 1953; id., 'Structural linguistics', *Studia linguistica* I (1947), 69–78; H. SPANG-HANSSEN, 'Glossematics', MOHRMANN, SOMMERFELT, and WHATMOUGH, 1961, 128–64. Criticism of some aspects of glossematic theory in E. FISCHER-JORGENSEN, 'Remarques sur les principes de l'analyse phonémique', *TCLC* 5 (1949), 214–234; B. SIERTSEMA, *A study of glossematics*, The Hague, 1955.

12. See further S. ULLMANN, *Principles of semantics*, Glasgow and Oxford, 1957, 152–70; J. LYONS, *Semantics*, Cambridge, 197, 250–69.

13. On the history of phonetics see further R. E. ASHER and E. J. A. HENDERSON (eds.), *Towards a history of phonetics*, Edinburgh, 1981.

14. *Works*, volume 3, London, 1807, 253–318 (264).

15. London, 1855.

16. A. M. BELL, *Visible speech: the science of alphabetics*, London, 1867; SWEET, *Primer of phonetics*, Oxford, 1890; cp. Sweet's general discussion of 'Sound notation', *TPS* 1880–1, 177–235.

17. WRENN, 1946. It is interesting to notice that Bernard Shaw, also knew Sweet and his work, took him as the model for Professor Higgins in *Pygmalion*; the same character appears again, of course, in the later musical adaption *My fair lady*.

18. cp. Sweet's Presidential Address, *TPS* 1877–9, 1–16.

19. SWEET, *Handbook*, 100–8, 182–3.

20. R. JAKOBSON, 'Henry Sweet's paths toward phonemics', *In memory of J. R. Firth* (eds. C. E. BAZELL, J. CATFORD, M. A. K. HALLIDAY, and R. H. ROBINS), London, 1966, 242–54; BAUDOUIN DE COURTENAY, *Versuch einer Theorie phonetischer Alternationen* (German translation), Strassburg, 1895; JONES, 1951; E. STANKIEWICZ, *Baudouin de Courtenay and the foundations of structural linguistics*. Lisse. 1976. The actual word *phonème* appears to have been first coined

by the French scholar. A. Dufriche-Desguettes (E. F. K. KOERNER, *Phonetica* 33 (1976), 222–31).

21. SWEET, *Handbook*, 105; JONES, 1950, chapter 29; W. F. TWADDELL, *On defining the phoneme*, Baltimore, 1935, and further references therein.

22. TRUBETZKOY, 1939 (page references are taken from Baltaxe's English translation).

23. ibid., 3, 31–45, 66–89; VOCHEK, 1966, chapter 3. Like Hjelmslev, Trubetzkoy was greatly influenced by the structural and relational theory of de Saussure, but this did not lead him to reject phonetic criteria in phonological analysis.

24. TRUBETZKOY, 1939, 77–83, 228–41; id., 'Die Aufhebung der phonologischen Gegensätze', *TCLP* 6 (1936), 29–45. id., 1939, 170–207, 273–97; id., *Anleitung zu phonologischen Beschreibungen*, Brno, 1935.

25. 'Functional sentence analysis' or 'functional sentence perspective', the analysis of the syntactic expression of different aspects of sentence meaning, derived ultimately from K. Bühler, has played an important part in post-war Prague School linguistics, and is acknowledged by Halliday as a major influence on his systemic grammar (VACHEK, 1966; HALLIDAY, 'Options and functions in the English clause', *Brno studies in English* 8 (1969), 81–8. The Prague School was one of the most prominent centres of theoretical linguistic research in the inter-war years in Europe. It was recons tituted after the second world war; see VACHEK, 1966.

26. 'Beitrag zur allgemeinen Kasuslehre', *TCLP* 6 (1936), 240–288; VACHEK, 1966.

27. cp. ROBINS, 'Distinctive feature theory', D. ARMSTRONG and C. H. VAN SCHOONEVELD (eds.), *Roman Jakobson: echoes of his scholarship*, Lisse, 1977, 391–402.

28. A. F. C. WALLACE and J. ATKINS, 'The meaning of kinship terms', *American anthropologist* n.s. 62 (1960), 58–80; E. A. HAMMEL (ed.), 'Formal semantic analysis', *American anthropologist* 67.5 (1965), part 2, special publication. This mode of semantic analysis bears some resemblances to the semantic field theories of European scholars, but componential analysis is primarily concerned with the analysis of the terms by reference to their semantic features, while field theory is concerned with the division of a semantic field among the terms (cp. p. 222, above).

29. JAKOBSON, 1962.

30. JAKOBSON and M. HALLE, *Fundamentals of language*, The Hague, 1956, 28–32.

31. JAKOBSON and J. LOTZ, 'Notes on the French phonemic pattern', *Word* 5 (1949), 151–8; CHOMSKY, 1964, 65–75; CHOMSKY and HALLE, 1968, 335–8. A valuable survey of phonological developments in this century is to be found in E. FISCHER-JØRGENSEN, *Trends in phonological theory: a historical introduction*, Copenhagen, 1975.

32. JAKOBSON, 'Prinzipien der historischen Phonologie', *TCLP* 4 (1931),

247–67 (and in JAKOBSON, 1962, 202–20 (French translation)); J.
FOURQUET, *Les mutations consonantiques en germanique*, Paris,
1948.

33. BLOOMFIELD, 1935, 385.

34. DE SAUSSURE, 1949, 124.

35. A. MARTINET, 'Structure, function, and sound change', *Word* 8
(1952), 1–32; A. G. HAUDRICOURT and A. G. JUILLAND, *Essai pour une
histoire structurale du phonétisme français*, Paris 1949.

36. E. J. SIMMONS (ed.), *The Soviet linguistic controversy*, New York
1951; L. C. THOMAS, *The linguistic theories of N. J. Marr, UCPL* 14
(1957), summary account in IVIĆ, 1965, 102–7.

37. T. A. SEBEOK (ed.), *Current trends in linguistics I: Soviet and East
European linguistics*, The Hague, 1963; F. KIEFER (ed.), *Trends in
Soviet linguistics*, Dordrecht, 1973. The 'glottalic hypothesis', as this
theory is sometimes called, must be left for future research. It has
been set forth in T. V. GAMKRELIDZE and V. IVANOV, *Indo-European
and the Indo-Europeans*, Moscow, 1968 (in Russian, but translations are in preparation into western European languages) See also
GAMKRELIDZE, 'Language typology and linguistic reconstruction',
Proc. 12th *International Congress of Linguistics*, Innsbruck, 1978,
480–2.

38. London, 1922; Oxford, 1932; Jena, 1934; Copenhagen, 1928; Aarhus, 1935.

39. cp E. CASSIRER, *Philosophie der symbolischen Formen*, Berlin, 1923–
1929; BLOOMFIELD, 'Language or ideas?', *Language* 12 (1936),
89–95.

40. C. C. FRIES in MOHRMANN, SOMMERFELT, and WHATMOUGH, 1961, 218;
Language 19 (1943), 198; see further P. Swiggers (*The Boas-Bloom-
field Correspondence*; Münster, 1988.

41. 'Sound patterns in language', *Language* I (1925), 37–51, 'La réalité
psychologique des phonèmes', *Journal de psychologie normale et
pathologique* 30 (1933), 247–65 (in English in SAPIR, 1951, 46–60)
On European influence on American linguistics, H.M HOENIGSWALD
(ed.), *The European background*, Dordrecht, 1979.

42. WEISS, *Theoretical basis of human behavior*, Columbus, 1929, chapter 13; BLOOMFIELD, 1935, preface, 28, 142; id., obituary of A. P.
Weiss, *Language* 7 (1931), 219–21.

43. *Indian linguistic families of American north of Mexico* (seventh annual report of the Bureau of Ethnology), Washington, 1891.

44. Washington 1911 (parts 1 and 2), New York 1938 (part 3).

45. SAPIR, 1921 and 1951; id., 'The status of linguistics as a science',
Language 5 (1929), 207–14; S. NEWMAN, *IJAL* 17 (1951), 180–6;
J. B. CARROLL (ed.), *Language, thought, and reality: selected writings
of Benjamin Lee Whorf*, New York, 1956. See further W. COWAN
et al (eds), *New perspectives in language, culture, and personality*,
Amsterdam 1986; R. A, HALL (ed.), *Leonard Bloomfield: essays on
his life and work*, Amsterdam 1987.

46. Critics were able to point out that the actual uses of these two types
of unit were not as parallel as the theory suggested (C. E. BAZELL,

'Phonemic and morphemic analysis', *Word* 8 (1952), 33–8); the development of American linguistic methods during this period can be traced in JOOS, 1958.

47. R. E. LONGACRE, *Language* 32 (1956), 301.
48. BLOOMFIELD, 1935, 178–89, 167, 194–7; O. JESPERSEN, *The philosophy of grammar*, London, 1924, chapter 7; R. S. WELLS, 'Immediate constituents', *Language* 23 (1947), 81–117.
49. HARRIS, 1951, 6.
50. C. F. HOCKETT 'Two models of grammatical description', *Word* 10 (1954), 210–34.
51. BLOOMFIELD, 1935, 161; HOCKETT, *Manual of phonology* (*IJAL* 21.4, part 1, 1955), 14–17; 'Linguistic elements and their relations', *Language* 37 (1961), 29–53.
52. G. L. TRAGER and H. L. SMITH, *Outline of English structure* (*Studies in linguistics* occasional papers 1, 1951); HOCKETT, 'A system of descriptive phonology', *Language* 18 (1942), 3–21. The term *grammatical prerequisite* is from K. L. Pike, who never accepted this restriction on phonemic analysis ('Grammatical prerequisites to phonemic analysis', *Word* 3 (1947), 155–72; 'More on grammatical prerequisites', *Word* 8 (1952), 106–21). On the separation of levels, TRAGER and SMITH, op. cit., 50, 53–4; HARRIS, 1951, 6.
53. H. L. SMITH, *Language* 28 (1952), 144–9; HARRIS, 1951, 16, CHOMSKY, 1964, 80.
54. So B. BLOCH, 'English verbal inflection', *Language* 23 (1947), 399–418.
55. New York, 1958; New York, 1955; New York, 1958.
56. JOOS, 1958; MOHRMANN, SOMMERFELT, and WHATMOUGH, 1961. A very useful account of this phase of American linguistics in D. HYMES and J. FOUGHT, 'American structuralism', SEBEOK, *Historiography*, 903–1176.
57. For a more detailed historical account of linguistics in this century, especially of work done or inspired by Chomsky, see NEWMEYER, 1986.
58. *An introduction to the study of language*, New York, 1914, 311.
59. *Linguistic aspects of science*, Chicago, 1939 (quotation from p. 76); ROBINS, 'Leonard Bloomfield: the man and the man of science', *TPS* 86.1 (1988), 63–87. Many of Bloomfield's articles and reviews have been helpfully published in one volume, C. F. HOCKETT (ed.), *A Bloomfield anthology*, Bloomington, 1970.
60. cp. K. L. PIKE, *Phonemics: a technique for reducing languages to writing*, Ann Arbor, 1947; E. A. NIDA, *Morphology*, Ann Arbor, 1948.
61. BLOOMFIELD, 1935, 140, 23.
62. cp. B. Bloch and C. L. Trager, *Outline of linguistic analysis*, Baltimore, 1942, 8
63. C. C. Fries in MOHRMANN, SOMMERFELT and WHATMOUGH, 1961, 212–7.
64. 1935, 18.

65. C. C. FRIES, *The structure of English*, New York, 1952, 3–4.
66. cp. CHOMSKY, *Language and mind*, New York, 1972, 1, and *Rules and representations*, Oxford, 1980, 4, 48.
67. cp. the full title of N. BEAUZÉE'S eighteenth-century work, *Grammaire générale ou exposition raisonnée des éléments nécessaires du langage pour servir de fondement à l'étude de toutes les langues*, Paris, 1767.
68. cp. CHOMSKY, 'Principles and parameters in syntactic theory', in N. HORNSTEIN and D. LIGHTFOOT (eds), *Explanation in linguistics*, London, 1981, chapter 2. Contrast BLOOMFIELD, 1935, 276.
69. BLOOMFIELD, 1935, 20; CHOMSKY, op. cit. in n. 68.
70. *Language in relation to a unified theory of the structure of human behavior*, Glendale, 1954–60; R. E. LONGACRE, *Grammar discovery procedures*, The Hague, 1964.
71. B. ELSON and V. PICKETT, *An introduction to morphology and syntax*, Santa Ana, 1962, 57.
72. V. WATERHOUSE, 'The grammatical structure of Oaxaca Chontal', *IJAL* 28.2 (1962), part 2. See further R. E. LONGACRE, 'String constituent analysis', *Language* 36 (1960), 63–88; V. PICKETT, *The grammatical hierarchy of Isthmus Zapotec* (*Language* 36.1, part 2, 1960); ELSON and PICKETT, op. cit.; W. A. COOK, *Introduction to tagmemic analysis*, New York, 1969; R. M. BREND, *A tagmemic analysis of Mexican Spanish clauses*, The Hague, 1968; id. (ed.), *Advances in tagmemics*, The Hague, 1974.
73. R. E. LONGACRE, 'Some fundamental insights of tagmemics', *Language* 36 (1960) 63–88 (quotation from p. 67); as an example of a tagmemic field manual, id., *Grammar discovery procedures*, The Hague, 1964.
74. MALINOWSKI, 'An ethnographic theory of language', *Coral gardens and their magic*, London, 1935, volume 2, chapter 1; FIRTH, 'Ethnographic analysis and language with reference to Malinowski's views', *Man and culture* (ed. R. W. FIRTH), London, 1957, 93–118.
75. FIRTH, 'The technique of semantics', *TPS* 1935, 36–72.
76. The inclusion of reference and denotation within the relations comprised by a Firthian context of situation is disputed by J. LYONS, 'Firth's theory of "meaning"'. *In memory of J. F. Firth*, 288–302; but it seems both compatible with his theory and, indeed, necessary, if the theory is to be sustainable.
77. F. R. PALMER, 'Linguistic hierarchy', *Lingua* 7 (1958), 225–41.
78. Based on HALLIDAY, 'Categories of the theory of grammar', *Word*, 17 (1961), 241–92.
79. HALLIDAY, op. cit.
80. For the details of the theory at this initial stage HALLIDAY, 'Categories', should be consulted. A more popular account is given in HALLIDAY, A. MCINTOSH and P. D. STREVENS, *The linguistic sciences and language teaching*, London, 1964.
81. There is now quite an abundant literature on and by Halliday. His article, 'Some notes on "deep" grammar', *Journal of linguistics* 2

(1966), 57–67, constitutes a bridge between the early and the later versions of his theory; perhaps the most readily accessible presentation by him of systematic grammar is to be found in his 'Language structure and language function', *New horizons in linguistics* (ed. J. LYONS), London, 1970, 140–65. See also R. A. HUDSON, *English complex sentences: an introduction to systemic grammar*, Amsterdam, 1971. Hudson has recently set out what he calls 'daughter-dependency grammar', deriving in part from systemic grammar (*Arguments for a non-transformational grammar*, Chicago, 1976). Most recently HALLIDAY, *An introduction to functional grammar*, London, 1985.

82. FIRTH, 'Synopsis of linguistic theory', *Studies in linguistic analysis*, 1957, 1–32; ROBINS, 'General linguistics in Great Britain 1930–60', C. MOHRMANN, F NORMAN, and A.SOMMERFELT, 1963, 11–37.

83. FIRTH, 'Sounds and prosodies', *TPS* 1948, 127–52; ROBINS, 'Aspects of prosodic analysis', *Proceedings of the University of Durham Philosophical Society*, series B (Arts), I (1957), 1–12.

84. SWEET, *Primer*, 41.

85. J. T. BENDOR-SAMUEL, *The verbal piece in Jebero* (*Word* 17, supplement, 1961), chapters 2 and 3.

86. E. J. A. HENDERSON, 'Prosodies in Siamese', *Asia major* n.s. I (1949), 189–215; PALMER, 1970.

87. PIKE, *Phonemics*, Ann Arbor, 1947, 63.

88. W. S. ALLEN, 'Some prosodic aspects of retroflexion and aspiration in Sanskrit', *BSOAS* 13 (1951), 939–46; N. C. SCOTT, 'A phonological analysis of the Szechuanese monosyllable', *BSOAS* 18 (1956), 556–60.

89. This apparent anticipation by Firthians of the basic transformational-generative view of the place of phonology in a full linguistic description is discussed by D. T. LANGENDOEN, *The London school of linguistics*, Cambridge Mass., 1968, 59. Langendoen's book contains a critical survey both of Firth's semantic theory and of prosodic analysis from a transformational-generative position. Some of these criticisms are discussed in ROBINS, *Language* 45 (1969), 109–16.

90. e.g. HENDERSON, op. cit.; further references in ROBINS, 'General linguistics in Great Britain 1930–1960'; see also PALMER, 1970.

91. J. A. GOLDSMITH, *Autosegmental and metrical phonology*, Oxford, 1988.

92. Stratificational theory was first made public in two papers by LAMB, 'The sememic approach to structural semantics', *American anthropologist* 66.3 (1964), part 2, 57–78; id., 'On alternation, transformation, realization, and stratification', *Monograph series on languages and linguistics* (Georgetown) 17 (1964), 105–22; id., *Outline of stratificational grammar*, Washington, 1966. See now D. C. BENNETT, *Spatial and temporal uses of English prepositions: an essay in stratificational semantics*, London, 1975; D. G. LOCKWOOD, *Introduction to stratificational linguistics*, New York, 1972. The

connection between stratificational linguistics and Prague theory is pointed out in VACHEK, 1966.

93. D. G. LOCKWOOD, *Introduction to stratificational linguistics*, New York, 1972, 281–6.

94. Z. S. HARRIS, 'Discourse analysis', *Language* 28 (1952), 1–30; id., 'Co-occurrence and transformation in linguistic structure', *Language* 33 (1957), 283–340. On the relation between Harris's and Chomsky's uses of transformation, CHOMSKY, 1964, 62–3 (n. 2).

95. R. B. LEES, *Language* 33 (1957), 375–408; W. O. DINGWALL, 'Transformational grammar: form and theory', *Lingua* 12 (1963), 233–75; W. HAAS, *Archivum linguisticum* 10 (1958), 50–4; CHOMSKY, 1964, 25: 'It should be obvious that its roots are firmly in traditional linguistics'.

96. *An integrated theory of linguistic descriptions*, Cambridge Mass., 1964, 1.

97. cp. HOCKETT, *Language* 18 (1942), 3: 'Linguistics is a classificatory science'.

98. On the corpus as a fair sample, HARRIS, 1951, 12–13.

99. The Hague, 1959.

100. CHOMSKY and HALLE, 1968.

101. CHOMSKY, 1965, 27–30; LYONS, 'Towards a "notional" theory of the "parts of speech"', *Journal of linguistics* 2 (1966), 209–36; E. BACH and R. T. HARMS (eds.), *Universals in linguistic theory*, New York, 1968

102. CHOMSKY, 1965, 132, 'Remarks on nominalization', in R. A. JACOBS and P. S. ROSENBAUM (eds.), *Readings in English transformational grammar*, Waltham, 1970, 184–221.

103. A reader who may be unfamiliar with recent and current developments in generative grammar may usefully consult HORROCKS, 1987, and, for a more detailed account of transformational-generative theory from its earliest days, F. J. NEWMEYER, 1986. In view of the rapidity with which generative theory has developed over the past twenty years attention should be paid to the dates of first publication of books and articles listed in Horrocks's and others' bibliographies. On Government and Binding, Generalized Phrase Structure Grammar, and Lexical-Functional Grammar, see HORROCKS, 1987, chapters 2.3–4, 3, and 4.

104. G. P. LAKOFF, *Linguistics and natural logic*, Ann Arbor, 1970; id., 'On generative semantics', D. D. STEINBERG and C. A. JAKOBOVITS (eds.), *Semantics*, Cambridge, 1971, 232–96; R. M. KEMPSON, *Semantic theory*, Cambridge, 1977, chapter 9; ROBINS, *Ideen- und Problem-geschichte der Sprachwissen-schaft*, Frankfurt a. M., 1973, 134–41; HORROCKS, 1987, 29–30.

105. See FIRTH, 'Personality and language in society' (1950), in his *Papers in linguistics* 1934–51, London, 1957, 182. On relevance theory, D. Sperber and D. Wilson, *Relevance*, Oxford, 1986.
1969. T. BYNON, *Historical linguistics*, Cambridge, 1985, chapters 1, 2, and 3 give accounts of the interpretations of language change by

the neogrammarians, by structural linguists of the Prague School, and by T-G grammarians, respectively; chapter 3 covers much recent work and has more up to date references than King. See also V. WEINREICH, W. LABOV, and M. I. HERZOG, 'Empirical foundations for a theory of language change' in (eds.) W. P. LEHMANN and Y. MALKIEL, *Directions for historical linguistics*, Austin, 1968, 95–188.

107. CHOMSKY, *Cartesian linguistics: a chapter in the history of rationalist thought*, New York, 1966 (review by V. G. SALMON, *Journal of linguistics* 5 (1969), 165–87); H. AARSLEFF, 'The history of linguistics and Professor Chomsky', *Language* 46 (1970), 570–85; E. COSERIU, 'Semantik, innere Sprachform und Tiefenstruktur', *Folia linguistica* 4 (1970), 53–63.

108. *Gnôthi seautón* (*know thyself*), PAUSANIAS 10.24.1; JUVENAL 11.27; BLOOMFIELD, *An introduction to the study of language*, New York, 1914, 325: 'Linguistic science is a step in the self-realization of man'.

Index

General Editors
R.H. Robins, *University of London*
Martin Harris, *University of Essex*

This well-respected text presents a comprehensive account of the history of linguistic studies up to the present day. Focussing on the history of linguistics in Europe, R.H. Robins also examines how linguistic science developed in interesting and important ways in Ancient India, Classical China, and among the Arabs and Jews in the first millenium A.D. All these traditions were extremely influential in the history of world linguistics, as scholars made contact with them.

Now, the third edition of this popular study has been revised and updated to give an account of the recent and current research in the history of linguistics that has led to a reevaluation of some traditional opinions and judgements on certain periods, such as late Antiquity and the early Middle Ages. The final chapter on *Linguistics in the Present* has been extensively revised in the light of current developments in the theory and practice of linguistics.

This succinct and highly accessible survey will prove invaluable to both undergraduate and graduate students of linguistics, as well as all those who wish to see the subject in the context of its history and to know what lies behind our present preoccupations.

Reviews of the second edition:

"Altogether an excellent book, at once interesting and authoritative."
THE YEAR'S WORK IN ENGLISH STUDIES

" . . . the most intelligent account of the history of the language sciences."
LINGUISTICS

R.H. Robins is Professor Emeritus of General Linguistics in the University of London.

Front cover: the Tower of Babel from the Bedford Book of Hours (early 15th century) (B.M. M.S. Add. 18, 850, f.17ᵛ). By courtesy of the Trustees of the British Library.

ISBN 0-582-29145-3

9 780582 291454

LONGMAN